Mortality and Society
in
Sub-Saharan Africa

The International Union for the Scientific Study of Population Problems was set up in 1928, with Dr Raymond Pearl as President. At that time the Union's main purpose was to promote international scientific co-operation to study the various aspects of population problems, through national committees and through the work of individual members. In 1947 the International Union for the Scientific Study of Population (IUSSP) was reconstituted in its present form. It expanded its activities to:

- stimulate research on population
- develop interest in demographic matters among governments, national and international organizations, scientific bodies, and the general public
- foster relations between people involved in population studies
- disseminate scientific knowledge on population.

The principal ways in which the IUSSP currently achieves its aims are:

- organization of worldwide or regional conferences and operations of scientific committees under the responsibility of the Council
- organization of training courses
- publication of conference proceedings and committee reports.

Demography can be defined by its field of study and its analytical methods. Accordingly, it can be regarded as the scientific study of human populations with respect to their size, their structure, and their development. For reasons which are related to the history of the discipline, the demographic method is essentially inductive: progress results from the improvement of observations, more sophisticated methods of measurement, and the search for regularities and stable factors which lead to the formulation of explanatory models. In summary, the three objectives of demographic analysis are to describe, measure, and analyse.

International Studies in Demography is the outcome of an agreement concluded by the IUSSP and the Oxford University Press. This joint series is expected to reflect the broad range of the Union's activities and, in the first instance, will be based on the seminars organized by the Union. The Editorial Board of the series consists of:

Mortality and Society in Sub-Saharan Africa

Edited by

Étienne van de Walle
Gilles Pison
and
Mpembele Sala-Diakanda

CLARENDON PRESS · OXFORD
1992

Oxford University Press, Walton Street, Oxford OX2 6DP
Oxford New York Toronto
Delhi Bombay Calcutta Madras Karachi
Petaling Jaya Singapore Hong Kong Tokyo
Nairobi Dar es Salaam Cape Town
Melbourne Auckland
and associated companies in
Berlin Ibadan

Oxford is a trade mark of Oxford University Press

Published in the United States
by Oxford University Press, New York

British Library Cataloguing in Publication Data
Data available

Library of Congress Cataloging in Publication Data
Mortality and society in Sub-Saharan Africa/edited by Étienne van de
Walle, Gilles Pison, and Mpembele Sala-Diakanda.
Includes bibliographical references and index.
1. Mortality—Africa, Sub-Saharan. 2. Africa, Sub-Saharan—Social
conditions—1960– . 3. Africa, Sub-Saharan—Economic
conditions—1960– . I. Van de Walle, Étienne, 1932– .
II. Pison, Gilles. III. Sala-Diakanda, Mpembele.
HB1491. A3M667 1992 304, 6'4'0967—dc20 91–26053
ISBN 0–19–828372–5

Typeset by Best-set Typesetter Ltd., Hong Kong
Printed in Great Britain by
Bookcraft Ltd
Midsomer Norton, Avon

List of Contributors

Peter Aaby, Institute of Ethnology and Anthropology, Copenhagen

Lawrence A. Adeokun, Obafemi Awolowo University, Ile-Ife

Eliwo Akoto, Institute of Demography, Catholic University of Louvain

Caroline H. Bledsoe, Northwestern University, Chicago

Anastasia Brandon, University of Pennsylvania, Philadelphia

John C. Caldwell, Australian National University, Canberra

Pat Caldwell, Australian National University, Canberra

Michel Caraël, WHO

Philippe Fargues, INED, Paris

Bamikale J. Feyisetan, Obafemi Awolowo University, Ile-Ife

Michel Garenne, ORSTOM, Dakar

Kuakuvi Gbenyon, Unité de Recherche Démographique, Lomé

Allan G. Hill, Centre for Population Studies, London School of Hygiene and Tropical Medicine

Althea Hill, The World Bank

Dan C. O. Kaseje, Aga Khan Health Service (Kenya)

Odile Leroy, ORSTOM, Dakar

Thérèse Locoh, INED, Paris

Cheikh Mbacké, CERPOD, Bamako

Ouaidou Nassour, CERPOD, Bamako

Peter Piot, WHO

Gilles Pison, Musée de l'Homme, Paris

Mpembele Sala-Diakanda, IFORD, Yaoundé

John Seaman, The Save the Children Fund (UK)

Dominique Tabutin, Institute of Demography, Catholic University of Louvain

Anton W. Teunissen, Regional Office of Public Health, Dordrecht

Jacques Vallin, INED, Paris

Étienne van de Walle, University of Pennsylvania, Philadelphia

Hendrik van der Pol, IFORD, Yaoundé

Jeroen K. van Ginneken, Netherlands Institute of Preventive Health Care, TNO, Leiden

Contents

List of Figures

List of Maps

List of Tables

List of Abbreviations

AIDS	Acquired Immunodeficiency Syndrome
ALRTI	Acute Lower Respiratory Tract Infections
BCG	Bacillus Calmette–Guérin
CERPOD	Centre d'Études et de Recherche sur la Population pour le Développement
CFA	Communauté Franc d'Afrique
DHS	Demographic and Health Survey
DPT	Diphtheria-Pertussis-Tetanus
EDCA	Endemic Disease Control Assistant
IFORD	Institut de Formation et de Recherche Démographiques
INED	Institut National d'Études Démographiques
INSERN	Institut National de la Santé et de la Recherche Médicale
IUSSP	International Union for the Scientific Study of Population
MCH	Maternal and Child Health
ORSTOM	Institut Français de Recherche Scientifique pour le Développement en Coopération
P/F ratio	Parity/Fertility ratio
PHC	Primary Health Care
PHN	Population, Health, and Nutrition
UNICEF	United Nations International Children's Emergency Fund
USAID	United States Agency for International Development
WFS	World Fertility Survey
WHO	World Health Organization

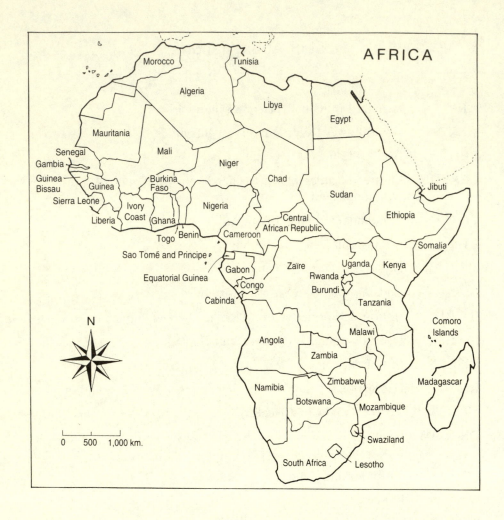

AFRICA

Morocco
Tunisia
Algeria
Libya
Egypt
Mauritania
Mali
Niger
Senegal
Gambia
Guinea
Bissau
Guinea
Burkina
Faso
Chad
Sudan
Jibuti
Sierra Leone
Ivory
Coast
Nigeria
Central
African Republic
Ethiopia
Liberia
Ghana
Togo
Benin
Cameroon
Somalia
Sao Tomé and Principe
Equatorial Guinea
Gabon
Congo
Zaïre
Uganda
Kenya
Rwanda
Burundi
Cabinda
Tanzania
Comoro
Islands
Angola
Malawi
Zambia
Madagascar
Namibia
Zimbabwe
Botswana
Mozambique
Swaziland
South Africa
Lesotho

N

0   500   1,000 km.

Introduction

Étienne van de Walle, Gilles Pison, and Mpembele Sala-Diakanda
University of Pennsylvania, Musée de l'Homme, and IFORD

1. Levels, Trends, and Differentials: The Need for Data

Africa remains largely *terra incognita* to the student of mortality. Vital registration data, the type of materials that provide direct mortality information for more developed countries, are almost completely lacking in Africa. As a rule censuses are not accurate enough to provide measures of intercensal survival. The best evidence on national levels and trends of mortality comes from indirect estimates based on census and survey data. Wherever the census has included a question to women on the number of their children ever born and surviving, it has been possible to estimate mortality levels and even trends for the recent past, using what is usually known as the Brass method of child mortality estimation. In Chapter 1 of this volume, Althea Hill uses census data and the indirect estimation technique extensively to draw a picture of infant and child mortality at the level of national units.

Unfortunately, there are still a great many countries that do not routinely include the Brass questions in their censuses; and of course, there are all the countries where a census worthy of this name has not been taken recently. Moreover, this type of information does not, as a rule, document the very recent past, because censuses are only taken at ten-year intervals in the most favourable case. Neither in time nor in space is the coverage complete. Because they must provide yearly demographic estimates on every country even in the absence of a minimum of empirical knowledge, the United Nations and other compilers of statistics have provided us with a false sense of coverage. And the sample of countries is not representative of mortality levels, since censuses are not taken when there is a civil war or a grave economic crisis. We must essentially extrapolate from peaceful and relatively prosperous countries to cover the countries without data. It is not implausible that the absence of data is correlated with a worse than average health situation.

The census data on children ever born and surviving are arguably underused, and could provide enormously more information at the local level, including a picture of the regional variation in mortality, which could be assessed with other regional data from censuses or other sources, to document the ecological correlates of mortality. They could also be used at the individual level, using a technique that Preston and Trussell have developed, and that has given results that are used by Tabutin and Akoto in Chapter 2 of this volume. But because of the limited quantity of relevant information in the census, the Brass questions can obviously not provide all the information we need on mortality differentials. And of course, mortality information from censuses on older children and adults remains very defective.

Thanks to the World Fertility Survey (the last one being the 1984 Nigerian Fertility Survey), census-type data on children ever born and surviving are no longer the only source of country-level child mortality data. In the process of reconstructing the maternity histories of women, information was collected on the deaths of their children. This information has generally proved of excellent quality, and it lends itself to the study of trends and differentials. The surveys have clearly represented a breakthrough for the study of the relationship between mortality and various characteristics of the mothers and their husbands (demographic characteristics, but also socio-economic ones such as education, urban or rural residence, and even cultural variables such as ethnic group and religion), even though they do not answer all our questions, as Tabutin and Akoto indicate in Chapter 2. There are clear differentials in child mortality by socio-economic characteristics of the parents, but the surveys do little in themselves to explain why, for example, the mother's education is more important than the father's, or why ethnic group affects mortality. There are a number of mechanisms that could be invoked. For example, education could be a proxy for a better understanding of disease processes and a more informed use of personal hygiene and available health facilities; but it could also reflect more power, initiative, and access to resources by the woman, who can use these resources for the benefit of her children. Similarly, mortality differences by ethnic group could reflect differences in child-rearing customs, but also in attitudes towards disease and the efficacy of traditional treatments.

One of the most important issues raised by the World Fertility Surveys is the exact role played by the socio-economic variables in influencing mortality, a question which may have a major impact on policy and budget allocations. Is it better to build a hospital or a school? The surveys do not answer such questions, they only lead to possibly misleading and partial answers. They were notoriously inadequate for the study of mechanisms, notoriously poor in their coverage of what Mosley and Chen (1985) have called the 'proximate determinants of mortality', or the 'intermediate variables'. Blaming the World Fertility Surveys on this failure to address the mechanism of mortality would be unfair, since they were meant to study fertility, with serendipitous inclusion of mortality questions. But we need more, and different data sets to study the mechanisms of mortality.

One of the unresolved issues raised by the World Fertility Surveys concerns the respective roles of access to health services and socio-economic factors in explaining mortality differentials. On the basis of their results, it has been hypothesized that the health advantage of urban dwellers is related not so much to their proximity to better medical facilities, as to the concentration of educated parents in cities. Several longitudinal surveys of infant and child mortality in French-speaking Africa, the IFORD surveys, have focused on an urban birth cohort; they are a useful tool to investigate this issue (Chapter 5, Mbacké and van de Walle). The IFORD surveys contain information of many proximate determinants of mortality, and they provide a framework to study mortality differentials among urban residents who can be hypothesized to have equal *access* to health services, and to differ only in their *use* of these services. In Bobo-Dioulasso (Burkina Faso), it would appear that mortality differentials are largely the result of the extent to which members of various socio-economic groups use the existing facilities; education of the mother, in particular, explains little when the use of health facilities is controlled. This is an important result, but it is weakened by the absence of large differences in education among women in Bobo-Dioulasso, and by deficiencies in the data which make it difficult to study perinatal mortality.

What are the prospects for better data collection in Africa? Something may yet come out of the much maligned vital statistics, as Fargues and Nassour demonstrate in Chapter 4. To the demographer, the research of causes and relationships must often be an indirect one. The patterns of mortality by age and the seasonality of deaths offer clues to the mechanisms at work. Fargues and Nassour focus on seasonality, and bring out the extreme regularity of the yearly measles epidemics in Bamako, until a vaccination campaign lowered the number of susceptibles, thus modifying the frequency of epidemics.

Several of the chapters in this volume illustrate the usefulness of various partial approaches to study specific health problems. The longitudinal surveys (van der Pol), retrospective surveys including questions on the proximate determinants and on perceptions and attitudes (Feyisetan and Adeokun), the special surveys investigating one single disease (Aaby), population laboratories or surveillance systems (Garenne, van Ginneken), and field research projects devised to test a disease control strategy (Kaseje) all have a role to play. It is unlikely that a full coverage of Africa by permanent vital registration systems or regular surveys paid by regular national budgets, will be installed soon. For the assessment of trends, it may well be that the only hope lies in the improvement and use of existing statistics from the health administration systems. In Chapter 3, Allan Hill argues that they may offer the best prospect for knowing more about age patterns of mortality (particularly for infants and adults, which the techniques of indirect estimation do not treat well) and about causes of death. What is needed are fairly sensitive indicators of changes over time, which are specific enough to be useful. Although different sources of administrative statistics taken separately are likely to suffer from various deficiencies, together and used in combination with periodic surveys and censuses, they are likely to come closest to a complete coverage allowing a study of trends.

Does it matter that our knowledge of mortality and health variables is so scanty? Clearly, we need more data to test our theoretical models, and to provide an empirical basis for policies and programmes, including the much touted Primary Health Care agenda which has been proposed on ideological grounds, but not fully tested.

Whither African mortality? A surprising result, which is conclusively drawn from available nation-wide statistics, is that mortality has declined steadily everywhere, irrespective of the course of the economy and the state of production, and perhaps, notwithstanding the inefficiency of public health systems and policies. On the basis of the available data in Chapter 1, the evidence of a general decline of mortality during the 1960s and 1970s is undeniable. It remains essentially a puzzle whether mortality has continued to decline into the 1980s, but Althea Hill argues that there is no reason to doubt that it has. The mechanisms behind the reduction of high mortality remain largely obscure.

The findings about the pervasiveness of the mortality decline raise fundamental questions about the relation between socio-economic development, public health policies, and the course of mortality, at a time when a concern about crises (drought, famine, AIDS, the economic problems) seems to dominate.

Have special programmes, such as the WHO's Expanded Programme on Immunization under which in 1986, 38 per cent of African infants had received the prescribed dose of measles vaccine, and 34 per cent that against diphtheria, pertussis, and tetanus (UNICEF, 1988), made up for the general poor quality of public health services in the region? Have private medicine and the free market in drugs taken over where governmental services proved to be defective? Have the understanding of disease processes, the confidence in allopathic medicine of Western origin (accompanied by a steady supply of modern drugs), the distrust in traditional recipes, and the resort to prevention and hygiene, increased amongst the public? Feyisetan and Adeokun explore the impact of perceptions of the aetiology of disease and of the need for prevention on infant mortality, and they find that for measles and diarrhoea at least, the 'modernity' of the public's views of disease and treatment makes a difference.

Alternatively, is it possible that post-independence prosperity has maintained its effect while the economic boom was going sour? In particular, since education (and particularly female education) appears in all surveys as one of the most important correlates of mortality, is it possible that the great increase of the length and the prevalence of schooling that has occurred in Africa has resulted in the observed decrease in child mortality and gain in life expectancy? The effect could be largely divorced from the quality of education. Tabutin and Akoto show that primary schooling already has some effect, well before the imparted teaching on health has the opportunity to have much impact on the minds of the pupils. It has sometimes been hypothesized that the effect of schooling is in nation-building, i.e. in preparing a public of individuals who will be open to the government's message on health, thus breaking the allegiance to traditional systems of health.

The most intriguing set of questions concerns the possible impact of the change in social arrangements which Africa is undergoing, particularly in the area of family relationships and child-rearing. We know little about the base situation, however, and can do no more than speculate on the impact of changes.

2. The Social Components of Mortality

The most common biological or demographic characteristics (sex, age, parity, twinhood, etc.) have two obvious types of connections with mortality. On the one hand, by themselves they constitute risk factors in any society, because they carry physiological consequences. Girls seem to benefit from a biological advantage over boys. The life of twins everywhere is especially endangered, because their birth weight is less than that of singletons. There may even be special physiological risks in certain societies. In Africa, as Gilles Pison shows in Chapter 11, there are more twins than in other human populations, and this appreciably increases infant mortality through a simple compositional effect.

But, on the other hand, mortality and health are also grounded in society and custom. Parents may discriminate against girls (although there is little evidence that this is the case in Africa, according to Gbenyon and Locoh in Chapter 10). Twins may be objects of terror or veneration, and this may affect their life chances (Pison in Chapter 11). Moreover, family structure and other patterns of interaction provide the matrix in which children are reared and health may or may not flourish. Social arrangements, however attractive they may look on other grounds, may have life-threatening potential.

Among all social factors, the patterns of daily interaction between family members, as they are regulated by custom or by the environment, appear to be the most crucial, and the least obvious to the persons concerned. In Chapter 14, Aaby suggests that patterns of measles infection do not fit the paradigm of synergism between disease and malnutrition to which the high measles mortality in Africa has often been attributed. He resorts to another paradigm, that of crowding, to explain the series of facts that his surveys have revealed. Aaby's new hypothesis, however tentative its empirical basis, offers exciting prospects for research, and was particularly germane to the

subject at hand, since it views a particular characteristic of social organization, crowding, as a key to the understanding of measles and perhaps other
diseases.

When the very structure of family relations affects the rearing of children,
there are bound to be consequences on their health. Changes in the African
family are clearly taking place. The existence of extra-marital relationships,
because they involve the system's support of children born out of wedlock,
are potentially crucial. On the other hand, the custom of child fosterage
represents in many respects a strength for the West African family because
it provides an element of flexibility and offers a way of distributing the
burden and cost of children on a larger kin group. Bledsoe and Brandon, in
Chapter 12, suggest that there may be hidden risks behind this a priori
attractive feature of extended networks of solidarity. Mothers remain the
best agents in the task of preserving the health of children. In the case of
fosterage, it may be that less knowledgeable or motivated persons inherit
the care of the child; the child suffers perhaps from unconscious forms of
discrimination when it is entrusted to other keepers. Most importantly,
the fosterage of very young children may lead to early weaning, with its
attendant risks.

One type of change in customs and maternal behaviour affects the components of the birth interval: the duration of abstinence and breast-feeding
may be declining in sub-Saharan Africa, and the introduction of supplementary feeding instead of breast milk has a potential to provoke diarrhoea
and malnutrition among young children. The relation between birth spacing
and mortality has been a controversial subject in recent years; the con-
troversy has been reviewed by Pebley and Elodu (1989). The problems of
measurement are daunting, and the present volume has not considered
the subject. Similarly, maternal mortality is an important subject from
our perspective, but it requires special techniques to assemble sufficient
unbiased information on what remains a rare event. In the absence of vital
registration, the main challenge is to find someone who will report on the
deceased mother. The most successful techniques of mortality measurement in Africa have been the so-called 'bereavement' techniques that use
retrospective reporting by persons with a close relationship to the deceased:
mothers reporting their children ever born and surviving, children reporting
on their parents, and so on. A similar procedure that would use networks of
informants reporting on the death of newly delivered mothers is still at the
exploratory stage.

A systematic review of the principal diseases which affect children in
Africa suggests the influence of social and cultural variables on mortality.
Tetanus, discussed in Chapter 7 by Leroy and Garenne, is universally
present, and yet it affects certain parts of the population more than others
and is more deadly during certain parts of the year. In the Ngayokheme
surveillance area of Senegal, the rainy season is the dangerous period, and

boys are more affected by tetanus than girls; and yet, there is no obvious social explanation of the difference.

The aetiology of diarrhoea is fairly well known, as van Ginneken and Teunissen establish in Chapter 8, but the specific characteristics of the disease in various parts of Africa exhibit striking variability. The impact of season, of climate, and of environment clearly contribute to the variability, but social factors intervene in efforts at prevention, in the circumstances of infection, in the care of sick children, etc. Our knowledge of the various child-rearing practices which affect diarrhoea remains grossly inadequate.

Malaria poses a particular epidemiological challenge, since strains of the disease have become resistant to chemotherapy. Kaseje and his collaborators in Kenya have designed various experimental studies of malaria control in community-based systems (see Chapter 9). The synergism of various diseases makes it difficult to isolate malaria, and to measure the effect of programmes on mortality.

The approach characterizing a large part of this volume is very much the piecemeal one, analytical, as it were, before a synthesis can be adopted. On the one hand, we have a series of chapters on characteristics of infants (sex, twinhood) or of their support in the family (the famous fosterage systems of West Africa). On the other hand, we have chapters on specific diseases, one by one: diarrhoea, measles, malaria, tetanus. This is not to suggest that a reduction of mortality in Africa will be achieved by the sequential attack of various diseases. Each of these diseases has much to tell us about the mechanism of morbid processes, but each retains its idiosyncrasies and none has yet revealed all its secrets. All appear to be greatly under-studied, in view of the toll they exert on the population. Although malaria or diarrhoea, for example, have some general characteristics throughout the continent, they behave quite differently in various contexts because of ecological differences, but also, and more importantly, because the social context is not the same everywhere. There is clearly a need to investigate these diseases outside of the few surveillance systems where pioneering studies have been made, and to relate them to the functioning of society at large.

Traditional African systems were shaped over time by hardship and crisis, and their ability to withstand particular risks has ensured their survival. The modern period has brought about new hazards, and social change has imposed new adaptations. Crisis mortality, however, has not disappeared and it may even have gained a new urgency in recent decades. Famine and drought, war and refugee movements have confronted some African populations with new versions of old scourges. John Seaman (Chapter 15) shows that the old adaptation mechanisms—migration, sale of cattle, use of wild foods—have functioned with uneven effectiveness; Sudanese villages were in general more resilient than Ethiopian ones, because reserves and alternative opportunities were more available. The existence of outside sources of relief has changed the mechanisms of adaptation. John and Pat Caldwell suggest in Chapter 16 that social adaptations to drought as a normal condition of the region can be jeopardized by continuous food aid. It is a moot point, however, whether long-term changes in climate or the lasting effect of population pressure on fragile environments can lead to successful, unaided adaptation. As for the new crisis described by Caraël and Piot in Chapter 17, AIDS, it offers an enormous challenge to the potential of adaptation of social systems, both at the macro level (the reaction of states, churches, and public opinion) and at the micro level (the adjustments of individual sexual practices, nuptiality patterns, and family support structures).

3. The Policy Orientation

The reorientation of public health policies towards primary health care is one of the great policy changes of the modern era. It was proclaimed ten years ago at Alma-Ata, and its impact on Africa was one of the questions raised by the conference which is the origin of this volume. The authors of the papers presented here had been asked, in advance, to spell out the implications of their findings for public health policy, particularly in a primary health perspective. Under the circumstances of a looming health crisis in Africa, there is a need to rethink health policies. The economic crisis too has had consequences for the setting of priorities and for implantation of a primary health approach, with its potential for relieving national budgets from the heavy load of infrastructures.

The primary health ideology visualizes better health in a community perspective, using simple and accessible technology, and integrating various health efforts in a holistic fashion. In treating the subject of malaria control in Kenya, Kaseje addresses the issues of community participation that were so dear to the Alma-Ata theoreticians. Community health workers have not fulfilled what was expected of them (except as a source of drugs for self-administered chemoprophylaxis), indicating perhaps a failure of a particular programme, but perhaps also that in general, health workers may constitute a weak link in the execution of health policies. Because of the complexity of continuing health programmes using permanent paramedical staff, because of the logistic problems of maintaining a steady supply of drugs to decentralized health units, and because of the relative failure of some of the flagship programmes of the primary health movement, it is too early to decide whether the instruments of the primary health care arsenal have won the day. Neither growth monitoring nor oral rehydration therapy have proved themselves; immunization has borne the brunt this far of the public health effort.

There seem to be two reasons why the chapters in this volume do little more than pay lip service to the primary health care movement, whatever the success of its implementation. The first reason is the absence of the evaluation capability that better statistics and research would provide. A major theme of this volume is that we have not reached the stage where a synthesis evaluation of the best health policies can be attained on the basis of available data. The second reason is that crisis mortality, rather than community-based public health with its strong preventive component, has come to dominate our thinking in recent years. Here too, there is a dearth of information and data-gathering capability. As John and Pat Caldwell write, one of the main demographic findings resulting from the African droughts was that we do not have the statistical data to evaluate their impact. This is obviously true also of the recent AIDS crisis. It may be true that there is little relation between the presence of crisis and mortality levels; the Caldwells suggest that the drought has not interrupted the mortality decline of the recent years; but we cannot be sure from the data at hand.

Nevertheless, crisis mortality has certainly the potential to overwhelm the feeble health care systems of Africa, and to force the revision of the carefully designed blueprints that were meant to ensure community-based medicine. We are learning more about the administration of famine relief systems than about the prevention of famine. Refugee populations, relief centres and camps have their own brands of medicine, designed for the treatments of acute malnutrition and epidemics. And AIDS, with its urban focus and it visibility among the patients of large city hospitals, is the antithesis of the primary health care model.

The chapters in this volume consist of a selection of papers presented at an international seminar held in Yaoundé, Cameroon, from 19 to 23 October 1987, and hosted by IFORD, the United Nations Demographic Training and Research Institute. Two committees of the International Union for the Scientific Study of Population sponsored the Seminar: the Committee on Comparative Mortality changes, consisting of Stan D'Souza (Chair), Borbor Kandeh, Shiro Horiushi, Alberto Palloni, Jacques Vallin, and Étienne van de Walle, and the Committee on Anthropology and Demography, consisting of Gilles Pison (Chair), Peter Aaby, Lourdes Arizpe, Caroline Bledsoe, Monica Das Gupta, Tim Dyson, and Valérie Hull. A French version of the volume appeared as G. Pison, É. van de Walle, and M. Sala-Diakanda (eds.) (1989), *Mortalité et Société en Afrique*, INED–PUF, Cahier 124.

References

Mosley, W. H. and Chen, L. C. (1984), 'An analytical framework for the study of child survival in developing countries', in *Child Survival: Strategies for Research*, supplement to vol. 10 of *Population and Development Review*, 25–45.
Pebley, A. and Elodu, I. (1989), 'The relationship of birth spacing and child health', *International Population Conference*, New Delhi, vol. 1, pp. 403–17.
UNICEF (1988), *The State of the World's Children 1988*, Oxford University Press.

1 Trends in Childhood Mortality in Sub-Saharan Mainland Africa

Althea Hill
The World Bank

1. Introduction

The intention of this chapter is to present a broad, comparative outline of levels, patterns, and trends of childhood mortality in sub-Saharan mainland Africa, over a period stretching roughly from the late 1940s to the late 1970s. The mainstay of the analysis is inevitably information on child survival collected in population censuses and demographic surveys. Methods of analysis have been standardized as much as possible in keeping with the focus on the overall pattern of differentials in mortality levels and trends. Thus, the estimates presented here may not be the best that could be obtained for any one country with the aid of more refined methodology and country-specific information from other sources. It is hoped, however, that the broad picture is substantially correct, and can be useful in suggesting and supporting further investigation into the determinants of childhood mortality in Africa.

2. Sources of Data and Method of Estimation

(a) The data

Africa is rich in data on child survival, as reported retrospectively by mothers in censuses and surveys.[1] Such data are available at the national level for almost all sub-Saharan African mainland countries at least once (the only exceptions being Namibia, South Africa, Mauritania,[2] and Equatorial Guinea), and for the majority at least twice. However, there are two major gaps to be borne in mind:

---

[1] A list of the data sets examined and used for each country is available from the author, together with print-outs and graphs.

[2] The Demographic Survey of 1965 excluded urban areas, without (as in other countries) collecting comparable urban data in a separate operation that could be combined with the rural data; the 1981 survey excluded the nomad population.

1. The most recent date of data collection for most countries is still in the 1970s, and only a few have both collected and published data from the early 1980s. Because child survival data yield reliable estimates of childhood mortality only up to two or three years prior to the date of data collection, the analysis of trends can be carried only up to the late 1970s. Therefore, the effect of the economic and climatic shocks of the early 1980s (recessions, debt crises, droughts) cannot as yet be studied.
2. Data for periods of social and political turmoil, or open war, are also scarce; hence, the effects of such disturbances cannot yet be traced with confidence.

(*b*) The methodology

The basic technique of analysis was the Trussell variant of the Brass child survival method, as described in Manual X (United Nations, 1983). It was applied, using the AFEMOPC computer program,[3] to all available sets of child survival data, including sub-national information. The resulting retrospective dated series of survival probabilities, expressed as matching levels in Coale–Demeny model life tables, were graphed and evaluated for consistency and regularity, both within each data set and between data sets collected at different times. Data from other sources, such as direct reports of child survival from World Fertility Survey maternity histories or direct observations from longitudinal or multi-round surveys, were also used for evaluation at this stage. Data sets that were clearly anomalous with respect to other data sets, or that presented both extreme irregularities and un-believable levels or trends, were excluded from further analysis. So also was all information from mothers aged under 20, since this is generally con-sidered highly unreliable on methodological grounds (United Nations, 1983). The remaining results from national series were then crudely sum-marized to make inter-country comparisons easier. This was normally done by first selecting the Coale–Demeny model family which gave the most consistent results for each country. Then, for each data set, two averages were taken of the values of q(5) (the proportion of children dying before age 5)[4] corresponding to the levels in that model family estimated from propor-tions dead reported by each age group of women. The first average is of the three age groups 20–24, 25–29, and 30–34, and the second average of the three age groups 35–39, 40–44, and 45–49. These two averages were then dated in a corresponding fashion by averaging dates of reference for the two groups (A. Hill, 1991).

[3] Developed by K. Hill to apply the Brass P/F ratio and child survival methods using the methodology recommended in *Manual X* (United Nations, 1983). An earlier mainframe version has been published in Zlotnik, 1981.
[4] This measure has been christened the 'Under-Fives Mortality Rate' by UNICEF in recent publications.

There are two reasons for neglecting the infant mortality rate, traditional and familiar to non-demographers though it is:

1. It cannot be measured reliably through the Brass child survival method, being heavily dependent on the model of age patterns of mortality in early childhood incorporated in the estimation procedure. The proportion dying in the first five years of life is a much robuster measure.
2. More importantly, there is strong evidence, as mentioned above, that in much of Africa child mortality after the first year of life is high, sometimes as high as or higher than mortality in infancy. It makes no sense, therefore, from either the analytical or the policy and programme standpoint, to focus exclusively on infant mortality.

3. Results of the Comparative Analysis

The continent-wide results of the comparative analysis are shown in Tables 1.1 and 1.2. The continental picture of trends in the mortality of children under 5 is displayed in Fig. 1.1, and separately for western and eastern Africa in Figs. 1.2 and 1.3.[5] (Zaïre is shown in both since it stretches from the Atlantic to the Great Lakes.)

Four very striking general features are at once obvious:

1. declines in childhood mortality since World War II in most countries where data are available;
2. much variation in the type of decline between countries;
3. much variation in levels of mortality between countries;
4. a very marked overall difference in mortality levels between eastern and western Africa.

There are also three interesting types of exception to these general patterns:

1. a few countries with static or rising mortality, notably Angola, Niger, Nigeria, Mozambique, Ethiopia, and Rwanda;
2. a few western African countries whose mortality has fallen to eastern African levels, Congo, Ghana, Cameroon;
3. one eastern African country, Malawi, with a western African level of mortality, indeed high even by western African standards.

We describe briefly first the four major features of the continental pattern, then the three types of outliers, and finally summarize the position of Africa with respect to other parts of the developing world.

---

[5] The World Bank definitions of western and eastern are used here. Zaïre is classified as eastern Africa and the split runs from Chad and CAR/Sudan north of Zaïre to Angola/Zambia, south of Zaïre: all countries to the south of Angola are considered eastern Africa also.

Table 1.1. (*a*) *Summary estimates of childhood mortality (q5) over time, eastern Africa: Horn of Africa countries*

	Coale–Demeny model used	Date of reference	Estimated value of q5 (%)	Sources of data + quality[d]	
Sudan[a]	North	1959.7	20.1	1973	Census (poor)
		1965.1	19.3		
Ethiopia[b]	North	1958.2	23.6		Demographic
		1964.3	23.2		Survey (good)
		1968.0	22.7	1978	Addis Ababa
		1972.4	22.6		Demographic
		1975.9	22.3		Survey (fair)
				1980/81	Rural Demographic Survey (good)
Somalia[c]	North	1967.9	24.1	1980	National
		1974.3	21.4		Population Survey

[a] To reflect the trend in the base data better, 3 averages of 2 points only were taken.

[b] To reflect trends in base data better, 3 averages of 2 points each were taken from 1980/81 rural data. National averages were estimated by weighting rural values by 0.89, Addis values by 0.03, and other urban centres (assumed to be midway between Addis and rural values) by 0.08, following the 1984 census distribution of population. These same weightings were maintained at earlier periods for convenience. Since Addis mortality appeared to approach rural then, and thus to have little impact on national values, Addis values for the 1950s were also assumed to be the same as in the 1960s—again with little potential impact on national values.

[c] 1975 census data examined but not used because lacking data for the nomadic half of the population. Value for women 20–24 not used because extremely high and out of line. Averages of next 3 points taken, then of last 2.

[d] 'Quality' refers to the regularity and consistency of the results. Single data sets are never labelled better than 'fair' since no external checks of consistency can be made.

Table 1.1. (*b*) *Summary estimates of childhood mortality (q5) over time, eastern Africa: East and Central African countries*

	Coale–Demeny model used	Date of reference	Estimated value of q5 (%)	Sources of data + quality	
Kenya[a]	North	1947.5	26.2	1962	Census
		1950.0	25.4		(good)
		1955.0	23.1	1969	Census
		1960.0	21.1		(good)
		1965.0	18.8		
		1970.0	16.7		
		1975.0	14.9	1979	Census (good)

Table 1.1. (*b*) *(cont.)*

	Coale–Demeny model used	Date of reference	Estimated value of q5 (%)	Sources of data + quality	
Uganda	North	1957.1	24.5	1969	Census (fair)
		1964.7	20.2		
Rwanda[b]	South	1956.2	26.8	1970	National
		1968.0	22.1		demographic
		1975.8	22.8		Survey
		1979.1	21.7		(poor)
				1978	Census (fair)
				1983	National
					Fertility
					Survey (fair)
Burundi	North	1959.0	26.1	1970/71	National
		1965.5	23.1		Demographic
		1969.5	22.3		Survey
		1976.5	22.4		(good)
				1979	Census
					(good)
Zaïre[c]	South	1944.4	30.5	1955–57	National
		1951.3	26.8		Demographic
					Survey (fair)
Tanzania[d]	North	1953.4	26.2	1967	Census
		1958.9	24.2	1978	Census
		1966.5	23.2		
		1973.0	21.9		

[a] Values taken from a child survival analysis reported in an unpublished paper by K. Hill, prepared for the National Academy of Sciences Committee on Population and Demography in 1981. Data from national surveys in 1977 and 1978 examined but not used because out of line with census results.

[b] Points from child survival data chosen to correspond best with trend from direct maternity history reports, given serious inconsistencies in child survival data (Hill, 1983: 2): these values were those for women aged 45–49 in 1970, 40–44 in 1978, 20–24 in 1978, and an average of 20–24 and 25–29 in 1983.

[c] Since data were tabulated only for age groups 35–44 and 45–54, the last point was not used and an average of the values for 35–39 and 40–44 (which were estimated from exactly the same raw values of children ever born and since dead) was taken.

[d] Some uncertainty over correct national figures for 1978 (no national aggregations were done for the census tabulations). Two separate aggregations were done at the US Bureau of the Census and at the Population Studies Centre, University of Pennsylvania; these gave differing results, the former highly consistent with the 1967 data, but irregular, the latter less consistent but smoother. The Pennsylvania aggregation was used here. To smooth the series, data for the 4 oldest age groups only in 1967 were used, in 2 averages of 2 points: and the point for women aged 20–24 in 1978 was also excluded, with an average of women aged 25–34 taken instead.

Table 1.1. (c) *Summary estimates of childhood mortality (q5) over time, eastern Africa: Zambezi countries*

	Coale–Demeny model used	Date of reference	Estimated value of q5 (%)	Sources of data + quality	
Malawi[a]	South	1958.1	36.7	1970/71	Population
		1964.2	35.5		Change
		1972.8	33.4		Survey (poor)
				1977	Census (good)
Zambia[b]	North	1956.0	22.3	1969	Census (good)
		1962.5	20.7	1974	Sample
		1965.0	20.3		Census (fair)
		1970.0	17.2		
Zimbabwe[c]	North	1957.5	16.2	1969	Census (good)
		1964.0	15.4	1982	Census (good)
		1971.1	14.9		
		1978.4	13.7		
Mozambique[d]	South	1936.7	26.1	1950	Census (poor)
		1942.5	26.3	1980	Census (fair)
		1966.9	28.1		
		1974.2	28.2		

[a] To smooth transition between highly irregular 1970 data and smooth 1977 data, points for mid-1960s taken are average of 1970 values for women aged 25–29 and 30–34 years and 1977 values for women aged 40–44 and 45–49. For details of full analysis, see Hill, 1986. The 1984 Family Formation Survey results have not yet been released and thus could not be used.

[b] Standard procedure followed: for details of analysis see A. Hill, 1985.

[c] Because of slight anomaly in value for women 20–24 in 1969 (too high), only average of 25–29 and 30–34 taken for the 1969 data series. Data from 1984 Reproductive Health Survey could not be used because published in insufficient detail (only one decimal point for children ever born).

[d] Data for women aged 20–29 from 1950 were not used because evidently poor (Hill, 1991): two points taken from averages of women aged 30–34 and 35–39, and women aged 40–44 and 45–49. Anomalous (too high) data for women aged 20–24 in 1980 not used; instead last point taken from average of women aged 25–29 and 30–34. Data from the 1970 census were not used because grossly out-of-line (lower) than 1950 and 1980 data, and reasons to suppose enumeration incomplete (from evidence of intercensal growth rates as well).

(a) Major Features of Childhood Mortality Patterns

Overall mortality declines. There appears to have been some degree of decline in childhood mortality between the end of World War II and 1980 in the vast majority of African countries for which post-war data exist. The overall magnitude of the fall can be summarized by noting that in the Africa of the 1950s countries were common where 30 to 40 per cent of children died before achieving the age of 5 years, while it was very rare to find

Table 1.1. (*d*) *Summary estimates of childhood mortality (q5) over time, eastern Africa: Southern African countries*

	Coale–Demeny model used	Date of reference	Estimated value of q5 (%)	Sources of data + quality	
Botswana[a]	South	1959.0	17.7	1971	Census
		1967.4	15.9		(good)
		1970.2	14.5	1978	Census
		1977.0	11.6		(good)
Swaziland[b]	South	1951.7	24.1		
		1959.1	22.6		
		1962.8	22.4	1966	Census
		1969.7	21.5		(good)
				1976	Census
					(good)
Lesotho[c]	West	1956.9	20.7	1968–69	Demo-
		1964.7	19.4		graphic
		1965.1	19.0		Survey
		1973.0	18.3		(good)
				1977	Fertility
					Survey
					(poor)

[a] To smooth transition between series, 1981 data from women aged 45–49 were not used: instead average of women aged 35–39 and 40–44 was used.

[b] Because in both data sets the values for women aged 20–24 years were anomalously high (possibly because of late marriage and hence a high proportion of first births), they were not used. Averages of women aged 25–39 and 40–49 were taken instead.

[c] Data from the 1971–73 Demographic Survey and 1976 Census were not used because they gave results much out of line with 68/69 and 77 (and with each other).

countries which lost less than 22 per cent. By the mid-1970s, however, very few African countries documented losses of more than 27 per cent of children before age 5, and losses of less than 22 per cent were common. This represents a major post-war achievement in African development.

Variations in declines. However, the observed declines vary greatly in size, timing, and pace, even taking into account the methodological difficulties of dating retrospective child survival data. In some countries, falls in mortality have been dramatic. The percentage of children dying before reaching their fifth birthday almost halved in Ghana over 30 years between the late 1930s and late 1960s (from 37 to 20 per cent), in Congo over 20 years between the late 1940s and late 1960s (from 29 to 15 per cent), and in Kenya over 25 years between the late 1940s and early 1970s (from 26 to 15 per cent). In other countries, observed declines have been much more gradual. In

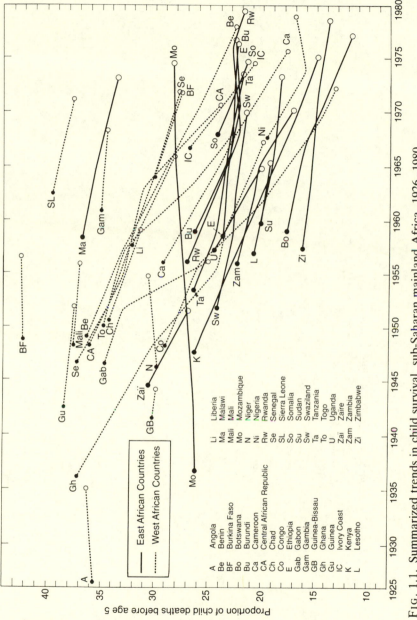

FIG. 1.1. Summarized trends in child survival, sub-Saharan mainland Africa, 1926–1980

Table 1.2. (a) Summary estimates of childhood mortality (q5) over time, western Africa: Sahel countries

	Coale–Demeny model used	Date of reference	Estimated value of q5 (%)	Sources of data + quality
Mali	South	1947.9	37.5	1960–61 Demographic Survey (fair)
		1955.7	36.9	
Niger	South	1945.9	29.7	1959 National Demographic Survey (fair)
		1954.6	30.5	
Chad	South	1950.4	34.2	1964 National Demographic Survey (fair)
		1958.8	31.3	
Senegal[a]	South	1946.2	37.3	1960 National Demographic Survey (poor)
		1951.6	34.3	
		1966.8	29.0	1978 Fertility Survey (poor)
		1971.7	27.6	
Gambia	South	1960.6	34.9	1973 Census (fair)
		1968.1	34.3	

Burkina Faso[b]	South	1960–61	Rural Demographic Survey (?)	42.1	1948.5
				42.3	1956.4
		1961	Ouagadougou Demographic Survey (?)	30.0	1963.7
				27.5	1971.4
		1976	Post-Censal Survey (?)		
Guinea-Bissau[c]	South	1950	Census (poor)	30.1	1941.4
				29.8	1943.9

[a] To smooth the very irregular series and conform as much as possible to the Ewbank analysis and the directly reported data only the data from the four oldest age groups of women in 1960 and 1978 were used (divided into 2 averages of 30–34 and 35–39, and 40–44 and 45–49 respectively).
[b] Quality of both survey and census problematic; both internally smooth and regular (would merit fair or good) but utterly inconsistent with each other. Two separate trend lines are used, since there is no internal basis for preferring one data set to the other (see A. Hill): 2). National estimates from 1960/61 data are obtained by weighting rural and Ouagadougou values by 0.976 and 0.024 respectively; on the assumption that the only other town, Bobo-Dioulasso (which together with Ouagadougou made up the estimated 2.4 per cent urban dwellers in the population at that date) had similar levels of childhood mortality to Ouagadougou.
[c] Due to exceptionally poor and erratic data, points for women 45–49, 20–24, and 25–29 were not used (all much lower values). The remaining four were grouped in two averages of two.

Table 1.2. (*b*) *Summary estimates of childhood mortality (q5) over time, western Africa: Coastal strip countries*

	Coale–Demeny model used	Date of reference	Estimated value of q5 (%)	Sources of data + quality	
Guinea	South	1942.2	38.4	1955	National
		1949.7	37.6		Demographic
					Survey (fair)
Sierra Leone	South	1962.2	39.4	1974	Census (fair)
		1969.4	37.8		
Liberia[a]	South	1957.3	32.1	1970/71	PGE Survey
		1965.6	28.1		(fair)
Ivory Coast[b]	South	1966.5	26.7	1978/9	National Multi
		1974.3	20.7		Round
					Demographic
					Survey (good)
Ghana[c]	South	1935.9	37.1	1948	Census, S.E.
		1948.0	30.1		(poor)
		1955.4	24.1	1960	Census, S.E.
		1959.2	23.3		(fair)
		1967.1	19.9	1970	Census, S.E.
					(good)
Togo[d]	South	1949.9	34.7	1961	National
		1957.2	32.8		Demographic
		1963.5	26.2		Survey (fair)
		1968.0	22.7	1971	National
					Demographic
					Survey (fair)
Benin	South	1948.8	36.3	1961	National
		1956.6	33.2		Demographic
		1970.2	25.8		Survey (good)
		1977.8	22.4	1981	Fertility Survey
					(poor)

[a] Child survival data were collected in both 1970 and 1971, giving somewhat different levels and trends (1971 generally higher mortality than 1970 except at youngest ages of women, but showing a fall over recent years as opposed to 1970, which showed a rise) that are difficult to interpret. (The cholera epidemic in 1971 would not have affected 1970 data, and 1971 only to a minor degree, and its effects are not consistent with the differential in trends.) An average of the two sets of data was taken. 1974 Census data were not used, because although close to 1970/71 levels in the data from the oldest women, they showed a fantastic decline in the data from the youngest women. Probably errors stemming from the imputation programs used for processing the census data are responsible.

[b] Point for women aged 30–34 from 1978/79 survey omitted because of obvious error in raw numbers in survey report table (mortality far too high as a result). Average taken of points for women aged 20–24 and 25–29 only. Child survival data from 1980/81 survey not used because inconsistent with both 1978/79 and its own direct maternity history reports (which are very consistent with 1978/79).

[c] The 3 points for the younger women in 1948 were not used.

[d] Points for 2 oldest age groups in 1971 omitted in order to smooth transition between the 2 series; averages taken of women aged 20–24 plus 25–29 and women aged 30–34 plus 35–39.

Table 1.2. (*c*) *Summary estimates of childhood mortality (q5) over time, western Africa: Central/western countries*

	Coale–Demeny model used	Date of reference	Estimated value of q5 (%)	Sources of data + quality	
Nigeria[a]	South	1967.5	19.6	1981–82	Fertility
		1973.6	16.0		Survey,
		1978.7	16.9		Individual
					Survey
					(poor?)
Cameroon[b]	South	1955.9	29.1	1978	Fertility
		1966.1	23.4		Survey (fair)
		1973.6	18.9		
Central	South	1948.0	36.0	1959	Demographic
African		1954.6	32.9		Survey of
Republic		1963.0	30.9		Centre-
		1970.4	23.9		Oubangui
					(fair)
				1975	Census (fair)
Gabon[c]	South	1946.3	34.6	1960	National
		1951.5	32.9		Demographic
		1956.1	24.9		Survey (poor)
Congo[d]	South	1948.0	28.9	1960–61	Rural
		1955.8	25.8		Demographic
		1961.8	19.9		Survey (good)
		1969.4	14.5	1961	Brazzaville
					Demographic
					Survey (good)
				1974	Census (fair)
Angola[e]	South	1926.4	35.6	1940	Census (fair)
		1934.8	36.2		

[a] South model taken because closest to the direct reports of child survival. Three averages of 2 points each taken in order to reflect trend of base data.

[b] The individual Survey child survival data were used in preference to the Household Survey data, though not on very strong grounds. South was selected because it fitted the directly reported trend better. The earliest point from the direct data was also used since no indirect estimates reached back that far.

[c] Because of very jerky, step-wise trend, averages were done in 3 pairs.

[d] National estimates from 1960/61 data were obtained by weighting values from each survey by the 1960 distribution of total population (16.1 per cent in Brazzaville, 8.4 per cent in Pointe-Noire, 75.5 per cent in the rest of the country covered in the Rural Survey), on the assumption (which is not very important) that Pointe-Noire child mortality levels were similar to the national average.

[e] Because of anomalously high value for women aged 20–24, this point was omitted and average of two points for 25–29 and 30–34 only taken.

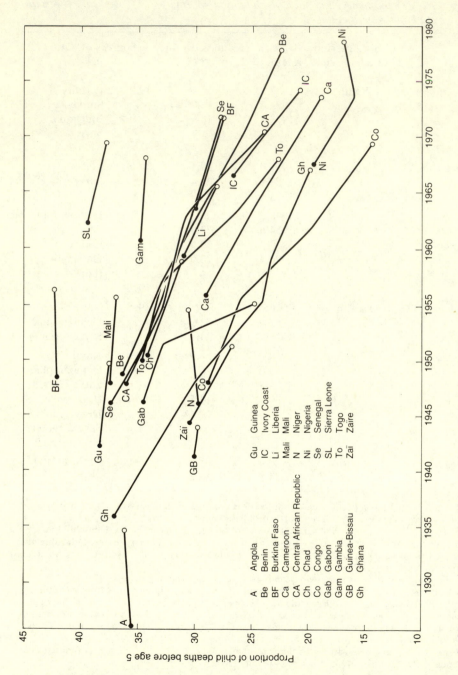

Fɪɢ. 1.2. Summarized trends in child survival, western Africa, 1926–1980

A   Angola
Be   Benin
BF   Burkina Faso
Ca   Cameroon
CA   Central African Republic
Ch   Chad
Gab   Gabon
Gam   Gambia
GB   Guinea-Bissau
Gh   Ghana

Gu   Guinea
IC   Ivory Coast
Li   Liberia
Mali Mali
N   Niger
Ni   Nigeria
Se   Senegal
SL   Sierra Leone
To   Togo
Zaï   Zaïre

Proportion of child deaths before age 5

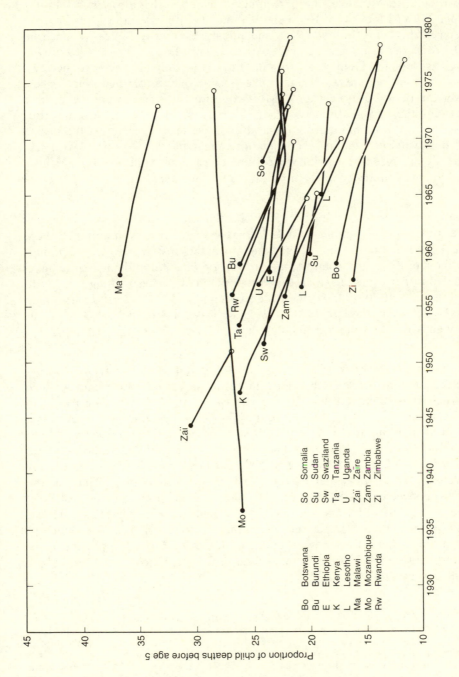

Fig. 1.3. Summarized trends in child survival, eastern Africa, 1926–1980

Swaziland, for example, the percentage of children dying by age 5 fell only from 24 to 21.5 per cent between 1950 and 1970; in Lesotho from 21 to 18 per cent between the mid-1950s and mid-1970s; and in Sierra Leone from 39.5 to 38 per cent over the decade of the 1960s. Indeed, in a few countries, such as Mali and Guinea (all with data available only for one early period), the observed decline was even smaller, being one percentage point or less over the period of observation. Most countries, however, were somewhere between these two extremes. Generally speaking, declines in eastern Africa have been slower and more gradual than in western Africa, over the period of observation: a tentative explanation might be that eastern Africa had already advanced to a point where further gains in child health were, in a developing country context, more difficult to achieve.

Variations in mortality levels.   The variations in mortality levels in Africa are truly impressive in all periods for which data exist, even although there has been some narrowing of the range over the post-World War II period. In the late 1950s, for example, the proportion of children dying before age 5 ranged rather evenly from 16 to over 40 per cent, corresponding roughly to a difference of 20 to 25 years in life expectancy (30–35 years versus 50–55 years). Even by the late 1970s, the range was still from 12 to 33 per cent, though with most countries falling below an upper limit of 27 per cent.

West/East differentials.   There is, beyond doubt, a marked and consistent differential between childhood mortality levels in eastern and western Africa. It is found throughout the post-war period, but has narrowed in more recent times. Childhood mortality has been generally much severer in western than in eastern Africa, with a rough gradient across the continent from north-west to south-east. The highest levels of childhood mortality are recorded in West and Sahel Africa, the next highest in Central Africa, lower levels in East Africa, and lowest of all in southern Africa.[6] Thus, in the 1950s, between 30 and 40 per cent of children died before 5 in most of West and Sahel Africa, between 25 and 30 per cent in Central and East Africa, and between 15 and 25 per cent in southern Africa. By the 1970s, much of West and Sahel Africa was experiencing losses of 22 to 30 per cent, compared with 20 to 22 per cent in Central and East Africa, and 12 to 20 per cent in southern Africa.

---

[6] South Africa and Namibia are not included in this analysis because of a lack of child survival data—indeed of any available large-scale survey or census demographic data. However, evidence from other sources indicates that the mortality of the black population of South Africa conforms to this general gradient, being rather similar to that of its neighbours Zimbabwe and Botswana. The national level is, of course, the lowest in Africa because of the European levels of childhood mortality enjoyed by the large white, Asian, and coloured minorities.

(*b*) Exceptions to the General Pattern

Static or rising mortality. There are six cases of persistent stagnation or rise in mortality shown in Figs. 1.1 to 1.3; namely Angola, Niger, Nigeria, Mozambique, Ethiopia, and Rwanda. To these we may add Sudan, for reasons to be shown later.

For Angola and Niger, only one data set is available, for an early period, and the rise is slight. In the case of Angola, further uncertainty is created by the generally very poor quality of Portuguese data collection in Africa (Brass *et al.*, 1968). The case of Nigeria also rests on one data set alone, since others had to be discarded because of obvious very poor quality. Thus, it is probably unwise to attach too much importance to these three cases.

For Ethiopia, Sudan, Mozambique, and Rwanda, two or more data sets exist (though in Sudan only for the north in recent times) and the observed trends must be taken more seriously. The data for Mozambique (another ex-Portuguese colony) are very doubtful and inconsistent, but the most likely inference by far is that childhood mortality did not fall in Mozambique between the late 1930s and the late 1970s, a trend explicable by lack of socio-economic development and the festering civil war over the period 1950–75.

The case of Sudan is also unclear. The data are incomplete, obviously of poor quality again, and inconsistent as regards levels of mortality in the north. The most prudent inference is that childhood mortality did not change greatly between the mid-1950s and mid-1970s; and again, this co-incides with a long-drawn-out and expensive civil war. However, doubts must remain at least till the child survival data from the 1983 census become available.

The case of Ethiopia is fairly straightforward. The data from 1970, 1978, and 1980 are consistent and appear of reasonable quality. Pending further data from the 1984 census,[7] a trend of long-term near-stagnation between the mid-1950s and mid-1970s must be accepted. Again, this stagnation coincides with a long-drawn-out and expensive civil war and a general lack of progress in socio-economic development.

The case of Rwanda, while complex, has been clarified recently by direct evidence on trends in child survival from maternity histories. Though doubts must remain over exact mortality levels and timing of trends, there is a clear overall trend of decline in childhood mortality during the 1950s followed by a plateau and then a rise between the early 1960s and mid-1970s, followed in turn by a recovery in the late 1970s. Again, these trends fit nicely as a somewhat lagged response to the country's history of rapid development in the 1950s and civil turmoil in the early 1960s, followed by an interruption

---

[7] Census results for Addis Ababa have already been published, but unfortunately do not include full raw data on child survival and hence cannot be used here.

of normal development until the 1970s, when socio-economic progress resumed.[8]

To summarize, then, these four cases of stagnating or rising childhood mortality are all individually subject to doubts or reservations. Taken together, however, they suggest (unsurprisingly) that the evolution of childhood mortality may be very sensitive to socio-political instability with accompanying interruptions or stagnation of socio-economic development. Data are lacking for most African countries in periods of such upheaval over recent decades, but it may be wisest to assume that the almost universal post-war declines observed in countries at peace are absent in times of severe instability.

Cross-over from western to eastern mortality level. Figs. 1.1 and 1.2 show, against the general background of higher mortality in western Africa and lower mortality in eastern Africa, three western African countries whose rapid mortality declines have brought them down from initial western levels to a position unequivocally within the eastern group. These countries are Ghana, Congo, and Cameroon. Nigeria is not included here, since the data are so uncertain in quality: in any case it would require separate classification as a West African country which had always been within the eastern range, if the directly reported child survival data were to be accepted.

The data from Ghana and Congo pose some difficulties of reconciliation and interpretation. However, according to the most plausible interpretation, these two countries began the post-World War II period already boasting the lowest childhood mortality in western Africa and then experienced (or continued to experience) dramatic declines throughout the 1950s and 1960s. By 1970, both had plunged well inside the eastern range; Ghanaian childhood mortality was comparable to the level in contemporary Uganda and Zambia, while Congolese childhood mortality had actually reached the very low level of contemporary Botswana and Zimbabwe. Trends since 1970 cannot be measured for Congo until the 1984 census results become available; for Ghana, the picture is unclear, but there was probably some levelling off in mortality, though still within the eastern range.

The interesting question is whether these two countries had always been unusual in their childhood mortality levels, or had simply experienced an earlier and steeper decline than the rest of western Africa. Very early data are not available for Congo, but 1930s data for Ghana do indicate mortality levels that were rather similar to the severe mortality characteristic of western Africa in the late 1940s. Perhaps, therefore, Congo and Ghana were

---

[8] One might mention here a somewhat similar response in Rwanda's 'twin' country of Burundi, where a similar decline in the 1950s, followed by only slow improvement in the 1960s and a plateau in the 1970s, can be linked to a history of rapid development in the 1950s, followed by civil unrest in the 1960s, which culminated in civil war and slowed development in the early 1970s (A. Hill, 1983*a* and *b*).

exceptional, not in any natural initial advantage in health conditions, but in an early start to their modern mortality decline. This early start could be explained for Ghana by its unusually early modern economic and social services development; and for Congo by the unusually high degree of urbanization long imposed by colonial development of the Congo railway.

Cameroon is a more recent and less spectacular case. Again, childhood mortality began (in the mid-1950s) at a comparatively low level for western Africa and then fell rapidly to within the eastern range by the mid-1970s. The same factors were operating in Cameroon as in Ghana and Congo, namely rapid economic and educational development and rather heavy urbanization, and may again have been responsible for the cross-over.

Finally, we note that several other West African countries (Ivory Coast, Central African Republic, Togo, Benin, Gabon) appear to have been heading for a cross-over at the last observed point in time. The Ivory Coast indeed had actually just passed the highest mortality eastern countries by 1975: no doubt its rapid economic development and heavy urbanization were again important factors.

A western mortality level in eastern Africa. In East and southern Africa, Malawi stands out as an exception to the general rule of relatively light childhood mortality.[9] While the earlier data are very rough, there can be no doubt of the overall high mortality level. The proportions of children dead before age 5 in the late 1950s and early 1970s (37 and 33 per cent respectively) are not only far above contemporary ranges in eastern Africa, but among the highest even in contemporary western Africa. There is no single obvious characteristic of Malawi that could be advanced to explain this anomaly.[10] The country has experienced political stability and good GNP growth over the past few decades, and appears broadly similar to the rest of eastern and southern Africa in climate, culture, and epidemiology.

(c) African Childhood Mortality Relative to the Rest of the Developing World

How does sub-Saharan Africa compare with the rest of the developing world in childhood mortality? It is often taken for granted that Africa is a continent of uniquely severe mortality. On the evidence presented above, there

---

[9] Mozambique is also within the western range, but only because of its lack of decline against a background of important falls in mortality elsewhere: whereas Malawi had apparently always been far outside the eastern range.

[10] It is interesting to note indications of exceptionally high childhood mortality also in neighbouring areas of Zambia, Tanzania, and Mozambique. In the ethnically and culturally similar Eastern Province of Zambia, for example, nearly 30 per cent of children died before the age of 5 in the mid-1960s, compared with around 20 per cent for Zambia as a whole. For further detail see A. Hill, 1985 and 1986.

can be no doubt that this assumption is generally true. This is the result of two special features:

1. Africa contains several countries that experience the severest peace-time childhood mortality currently to be found in the world, notably Sierra Leone, Gambia, Malawi, and probably a few others in western Africa. Only Afghanistan (at national level and in peacetime) has approached these levels in recent decades.[11]

2. Africa still possesses only a very few countries which have attained the moderately low mortality common in much of East and south-east Asia, Central and South America, and the Middle East. Moreover, in one of those, South Africa, the low national level is partly the result of the European level of childhood mortality enjoyed by the large non-Black minorities.

However, it is equally important to emphasize that many African countries are not exceptionally disadvantaged in childhood mortality. Much of eastern and southern Africa, as well as a few western African countries, compare well with many parts of the Indian subcontinent, with Indonesia, and with several countries in Latin America, North Africa, and the Middle East. It is misleading, therefore, to portray Africa as a homogeneous continent uniformly trailing behind the rest of the world in mortality, or to conclude that improvements in health conditions are necessarily more difficult to achieve in Africa than elsewhere.

4. Conclusion

The results presented above have brought out two dominant characteristics of childhood mortality in Africa, namely general but uneven post-war progress, and an enormous heterogeneity of levels and trends between countries. In this paper, only national-level estimates have been considered, but heterogeneity within countries is just as impressive. Two illustrations are given in Figs. 1.4 and 1.5 which display proportions of children dead by age 5 for districts of Zaïre in the early 1950s (from the 1955–7 Demographic Inquiry) and for provinces of Zambia in the mid-1960s (from the 1969 census); these range from 15 to 38 per cent in Zaïre and from 13 to 29 per cent in Zambia.

Information on the determinants underlying these patterns of heterogeneity is almost totally lacking. Analysis at the micro level, notably of WFS data, has shown general patterns of individual variation common to the rest of the developing world. As regards socio-economic variables, childhood mortality is lower for urban residents, educated mothers, educated fathers

[11] See, for crude comparisons, the tables of mortality indicators in World Bank, 1986, and UNICEF, 1987.

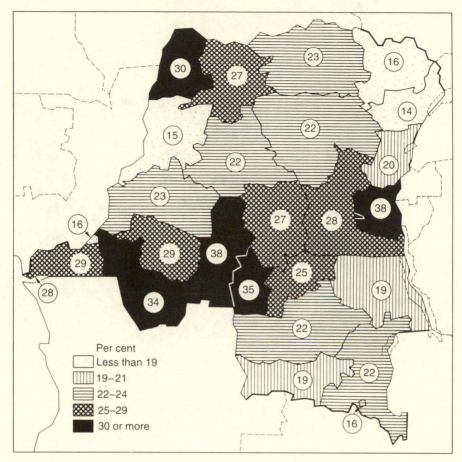

FIG. 1.4. Percentage of children dying in the first five years of life (q5) by district, Zaïre, 1950–1953

(to a lesser degree), and higher income and higher socio-economic status families. As regards biological variables, infant and child mortality is higher for teenage mothers, high-parity mothers, and mothers with short birth intervals. Scattered small-scale studies have indicated the crucial importance of infant and child feeding practices, severe seasonal food shortages, and the burden of various diseases such as malaria, measles, tetanus, and gastro-intestinal infections, in determining the level and pattern of childhood mortality.

At the national and regional level by contrast, it is known that most of the variation in levels and trends between regions and countries, particularly the basic West/East contrast, cannot be explained by standard economic or

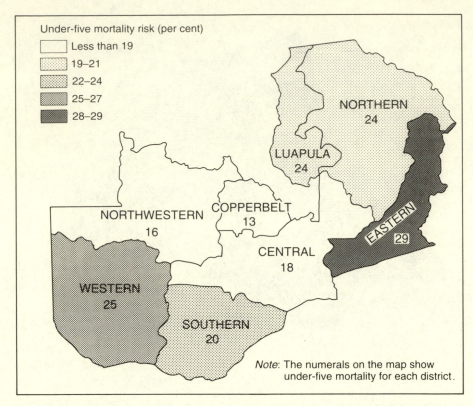

Under-five mortality risk (per cent)

Less than 19
19–21
22–24
25–27
28–29

NORTHERN
24

LUAPULA
24

NORTHWESTERN
16

COPPERBELT
13

EASTERN
29

CENTRAL
18

WESTERN
25

SOUTHERN
20

Note: The numerals on the map show under-five mortality for each district.

FIG. 1.5. Percentage of children dying in the first five years of life (q5) by province, Zambia, mid-1960s

social variables such as GNP per person (K. Hill, 1985) or level of education, but there is no general agreement as to what are the other important variables. Many candidates have been proposed, including climate, altitude, ecology, epidemiology, basic diets, and patterns of population settlement, as well as various cultural, social, political, and historical factors. However, few systematic, integrated studies even of regional differentials within countries have been done, let alone of differentials between countries or cultural or ecological groups across country boundaries. Yet countries, and still more regions and districts within countries, are the administrative, financial, and political units in the framework of which policies and programmes aimed at improving health and survival will be designed, targeted, and implemented. Studies using these units as units of analysis are thus needed in order to elucidate the determinants of childhood mortality in Africa and to assist in the design of strategies and interventions to improve child survival still further.

References

Brass, W. A., Coale, J., Demeny, P., Heisel, D., Romaniuk, A., and van de Walle, E. (1968), *The Demography of Tropical Africa*, Princeton University Press.

Hill, A. (1983a), 'The Demographic Situation', PHN Technical Note, The World Bank.

—— (1983b), 'The Demographic Situation in Burundi', PHN Technical Note, The World Bank.

—— (1985), 'The Demography of Zambia', PHN Technical Note 85–9, The World Bank.

—— (1986), 'The Demography of Malawi', PHN Technical Note 86–20, The World Bank.

—— (1991), 'Childhood mortality', in R. G. Feachem and D. Jamison (eds.), *Disease and Mortality in Sub-Saharan Africa*, Oxford University Press for the World Bank (in press).

Hill, K. (1985), 'The pace of mortality decline since 1950', in J. DaVanzo, J. P. Habicht, K. Hill, and S. Preston, *Quantitative Studies of Mortality Decline in the Developing World*, World Bank Staff Working Paper 683, Population and Development Series, 8: 57–95.

UNICEF (1987), *The State of the World's Children 1987*, Oxford University Press.

United Nations (1983), *Indirect Techniques for Demographic Estimation: Manual X*, Population Studies 81, Department of International Economic and Social Affairs, New York.

The World Bank (1986), *World Development Report 1986*, Oxford University Press.

Zlotnik, H. (1981), *Computer Programs for Demographic Estimation: A User's Guide*, National Academy Press, Washington, DC.

2 Socio-Economic and Cultural Differentials in the Mortality of Sub-Saharan Africa

Dominique Tabutin and Eliwo Akoto
Institute of Demography, Catholic University of Louvain

1. Introduction

Scientific research on African mortality is hindered by the lack of good quality data and by the insufficient use of the information that has been collected, however imperfect or indirect it may be. As a rule, overall mortality remains poorly known (Waltisperger, 1988). By contrast, within the last ten years, there has been an increase in information about the mortality of children (levels, differentials, and determinants) thanks to several censuses which have been used for that purpose, and thanks even more to various fertility surveys which allow the studies of differences at the national level.[1]

Here we are interested in socio-economic and cultural differentials in mortality, and not in bio-demographic factors such as age and fertility of the mother, birth order, birth intervals, or breast-feeding, the role of which is well enough known (Hobcraft et al., 1983, 1985; United Nations, 1985; Rutstein, 1984; see Akoto, 1985: 141–55, for a review of the literature on infant mortality in Africa from 1960 to 1983). We shall focus on the differentials by level of education (of father and mother), occupation, employment status of women, place of residence, region, religion, and ethnic group. In this comparative review of the whole of sub-Saharan Africa, we bring together results which were published in many different places, and proceed to additional analyses of certain World Fertility Surveys (Ghana, Kenya, and Cameroon), and to one new analysis (Rwanda).

We shall first examine inequalities in child mortality at the national level variable by variable, and then use a multivariate approach (Multiple Classification Analysis) in an attempt to measure the role of each of the

---

This chapter was translated by Mark Hereward.

[1] The results of retrospective fertility surveys must always be interpreted with caution, because of the possibility of recall lapses and age misreporting, and because of the small sample size. In comparing sub-populations, it is questionable to assume that the data have similar biases. Finally, the results refer to a more or less distant period in the past. We will limit ourselves most often to women between 20 and 34 years of age, or to birth cohorts of the last 15 years, and rely mainly on $_5q_0$, the probability of dying between 0 and 5 years.

socio-economic variables. The dependent variable will be an individual woman's index of child mortality (Preston and Trussell, 1982). This analysis will be conducted for Kenya and Cameroon.

2. The Effect of Education

Educational level is probably the most commonly used variable in the study of mortality differentials. And indeed, education generally plays a direct role in shaping behaviour toward children, as it is a proxy for socio-economic status. We shall not only examine the role of the mother's education, but also the role of the father's, and then we shall look at the combination of two. Table 2.1 gives infant and child mortality by mother's education in nine countries, Table 2.2 shows the mortality between 0 and 5 years of age by the father's education in six countries, while Table 2.3 combines the education of both parents. Figs. 2.1 and 2.2 illustrate the relationship for mortality between 0 and 5.

(a) Mother's education

Everywhere, mortality falls as expected, more or less strongly and more or less rapidly, with an increase in the mother's education. For 0–5 years of age, the excess mortality of the children of illiterate women over that of children whose mothers had at least seven years of schooling ranges from 190 in Benin and 160 per cent in Senegal to only 40 per cent in Ghana and Lesotho (Fig. 2.1). According to these data, the role of the mother's education varies greatly by country. These inequalities by educational level differ also for the two subgroups under 5 years: except in Benin and Kenya, the inequalities are clearly more marked between 1 and 5 years than under 1 (Table 2.1). It is above 1 year that the child runs the greatest risks, because of weaning or the arrival of another child, and it is at those ages that the mother's education can exert its full impact.

The level of education after which noticeable declines in mortality are observed also varies according to the country. In Senegal, Sudan, or Benin, which are high mortality countries, three years of elementary school already give a great advantage over being illiterate, whereas in Rwanda, also a country of high mortality, maternal education plays a genuine role only after four years of schooling. Similarly, in Kenya and Lesotho, which have a lower level of mortality, it is only after at least four years in school that a clear effect of the woman's education appears.

(b) Father's education

In the six countries examined (Table 2.2 and Fig. 2.1), mortality generally falls with the increased education of fathers, but here too we find a great

Table 2.1. *Infant and child probabilities of dying (per 1,000), by mother's education*

Country		Years of Schooling				
		0	1–3	4–6	7+	Total
Benin (1982)	$_1q_0$	130	86	46	30	123
	$_4q_1$	140	115	83	59	137
	$_5q_0$	252	191	125	87	243
Cameroon (1978)	$_1q_0$	112	100	84	66	99
	$_4q_1$	87	65	57	36	72
	$_5q_0$	189	159	136	101	163
Ghana (1979)	$_1q_0$	74	59	66	64	70
	$_4q_1$	60	(63)	36	31	49
	$_5q_0$	130	119	100	93	116
Kenya (1978)	$_1q_0$	112	105	88	64	101
	$_4q_1$	81	70	46	52	70
	$_5q_0$	184	168	130	113	163
Lesotho (1978)	$_1q_0$	168	167	136	141	143
	$_4q_1$	(75)	65	62	37	59
	$_5q_0$	230	221	190	173	194
Nigeria (1981–82)	$_1q_0$	127	n.a.	97	67	104
Rwanda (1983)	$_1q_0$	120	114	107	(88)	116
	$_4q_1$	132	133	88	(40)	124
	$_5q_0$	236	232	186	124	225
Senegal (1978)	$_1q_0$	130	68	92	—	127
	$_4q_1$	194	(119)	(26)	(19)	186
	$_5q_0$	299	179	116	—	289
Sudan (1973)	$_5q_0$	218	170	135	108	195

Notes: (□): Rates calculated on 200–500 survivors.
—: Fewer than 200 survivors.
n.a. Not available.

Sources: Benin: National fertility survey; all births. Educational categories are: no schooling, incomplete primary education, complete primary education, secondary education and more. Cameroon and Ghana: National fertility surveys data tapes; women 20–34. Kenya, Lesotho, and Senegal: Hobcraft *et al.*, 1984, births of 5 to 15 years preceding the survey. Nigeria: Ayeni, 1985, and National fertility survey; all births. Rwanda: National fertility survey; births of 1965–78. Educational categories are 0, 1–2, 3–5, 6 and more years of schooling. Sudan: Farah and Preston, 1982.

variety of situations. In Ghana, Rwanda, and Lesotho, the father's education has only a weak effect on mortality from 0 to 5 years of age; it plays a more important role in Cameroon and Kenya, and becomes crucial in Senegal. Differences between the lowest and the highest level of fathers' education varies from 'only' 21 per cent in Ghana to 251 per cent in Senegal.

Table 2.2. *Infant and child mortality by father's education*

Country	Years of Schooling				
	0	1–5	4–6	7+	Total
Cameroon	196	153		114	164
Ghana	129	117		106	116
Kenya	185	208	159	127	162
Lesotho	185	212	196	169	190
Rwanda	254	200			226
Senegal	299	254	135	85	270

Sources: Hobcraft *et al.*, 1984; Cantrelle *et al.*, 1986; WFS Data tapes.

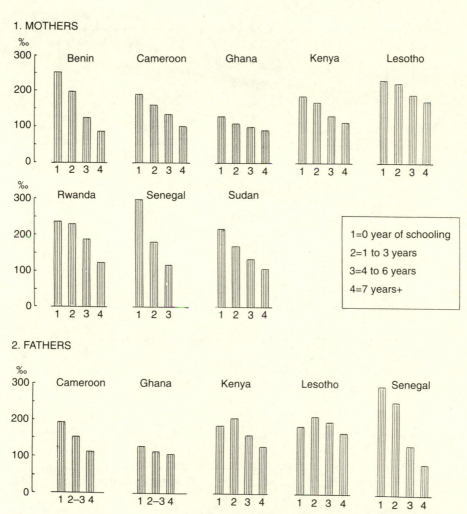

FIG. 2.1. Probability of dying before age 5 by mother's or father's education

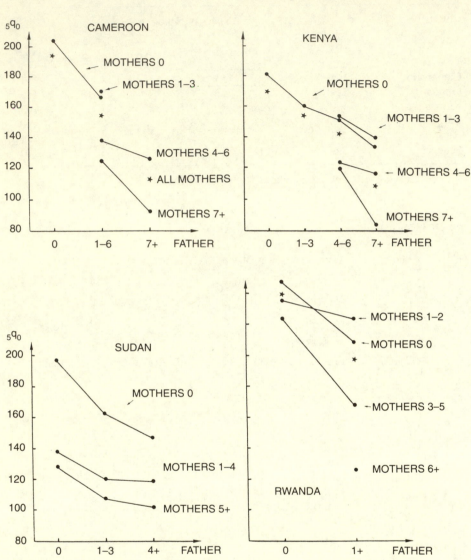

FIG. 2.2. Probability of dying before age 5 by mother's and father's education combined

There are even two countries, Kenya and Lesotho, where the mortality of the children of fathers who have started primary school is higher than that of the children of illiterates.[2] Rather like that of mothers', the influence of fathers' education does not really make itself felt until after four years of

---

[2] The differences are statistically significant, but this may well be due to problems of data quality.

Table 2.3. *Probability of children dying aged 0–5 by education of mothers and their partners*

Years of schooling of mother	Years of schooling of partner				
	0	1–3	4–6	7+	Total
Cameroon 1978					
0	204	166		—	190
1–3	(137)	171		—	158
4–6	(166)	138		125	137
7+	—	(123)		92	97
Total	196	153		114	164
Kenya 1978					
0	181	160	150	133	157
1–3	(140)	—	152	140	139
4–6	(155)	—	123	116	126
7+	—	—	120	80	88
Total	171	158	141	108	133
Sudan 1973					
0	0.197	0.162	0.147		n.a.
1–4	0.139	0.120	0.119		n.a.
5+	0.127	0.109	0.101		n.a.
Total	n.a.	n.a.	n.a.		n.a.
Rwanda 1983					
0	259	208			236
1–2	242	227			232
3–5	(234)	166			186
6+	—	124			124
Total	254	200			226

Notes: Women 30–34 years; in Rwanda, births cohorts 1965–78:
  (□): Rates computed on 200–500 births.
  —: Fewer than 200 births.
  n.a. Not available.

Sources: National fertility surveys except for Sudan: Farah and Preston, 1982.

primary school, but overall the father's education, considered separately, plays a lesser role than that of the mother. So what happens if we combine the two?

(c) Combined education of the father and the mother

Fig. 2.2 and Table 2.3 present for four countries (Cameroon, Kenya, Sudan, and Rwanda) the pattern of mortality at 0–5 according to the level of education (number of years of schooling) of the two spouses. In Fig. 2.2, we can observe the joint role of the education of each partner. Horizontally,

the mothers at a given level of education always have lower mortality than
those who are at a lower level;[3] vertically, mortality declines, for all levels of
the mother's education, with an increase in education of the father. We
have, therefore, an additive effect of the education of the two partners.

Having said this, the influence of the father's education (slopes of the
lines) is more or less strong according to the mother's education. According
to Fig. 2.2, the mother's education seems important at the two extremes,
when the mothers are illiterate, and when they are highly educated. By
contrast, when they have only had from one to four (or one to six) years of
schooling (Cameroon, Kenya, and Sudan), whether the men have attended
secondary school or whether they stopped at primary school does not
fundamentally alter child mortality. In summary, the mother's education
appears always to be a decisive factor, while that of the father comes into
play most of all at the two extremes of the mother's education (illiterate or
very well educated). The three situations doubtless correspond to different
positions on the social ladder. When husband and wife are both illiterate,
mortality is very high; when the wife has an elementary level of education,
the husband's education does not seem to matter very much; and when
husband and wife are both very educated, they belong to a privileged social
class which has low mortality in comparison to the others.

(d) Father's income and mother's education: The example of Nigeria

The education of the father is often considered a proxy for the socio-
economic status of the couple in place of income, which (and with reason) is
rarely asked in surveys. For Nigeria, where income was asked in a survey,
Table 2.4 presents the trends in mortality (Preston–Trussell indices) according to father's income and mother's education (United Nations, 1985). The
two extreme situations (on the one hand, a small paternal income and an
illiterate mother, or, on the other hand, both education and income quite
high) offer the clearest contrast. The mortality of these two groups varies by
a factor of two (one might have expected much more). Having said this,
at each level of income, mortality falls noticeably with rises in maternal
education, the role of which is confirmed once again. For example, Nigerian
families with a very small income (less than $70 per year) have markedly
lower mortality than richer ones ($300 or more) where the mother is
illiterate. Furthermore, when the mothers are literate, income is not an
important factor, except when it is high (more than $500). Only very high
standards of living,[4] corresponding to the privileged social class of that
country, have a clear effect on child mortality. Thus, the conclusion might

---

[3] Except in Kenya and Rwanda, where if the fathers are well educated, the mothers with one
to three years of schooling have children whose mortality is slightly higher than that of the
children of illiterate mothers.

[4] Calculated here only on the base of paternal income, which is of course much too narrow.

Table 2.4. *Preston and Trussell's relative mortality index by father's income and mother's education, Nigeria*

Father's income (US $)	Mother's education		
	0	1–6	7+
0–69	1.20	0.98	0.73
70–139	1.30	—	—
140–299	1.16	0.57	—
300–499	1.11	0.90	0.86
500+	1.02	0.66	0.59

Source: United Nations, 1985: 206.

be that it is better (in Nigeria, and perhaps elsewhere) to be poor but educated than rich and illiterate.

3. Effect of Husband's Occupation

This is a variable which determines social class, way of life, and standard of living. Table 2.5 presents differences in infant and child mortality between ten occupational groups of Cameroon and of Kenya. Fig. 2.3 illustrates differences in child and infant mortality between these groups (expressed in per cent of the reference category, the professionals).

Despite the differences in context and in levels of mortality ($_5q_0$ of 215 per thousand in Cameroon and 166 per thousand in Kenya), the two countries present similar profiles of inequality between occupational groups (Fig. 2.3). The agricultural category has very high excess mortality (from 190 to 220 per cent) in comparison with the wives of those in technical and managerial positions, with little difference between self-employed and salaried agricultural workers; in practice, those who have no work and the household workers are also at this end of the scale. At the other end, we find wives of clerical workers (who are quite close, especially in Kenya, to the professional group) and, not quite so well off (with an excess mortality of 40 per cent), wives whose husbands are in sales and services. Only one category, the manual workers, whether skilled or unskilled, has a very different relative position in the two countries. In Cameroon, the manual workers are better off than those in sales and services, with an excess mortality of 25 to 30 per cent, while in Kenya their mortality is close to that of agricultural workers and the 'never worked' category. (The cause of this difference between the two countries deserves to be investigated.) In Cameroon, as in Kenya, skilled workers have better conditions than non-skilled and manual

Table 2.5. *Variations in infant and child mortality by occupation of partner*

Occupation	Cameroon 1978			Kenya 1978		
	$_1q_0$	$_4q_1$	$_1q_0/_4q_1$	$_1q_0$	$_4q_1$	$_1q_0/_4q_1$
Professional	78	57	1.37	64	37	1.73
Clerical	115	57	2.09	67	41	1.63
Sales	113	80	1.41	93	45	2.07
Other services	109	78	1.40	98	50	1.96
Skilled manual	97	73	1.33	104	64	1.63
Unskilled manual	102	77	1.32	115	77	1.49
Self-employed agricultural	149	124	1.20	108	70	1.54
Agricultural workers	(100)	(79)	(1.27)	122	73	1.67
Private household workers	—	—	—	124	63	1.96
Never worked	(130)	(116)	1.12	98	69	1.42
Total	128	100	1.28	101	61	1.66

Notes: (□): Computed on 200–500 births.
—: Fewer than 200 births.
Source: Akoto, 1985.

workers. Setting aside the case of Kenyan manual workers, this scheme of inequalities reflects the social structure quite well.

Furthermore, in Kenya, as in Cameroon, the least favoured groups (the agricultural workers, the 'never worked' category, the unskilled workers in Kenya) present a higher excess child mortality than infant mortality. In other words, the differentials between the classes at either end of the social scale are greater for ages 1 to 5 than for the first year of life, while the opposite is usually true for managers and the intermediate class of clerical workers. This confirms that the greatest sensitivity to the economic and cultural environment is at the ages of 1 to 5 years.

For Rwanda (Table 2.6), in the three large sectors where mortality at 0 to 5 years can be distinguished by the occupation of the father, we find rates of 230 per thousand for agricultural workers, 163 per thousand for the informal sector, and 129 per thousand for the wage-earners and the self-employed in the modern sector. This represents a difference of 80 per cent between the two extremes. When the mother's occupation is also taken into account, mortality ranges from 230 per thousand when the two partners are in agriculture, to 145 per thousand when the two are outside agriculture. The important factor in explaining the level of mortality is whether or not the father is in the agricultural category.

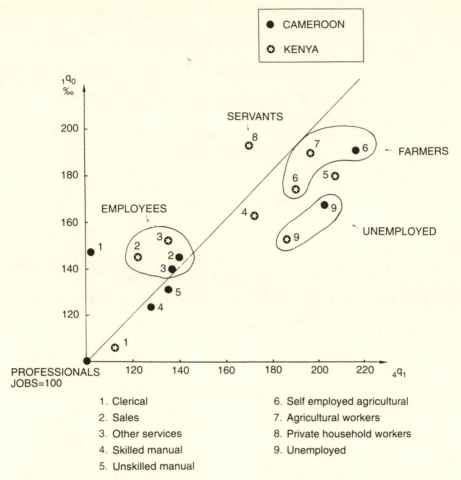

FIG. 2.3. Infant and child mortality differentials by father's education (in per cent of professionals)

1. Clerical
2. Sales
3. Other services
4. Skilled manual
5. Unskilled manual
6. Self employed agricultural
7. Agricultural workers
8. Private household workers
9. Unemployed

4. Effect of the Region

Table 2.7 presents data for eight countries. There are very large regional differences for child and for infant mortality, by a factor of three or four, or of two and a half if the region which contains the capital city is left out. Even in Mauritius, a small country with relatively low mortality, infant mortality ranges from 37 to 53 per thousand.

Fig. 2.4 shows the case of Kenya in 1979 for which mortality between 0 and 2 was estimated by district and mother's level of education (Ewbank *et al.*, 1986). Everywhere, the children of illiterate women have a higher

Table 2.6. *Mortality rates 0–5 years by occupation of father and combined sectors of father and mother, Rwanda*

Occupational group	$_5q_0$
Father	
In agriculture	230
In informal sector	163
In modern sector (salaried and self-employed)	129
Total	212
Father and mother	
In agriculture	230
Father not in agriculture, mother in agriculture	153
Both outside agriculture	145
Total	217

Source: National fertility survey, birth cohorts 1965–78.

Table 2.7. *Extreme rates of infant and child probabilities of dying by region*

Country	Number of regions	$_1q_0$	$_5q_0$
Benin (1982)	7	51–179 (123)	136–315 (243)
Cameroon (1978)	9	80–135 (113)	147–238 (203)
Kenya (1979), regions[a]	8	67–177 (125)	n.a.
Kenya (1979), districts[a]	40	49–216 (125)	n.a.
Mauritius (1975–76)	7	37–53 (46)	n.a.
Rwanda (1983)	10	86–151 (116)	188–280 (226)
Senegal (1978)	8	n.a.	172–430 (325)
Sudan (1973)[a]	10	121–253 (170)	n.a.
West Zaïre (1975–77)	10	n.a.	102–248 (184)

Notes: (□): National average.
  n.a. Not available.

  [a] $_2q_0$.

Sources: Benin: National fertility survey; Cameroon: National fertility survey; Women 20–34; Kenya: Ewbank *et al.*, 1986, and census of 1979; Mauritius: Etat Civil and WHO, Ministry of Health, 1981; Rwanda: National fertility survey, 1982, data provided by A. Ilinigumugabo; Senegal: National fertility survey and Charbit *et al.*, 1985; Sudan: Census of 1973 and Farah and Preston, 1982; West Zaïre: Survey, and Tabutin, 1979.

mortality than those of women with a primary level of education; and everywhere, the latter have a higher mortality than children of those with a secondary education. However, in the 49 districts and provinces, which have very different levels of mortality, there is quite a close correlation between mortality and educational levels. In other words, even when the key variable

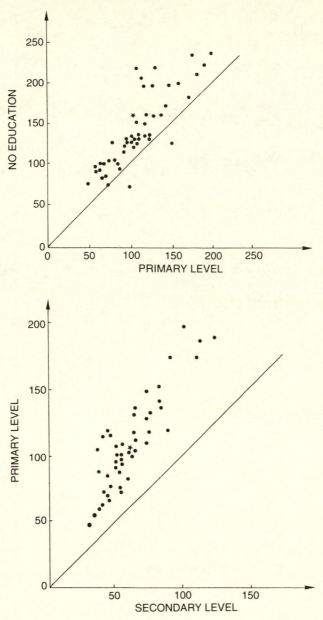

FIG. 2.4. Mortality differentials by mother's education in 49 districts of Kenya, 1979
☆: average (Kenya).
Source: Ewbank *et al*. (1986).

Dominique Tabutin and Eliwo Akoto

Table 2.8. *Infant and child probabilities of dying by place of residence*

Country	Large cities			Urban			Rural			Total		
	$_1q_0$	$_4q_1$	$_5q_0$	$_1q_0$	$_4q_1$	$_5q_0$	$_1q_0$	$_4q_1$	$_5q_0$	$_1q_0$	$_4q_1$	$_5q_0$
Benin 1982	70	90	154	105	138	229	138	147	265	123	137	243
Cameroon 1978	84	50	130	89	50	134	103	80	175	99	72	163
Ghana 1979–80	48	60	105	77	46	120	81	59	135	76	57	129
Ivory Coast 1979	53	43	99	72	65	132	94	80	166	84	73	151
Kenya 1978	(94)	(59)	147	95	37	128	102	72	167	101	70	163
Lesotho 1977	n.a.	n.a.	n.a.	132	(72)	194	145	58	195	143	59	194
Mauritania 1981	77	n.a.	n.a.	85	n.a.	n.a.	97	n.a.	n.a.	91	n.a.	n.a.
Mauritius 1975–6	48	n.a.	n.a.	37	n.a.	n.a.	48	n.a.	n.a.	46	n.a.	n.a.
Nigeria 1981–2	n.a.	n.a.	n.a.	62	n.a.	n.a.	119	n.a.	n.a.	104	n.a.	n.a.
Rwanda 1983	n.a.	n.a.	n.a.	81	81	156	118	126	229	116	124	225
Senegal 1978	82	94	167	81	116	187	146	222	336	127	186	289
Sudan 1979	81	45	122	66	60	121	83	72	148	81	67	143
Zaïre West 1976	87	39	123	106	54	155	144	83	215	118	66	176

Notes: (□): Computed on fewer than 500 survivors.
n.a. Not available.

Sources: Benin: National fertility survey; all births; Cameroon: National fertility survey; women 20–34; Ivory Coast: Antoine and Herry, 1984; Ghana: Akoto, 1985; all births; Kenya, Lesotho, Senegal, and Sudan: Hobcraft *et al.*, 1984; births of 5 to 15 years preceding survey; Mauritania: National fertility survey; births of 5 in year preceding the survey; Mauritius: WHO, Ministry of Health, 1981; Zaïre: Département de Démographie and SICAI, 1978.

of education is controlled, the regional differentials remain very large: mortality between 0 and 2 for illiterate mothers varies by district from 70 to 250 per thousand, with an average of 163, and for mothers with secondary education from 31 to 140 per thousand, with an average of 61.

The multivariate analyses conducted at the national level in sub-Saharan Africa (in Senegal and Kenya, for example) all bring out the importance of the variable 'region' among the explanatory variables of infant mortality. In terms of action programmes and health planning, this is obviously an important finding.

5. Effect of the Place of Residence

(a) Large cities, smaller urban areas, rural areas

In general, in all bivariate analyses in the Third World, mortality rates are lower in urban than in rural regions, and lower in large cities than in medium-sized ones (Hobcraft *et al.*, 1984). These results are not surprising in view of the higher concentration of resources (health, education, income) in urban areas. What about sub-Saharan Africa? Table 2.8 presents, for 13 countries, the variation in infant mortality by three categories: large cities, other cities, and rural areas. Fig. 2.5 illustrates the mortality differences by these three categories for 11 countries, with a base of 100 for the large cities. It shows differences for mortality under 1 year of age, from 1 to 5, and for the whole 0 to 5 age group.

Overall, in sub-Saharan Africa, large cities enjoy the best situation, with the exceptions of Kenya and Ghana,[5] where child mortality in smaller cities is appreciably less than in metropolitan areas, and of Mauritius where the child mortality in the capital, Port Louis, is higher than in Plaines Wilhems.

The differences between large cities and other urban areas, and between urban and rural areas, vary considerably from one country to another, at least from the results shown in Table 2.8 and Fig. 2.5. Furthermore, the differences are generally larger for mortality at one to five than at less than one year. The greater sensitivity of child mortality to the social and economic environment appears once again. For infant mortality, in four countries (Cameroon, Kenya, Mauritania, and the Sudan) there are only small differences between the three categories (mortality rates reduced by only 10 to 25 per cent in large cities), while in six other countries, the observed excess mortality ranges from 30 to 75 per cent in other cities, and from 75 to 110 per cent in the rural areas. For child mortality (between 1 and 5 years of age) the gap increases everywhere, even in Cameroon and the Sudan where we now find an excess mortality of 60 per cent in the rural areas, while the difference reaches 100 to 150 per cent in Senegal and Zaïre.

[5] Mortality data for Ghana seem unreliable, and appear to be underestimates.

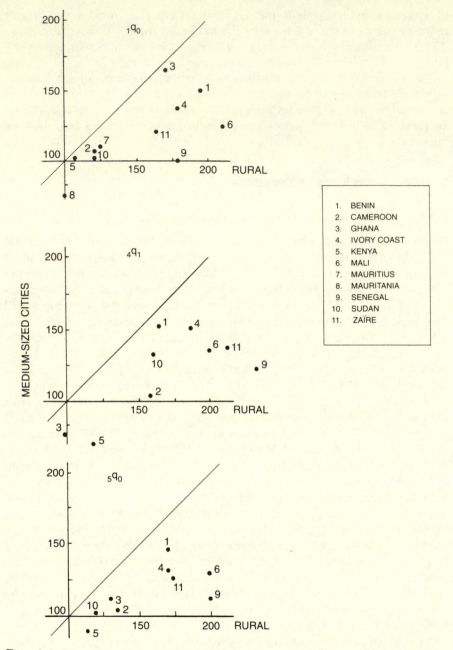

FIG. 2.5. Mortality of medium-sized cities and rural areas (in per cent of large cities)

For the overall mortality between 0 and 5 years of age, large cities show higher mortality than other urban areas only in Kenya. In three countries, Cameroon, Ghana, and the Sudan, they show only a small advantage. On the other hand, in the four other countries for which we have data, the metropolitan areas are clearly different from the rest of the country, with a very high excess mortality in rural areas.

In sum, the place of residence remains a key variable for child mortality. In Senegal (Cantrelle *et al.*, 1986), perhaps an extreme case, it is even the most important of all the socio-economic variables that are considered.

(b) Inequalities within large cities and capitals

Inequalities within large cities and capitals themselves are very large. In Pikine (a suburb of Dakar), mortality between 0 and 5 can be up to two and a half times higher, according to the type of area or, in other words, according to the social group or the parents' wealth (Antoine and Diouf, 1986). In Abidjan, child mortality can be up to twice as high, according to the type of housing, and mortality between one and five years of age varies by as much as a factor of 6 (Antoine and Herry, 1984). Child mortality is a better indicator of differentials than infant mortality. Everywhere (except in Yaoundé, for which see Dackam-Ngatchou, 1986, and this seems very surprising to us), the education of mothers is an important variable: mortality ($_5q_0$) is 40 to 50 per cent higher for illiterate mothers than for educated mothers in Luanda (Sousa Colaço, 1986) and Pikine. Perinatal mortality is 60 per cent higher in Kinshasa for the children of illiterate mothers than for the children of mothers with at least four years of secondary schooling. Everywhere, the source of water, which is merely another indicator of the quality of housing, also plays a non-negligible role, even if one controls for education, as in Pikine (Antoine and Diouf, 1986). In a study restricted to perinatal mortality in Kinshasa, the most important variable appeared to be the social status of the father, a proxy for social class. Between a manager or employer and a head of household without occupation, the proportion of still births and of deaths within the first week of life varied from 21 to 47 per thousand (Nzita Kikhela, 1986).

The small province of Luanda (2,400 square kilometres) of approximately one million inhabitants includes nine municipalities and 27 communes, of which 21 are urban. As in other large African cities, one can distinguish a modern zone, a transitional zone, a marginal zone, and a green belt (rural zone) in this urban region. In his analysis of the 1983 census of Luanda, L. F. Sousa Colaço (1986) studied the differences in mortality within the urban region. There as elsewhere, the mortality of children ($_2q_0$) clearly increases from the most modern and privileged to the poorer neighbourhoods and to the rural belt (Table 2.9). There also, the education of mothers plays an important role: in all neighbourhoods the children of illiterate mothers show

Table 2.9. *Child mortality ($_2q_0$) by urban district in Luanda, 1983*

District	$_2q_0$	% excess mortality of illiterate over educated mothers	% increase in mortality 1975–1980
Ingombota	121	57	17.5
Maianga	163	48	23.5
Rangel	148	33	13.8
Kilamba-Kiaxi	165	48	16.2
Sambizanga	183	30	17.3
Cazenga	184	27	18.7
Samba	179	14	−2.2
Viana	186	21	8.1
Cacuaco	255	11	10.4
Total	169	38	18.9
Urban communes	167	n.a.	19.3
Rural communes	231	n.a.	8.5
Illiterate	189		13.8
Educated	137		25.3

Note: Districts are ranked from the most modern to the most rural.
Source: Sousa Colaço, 1986.

excess mortality, but the differences between the illiterates and the educated are more important in the privileged zones. The differences range from 57 per cent in Ingombota (the modern sector) to only 11 per cent in Cacuaco (the green belt). Inequalities, then, increase with the modernization of the neighbourhood. The mortality of illiterates varies relatively little from one municipality to another (about 11 per cent between Ingombota and Samba), that of educated mothers much more (54 per cent). Education does not really play a role except in privileged and well-provided zones. In other words, the poorest social classes benefit much less than others from the social and health environment. These problems are perhaps cultural and behavioural, but they are certainly also economic (lack of resources).

Moreover, in Luanda infant mortality has increased since Independence (1975) because of war and a notable deterioration of the general conditions of life (health, diet). Mortality between 0 and 2 increased by nearly 20 per cent in five years. But contrary, perhaps, to what one might have expected, this increase in mortality was much higher in the modern than in the poor neighbourhoods, and higher in urban communes than in the rural communes of the province. The dramatic downturn in the conditions of life seems to have had a more clearly visible impact on the monetary economy (among salaried office workers in the centre) than on the subsistence economy (the rural or semi-rural sector of the periphery and the green belt). This demonstrates, if there was any need to do so, 'the fragility of health' in a very difficult economic and political climate, as exists currently in Luanda.

6. Effect of the Type of Economic Activity of the Wife

On the face of it, the fact that the woman works or not and, if so, whether she works at home or outside, should be an important variable. There may be consequences on the feeding of young infants (breast-feeding, weaning), on the attention and the care they receive, and, ultimately, on mortality. In fact, when the mother works outside the home, the child is often left in the care of other members of the family such as its brothers or sisters. For example, in rural Gambia, a good correlation has been observed between a rise in infant mortality and the periods of agricultural activity of the women, as well as between these periods and episodes of diarrhoea and malnutrition (quoted by Akoto and Hill, 1988).

In four of the six countries that were the subject of a 1985 United Nations study using the Preston–Trussell index of mortality, the mother's activity seemed to be more harmful to the child than her non-activity. This depended, however, upon the type of activity, because female family workers showed a clear excess mortality everywhere (except in Ghana), while the mothers who declared themselves 'clerical workers' had a great advantage over those who were either in other activities or non-active.

In Table 2.10, we present the results for six countries, this time using mortality rates between 0 and 5 years of age. Except in Ghana (again!) and perhaps in Kenya, working women have generally higher risks than others. But this average excess mortality among economically active women, here too, is a clear result of excess mortality among family workers. Mothers working outside the home have the lowest mortality of the three groups, even if the differences are not always very large.

Table 2.10. *Infant and child mortality rates by working status of mother*

Working status	Countries					
	Senegal	Lesotho	Kenya	Sudan	Cameroon	Ghana
Mother does not work	190	185	166	130	159	141
Works at home	322	226	(167)	161	170	119
Works outside home	(181)	189	138	(155)	130	106

Note: (□): fewer than 500 births.

Sources: For Senegal, Lesotho, Kenya, and Sudan: Hobcraft *et al.*, 1984; for Cameroon and Ghana: National fertility surveys; women 20–34.

Table 2.11. *Variations in child mortality ($_5q_0$) by place of last occupation, education, and place of residence of mother, Cameroon*

Place of occupation	Place of residence		Education		Total
	rural	urban	0–3	4 years +	
Farm or home	126	135	186	138	170
Outside home	(141)	123	(194)	106	130
Never worked	179	134	186	127	159
Total	175	132	186	127	164

Note: (□): fewer than 500 births.
Source: National fertility survey; women 20–34.

If one controls the variable 'mother's activity' for type of residence and the level of education (Cameroon in Table 2.11), the differences diminish somewhat. In rural or urban areas, or among women with little education, any significant difference between women working in the home and women who have never worked disappears. A difference remains only for women who are relatively well educated: for them, not to work is better than to work at home. As for work outside the home, it presents a clear advantage only in the urban areas and for women who have received more than four years of schooling (many of whom are to be found among the office workers).

In sum, except for white-collar workers with a higher level of education, the differences in child mortality according to the mother's activity are not large in Africa today. Having said this, might it not be feared that the future increase in female employment (as a result of education and modernization, or because of the economic crisis), in itself a good thing, may have deleterious consequences for the health of children, given the almost complete lack of non-familial structures for child care and family planning?

7. The Effect to Two Cultural Variables: Religion and Ethnicity

(a) Religion

As E. Akoto (1985: 185) has written:

religion carries with it a certain number of values and norms which govern the lives of believers on behavioural, physiological, and psychic levels. It may reflect an openness to western civilization (for Catholic and Protestant religions), adherence to customs (traditional religion), and sometimes the position of individuals in the social hierarchy (for example, in a very Christian country, Catholics and Protestants

Table 2.12. *Probability of dying at 0–5 years by religion of parents*

Religion	Number of deaths				
	Cameroon	Ghana	Kenya	Lesotho	Senegal
Catholic	205	104	192	161	162
Protestant	201	112	174		
Anglican				163	
Lesotho Evangelical Church				155	
Muslim	224	128	233		276
Traditional and others	274	166	207	182	
No. of births	23,101	18,189	24,811	11,473	n.a.

n.a. Not available.

Sources: Four first countries: Akoto, 1985, all births. For Senegal: Cantrelle *et al.*, 1986; birth cohorts 1967–72.

will benefit from a privileged position in society in comparison with Moslems or adherents to other religions).

Certainly, then, religion is not a variable to be neglected in a study of mortality differentials.

If one controls for no other variable, in Cameroon, Ghana, Kenya, Lesotho, and Senegal, Catholics and Protestants appear to show a lower mortality rate for their children (from 0 to 5 years) than Muslims or followers of traditional religions (Table 2.12). The latter show an excess mortality of 20 to 60 per cent, reflecting mostly differences in mothers' education. But when other socio-economic and cultural factors are included in a multivariate analysis for Senegal (Cantrelle *et al.*, 1986) or Kenya (Ewbank *et al.*, 1986), the variable 'religion' loses much of its explanatory force, and may even become insignificant. We shall see, however, that its role remains relatively important in Cameroon.

(*b*) Ethnic Group

In the five countries shown in Table 2.13, the ethnic groups have very different mortality rates. In Cameroon, the mortality rates for children under 2 years of age range from 116 per thousand among the Boulou (an ethnic group of the South) to 251 per thousand among the Bénoué (an ethnic group of the North), although the majority of ethnic groups have rates between 140 and 170 per thousand. In Kenya, the differences are still larger: from 74 per thousand among the Nandi to 197 among the Luo. In Ghana, they range from 74 to 158 per thousand, and in Senegal, at an entirely different level, from 261 among the Wolof to 452 per thousand

Table 2.13. *Probability of dying of children 0–2 or 0–5 by ethnic group of mother*

Cameroon		Kenya		Ghana		Senegal		Rwanda	
Ethnic group	$_2q_0$	Ethnic group	$_2q_0$	Ethnic group	$_5q_0$	Ethnic group	$_5q_0$	Ethnic group	$_2q_0$
Douala	135								
Bafia East and South	131								
Bassa	136	Kikuyu	93	Fanté	137	Wolof	261		
Baya	156	Luo	197	Twi	97	Poular	273		
Boulou	116	Luhya	140	Other Akan	158	Serer	326	Tutsi	168
Kaka	205	Kamba	131	Mole-Degani	131			Hutu	234
Maka	187	Kisii	125	Ewe	81	Mandingue	452		
Yaoudé	137	Meru	88	Ga-Adangbé	74	Others	291		
Bamenda	136	Mijikenda	164	Guané	104				
Bamiléké	140	Kipsigis	79						
Bamoun	178	Nandi	74						
Bénoué	251								
Toupouri-Guiziga	165								
Mendara	173								
Peul	171								
Fang	140								
Ratio of extremes	(2.16)		(2.66)		(2.13)		(1.73)		(1.39)

Notes: Cameroon, Kenya, and Ghana, all births; Senegal, births of 1968–78; Rwanda, births of 1965–78.

Sources: Cameroon, Kenya, and Ghana: Akoto, unpublished; Senegal: Charbit *et al.*, 1985; Rwanda: data provided by A. Ilinigumugabo.

Table 2.14. *Probability of dying of children 0–2 by ethnic group and place of residence of the mother*

Ethnic group	Cameroon			Ethnic group	Kenya		
	Urban	Rural	Rural/Urban		Urban	Rural	Rural/Urban
Bafia East and South	108	143	1.32	Kikuyu	83	96	1.16
Bassa	110	162	1.47	Luo	147	211	1.43
Yaoundé	123	141	1.15	Luhya	114	144	1.26
Bamenda	93	150	1.61	Kamba	95	135	1.42
Bamiléké	106	163	1.54	Mijikenda	111	183	1.65
Bamoun	126	199	1.58				

Source: National fertility surveys, Akoto (unpublished).

Table 2.15. *Mortality rates of children 0–5 years by ethnic group and education of the mother, Rwanda*

Ethnic group	Years of schooling			
	0	1–2	3 and +	Total
Tutsi	179	(232)	115	168
Hutu	242	231	194	234
Total	237	231	175	226
Ratio	1.35	(1.00)	2.01	1.39

Note: (□): Fewer than 500 births.
Source: National fertility survey, 1983. Data provided by A. Ilinigumugabo, births of 1965–78.

among the Mandingue. In Rwanda, the ethnic group both in the majority and in power (the Hutu) show a marked excess mortality, nearly 40 per cent higher than the Tutsi.

When one controls for place of residence, the differences diminish but do not disappear (Table 2.14). The ethnic groups that are most advantaged in rural areas are equally so in urban areas. The same is true in Rwanda when one controls for education; the excess mortality of the Hutu even increases with education of the women (Table 2.15). Ethnic differences of the order of 35 per cent have been found in two rural surveys, in Senegal and Mali (Table 2.16). In the Malian study (Hill and Randall, 1984), the Tamasheq nomads have lower mortality than the settled Bambara; in addition, the rich and noble caste has a higher mortality than the former slaves, the Bella. Although economic factors may also be relevant, these results argue for the relevance of cultural variables, acting through child care, in a context of 'natural mortality'. The ethnic variable should always be controlled in a study of mortality. And its importance persists after the effect of other variables has been accounted for, as we shall see below.

Table 2.16. *Probability of dying of children 0–2 years by ethnic group of mother in rural Mali and Senegal*

Mali (central)		Senegal (Saloum)	
Ethnic group	$_2q_0$	Ethnic group	$_2q_0$
Bambara	257	Wolof	251
Tamasheq	209	Serer	246
Peul	280	Peul	184

Sources: For Mali: Hill and Randall, 1984; for Senegal: Cantrelle and Livenais, 1980.

8. Multivariate Analysis

In this section, we perform a Multiple Classification Analysis (MCA) of the World Fertility Survey data for Kenya and Cameroon.[6] The purpose is to compare the predictive value of the variables that have been previously examined one by one. The dependent variable is the individual mortality index computed for each woman (Preston and Trussell, 1982). We have reduced the number of possible categories for each characteristic, in order to include as many variables as possible in the models.[7]

Significant child mortality differences appear only after three to four years of schooling; hence, we have retained only two categories for the variable education: women who have completed less than four years of schooling, and those who have more. Paternal education was similarly divided in two categories: 'less than ten years' and 'ten years and more'. As for religion, we have distinguished between Christian denominations, Islam, and the traditional religions. Always on the basis of the results of the univeriate analysis, we reduced the number of socio-occupational categories of the husband, by regrouping the professional and the clerical workers; the sales and other services; all those who work in the agricultural sector; all manual workers (skilled or unskilled); and those who never worked and the household workers.

Ethnic groups are arranged by the Ward method according to twelve economic, social, or cultural characteristics (see note 7), and we have ended up with six large groups for Cameroon, three large groups for Kenya, and a residual category for each.

(*a*) General Results

First of all, one observes a slightly different order among variables considered the most 'predictive' in the two countries. In Kenya (Table 2.17), women's education comes in first place (with an η coefficient of 0.12), followed closely by ethnicity, husband's education, and occupational category. By contrast, in Cameroon (Table 2.18) ethnic membership occupies first place, followed, though not far behind, by mother's education and partner's occupation. The most notable difference is the minor role played

[6] This technique is an analysis of variance which, like multiple regression, explains the variation in a dependent variable on the basis of a linear additive model which estimates the gross and net effects of each of the categories of the independent variables on the dependent variable.

[7] This was done on the basis of the results of the univariate analysis for most variables; ethnic group was an exception. In the latter instance, we have use Ward's classification method on 12 characteristics by ethnic group: the proportion of rural residents, the average number of years in school, the mean number of marriages, the average duration of breast-feeding, the proportion in agriculture, the proportion of women not using contraception, final parity, mortality level ($_q0$), and the proportions of Catholics, Protestants, Muslims, and animists. Detailed results are not presented here for lack of space.

Table 2.17. *Multiple classification analysis of individual mortality, Kenya*

Independent variables	N	Deviations from the mean			
		Gross	η	Net	β
Educational level of mother			0.12		0.07[a]
1. Less than 4 years of schooling	2,382	0.13		0.08	
2. 4 years of schooling and more	1,710	−0.18		−0.11	
Educational level of partner			0.11		0.05[a]
1. Less than 10 years of schooling	3,300	0.07		0.03	
2. 10 years of schooling and more	792	−0.30		−0.14	
Place of residence			0.07		0.04[a]
1. Rural	3,301	0.04		0.02	
2. Urban	791	−0.18		−0.10	
Religion			0.04		0.00
1. Christian	3,672	−0.02		−0.00	
2. Muslim	195	0.13		0.00	
3. Traditional	225	0.18		0.01	
Ethnic Group			0.11		0.12[a]
1. Kikuyu-Kamba-Luo-Luhya	2,856	0.06		0.08	
2. Kisii-Kipsigis-Nandi-Meru	728	−0.21		−0.28	
3. Mijikenda	216	0.31		0.22	
4. Others	292	−0.24		−0.26	
Occupation of Partner			0.11		0.06[b]
1. Professional and clerical	748	−0.30		−0.15	
2. Sales and other services	731	−0.03		−0.04	
3. Agricultural	1,413	0.10		0.06	
4. Skilled and unskilled manual	964	0.07		0.04	
5. Never worked and household workers	236	0.19		0.11	
Total number of women	4,092				
General mean	0.82				
Per cent of explained variance	3.6[a]				

Notes:
[a] Significant at 1 per cent level.
[b] Significant at 5 per cent level.

in Cameroon by the husband's education, which is quite important in Kenya. As far as religion is concerned, it remains the least predictive variable in both countries, with an η coefficient of 0.04.

To determine the most 'explanatory' variable among the six considered, let us examine the net contribution of each variable as a percentage of the variance of the individual mortality index explained by the model when the other predictive factors are already included (Table 2.19). It becomes clear that the ethnic group of the mother (with a contribution of 33 per cent in

Cameroon and of 39 per cent in Kenya) is the factor with the highest explanatory power. The mother's education takes second place (14 and 10 per cent respectively), and the occupational category of the husband is third (10 and 8 per cent). In Kenya, for example, if one includes successively in this order the variables mother's education, partner's education, place of residence, religion, ethnic group, and occupational category of the husband, the models 'explain' respectively, 1.3, 1.8, 1.87, 1.9, 3.3, and 3.6 per cent of the variance of the individual index of infant mortality. When one introduces occupation last, it explains only 0.3 per cent of the variance, that is 8.3 per cent of the explained percentage, while in the absence of inter-action, it accounts for 34 per cent of the variance (Table 2.20). The overall contribution of religion (for Kenya) and of the husband's education (for Cameroon) turn out to be least significant.

It is clear then that in addition to classic variables such as the mother's education and the husband's occupation, ethnic group should not be ignored in a study of mortality differentials in sub-Saharan Africa. However, the explanatory force of various variables diminishes or increases in the absence or presence of certain other predictive factors. Thus in Kenya there is a significant association (at the 5 per cent level) between the mother's education and the place of residence, between the mother's level of education and the partner's occupation, and between this latter factor and religion. In Cameroon, by contrast, no association is significant at a level of less than ten per cent.

Let us now examine the effect of an adjustment for the interdependence between explanatory variables (net deviations in Tables 2.17 and 2.18) in Kenya and Cameroon.

(b) Kenya

Table 2.17 shows that controlling for the other variables diminishes noticeably the advantage of educated women over the women with little or no education. The negative difference between their number of deaths and that of the standard pattern derived from model life tables changes from 31 to 19 per cent. The better survival of children born to educated mothers is due mainly to the fact that they tend to reside in the more favoured urban areas rather than in rural areas, and that they attract, much more than the women of little or no education, men belonging to higher social and occupational classes. Because of this, they are more apt to make efficient use of the health infrastructure and other advantages of the city (see, for example, Chapter 5 by Mbacké and van de Walle in this volume).

After adjusting for confounding factors, a reduction in the difference between the mortality of children of the wives of men with little or no education, and that of children whose mothers live with an educated man, can also be observed. The same is true for place of residence. The

Table 2.18. *Multiple classification analysis of individual mortality indices, Cameroon*

Independent Variables	N	Deviations from the mean					
		Gross	η	Model A		Model B	
				Net	β	Net	β
Educational level of mother			0.09		0.07[a]		0.06[a]
1. Less than 4 years of schooling	2,287	0.09		0.07		0.06	
2. 4 years of schooling and more	1,364	−0.15		−0.12		−0.11	
Educational level of partner			0.05		0.01		0.00
1. Less than 10 years of schooling	3,237	0.02		0.00		0.00	
2. 10 years of schooling and more	414	−0.17		−0.03		0.01	
Place of residence			0.08		0.03		0.02
1. Rural	2,678	0.06		0.02		0.03	
2. Urban	973	−0.17		−0.06		0.04	
Religion			0.04		0.04		
1. Christian	2,690	−0.03		−0.02			
2. Muslim	576	0.07		0.02			
3. Traditional	385	0.11		0.14			

		0.10	0.09^{a}	0.08^{a}
Ethnic group				
1. Douala-Bassa	220	−0.19	−0.07	−0.06
2. Bafia-Yaoundé-Boulou	608	−0.04	−0.03	0.03
3. Baya-Kaka-Maka-Fang-Benoué	551	0.24	0.23	0.20
4. Bamenda-Bamiléké-Bamoun	1,175	−0.12	−0.10	−0.10
5. Toupouri-Guiziga-Mou-Mandara	412	0.00	−0.15	−0.09
6. Peul	221	0.10	0.06	0.04
7. Others	464	0.13	0.09	0.08
Occupation of partner		0.09		0.05
1. Professional and clerical	501	−0.18		−0.11
2. Sales and other services	391	−0.15		−0.09
3. Agricultural	1,791	0.11		0.06
4. Skilled and unskilled manual	879	−0.08		−0.03
5. Never worked and household workers	98	0.09		0.13
Total number of women		3,651		3,660
General mean		0.87		0.87
Per cent of explained variance		1.8^{a}		1.9^{a}

[a] Significant at 0.01 level.

Table 2.19. *Net contribution in per cent of each variable to the variance explained by the model when the 5 other variables are already included*

Variable	Kenya	Cameroon	
		Model A	Model B
Level of mother's education	9.5[a]	19[a]	13.8[a]
Level of partner's education	4.9[a]	0.2	0
Place of residence	3.3[b]	3	1
Religion	0	5	
Ethnic group	38.8[a]	40.5[a]	32.8[a]
Occupation of partner	8.2[b]		10.1

[a] Significant at 0.01 level.
[b] Significant at 0.05 level.

Table 2.20. *Contribution of each variable assuming no interaction, Kenya and Cameroon*

Independent variable	Kenya	Cameroon	
		Model A	Model B
Education of mother	40	45	42.6
Education of partner	34	14	13.2
Place of residence	14	35.6	33.7
Religion	44	8.9	
Ethnic group	34	55.6	52.6
Occupation of partner	34		42.9

advantages of city dwellers over their counterparts in the country diminish but do not disappear. Living in the city would seem to be inherently beneficial for the survival of children. (See also Cantrelle *et al.*, 1986 about Senegal.)

The effect of the religious persuasion of the mother disappears entirely. At the bivariate level, Christians show an undeniable advantage in child survival when compared with Muslims and followers of traditional religions. Their children enjoy a mortality level 20 per cent less than the standard pattern, as opposed to 5 per cent and 0 per cent respectively for children of Muslims and of 'traditionalists'. After controlling for other variables, especially the social and occupational class of the husband, the differences between the three groups of mothers disappear. Religion, therefore, has an impact on infant mortality only through other variables.

In contrast, the differences between the various ethnic groups remain after controlling for the other factors in Kenya. The ethnic group of the mother thus exerts its own influence on infant mortality (via the customs, beliefs, family structures, etc. specific to the group).

With respect to the social and occupational class of the husband, the wives of 'upper-level management, professionals, or clerical workers' enjoy the greatest survival of their children (with a mortality that is lower by 48 per cent). Those whose husbands work in the agricultural sector fall at the other end of the scale. After controlling for other variables, the differences between the first group and the others diminish noticeably while remaining quite high. This is probably due to the association between husband's occupation and maternal education.

(c) Cameroon

As we cannot consider six variables at once, because of the large number of categories, we shall posit two models (A and B) containing five variables each. Model A includes mother's education, husband's education, place of residence, ethnic group, and religion. Model B considers the first four variables listed above for model A and occupation of the husband.

Table 2.18 shows that children of mothers who have at least four completed years of schooling are favoured in comparison with those whose mothers have attended school little, if at all. This notable advantage remains even after controlling for other variables. The mother's education seems to have a more important effect in Cameroon than in Kenya. By contrast, the role of the husband's education, which was important in Kenya, disappears entirely in Cameroon after controlling for other factors.

With respect to place of residence, the cities of Cameroon ensure a distinct advantage in the survival of children. However, after the introduction of controls, the difference between urban and rural areas diminishes notably. In contrast, religion constitutes one of the most important differentiating factors of child mortality in Cameroon: after controlling for other factors, there is no difference left between Christians and Muslims, but the disadvantage of the 'traditionalists' is still clearly apparent.

It is clear from Table 2.18 that the explanatory force of the ethnic identity of the mother remains intact after controlling for other variables. The analysis of occupation reveals important differences which favour the wives of upper-level management, professionals, and clerical workers. Part of that advantage seems to be linked to the ethnic group of the mother. The next category consists of women married to shopkeepers, salesmen, or employees in other service activities. Wives of manual workers hold the third place. As in Kenya, children of the unemployed, of domestics, and of self-employed agricultural workers remain most disadvantaged, even though the differences diminish somewhat.

9. Conclusion

In sub-Saharan Africa, as elsewhere, there exist important differentials in mortality between sub-populations. This study has focused on several large socio-cultural factors.

Of the variables that we used, ethnic group, maternal education, occupation, and to a lesser degree, the place of residence, turned out to be the most important. That the list includes the variables 'education' and 'occupation' hardly seems surprising, but the presence of 'ethnic group' merits comment. The ethnic group is clearly a variable that must be controlled in studies of mortality as well as in studies of fertility in Africa. The results confirm, in fact, those of several previous studies (United Nations, 1985; Cantrelle *et al.*, 1986, for Senegal; Wenlock, 1979, for rural Zambia).

The way in which this factor operates should not remain a 'black box'. It is important to explore the paths by which its influence is likely to be exerted. The ethnic group may act upon child mortality through a series of variables such as attitudes towards sickness and death, use of health services, beliefs relative to the aetiology and treatment of disease, feeding and child care practices (see on this subject, Hill and Randall, 1984), family structures, age of mother at birth, etc. Vimard (1980) writes, for example, on the subject of the different behaviour of the Ewe and the Kabye (plateau of Dayes in Togo) toward Western medicine, that 'the physical distance which separates a population from health services is often only of small importance compared with the cultural distance'.

Will these inequalities, which are already important, increase in the coming decades? This is a difficult question, that many will answer affirmatively. But additional surveys will be necessary before a scientifically valid answer can be given.

Acknowledgements

We would like to thank our colleagues Evina Akam and Aloys Ilinigumugabo of the Institute of Demography of the Catholic University of Louvain for their help in computer analysis of the surveys of Ghana, Kenya, and Cameroon, and of Rwanda.

References

Akoto, E. (1985), *Mortalité infantile et juvénile en Afrique: Niveaux, caractéristiques, causes et déterminants*, Ciaco Editor, Department of Demography, Louvain-la-Neuve.
—— and Hill, A. G. (1988), 'Morbidité, malnutrition et mortalité des enfants', in D. Tabutin (ed.), *Population et sociétés en Afrique au sud du Sahara*, L' Harmattan, Paris, 309–34.

Antoine, P. and Diouf, P. D. (1986), 'Indicateurs de mortalité des enfants et conditions socio-économiques en milieu urbain (Pikine)', Paper presented at a Seminar on Urbanisation and Health in Third World Countries, 2–9 Dec., Pikine.

—— and Herry, C. (1984), 'Mortalité infantile et juvénile à Abidjan', in *La Mortalité des enfants dans les pays en développement*, Éditions de l'ORSTOM, Paris, 141–55.

Ayeni, O. (1985), 'Geographic and socioeconomic differential characteristics of infant and child mortality in Africa', in IUSSP, *International Population Conference*, Florence, vol. 2, pp. 261–73.

Cantrelle, P. and Livenais, P. (1980), 'Fécondité, allaitement et mortalité infantile; différences inter-ethniques dans une même région: Saloum (Sénégal)', *Population* 3: 623–48.

—— Diop, I. L., Garenne, M., Gueye, M., and Sadio, A. (1986), 'The profile of mortality and its determinants in Senegal, 1966–1980', in United Nations, *Determinants of Mortality Change and Differentials in Developing Countries*, Population Studies 94: 86–116.

Charbit, Y., Gueye, L., and Ndiaye, S. (1985), *Nuptialité et fécondité au Sénégal*, INED–PUF, Cahier 112.

Dackam-Ngatchou, R. (1986), 'Niveau et déterminants de la mortalité infanto-juvénile à Yaoundé', in *Estimation de la mortalité du jeune enfant (0–5 ans)*, Séminaire de l'INSERM 145, Paris, 355–69.

Département de Démographie, SICAI, République du Zaïre (1978), *Synthèse des études démographiques de l'Ouest du Zaïre 1974–77*, Louvain-la-Neuve.

Ewbank, D., Henin, R., and Kekovole, J. (1986), 'An integration of demographic and epidemiologic research on mortality in Kenya', in United Nations, *Determinants of Mortality Change and Differentials in Developing Countries*, Population Studies 94: 33–85.

Farah, A. A. and Preston, S. H. (1982), 'Child mortality differentials in Sudan', *Population and Development Review* 8/2: 365–83.

Hill, A. and Randall, S. (1984), 'Différences géographiques et sociales dans la mortalité infantile et juvénile au Mali', *Population* 6: 921–45.

Hobcraft, J. N., McDonald, J. W., and Rutstein, S. O. (1983), 'Child spacing effects on infant and early child mortality', *Population Index* 49: 585–618.

—— —— —— (1984), 'Socio-economic factors in infant and child mortality', *Population Studies* 38/2: 193–223.

—— —— —— (1985), 'Demographic determinants of infant and early child mortality: A comparative analysis', *Population Studies* 39/3: 363–86.

Institut National de la Statistique—Enquête Mondiale sur la Fécondité (1985), *Enquête sur la fécondité au Bénin 1982, rapport national*, vol. 1, *Analyse des principaux résultats*, Cotonou and London.

Ministère du Plan et de l'Aménagement du Territoire—World Fertility Survey, (1984), *Enquête nationale mauritanienne sur la fécondité 1981*, Main Report, Analysis of Results.

Nzita Kikhela, D. (1986), 'La Mortalité périnatale à Kinshasa: Niveaux, déterminants et familles à risque', Ph.D. thesis, Department of Demography, Louvain-la-Neuve.

Preston, S. H. and Trussell, J. (1982), 'Estimating the covariates of childhood mortality from retrospective reports of mothers', *Health Policy and Education* 3/1: 1–36.

Rutstein, S. O. (1984), *Infant and child mortality: Levels, trends and demographic differentials*, Comparative Studies, WFS, 3.

Sousa Colaço, L. F. (1986), 'La Mortalité des enfants à Luanda, étude exploratoire', MA thesis, Department of Demography, Louvain-la-Neuve.

Tabutin, D. (1979), 'Fécondité et mortalité dans l'Ouest du Zaïre', Working Paper, Department of Demography, Louvain-la-Neuve.

United Nations (1985), *Socio-economic Differentials in Child Mortality in Developing countries*, ST/ESA/SER.A/97, New York.

Vimard, P. (1980), 'Nuptialité, fécondité et mortalité dans l'enfance en économie de plantation: Le Cas du plateau de Dayes', Thesis for the 3rd cycle, IDP/Paris, ORSTOM.

Waltisperger, D. (1988), 'Tendances et causes de la mortalité', in D. Tabutin (ed.), *Population et sociétés en Afrique au sud du Sahara*, L'Harmattan, Paris, 279–307.

Wenlock, R. W. (1979), 'Social factors, nutrition and child mortality in a rural subsistence economy', *Ecology of Food and Nutrition* 8: 227–40.

WHO Ministry of Health (1981), *Infant Mortality in Mauritius 1975–76*, Port Louis.

3 Making Better Use of Demographic Data and Health Statistics in Primary Health Care

Allan G. Hill
Centre for Population Studies, London School of Hygiene and
Tropical Medicine

At the international conference in Alma-Alta in 1978, all developing countries accepted that primary health care (PHC) was the key to 'the attainment by all peoples of the world by the year 2000 of a level of health that will permit them to lead a socially and economically productive life' (WHO/UNICEF, 1978: 3). This public declaration of general intent accompanied by only a vague description of the exact composition of the proposed primary health care programme none the less represented a major switch of emphasis in the approach of health ministers and official agencies, both public and private, to the delivery and content of health services. The change, it must be said, has taken place largely on ideological grounds since prior evidence that a community-based health care delivery system based on 'practical, scientifically sound and socially acceptable methods and technology' (WHO/UNICEF, 1978: 3) can be more effective in maintaining good health than centrally organized, hospital and clinic-based services is thin, certainly, in most developing countries. This ideological shift is seen by historians as the final stage in a much longer process involving the abandonment of the Cartesian paradigm with its emphasis on mechanistic aspects of the human organism and its replacement by the 'socio-ecological' paradigm which emerged as a result of work by medical sociologists and epidemiologists (see Noack, chapter 1, in Abelin et al., 1987, for a good account). The difficulty with the assessment of the effectiveness of the primary health care approach is that the idea of devolving prime responsibility for health care to the community has been confused with an additional body of assertions about the factors responsible for the maintenance of good health; these include health education, adequate nutrition and clean water, maternal and child health and family planning, immunization, treatment for disease and injuries, and provision of essential drugs. Other factors are also cited in the basic PHC document so that effectively all aspects of the economy, society, and politics of a country are considered relevant in some way or another to the development and maintenance of a state of 'complete physical, mental and social well-being' (WHO/UNICEF, 1978: 2 and 4). Now there is nothing wrong with the view that all these assorted variables do indeed have some bearing on the health of individuals and communities. Problems only arise when these general statements have to be translated into intervention programmes or when evaluation and monitoring studies have to be designed and implemented.

The first of these problems was circumvented by adoption of an approach now known as 'selective primary health care' by the major international agencies following an influential article by Walsh and Warren (1979). The UNICEF programme, for example, known as the 'child health revolution', consists of only a few well-established interventions, most of which have been components of pre-PHC systems. The strong reaction to Walsh and Warren's advice from many quarters (see Rifkin and Walt, 1986, for a recent review) has not produced much solid evidence one way or another. The data from the Matlab Thana surveillance project in Bangladesh have been cited in this context but the overall argument is unconvincing because of the short time-lag between intervention and evaluation and because of several factors peculiar to the very poor living conditions in Bangladesh (Chen, 1986). Much more thought-provoking are the writings by Caldwell (1986), on the one hand, and the report of a Rockefeller Foundation conference entitled 'Good Health at Low Cost' (edited by Halstead *et al.*, 1985), on the other, which suggested that both wealth and the nature of the health care services had a more tenuous link to health than previously imagined. This is not the place to discuss in detail the case these authors build for the importance of education, female autonomy, and local democracy for good health. What this brief summary of the wide-ranging debate about the merits of the selective PHC approaches is intended to do is to draw attention to the lack of a workable theory for the design of more effective health care interventions or indeed for the assessment of any measures implemented. This is the central problem in trying to draw up a protocol for the collection and analysis of appropriate demographic and health data for a PHC system. Although the required empirically based model of the determinants of health care cannot be constructed without much more work, there is, however, some consensus about the overall structure of the major components. The ordering of the biological and behavioural factors contained in the schema by Van Norren and Van Vianen (1986) seems inherently sensible and points to some testable hypotheses (see Fig. 3.1). If good health really is the outcome of such a diversity of socio-economic and biological factors, as the Alma-Ata declaration stated, then there is an immense job to be done if the measure of even a few key variables is to be taken. Can the theoretical data needs for testing such a broad model be reconciled with current practice and the realistic capacity of developing countries to collect and analyse health and health-related statistics? And on what basis can key variables be identified?

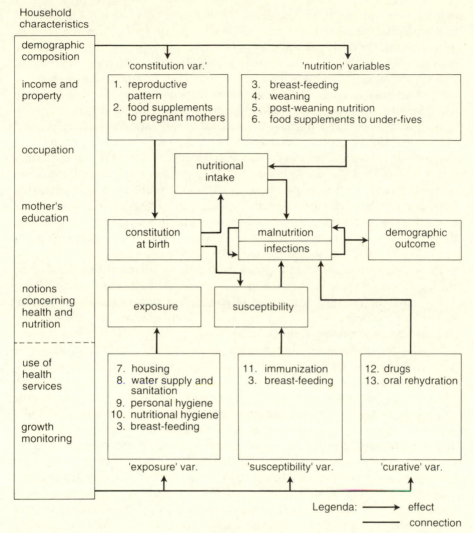

FIG. 3.1. A model of the malnutrition–infections syndrome and its demographic outcome in terms of categories: risk factors, intermediate variables, and household characteristics

1. Outcome versus Process Variables

Whilst a life table is an unambiguous measure of the risks of dying in a population, permitting easy comparison between and within major groups, there are problems in using such measures for the evaluation or monitoring of the effects of health interventions of any kind. One general problem is that life tables calculated from conventional sources, that is, recorded deaths by age from a vital registration system and a mid-year population from a census, only describe the risks of dying in a particular year or group of years. As in fertility analysis, period and cohort effects intersect in complex ways, particularly when both the age pattern and level of mortality are changing rapidly—the normal situation in most developing countries.

In most developing countries, where death registration is incomplete and inaccurate, childhood and adult mortality are mostly measured by indirect methods or through data collected in special surveys (e.g. the full maternity histories collected by the WFS or the DHS). The exact time location of these estimates is always approximate and again there is the problem that period and cohort changes are entangled in the aggregate reports on, for example, children ever born and surviving. The indirect methods too have the important disadvantage that they tell us little about age patterns of mortality within either the childhood or the adult age groups.

In addition to these largely practical problems in measuring levels and trends in mortality described in greater detail in Hill and David (1988), much more difficult problems arise in connection with cause of death attribution in developing countries. It has been widely recognized for some time that the ultimate causes of death which may appear on the death certificate are rarely the same as the determinants of mortality in a population. Many careful studies, some incorporating pathological and clinical observations, have shown that each childhood death is simply the last link in a long chain of events which include infection and malnutrition working in a synergistic relationship (see Puffer and Serrano, 1975, for results from several Latin American studies, and further sources cited by Mosley, 1985, or van Norren and van Vianen, 1986). This makes it extraordinarily difficult to calculate the 'deaths averted or postponed' which may be associated with a particular health intervention such as oral rehydration therapy or measles immunization. These two interventions, both part of the core PHC programme, illustrate very neatly the importance of the aetiology of diarrhoeal disease and measles for impact and assessment studies. Very briefly, oral rehydration therapy does little to reduce the exposure to the risks of catching a diarrhoeal infection and may, by reducing the mean duration of each attack, return the child more quickly to the pool of exposed children. Thus, the mortality effects of even an effective oral rehydration therapy programme may be quite modest, as Rashad (1987) and others (e.g. Black, 1984) are suggesting. Compare this with the cumulative benefits of avoiding exposure to measles by immunization, which include protection from the quite debilitating sequelae of measles as well as a reduced risk of catching an intense dose of the virus when the exposed population is small (Foster, 1984; Aaby *et al.*, 1984 and 1986). Moreover, the lethality of a disease is closely associated with socio-biological factors such as the susceptibility and resistance of the host as well as the individual behavioural response on catching the infection. There are thus many reasons for urging caution in the use of mortality improvements alone as a measure of the effectiveness of a primary health care programme and its individual components; indeed, it would be disastrous if decisions on the cancellation or continuation of PHC programmes generally were to be based entirely on the achievement of stated mortality goals, particularly such ambitious targets for the sharp reduction of mortality in early childhood as are set out in the UNICEF programme. The question is what supplementary indicators are likely to be accepted as good indicators of achievement of an improved level of health?

2. The Search for Health Indicators

Despite considerable effort internationally, a recent WHO review of indicators and methods for the evaluation of health interventions draws attention to the

difficulty in devising methods to measure appropriate indicators of health status change which could be carried out at the national level in a precise and cost-effective fashion. In addition, several programmes not dealing with specific disease prevention and control have had difficulties in defining the specific health changes which could be associated to health interventions carried out by the programme (WHO, 1986: 7).

To be useful, indicators have to be both sufficiently *sensitive* to measure change and *specific* enough to measure only the change in the variable being studied.

The literature on health indicators is now large and diverse as well as being full of semantic problems (the distinction between health statistics, health indicators, and health indices is one). In developed countries, indicators are important because the low death rates are no longer useful for identifying special needs; decisions of resource allocation and service provision rather than mortality levels are of paramount importance to health planners there (Graham and Arthur, 1986: 5). The situation in developing countries is very different. Further, the introduction of new concepts such as 'ill-health versus positive health' (Hansluwka, 1985) and the idea of health as a continuum create confusion in an already unorganized field.

Several sets of health status indicators have been proposed (see Appendix 3.1, Tables A–D from Graham and Arthur, 1986) but many are very demanding in terms of data collection requirements and are certainly not easily added to a community-based PHC system. Ideally, planners are searching for a few composite measures but the early work done on 'indices of health' (Stouman and Falk, 1936) and more recently on indices of the 'quality of life' (Culyer, 1983) have not produced any general agreement on key measures. Essentially, what is lacking is, first, a model of the social and biological determinants of health, and second, a good deal of systematic work on the way the relationships between selected variables change as health improves.

3. What Health Statistics are Already Being Collected?

In many of the developing countries, the health services provide the principal source of continuous information on morbidity, specially for children under five and pregnant women. Although the structure of these services obviously varies from country to country, generally it is possible to recognize five major sources of data:

1. hospital (mostly in-patients) services;
2. maternity clinics;
3. clinic and other lower order health units e.g. dispensaries and treatment centres (mostly for out-patients);
4. primary health care services;
5. the transmissible disease surveillance system.

Equally, there are two levels of information available from these sources: first, individual's records, and secondly, aggregated data. The potential uses of these data are enormous, both in terms of patient management and the design, implementation, and evaluation of health policies and programmes, as well as for epidemiological research. Actual uses, by comparison, are often very limited despite the considerable amount of time and money spent on improving the health information system at all levels.

One of the major considerations affecting the use of health services' sources for mortality and morbidity research is the question of selectivity. This is all the more critical in view of the inequitable distribution of and access to health facilities, both governmental and non-governmental, found in most developing countries. In trying to assess the relevance of the selection factors, it is important to note the distinction between the community-based reporting system derived, for example, from the outreach facilities of a primary health care programme or through community disease surveillance, and the information from fixed facilities such as major referral hospitals. Obviously, the former sources are likely to provide a more representative picture overall, although the quality of the diagnostic information is likely to be poorer than from the latter sources. Moreover, without the full integration of data derived from these various sources, there are a number of problems related to the question of catchment populations for the calculation of rates, with the potential for both double reporting and losses due to referrals.

(*a*) **Mali**

Although the responsibility for the collection and interpretation of all the service and health statistics produced by the nation's hospitals, clinics, and other centres is concentrated within a single ministry, in practice, each of the Directorates has an almost independent system of reporting. A *médecin-chef* is often faced with demands for a monthly report by several Directorates, each requiring a common set of background statistics (population, health personnel, equipment, etc.) together with information on the work of specific interest to the Directorate. Thus, for instance, a quite comprehensive report required by the Directorate of Family Health overlaps considerably with the reports demanded by the Immunization Service and the Service des Grandes Endémies. More co-ordination would lighten the reporting load for the health service employees at all levels as well as produce a series of statistics of greater analytic value.

An *Annuaire Statistique* is published at irregular intervals. The tables available in the 1983 edition, published in 1985, are as follows:

- deaths by cause;
- morbidity by cause;
- total persons seen;
- infrastructure by region;
- health personnel.

The regions also publish statistical abstracts; for Mopti in 1975 (published 1981), deaths are shown by cause, sex, and broad age groups (0, 1–4, 5–14, 15 and over). The total numbers of vaccinations by type are also reported.

None of these data are easy to interpret principally because statistics on the population at risk are lacking. Even assuming constant coverage rates and unchanging definitions of morbid states, the time series is too short to permit trend analysis of the numerators alone.

By far the most interesting series of statistics on child mortality is contained in the registers maintained in the country's maternity clinics. In the urban areas, covering perhaps a fifth of the total population, it appears that about two-thirds of the mothers give birth in a maternity clinic or a hospital (Hill *et al.*, 1986). In most clinics, mothers are asked to give their age, parity, and the number of their children still alive, whilst the birth-weight of the new-born, its sex, and mode of delivery are also collected. Lefèvre (1986) has demonstrated how a simple analysis of the birth-weights might be used to identify clinics where low birth-weights are common. Abstracting the figures on children ever born and surviving for mothers of different ages would be an obvious way of obtaining an estimate of child mortality for the group of mothers giving birth in maternity clinics. Some additional work involving a subsidiary enquiry amongst a sample of mothers giving birth in the clinics would allow other systematic relationships to be examined (e.g. birth-weight, birth intervals, and child survival), as Hill *et al.* (1986) have already demonstrated. Unfortunately, all these analyses concern only the sub-population of mothers who are in contact with the health services. For research on child mortality amongst the general population, a more representative sample of mothers is needed (see later).

(*b*) Senegal

The general position in Senegal, apart from Cap Vert, is not unlike that in Mali except that the health services, both private and public, are much better developed and, as a result, a higher proportion of the population of greater Dakar is covered by these services. The existence of a flourishing private sector in Dakar complicates the task of collecting and analysing the available data. Hospital reports for three of Senegal's twelve hospitals are not in fact submitted to the Ministry of Health.

In the statistical year-books for Senegal, the health sector is discussed in a few pages of text with figures interspersed. Some coverage figures are presented in the 1983 edition of *La situation économique du Sénégal* (published in 1985). There we read that 60 per cent of the health personnel were in the Cap Vert region, and that 77 per cent of births to women in urban areas occur in maternity clinics, compared with 15 per cent for rural mothers. Only about a third of all pregnant mothers make a pre-natal visit. More disturbing is the decline during the 1980s in the number of vaccinations performed, BCG excluded. The explanation is also included in the year-book: the public health sector's share of the national budget declined from 9 per cent of the total in 1970–1 to 5.8 per cent in 1980–1. Of this budget in the 1977–81 Plan period, 55 per cent was allocated to hospitals (Garenne *et al.*, 1985).

More detailed information is available in a report entitled *Statistiques sanitaires et démographiques* which seems to appear biennially. These data concern the public and not the private sector. The privileged position of Cap Vert emerges very clearly; with 22 per cent of the nation's population, the region consumes 40 per cent of the health budget and contains 64 per cent of the country's doctors (Senegal, 1985). Whilst much of the report consists of service statistics, there is some attempt to estimate immunization coverage rates although the size of the target population is quite uncertain. Using the narrowest definition of the target population, we obtain the following coverage rates: BCG, 60 per cent; measles, 56 per cent; yellow fever, 57 per cent; and DPT3, 51 per cent (Senegal, 1985: 107).

The edition of 1983 (Senegal, 1984) contains the results of a special survey conducted to supplement the statistics routinely reported. Health personnel at all levels were asked about the services they were involved in providing as well as about more general issues concerning the 'politics' of health care. The detailed findings are not of particular interest here, but the idea of conducting a small survey amongst a sample of health units is an interesting one. When reporting from the periphery to the central ministry is poor, this may be an economic way to obtain some useful epidemiological information.

(c) The Gambia

The government health services of the Gambia are organized in a pyramidal system, with two general hospitals at the apex functioning as major referral centres, but also providing out-patient clinics. Below this level, and apart from certain specialist units, there is a network of health centres, dispensaries, sub-dispensaries, and health posts. The health centre is the main health institution in the rural areas, providing maternal and child health (MCH) and immunization services, curative out-patient care, and environmental health education, and staffed by qualified medical personnel, mostly nurses. Dispensaries primarily run basic out-patient care facilities and are staffed by nurse-dispensers, whilst maternal and child health and immunization services are provided by visiting mobile teams. At the base of the pyramid of fixed health facilities are the health posts staffed by village health workers. Next is the sub-dispensary, which may have a resident community health nurse, but, in her absence, they are lock-up units, visited regularly from the nearest health centre. The implementation of PHC in the Gambia, which was scheduled for national coverage in 1986, is based on the establishment of village health workers and traditional birth attendants who are supervised by community health nurses located in key PHC villages (Gambia, 1985). In addition to the above governmental health services, there are a number of private facilities providing in-patient and out-patient care.

A major component of the health information system is the Health Statistics and Epidemiology Unit, referred to earlier in the review, which receives data from health facilities. The unit was set up in 1979 with the objectives of providing for the collection and feedback of morbidity and mortality data, and maintaining disease surveillance and control nationally. The basis of the reporting system are monthly returns provided by all levels of the health service. In the two major in-patient facilities in the country, there are records departments staffed by clerks with specific responsibility for maintaining both patient records and aggregate returns. This contrasts with the management of data at all other units which depends on personnel whose principal task is not seen as health reporting and who often regard such an activity as an undue added burden.

At the level of the PHC villages, reporting of health and mortality information is carried out by the community health nurses, village health workers, and traditional birth attendants using tally forms. Similarly, at health centres, dispensaries, and hospital out-patient clinics, a tally sheet is used to report a range of 29 conditions, including reportable diseases, divided into cases aged under and over 5 years. At the end of each month, these various tally sheets are used to produce totals for forwarding to the central office in that region, and from here the information is passed to the Health Statistics and Epidemiology Unit in Banjul. The monthly return for the PHC villages is completed by the supervising community health nurses, with separate out-patient and reportable diseases returns being made by the other health facilities.

In addition to the above reporting system, two levels of information are available through the activities of the maternal and child welfare clinics. First, there are monthly returns based on child welfare, antenatal care, and immunization services. The material for these returns is derived from registers kept at the health centre or dispensary, including a birth register. The second level of information refers to individually held records, specifically child welfare cards and antenatal cards. The situation in the Gambia is quite exceptional by African standards with regard to the high degree of contact between maternal and child health and immunization services and the population of under-five children and pregnant women. A review of the PHC system (Gambia, 1985) revealed that almost all women are examined at least once during their pregnancy and issued with antenatal cards. Equally, there is a high degree of contact with traditional birth attendants, who deliver well over three-quarters of all babies in the Gambia and who see a slightly smaller fraction of mothers at least three times during the antenatal period. As regards the under-five population, in 1982 it was found that infant-welfare card possession and retention was over 90 per cent, and this can be tied in with the unusually high immunization coverage rates in the Gambia. In 1984, the national coverage rates for DPT3, Polio 3, measles, and BCG were 82, 87, 79, and 98 per cent respectively. Infant-welfare and antenatal cards represent a rich source of information which is sadly under-used both at the individual level and for building up an aggregate picture. Moreover, it should be possible to obtain from both cards the information on the survival of the preceding child. This could be of practical use in the identification of 'at risk' children and mothers, and for the calculation of mortality rates using the adaptation of the preceding birth technique described above for Mali (Aguirre and Hill, 1987 and 1988).

In seeking to use the health and mortality data available from the health services in the Gambia, the problems of selectivity in the recorded population are further complicated by the difficulty of establishing the catchment area of each reporting unit. The latter is a difficulty arising partly out of the development of parallel health facilities which may overlap in terms of the population within access but which are not necessarily linked in any formal way with regard to reporting information. Thus, for example, there is potential for some conditions and events to be recorded both by a village health worker or a community health nurse, and through, say, a health centre. At the same time there appear to be gaps in the reporting system as, for example, with the monthly returns submitted from health centres and dispensaries which do not provide the same information, especially with regard to deaths, as that given by the PHC workers. Moreover the latter information system does not operate in the area of Greater Banjul, although there are plans to introduce urban PHC. In the Gambia, the opportunity for vital registration to be facilitated through village health workers and traditional birth attendants, who are already recording some births and deaths, does seem to be wasted at present.

(d) Sierra Leone

Health and medical services in Sierra Leone are mainly provided by the government, but with additional facilities available in some localities from missions, mining companies, and private organizations. As with the health structure in the Gambia, the services are arranged in a hierarchy, headed by hospitals at provincial and district levels and with the main referral centres found in Freetown. At the chiefdom level there are three principal alternative levels of services—health centres, dispensaries, and treatment centres, with staff including nurses, dispensers, maternal and child health aides or endemic disease control assistants (EDCAs). These services are unevenly distributed throughout the country, with fourteen out of the 147 chiefdoms without any health facilities and an estimated 70 per cent of the population without access to hospital services. Transport problems and seasonal inaccessibility contribute to these inequalities.

A PHC programme began in Sierra Leone in 1978, operating through a number of pilot projects primarily in three districts of the country, and expanded further in 1986. The PHC delivery system which has been adopted is similar to that described for the Gambia, and is based on village health services provided by village health workers and traditional birth attendants, serving populations of around 500, and supervised by community health officers and maternal and child health aides located at fixed units at the chiefdom level.

Information gathered at the various levels of the health services are intended to be collected centrally by the Medical Statistics Unit of the Ministry of Health located in Freetown. In practice, it is estimated that at least a quarter of health units do not submit any returns and the reports which are received are often long overdue and clearly incomplete. The monthly returns which are expected from hospitals are extremely detailed and provide in-patient and out-patient statistics, coded to the International Classification of Diseases (Eighth Revision) without an age breakdown but including births and deaths. The completion of these forms (which are often in short supply) is the responsibility of the records department in the hospital, where registers of admissions and discharges are also maintained. In terms of published statistics derived from hospital returns, those most readily accessible are for the units in Freetown, and are usually presented as number of cases by diagnosis, without any age breakdown or attempt to calculate rates.

At the lower order health units, the monthly reporting system is based on forms completed by one of the senior health personnel, which are forwarded to Freetown. Maternal and child health and immunization services are provided at fixed centres and through mobile teams, with maternal and child health aides collecting information on births from traditional birth attendants, who deliver an estimated 70 per cent of all births (Sierra Leone, 1981). There is also a reporting network for immunizations delivered and for cases and deaths attributable to notifiable diseases, which in theory passes information to the Expanded Programme of Immunization Co-ordinating Office in Freetown. A recent UNICEF (1985) report indicated that this network had essentially collapsed, with complete immunization of only 5.3 per cent of the total target population of under-2-year-olds.

In those parts of the country where PHC programmes are under way, there are additional systems for reporting of health and mortality information. The most highly developed of these seems to be in the Bo-Pujehun PHC project (Sierra Leone and Federal Republic of Germany, 1985), where a central monitoring and evaluation unit has been set up to co-ordinate the data collection activities and to aggregate results. The system is based on individually held records and on registers and monthly summary sheets maintained by 29 peripheral health units (PHUs), including health centres and treatment centres. Child welfare and antenatal records, similar to those used in the Gambia, are issued during the initial contact with the maternal and child health and immunization clinic at the peripheral health unit. Duplicate records are kept of any further consultations, with one copy being issued to the mother for retention. Each month, summary sheets of the activities of the peripheral health units are prepared. The births and deaths include those notified to the peripheral health unit through traditional birth attendants or village health workers in the villages falling within a three-mile radius, which is felt to reflect the catchment area. Although this monthly reporting system has been in operation since October 1983, the procedures for routinely aggregating the data to produce a district-level picture are not yet firmly established. Moreover, whilst the identification of catchment areas provides the potential for calculating certain morbidity and mortality rates, this is undermined by the presence of certain health services not integrated into the PHC reporting network, a problem which was noted earlier for the Gambia.

This brief review of the health data being routinely collected in just four West African countries makes the essential point that considerable amounts of time and money are already being expended on these information systems. Such data are, however, rarely used and analysed in any systematic way for a number of reasons. First, there are the basic problems of incomplete coverage of the total population and strong selection bias since most of the statistics come from fixed centres like clinics and hospitals. Secondly, there is the problem of handling such a diverse mass of miscellaneous reports and sifting out the indicators of value. Finally, there is the lack of a capacity to analyse these data in most health ministries. Although simple tabulations of a few key variables on a regular basis is an extremely helpful start, the task of assembling information of varying reliability not only from the health services themselves but also from complementary sources such as the census, the vital registration system, surveys, and longitudinal studies is very demanding.

4. Examples of the Use of Routinely Collected Health Statistics and Survey Data for Evaluation

One of the major problems in using routinely collected health data to discern trends in mortality and morbidity is that the greater part of the data is obtained only from the ill. There are several circumstances, however, in which healthy individuals may encounter one or more of the public health services, including mothers who routinely give birth in hospitals and clinics, or young children who are presented for vaccination. For some time, more consideration has been given to making fuller use of information obtained in the course of providing such services. Neither maternity clinic data nor data obtained from mothers of children being vaccinated are free of selection bias unless the coverage of the exposed population is complete. There are a surprising number of circumstances where the coverage even in sub-Saharan Africa is reasonably complete. In many francophone African countries, perhaps two-thirds to three-quarters of all births to urban women may occur in a clinic or in a hospital, and in the country as a whole, coverage of some vaccination programmes (not necessarily the full immunization cycle) is over 80 per cent. Methods of measurement adjusted to these circumstances are sorely needed.

Using an idea by Brass and Macrae (1984) which showed that the proportions of preceding children dead at the time of a subsequent maternity is a good index of mortality in early childhood, approximating $_2q_0$, a small trial was arranged in four maternity clinics and one maternity hospital in Bamako, Mali. Previous research had indicated that in many countries, the key question on the survival of the preceding child was already being routinely collected in addition to a good deal of other valuable information. For the Bamako experiment, a short questionnaire was designed including several supplementary questions on data of previous births amongst other items but the revised form of the register approved by the Ministry of Health at the end of the trial is quite simple (Fig. 3.2). The trial demonstrated that plausible childhood mortality measures could be obtained by midwives in the course of their regular duties and that mothers

No.	Date and time of entry	MOTHER								THIS PREGNANCY										DEATH OF MOTHER		EXIT		
		Name, first name and CPN code	Age	Number of children born alive	Number of children still living	Number of abortions and still births	Sex of last child	Last born child alive (Y/N)?	Date and time of childbirth	Location of childbirth	Full term or premature	Type of delivery	Vitality	One baby or more?	Sex	Weight at birth	Height	BCG	Before, during or after?	Cause	Date and time of exit	Child still living?	Observations
(1)	(2)	(3)	(4)	(5)	(6)	(7)	(8)	(9)	(10)	(11)	(12)	(13)	(14)	(15)	(16)	(17)	(18)	(19)	(20)	(21)	(22)	(23)	(24)

FIG. 3.2. Questionnaire devised for collecting information from mothers at time of confinement on previous births

Table 3.1. *Child mortality estimated from proportions dead of last and second-to-last births by mother's age*

(a) Last births			
Age of mother	Births	Deaths	Proportions dead ($_2q_0$)
15–19	362	79	0.218
20–24	1,248	198	0.159
25–29	1,549	213	0.138
30–34	949	118	0.124
35–39	529	55	0.104
40–44	111	11	0.099
45+	15	2	0.133

(b) Second-to-last births			
Age of mother	Births	Deaths	Proportions dead ($_2q_0$)
15–19	59	18	0.305
20–24	697	163	0.234
25–29	1,394	238	0.171
30–34	929	125	0.135
35–39	525	57	0.109
40–44	110	16	0.145
45+	15	2	0.133

provided the necessary information without difficulty. The results are valuable both for the identification of clinics or clinic-attendance with higher than average childhood mortality and for discerning trends over time.

The factors of selection, even in a population in which an estimated 80 per cent of births occur in clinics and hospitals, operate in quite a subtle and potentially misleading way. For example, the data in Table 3.1 suggest that childhood mortality is lower amongst older mothers. This unlikely result is in fact due to the over-representation of higher class women amongst the clinic-attending mothers and the proportion of such women rises with maternal age. Other effects in the data such as the unlikely trend in the proportions of previous children dead by parity (Table 3.2) also stem from these selection biases. Clearly, census and survey data are needed to properly calibrate and adjust the clinic results but the recording of the details shown on the form in Fig. 3.2 should continue, since with unchanging coverage, the selection bias can be regarded as more or less constant. Apart from the cheapness of the method, it is possible to obtain key measures

Table 3.2. *Child mortality estimated from proportions dead of last and second-to-last births by mother's parity*

Parity	N	Proportions dead of last births ($_2q_0$)	N	Proportions dead of second-to-last births ($_2q_0$)
1	1,012	0.185		
2	825	0.156	807	0.252
3	751	0.117	746	0.178
4	620	0.135	620	0.116
5	493	0.134	492	0.146
6	389	0.123	388	0.129
7	263	0.118	263	0.133
8+	422	0.109	420	0.129
Total	4,775	0.142	3,736	0.166

unobtainable in cross-sectional surveys. In clinics and hospitals, the birth-weight and less commonly the length of the new-born are routinely recorded but other variables collected here and there include maternal weight and height, blood pressure, anaemia, etc. These can be valuable clues to the identification of health needs amongst mothers and young children. More recently, Aguirre and Hill (1987 and 1988) have developed adjustment factors so that the data on the survival of the previous born children can be converted into an index of early childhood mortality, again approximately $_2q_0$, even when the informants are mothers interviewed a year or two after a subsequent birth. This means that the question on the survival of the previous born child can be posed in a wide variety of circumstances and particularly in the context of primary health interventions which aim explicitly at covering the whole population. The method depends on the calculation of adjustment factors for two biases which fortunately operate in opposite directions and in some cases will cancel. The biases are:

1. the well-known association between the survival chances of successive children born to the same woman;
2. the extra exposure to the risks of dying experienced by the preceding born child when the data on the survival of these children is obtained from mothers interviewed some time after the birth of the last child rather than at the time of the last delivery.

Thus, if village or community health workers asked about the survival of the previous child during their regular visits to mothers with young children (for immunization, health examination, distribution of oral rehydration salts, etc.), very soon a series of indices of early childhood mortality could be established for each locality which would be a better description of child health by district than the much less representative reports obtained only from clinic and hospital attendance.

5. Are Surveys the Answer?

A whole variety of different surveys are now undertaken in an attempt to estimate the effectiveness and the efficiency of health interventions. The range includes the very specific studies of immunization coverage or of oral rehydration therapy programmes as well as much broader health surveys conducted independently by individual ministries of health or as part of a joint programme such as the Demographic and Health Surveys project. Most of these studies are single-round enquiries, usually involving a clustered sample of the general population. Hence, the surveys share all the problems of poor recall and selective omission of events which are commonly found in most retrospective surveys. In addition, simple cross-tabulations of, say, immunization coverage by single characteristics of the mother or of the household will be inadequate due to correlation between sets of variables as well as other technical problems associated with small numbers. Even in populations with poor health, the proportion reporting themselves ill in the two weeks before the interview is generally quite small and so rare events, such as maternal deaths, are hard to measure in small- and medium-sized surveys.

Recently, however, some newer forms of regression analysis have emerged making it possible to look simultaneously at a number of characteristics related to compliance with selected health care messages.

(*a*) **A household survey with health questions from Mali**

By way of illustration, some examples of the analysis of just a few health status variables have been taken from a survey in two towns in central Mali, Mopti and Sevare in 1985. The analysis was carried out by Dollimore (1987), using the relative risk approach with appropriate controls for education (E: 0 = none, 1 = some) and social class (S: 0 = no radio, refrigerator, moped, or cupboard, 1 = owning one of these items, 2 = owning two or more).

Looking at the data for the last born child in each household, she found significant differences in the relative risks of dying comparing monitored with unmonitored pregnancies (Table 3.3). The person delivering the child affected its survival although of course the difficult birth delivered in hospital by doctors displayed very high neonatal mortality (Table 3.4). Overall, full vaccination coverage was found to be less than one per cent for all vaccines but the excess mortality risks of the unvaccinated are clear at all

Table 3.3. *Relative risk of dying (R) for children of unmonitored compared with monitored pregnancies*

Subgroups Education, E Social class, S	0–1 month		0–5 years	
	R	95% Confidence interval	R	95% Confidence interval
E = 0, S = 0	1.27	0.66– 2.43	1.24	0.95– 1.63
E = 0, S = 1	2.12	0.84– 5.36	1.59[a]	1.12– 2.28
E = 0, S = 2	3.85[a]	1.06–13.92	1.99[b]	1.24– 3.21
E = 1, S = 0	4.07	0.67–24.62	1.85	0.76– 4.50
E = 1, S = 1	—	—	1.35	0.46– 3.95
E = 1, S = 2	3.20	0.12–84.25	4.19[b]	1.56–11.22
Weighted average	1.66[a]	1.04– 2.55	1.52[b]	1.26– 1.83

Note: —: Insufficient cases for analysis.
[a] $p < 0.05$.
[b] $p < 0.01$.

Table 3.4. *Relative risk of dying (R) for children delivered by an untrained compared with a trained assistant*

Subgroups Education, E Social class, S	0–1 month		0–5 years	
	R	95% Confidence interval	R	95% Confidence interval
E = 0, S = 0	2.59[a]	1.30– 5.14	1.73[a]	1.31–2.30
E = 0, S = 1	1.82	0.69– 4.78	2.06[a]	1.43–2.97
E = .0, S = 2	1.21	0.35– 4.21	2.13[a]	1.21–3.75
E = 1, S = 0	3.63	0.63–20.89	2.51[b]	1.01–6.29
E = 1, S = 1	—	—	1.34	0.40–4.48
E = 1, S = 2	—	—	—	—
Weighted average	2.16[a]	1.32– 3.52	1.89[a]	1.55–2.31

Note: —: Insufficient cases for analysis.
Trained assistant here refers to a midwife only. Deliveries by a doctor are excluded.
[a] $p < 0.01$.
[b] $p < 0.05$.

ages and for all social classes (Table 3.5). By contrast, only modest effects on child survival were attributed to water source or toilet facilities.

In summary, a survey of this kind provides a useful description of health conditions and related variables from some sections of the population, particularly young children. The data can also serve as a baseline before

Table 3.5. *Relative risk of dying (R) for unimmunized compared with partially immunized children*

Subgroups Education, E Social class, S	0–6 months		0–12 months		0–2 years		0–5 years	
	R	95% confidence interval	R	95% confidence interval	R	95% confidence interval	R	95% confidence interval
E = 0, S = 0	4.34[a]	2.56– 7.35	4.88[a]	3.17– 7.52	3.26[a]	2.27– 4.70	3.34[a]	2.77– 5.33
E = 0, S = 1	1.84	0.96– 3.54	2.27[a]	1.43– 3.59	1.97[a]	1.33– 1.93	2.18[a]	1.50– 3.18
E = 0, S = 2	3.64[a]	1.60– 7.07	2.45[a]	1.41– 4.25	2.84[a]	1.77– 4.57	2.64[a]	1.65– 4.23
E = 1, S = 0	3.88[b]	1.06–14.26	3.40[b]	1.06–10.85	5.68[a]	2.14–15.07	—	—
E = 1, S = 1	10.22	1.10–94.83	7.19[b]	1.29–40.01	2.85[b]	1.00– 8.10	2.26[b]	0.92– 5.51
E = 1, S = 2	5.08	0.93–27.94	5.97[a]	1.55–22.97	7.81[a]	2.17–28.11	5.92[a]	2.60–13.50
Weighted average	3.35[a]	2.39– 4.68	3.29[a]	3.21– 3.38	2.85[a]	2.27– 3.56	3.01[a]	2.45– 3.69

Note: —: Insufficient cases for analysis.

[a] $p < 0.01$.
[b] $p < 0.05$.

intervention. Even with relatively sophisticated analysis, however, the data are limited in the way they can be used for PHC monitoring. There is no guarantee, for example, that the relationships between social class and health service utilization will remain stable as general levels of education and living improve. Key measures such as birth-weights are impossible to collect in retrospective surveys and even data on immunizations received are of doubtful validity unless mothers can produce health cards. None the less, such a survey used in conjunction with other sources of information such as data from maternity registers can be a relatively quick and cheap way of learning a good deal about current health problems and needs as well as providing denominators and adjustment factors for the data from the health services.

(b) The Gambian primary health care review

Many African countries have embarked on PHC programmes following the Alma-Alta conference in 1978. In practice, under the PHC rubric several countries have simply tried to extend the coverage of centrally administered services such as immunization and mother and child health clinics without making very vigorous attempts to build up the community and individual participation in health care provision which is the essence of the PHC message. In the Gambia, the commitment to local-level participation in health care is well established and was reiterated in the PHC Action Plan formulated for the period 1980/1–1985/6. In late 1984, the Gambian Ministry of Health, Labour and Social Welfare undertook a national review of the progress made towards achieving the goals in the Action Plan and of 'ensuring an equitable redistribution of the limited health resources in the country in favour of the under-served majority who live and work in the rural areas' (Gambia, 1985: 8). The review included an examination of existing data sources and a series of interviews conducted with health personnel at all levels throughout the country. In addition, 588 households were visited in 56 villages (28 with PHC services and 28 without) with a questionnaire for both the household head and for mothers with a child under 5. The sampling design was a slightly modified version of the Expanded Programme of Immunization cluster methodology (Lemshaw and Robinson, 1985). In 456 of the 581 households successfully interviewed, one index child (the youngest child under 5) was located and a full interview conducted.

In terms of outcome measures, the two variables considered were an index of early childhood mortality (proportion dead of children ever born) and a measure of mean upper arm circumference for children (three bands: green, yellow, and red). Both these measures are poor indicators of the impact of PHC, particularly because the Gambian programme is quite recent. At the time of the survey, about 200 villages in all had village health services including a village health worker and a trained traditional birth attendant, forming part of a village Development Committee. Both the measure of childhood mortality and of nutritional status are likely to pick up effects which precede the beginning of PHC. There is an additional technical problem with the mortality measure which occurs quite commonly in surveys designed to measure the impact of a health intervention. The problem arises when the target population is the basis for sampling—in many cases, a child or children under the age of 5. By choosing households with a living last-born child, the results cease to be representative of childhood mortality in the general population unless the adjustments proposed by Aguirre and Hill (1987 and 1988) are applied to the data from mothers with a recent subsequent birth. Larger samples are needed to screen eligible cases and at the same time collect some basic data from households passed over.

Apart from the general problem of choosing reliable outcome measures, the measures selected to identify the reach of various PHC components were able to identify several major achievements in the Gambia since parts of the PHC message were entirely new. Immunization compliance has been very high by West African standards for some years but by asking about vaccine knowledge, the PHC review was able to discern the educational effects of village health workers (for example, 27 per cent of mothers in PHC villages named three or more vaccines compared with just 17 per cent elsewhere).

A summary of some of the results analysed by Chambers (1986, 1987) appears on Fig. 3.3 to 3.13. The diagrams show how the location of a

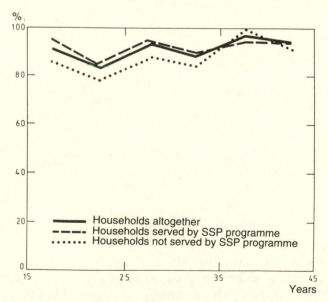

FIG. 3.3. Percentage of women examined during pregnancy by age

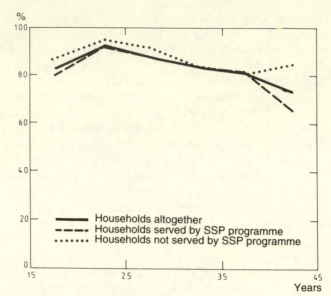

FIG. 3.4. Percentage of mothers delivering at home by age

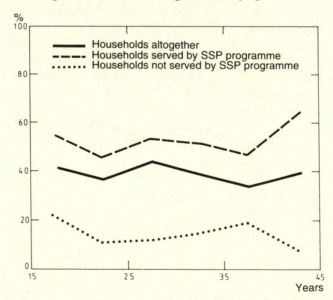

FIG. 3.5. Percentage of mothers assisted at birth by a trained health worker

trained person in the village has affected behaviour related to immediate
health needs (regular examination during pregnancy and thereafter; assistance at delivery; the diarrhoea treatment messages); but other aspects of
health care which may involve travel to a higher order centre for treatment

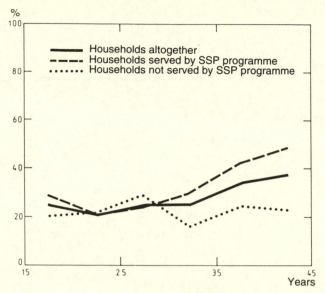

FIG. 3.6. Percentage of children weighed at birth by mother's age

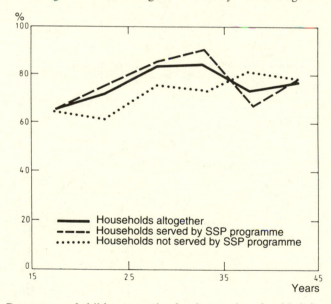

FIG. 3.7. Percentage of children examined at least twice after birth by mother's age

are as yet not greatly affected. The details of the review need not concern us here but several general points are worth some emphasis.

First, it is an enormously complex job to attribute causes to particular effects such as changes in attitudes and behaviour if not in outcome vari-

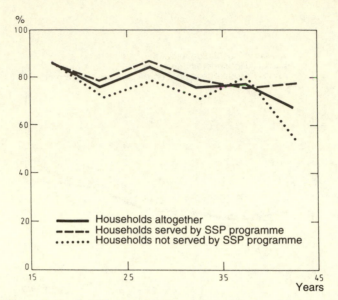

FIG. 3.8. Percentage of children weighed at least twice since birth by mother's age

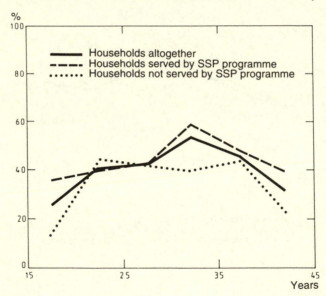

FIG. 3.9. Percentage of children receiving one or more vaccines by age of mother

ables. The Gambian PHC review, like many others of its kind, is beset by problems of confounding. For example, PHC villages have at least a population of 400 and will therefore begin with more services and easier access to towns than smaller places. The key element in a successful PHC review based on a survey will be the design of the sample of households for

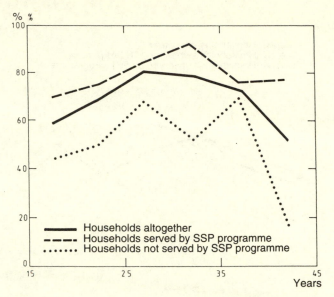

FIG. 3.10. Percentage using ORT by mother's age

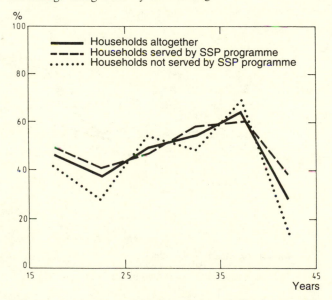

FIG. 3.11. Percentage of women with knowledge of diarrhoea treatment rules by age

interview. Only by trying to anticipate possible confounding effects and by designing the sample accordingly can false conclusions be avoided. Secondly, it is extremely important to consider the effects of household size and structure on health not only because of increased risks of cross-infection

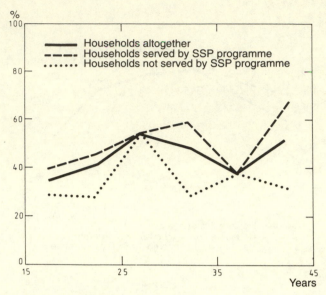

Fig. 3.12. Percentage of mothers knowing one or more methods for diarrhoea prevention by age

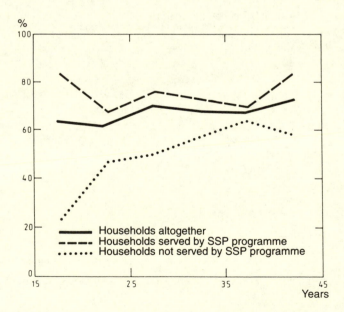

Fig. 3.13. Percentage of mothers providing solid food before 6 months by age of woman

in large households but also because household size and structure are connected with wealth, income, and other social class variables. Thirdly, it is important to be clear about the level of predicted impact. In other words, if PHC is aimed at improving the health of a whole community, then it is wrong to attempt to evaluate the effect using individual-level data. The analysis, even though reports come from individual householders, must be conducted at the community level. This has important implications for the size of the sample survey. Finally, it is important to understand pre-existing differentials in health care status and access to health facilities in reviewing the success of PHC in reaching different countries. The study of the diffusion of other innovations shows that there are districts which lag and others which lead; they differ in both location (distance from the centre) and in character (level of education and income, for example). The Gambian review highlighted the difference between the Western Region and the more isolated parts of the country. It would be wrong to expect the PHC messages to be received with the same clarity everywhere and indeed this lag by region could be exploited as a means of evaluating the progress of the PHC programme.

6. Conclusion

This paper began by indicating some of the difficulties in developing appropriate data collection and analysis methods for the monitoring and evaluation of PHC, difficulties which in larger part stem from the diverse nature of the PHC message. By including such broad goals and announcing such a general programme of action, the authors of the Alma-Alta declaration have set the health assessment community including demographers an enormous task. Many of the measurement techniques are poor at picking up early significant changes in mortality and morbidity, and the development of theory about the broader socio-economic and medical determinants of health is at a very early stage.

None the less, there is a rapidly growing body of experience now with the assessment of the impact of family planning programmes, oral rehydration therapy programmes, and the like, and some lessons for the future are emerging. One is that a single source of information is unlikely to be adequate since analysis needs are so diverse (planning, setting priorities, routine management, patient care, evaluation) and each of the usual sources of information is imperfect in some way. Censuses are expensive and take a long time to analyse; vital registration is generally incomplete and urban-biased; clinic and hospital records are beset by selection effects; household surveys are complex to organize and analyse, and are poor at measuring recent changes in behaviour and attitudes. Taken together, however, these diverse sources can be extremely informative about the progress of PHC, particularly when steps are taken to standardize terms and definitions and when household surveys or more detailed investigations are fitted within a nested system.

A second general point for future PHC evaluation is that the trend away from measuring episodes or isolated events towards an information system based on individuals is to be encouraged. Even in developed countries, several health authorities are moving towards patient-held medical records. The Gambian experience shows that card-retention by largely illiterate mothers in rural areas can be extraordinarily good—93 per cent of mothers in PHC villages could produce a child-welfare card. The data on these cards, which can be abstracted for analysis either during a special household survey or when the patient contacts the health services, will be of better quality than those obtained by simple interview (exact dates, specified treatment, height and weights of children) and will all refer to a single individual. Since excess health risks run in families, the information on the cards used in conjunction with census or survey data providing supplementary information on characteristics of the household, will be invaluable in identifying groups at risk as well as for directing and assessing the effect of the PHC message towards the most needy. The way ahead, it seems, for primary health care evaluation must be to try to install a community-based information system in which as many as possible of the records are held by individuals. This switch from a concentration on illness episodes, treatments, and vital events counted in isolation to aggregate statistics centred around individuals and families is the way for poor countries to emulate but at less expense the elaborate record linkage systems which many European countries are now using to great effect (see Baldwin *et al.*, 1986, for the first textbook on methods). When essential information about the individual's characteristics (age, place of birth, birth-weight, etc.) are assembled on a single record card together with information on health care received (immunization record, nutritional surveillance, clinic visits, etc.), there are a number of possibilities for the retrieval and analysis of this information. The simplest will be the cross-sectional survey but the techniques exist for longitudinal studies or follow-up of groups. The one casualty of these recommendations is the conventional civil registration system. If PHC does intend to extend to most of the population, then the PHC updating system itself should provide complete coverage of births and deaths, usually making the official registration system run by the Ministry of the Interior in most cases largely redundant.

Acknowledgements

Many of the ideas in this paper stem from collaborative work with Dr Wendy Graham. Nicola Dollimore and Mike Chambers, students in the Centre for

Population Studies, were responsible for the analysis of the Mopti survey and the Gambian PHC review respectively. Thanks go to the Gambian Ministry of Health and UNICEF for use of the PHC review data. The UK Overseas Development Administration and the Sahel Institute supported the field research in Mali.

References

Aaby, P., Bukh, J., Lisse, I. M., and Smits, A. J. (1984), 'Measles vaccination and reduction in child mortality: A community study from Guinea-Bissau', *Journal of Infection* 8: 13–21.

—— —— Hoff, G., Leerhoey, J., Lisse, I. M., Mordhorts, C. H., and Pederson, I. R. (1986), 'High measles mortality in infancy related to intensity of exposure', *Journal of Paediatrics* 109: 40–4.

Abelin, T., Brzezinski, Z. T., and Carstairs, V. D. L. (1987), *Measurement in Health Promotion and Protection*, WHO Regional Publications, European Series 22, Geneva.

Aguirre, A. and Hill, A. G. (1987), 'Childhood mortality using the preceding birth technique: Some applications and extensions', Research Papers 87–2, Centre for Population Studies, London School of Hygiene and Tropical Medicine.

—— —— (1988), 'Child mortality estimated by the preceding birth technique: Further developments', *UNICEF Social Statistics Bulletin*, Nairobi.

Baldwin, J. A., Acheson, E. D., and Graham, W. J. (1986), *Textbook of Medical Record Linkage*, Oxford University Press.

Black, R. E. (1984), 'Diarrhoeal diseases and child morbidity and mortality', in W. H. Mosley and L. C. Chen (eds.), *Child Survival: Strategies for Research*, Supplement to vol. 10 of *Population and Development Review*, 141–61.

Brass, W. and Macrae, S. (1984), 'Childhood mortality estimated from reports on previous births given at the time of a maternity: I—Preceding births technique', *Asian and Pacific Census Forum* 11/2: 5–8.

Caldwell, J. C. (1986), 'Routes to low mortality in poor countries', *Population and Development Review* 12/2: 171–220.

Chambers, M. (1986), 'A report on the household survey of the Gambia primary health care review (1984–5)', unpublished report for the Ministry of Health and UNICEF, Centre for Population Studies, London School of Hygiene and Tropical Medicine.

—— (1987), 'The effect of different types of contact with the medical services on health and health-related behaviour in the Gambia', unpublished report, Centre for Population Studies, London School of Hygiene and Tropical Medicine.

Chen, L. C. (1986), 'Primary health care in developing countries: Overcoming operational, technical and social barriers', *Lancet*, 29 Nov., 1260–5.

Culyer, A. J. (ed.) (1983), *Health Indicators*, An international study for the European Science Foundation, Martin Robertson.

Dollimore, N. (1987), 'The effects of health interventions upon childhood mortality in Mopti and Sevare, Mali', M.Sc. thesis, Centre for Population Studies, London School of Hygiene and Tropical Medicine.

Foster, S. O. (1984), 'Immunizable and respiratory diseases and child mortality', in

W. H. Mosley and L. C. Chen (eds.), *Child Mortality: Strategies for Research*, Supplement to vol. 10 of *Population and Development Review*, 119–40.

Gambia, Ministry of Health (1985), *Primary Health Care Review*, Banjul.

Garenne, M., Cantrelle, P., and Diop, I. (1985), 'Le Sénégal', in J. Vallin and A. Lopez (eds.), *La Lutte contre la mort: Influence des politiques sociales et des politiques de santé sur l'évolution de la mortalité*, Travaux et documents 108, INED–PUF, Paris, 307–30.

Graham, W. J. and Arthur, M. (1986), 'Health Status Indicators in Developing Countries: A Selective Review', The Commonwealth Secretariat, London.

Halstead, S. B., Walsh, J. A., and Warren, K. S. (1985), *Good Health at Low Cost*, Rockefeller Foundation, New York. (Republished in 1987.)

Hansluwka, H. E. (1985), 'Measuring the health of populations: Indicators and interpretations', *Social Science and Medicine* 20/12: 1207–44.

Hill. A. G. and David, P. H. (1988), 'Monitoring early changes in childhood mortality in developing countries', *Health Policy and Planning* 3/3: 214–26.

—— Traoré, S., Cluzeau, F., and Thiam, A. (1986), 'L'Enquête pilote sur la mortalité aux jeunes âges dans cinq maternités de la ville de Bamako', in *Estimation de la mortalité du jeune enfant pour guider les actions de santé dans les pays en développement*, Éditions de l'INSERM 145, Paris, 107–29.

Lefèvre, D. (1986), 'Étude de la nutrition au Mali et perspectives', Save the Children Fund, Bamako.

Lemshaw, S. and Robinson, R. (1985), 'Surveys to measure programme coverage and impact: A review of the methodology used by the Expanded Programme of Immunization', *World Health Statistics Quarterly* 38/1: 65–75.

Mosley, W. H. (1985), 'Will primary health care reduce infant and child mortality? A critique of some current strategies with special reference to Africa and Asia', in J. Vallin and A. D. Lopez (eds.), *Health Policy, Social Policy and Mortality Prospects*, IUSSP–INED, Ordina, Liège, 103–38.

Puffer, R. R. and Serrano, C. V. (1975), *Patterns of Mortality in Childhood*, Pan-American Health Organization, Washington, DC.

Rashad, H. (1987), 'Oral re-hydration therapy and its effect on child mortality: The Egyptian experience', Paper presented at the British Society for Population Studies Conference on Health Interventions and Mortality Change in Developing Countries, 9–11 Sept., Sheffield.

Rifkin, S. B. and Walt, G. (1986), 'Why health improves: Defining the issues concerning "comprehensive primary health care" and "selective primary health care"', *Social Science and Medicine* 23/6: 559–66.

Senegal, Ministère de la Santé (1984), *Situation sanitaire et démographique 1983*, Dakar.

—— (1985), *Statistiques sanitaires et démographiques du Sénégal 1981–2*, Dakar.

Sierra Leone, Ministry of Health (1981), *The Health Services of Sierra Leone*, Report no. 66, Freetown.

Sierra Leone and Federal Republic of Germany (1985), Bo-Pujehun Rural Development Project, Health and Nutrition programme, Plan of operation, Freetown.

Stouman, K. and Falk, I. S. (1936), 'A study of the objective indices of health in relation to environment and sanitation', *Quarterly Bulletin of the Health Organizations*, League of Nations 5: 901–66.

UNICEF (1985), *Sierra Leone—Annual Report*, Freetown.
van Norren, B. and van Vianen, H. A. W. (1986), 'The malnutrition–infections syndrome and its demographic outcome in developing countries', Programming Committee for Demographic Research, Publication no. 4, Geographical Institute, State University of Groningen.
Walsh, J. A. and Warren, K. S. (1979), 'Selective primary health care: An interim strategy for disease control in developing countries', *New England Journal of Medicine* 301/18: 967–74.
WHO/HST/86.2 (1986), 'Indicators and methods for evaluating the effectiveness of health interventions', *Health Situation and Trend Assessment Programme*, Geneva.
WHO/UNICEF (1978), *Primary Health Care*, Health for All Series, no. 1, Geneva.

Appendix 3.1

Table 3.A. *Health status indicators, and useful classifying variables, proposed by the United Nations Statistical Office*

Indicator	Classifying variables
1. Mortality and length of life	
(*a*) Number of rates of death (annually; some classifications less frequently)	Sex, age, urban, rural, national or ethnic origin, causes of death, socio-economic group
(*b*) Expectation of life, selected ages, (annually or less frequently)	Sex, age, urban, rural, national or ethnic origin, socio-economic group
2. Morbidity, impairments and handicaps	
(*a*) Spells of bed disability and restricted activity for specified periods (annually or less frequently)	Sex, age, urban, rural, national or ethnic origin, diseases and injuries (broad and/or selected groups), socio-economic group
(*b*) Duration of spells of bed disability and restricted activity for specified period (annually or less frequently)	Sex, age, urban, rural, diseases and injuries (broad and/or selected groups), socio-economic group
(*c*) Number and proportion of persons with selected chronic functional disabilities for specified period (annually or less frequently)	Sex, age, urban, rural, national or ethnic origin, impairments and handicaps, socio-economic group
(*d*) Number and/or incidence of communicable diseases of public health importance, (annually)	Sex, age, urban, rural, geographical area, selected diseases

Source: Graham and Arthur, 1986.

Table 3.B. *Health status indicators, by principal sources of data, proposed by the World Health Organization*

Indicators	Possible sources of data					
	Vital events register	Population and household censuses	Routine health service records	Epidemiological surveillance data	Sample surveys	Disease registers
Birth weight*	P	—	P	—	A	—
Weight & height*	—	—	P	A	A	—
Arm circumference	—	P	—	A	A	—
Infant mortality*	P	P	—	A	—	—
Child mortality	P	P	—	—	A	—
Under-5 mortality	P	P	—	—	A	—
Under-5 proportionate mortality	P	—	—	—	A	—
Life expectancy at given age	P	P	—	—	A	—
Maternal mortality	P	P	P	—	A	A
Crude birth rate	P	P	—	—	A	—
Disease-specific death rates	P	—	P	P	A	A
Proportionate mortality from specific disease	P	—	P	P	A	A
Morbidity:						
incidence rate	—	—	P	P	A	P
prevalence rate	—	—	P	P	A	P
Prevalence of long-term disability	—	—	P	—	A	—

Notes: P = Primary source.
A = Alternative source.
* = Global indicator.
Source: Graham and Arthur, 1986.

Table 3.C. *Health status indicators for measuring impact and effectiveness at different levels, drafted by WHO Informal Working Group (1985)*

Level	Indicator
Local Health Area	1. Probability of dying by age 2 years 2. % of infants with birth weights < 2,500 g. 3. Weight for age 12–23 months 4. Measles cases 5. Measles vaccine efficacy 6. Number of cases with severe dehydration 7. % severe dehydration among diarrhoea cases
Regional	1. Probability of dying by age 2 years 2. % of infants with birth weights < 2,500 g. 3. Weight for age 12–23 months 4. Neonatal tetanus mortality 5. Measles morbidity 6. Poliomyelitis morbidity 7. Number of cases with severe dehydration 8. % severe dehydration among diarrhoea cases 9. Diarrhoea case fatality 10. ALRTI case fatality 11. Malaria mortality
National	1. Birth rate 2. Infant mortality 3. Child mortality 4. Life expectancy at birth* 5. % of infants with birth weight < 2,500 g. 6. Weight for age 12–23 months 7. Maternal mortality 8. Measles cases prevented 9. Neo-natal tetanus mortality 10. Poliomyelitis morbidity 11. Diarrhoea mortality 12. ALRTI mortality 13. Malaria mortality
International	1. Birth rate 2. Infant mortality* 3. Child mortality 4. Life expectancy at birth 5. % of infants with birth weight < 2,500 g.* 6. Weight for age 12–23 months* 7. Maternal mortality 8. Measles cases prevented 9. Neo-natal tetanus mortality 10. Poliomyelitis morbidity 11. Diarrhoea mortality 12. ALRTI mortality 13. Malaria mortality

* Global indicator.

Source: Graham and Arthur, 1986.

Table 3.D. *Health status indicators recommended for use by selected WHO Regional Offices*

Indicator	WHO Regional Office			
	Eastern Mediterranean	Europe	American	Western Pacific
Life expectancy at birth separately for males and females	Yes	—	—	—
Life expectancy at ages 1, 15, 35, and 65 by sex	—	Yes	—	—
Maternal mortality	Yes	Yes	Yes	Yes
Mortality rates by sex and 5-year age groups for 10 selected causes of death	—	Yes	—	—
General mortality by cause and age	—	—	Yes	—
Mortality from chronic diseases by cause	—	—	Yes	—
Mortality for EPI diseases	—	—	Yes	—
Incidence of EPI diseases	—	—	Yes	—
Annual incidence rate of each of the 6 EPI target diseases for the most recent 5 years	Yes	—	—	—
Latest available data on the annual number of cases of diphtheria, tetanus, whooping cough, measles, poliomyelitis, or tuberculosis	—	—	—	Yes
Incidence of infectious diseases	—	Yes	—	—

Source: Graham and Arthur, 1986.

4 Seasonal Variation in Urban Mortality: The Case of Bamako, 1974 to 1985

Philippe Fargues and Ouaidou Nassour
Institut National d'Études Démographiques, Paris and
CERPOD, Bamako

1. Introduction

The struggle against death is a fight primarily against nature. The seasons, which form an integral part of nature, have always influenced mortality. As mortality declines, to what extent are these seasonal cycles of nature overcome? Do city dwellers, for whom life is less and less ruled by the seasons, still die according to seasonal rhythms, especially when in Africa the cities have particularly benefited from progress in health?

Certain epidemic diseases, and all diarrhoeal diseases, are more prevalent in particular seasons. Have the programmes to combat these diseases flattened the peaks in mortality which once recurred regularly with that season?

The replacement of the subsistence economy by a market economy and the increase in the number of agricultural regions supplying the urban market have protected the cities from the vagaries of production of each individual region. This has stabilized the stocks and the prices of essential products. Has mortality related to food intake similarly lost its correspondence with the seasonal cycles of crop production?

The observation of 12 years of mortality in Bamako[1] offers a precise picture of the change in this phenomenon over time in a large city of the Sahel. Because the period was characterized by a dramatic drop in mortality (Fargues and Nassour, 1988), it is possible to examine whether or not the seasonal variation in mortality tended to be reduced, to remain the same, or to increase, when mortality decreased.

The material analysed comes from the death records kept by the Bureau of Hygiene of the city of Bamako, which we examined exhaustively for the period between 1 January 1974 and 31 December 1985. 55,256 events were

---

This chapter was translated by Mark Hereward.

[1] A joint project of the French National Institute of Demographic Study (INED) and the Sahel Institute.

recorded during the period, of which 5,427 were still births, and 49,829 were deaths. The following information was recorded:

- date of death (day, month, and year);
- sex of the deceased;
- age at death (in days up to one month, months up to 1 year, and years after 1 year);
- place of death (home or health facility);
- place of birth;
- cause of death.

The coverage of these records is incomplete.[2] The analysis is based on absolute numbers of deaths, or on indices taken from life tables obtained after adjustment of the raw data (Fargues, 1984; Fargues and Nassour, 1988). Here, we present only the results which are not sensitive to biases arising from the methods of estimation. After a review of the seasonal variations of overall mortality, we shall examine in more detail a specific disease, measles, which remains the most important cause of death in Bamako.

2. Seasonal Variations in Overall Mortality

We shall first consider variations in mortality according to the month of death and then according to the month of birth among children under 1 year of age.

(*a*) The month of death

The monthly index of mortality[3] (Table 4.1 and Fig. 4.2) shows that both the size and the direction of the seasonal effect vary with age. At all ages except for the first day of life, the risk of death follows a curve more or less parallel to that of atmospheric temperature (Fig. 4.1): the warmest months are the most deadly. The excess mortality at the end of the dry season is moderate before the age of 1 month, very strong from 1 month to 5 years (ages at which the risk of death is three times as high in April or May as during the 'cold' months of September to January), then moderate again after 5 years of age.

Each of these seasonal patterns is the result of the specific pattern of different causes of death (Fig. 4.3), which combine in varying proportions according to age. It can only be understood by examining deaths classified

---

[2] The average coverage of registration was estimated to be 57.1 per cent for 0–5-year-olds and 77.1 per cent for those aged over 5 (Fargues and Nassour, 1988).

[3] The index is equal to the number of deaths that occur in one month, adjusted for month's length, over the average number of deaths per month, times 100.

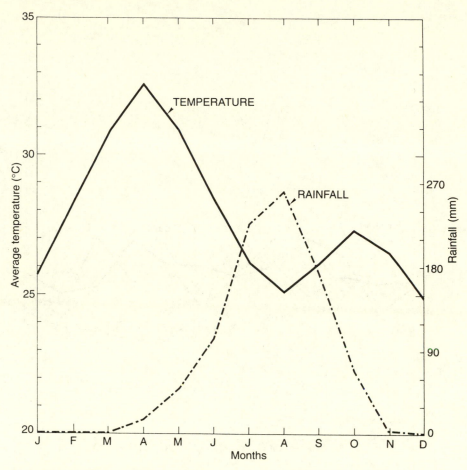

FIG. 4.1. Monthly average temperature and rainfall, Bamako, 1974–1985

by cause at each age. The classification of deaths by cause provided by this registration system is not absolutely reliable, because various sources of bias affect it, among which are:

1. The recording of only a single cause of death, whether this cause is in fact immediate, underlying, or contributing. Any one of these is used alternatively to describe the same particular cause of death.
2. The incompleteness of registration. The overall coverage rate may not be the same as the coverage rate for any one cause.
3. The absence of medical supervision, while they were still alive, of some of those who died. On a death certificate, the reported cause of death

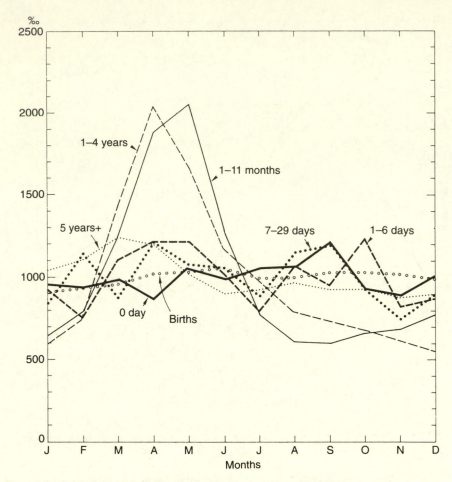

Fɪɢ. 4.2. Seasonality of deaths by age, both sexes together, Bamako, 1974–1985

is sometimes derived from a medical observation and sometimes from symptoms described by the deceased's relatives to the clerk of the Bureau of Hygiene. The frequency of these two kinds of reports varies with the sickness.

The second kind, a sort of 'verbal autopsy', applies generally to deaths that occur in the home (39.9 per cent of cases). This explains why a small number of diseases recur with great frequency among the causes of death reported in the registers. Fourteen of them appear more than 500 times between 1974 and 1985, representing 30,781 deaths or 61.8 per cent of the total (Table 4.2). However, in the case of illnesses which are well known to the population, such as measles (Garenne and Fontaine, 1986), diagnosis

Table 4.1. *Seasonal index of deaths by sex, and of births, Bamako, 1974, both sexes together (Yearly average = 100)*

Age	January	February	March	April	May	June	July	August	September	October	November	December
Deaths by month of death												
0 days	95	94	99	87	106	99	106	107	121	93	89	101
1–6 days	92	76	110	122	122	102	98	107	95	123	83	87
7–29 days	85	115	88	121	108	105	89	115	120	92	75	90
1–11 months	65	79	125	188	205	129	78	61	60	66	69	78
1–4 years	60	75	144	204	167	117	98	79	73	68	62	55
5+ years	104	110	124	120	102	90	93	97	93	93	88	90
Deaths by month of birth												
0 months	99	98	103	108	109	97	93	109	109	98	81	95
1–11 months	99	85	76	73	82	106	122	126	117	116	98	95
Births	91	94	96	102	103	106	100	100	103	104	102	98

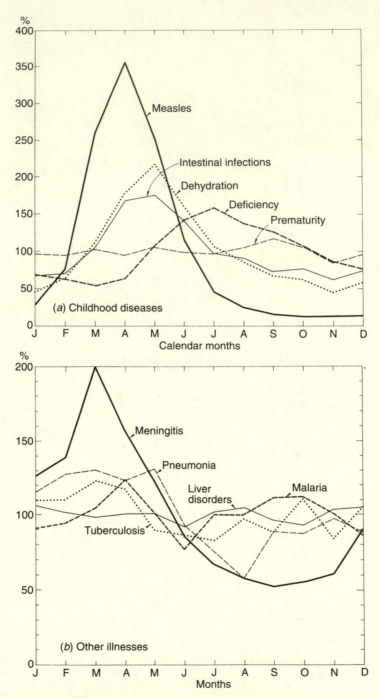

FIG. 4.3. Seasonality of deaths by cause, Bamako, 1974–1985

Table 4.2. *Distribution of deaths by cause and place of death, Bamako, 1974–1985, both sexes together*

Cause of death			Place of death		N
Classified as	Reported as	Code	hospital	domicile	
1. Measles	'Rougeole'	55	23.8	76.2	5,910
2. Malaria	'Accès pernicieux' 'Paludisme'	84	30.6	69.4	4,652
3. Infectious intestinal diseases	'Diarrhée' 'Diarrhée infectieuse'	1–9	51.0	49.0	3,290
4. Prematurity	'Prématurité'	765	69.7	30.3	2,920
5. Diseases of the liver	'Hépatite'	70	90.5	9.5	127
	'Cancer du foie'	155	75.3	24.7	195
	'Cirrhose'	571–2	79.6	20.4	1,347
	'Ictère'	782	35.7	64.3	742
Subtotal		5	68.3	31.7	2,411
6. Senility	'Sénilité'	797	2.9	97.1	2,328
7. Nutritional deficiency	'Malnutrition' 'Kwashiorkor'	260–9	58.6	41.1	1,990
8. Heart disease	'Insuffisance cardiaque'	428–9	64.6	35.4	1,606
9. Pneumonia	'(broncho) pneumonie'	485–6	52.2	47.8	1,206
10. Tuberculosis	'Tuberculose'	10–18	56.0	44.0	1,199
11. Meningitis	'Méningite'	320–2	93.2	6.8	1,190
12. Dehydration	'Déshydratation'	276	85.6	14.4	833
13. Anaemia	'Anémie'	285	72.8	27.2	675
14. Tetanus	'Tétanos' (sauf ombilical)	37	91.2	8.8	520
Other causes			80.9	19.1	19,048
Total with known place of death			60.1	39.9	49,829

error is probably rare, even when the deaths occur mainly in the home (76.2 per cent of measles deaths).

Despite some reservations about the accuracy of recorded information, the classification of death by cause and age (Figs. 4.4 and 4.5) makes it possible to distinguish three large age groups.

1. Children (less than 15 years of age), for whom mortality is dominated by measles and malaria. During the first year of life (Fig. 4.4), prematurity constitutes the primary cause of death: it accounts for 25

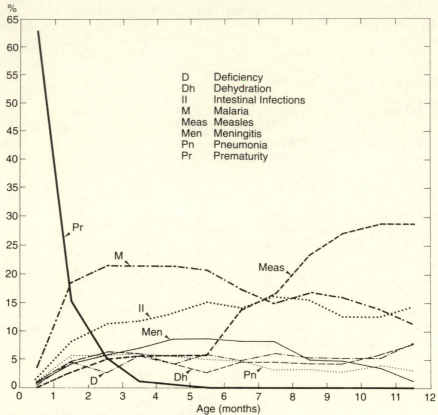

FIG. 4.4. Proportion of deaths by month of age due to the main causes of infant
mortality, both sexes together, Bamako, 1974–1985

per cent of all infant deaths and for 63 per cent of neonatal deaths.
Then follow, respectively, malaria, infectious intestinal diseases, and
measles. Between 1 and 4 years of age, measles causes more than one
in every three deaths (34 per cent). Among children older than 5,
malaria, real or presumed, is the primary cause of death, causing, on
average, one in five deaths.

2. Adults (15 to 59 years of age). Malaria takes the back seat to 'diseases
of the liver', the primary cause of death between 15 and 65 years of
age, responsible for 13 per cent of all deaths to adult males, and for 8
per cent of all deaths to females. After 25 years of age, tuberculosis
becomes the second most important cause of death.

3. The elderly (60 years of age and more). If 'senility' (26 per cent of
deaths) is excluded—a cause which we have omitted from Fig. 4.5
because of its inherently suspect nature—mortality of the old is

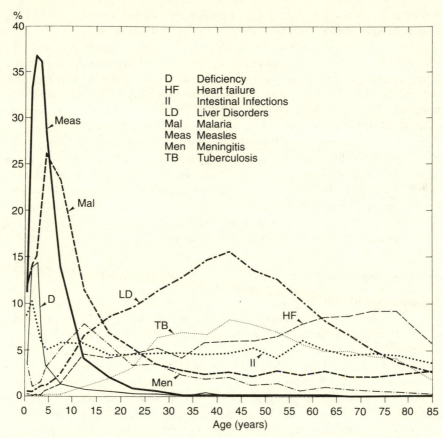

FıG. 4.5. Proportion of deaths by year of deaths due to the main causes of infant mortality, both sexes together, Bamako, 1974–1985

characterized by a great variety of causes. First among these is cardiac failure (8 per cent).

Together, variations in the distribution of causes of death by age and by season explain the seasonal variation in mortality by age (Figs. 4.2 and 4.3). In the course of the first month, the principal cause of death, prematurity, is virtually unaffected by the seasons. The child, moreover, protected by maternal antibodies, is relatively less vulnerable to the infectious and parasitic diseases of the warm season. The impact of malaria can still be discerned in the seasonal distribution of death at 0 days (a single peak in September, which is one month after the big rains of August), but as a cause of death, malaria is almost non-existent in the records before the age of 15 days. (At that age, the reported malaria deaths are spurious.) It could well be that it is the mother's malaria which increases the risks of perinatal

mortality. Between 7 and 29 days, two slight peaks are noted, of which the
second, in September, may well indicate early malaria deaths.

Between 1 month and 5 years of age, three warm-weather diseases take
the greatest toll: measles (peak in April), infectious intestinal diseases (peak
in May), and meningitis (peak in March). One may also note a frequent
cause of death during the rainy months: the mortality from malnutrition is
greatest in June and July, which in the agricultural economy at this latitude
is the traditional period for food shortages before the new harvest.

After 5 years of age, and especially in adults, the warm-season illnesses no
longer outweigh the causes of death for which seasonal variations are either
weak (tuberculosis, for example, where the death results from a long-drawn-
out process, and diseases of the liver) or inverted (malaria with its two
peaks, one at the end of the rainy season, and one in the middle of the
warm season, where its frequency is often over-estimated because of the
possible confusion with fevers from other causes).

(b) The month of birth

The variations in mortality are less marked when classified by month of birth
than by month of death (Table 4.1). Instead of the peak in 1–11 month
mortality observed during the months of April and May, we see a peak in
mortality (at the same ages) among children born in July and August. In
March and April, at the time when measles epidemics occur, they are 8
months old. They have lost the immunity conferred upon them by their
maternal antibodies, but they have not yet attained the age for measles
vaccinations (9 months), and hence they are particularly vulnerable.

In order to analyse the excess mortality of people born in July and
August, we should bear in mind a widespread finding in tropical Africa
(Cantrelle and Ly, 1980), confirmed by the curve of infant mortality in
Bamako: the distribution of infant mortality by month of age is bimodal
(Fig. 4.6). The first peak, at 0 months (in fact 0 days in Bamako, where
umbilical tetanus has become quite rare,[4] thanks to the high frequency of
births in maternity clinics, for which see Hill *et al.*, 1986), corresponds to the
deaths of low birth-weight children (regrouped here, for convenience, under
the term 'prematurity', although there may be children of low birth-weight
who were born at term). The second peak, at 8 months, corresponds with
deaths from infectious and parasitical diseases in children who have lost
their maternal antibodies. It remains to be verified whether or not the
resurgence in mortality invariably occurs at the particular age of 8 months in
all the birth cohorts examined.

On the basis of the exact date of death and the age at death in complete

---

[4] Leroy and Garenne report in Ch. 7 about villages where umbilical tetanus is the major
cause of neonatal death, and where the peak in mortality is on the 7th and 8th days of life.

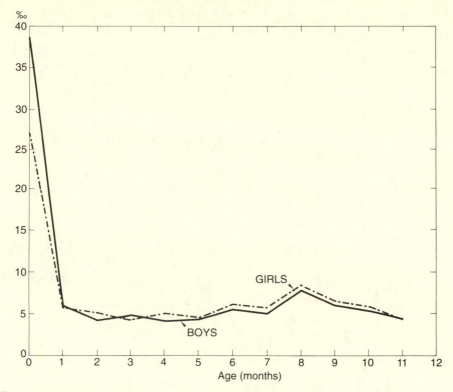

F IG . 4.6. Monthly probability of dying before 1 year, by sex, Bamako, 1974–1985

months, it is possible to infer the month of birth (within one month) of children who have died between 0 and 11 months of age. Having thus recreated the series of infant mortality according to age in months by month of birth, we then corrected the series for under-registration. As the number of registered births was available in Bamako month by month, we were able to construct life tables for children up to the age of 1 year, for each monthly birth cohort.

The mortality rates in these tables (Table 4.3 and Fig. 4.7, on which only half the curves have been shown, for clarity), highlight the bimodal distribution of mortality under the age of one year. While the first peak is always located at 0 months, the second, by contrast, changes position with the month of birth.

Births in January   maximum at 4 months of age
Births in February   maximum at 3 months of age
Births in March   maximum at 2 months of age
Births in April   maximum at 11 months of age
Births in May   maximum at 11 months of age

Table 4.3. *Monthly rates of mortality (per 1,000) by month of birth, Bamako, both sexes together, 1974–1985*

Exact age in months	January	February	March	April	May	June	July	August	September	October	November	December	Total
									Month of birth				
0– 1	33.0	32.7	34.4	36.1	36.3	32.5	31.1	36.4	36.5	32.8	27.1	31.8	33.4
1– 2	7.7	6.4	7.0	5.0	4.8	5.8	5.6	6.3	6.2	5.5	5.2	4.0	5.7
2– 3	5.4	7.7	7.3	5.0	3.5	3.6	3.0	2.7	3.4	5.4	4.6	4.3	4.6
3– 4	8.6	8.4	4.7	2.4	2.5	3.0	3.7	3.7	4.6	3.4	3.3	6.8	4.5
4– 5	9.5	5.4	3.5	3.2	3.4	3.0	3.7	4.3	3.3	3.7	5.5	6.8	4.5
5– 6	5.3	3.0	2.8	2.6	3.5	4.1	3.6	3.2	2.7	5.5	7.1	9.0	4.4
6– 7	5.1	3.4	2.8	4.5	4.7	5.4	3.7	3.2	6.3	11.0	10.9	7.2	5.8
7– 8	2.7	2.3	2.9	3.2	4.9	2.9	2.9	6.0	9.7	13.4	7.2	4.5	5.3
8– 9	3.7	5.2	4.7	4.7	5.0	4.9	9.9	16.7	17.0	10.8	6.4	4.7	8.0
9–10	3.6	2.6	3.2	2.4	2.7	8.2	14.0	15.2	9.4	5.0	2.7	3.7	6.1
10–11	3.2	2.9	2.6	3.6	6.3	10.5	15.2	8.9	3.7	2.8	2.2	3.3	5.5
11–12	2.9	1.5	2.7	6.2	7.2	10.9	6.1	3.8	2.6	2.0	2.2	1.4	4.2
0–12	87.4	79.3	76.3	76.6	82.0	91.1	98.4	105.7	100.9	97.1	81.3	84.4	88.6

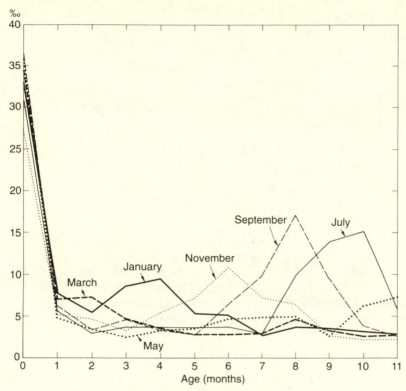

Fɪɢ. 4.7. Monthly probability of dying before 1 year, by month of birth, both sexes together, Bamako, 1974–1985

Births in June	maximum at 11 months of age
Births in July	maximum at 10 months of age
Births in August	maximum at 8 months of age
Births in September	maximum at 8 months of age
Births in October	maximum at 7 months of age
Births in November	maximum at 6 months of age
Births in December	maximum at 5 months of age

Unfortunately, our data do not indicate age in months after the first birthday. It is quite likely that the second peak in mortality occurs at the ages of 13 and 12 months, respectively, for children born in April and in May. As for the modal value of 8 months for those born in August, it may occur in reality at 9 months, but there may be heaping on the age of 8 months, identified by popular lore as a dangerous age. These three peaks constitute exceptions to the general pattern. From the April to the March birth cohort, the second modal age decreases regularly by one month.

Similarly, it will be noted that the level of the second mode varies by a

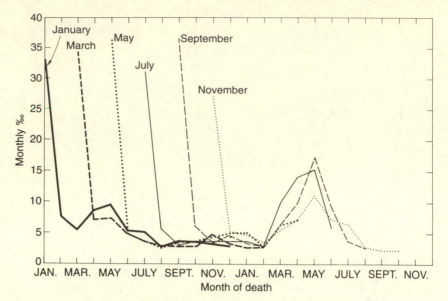

FIG. 4.8. Monthly probability of dying before 1 year, by month of birth and month of death, both sexes together, Bamako, 1974–1985

factor of two according to the monthly birth cohort. The resurgence in mortality is never stronger than when it occurs at the age of 8 or 9 months for those born in August, or at 8 months for those born in September.

Rather than considering variation by age at which this resurgence of mortality is evident, we should underline the consistency in its season of occurrence. To do this, we present the curves of Fig. 4.7 by calendar month of death, rather than by month of age; the result is Fig. 4.8. Beyond the first month of age, the curves for each birth cohort can be superimposed almost perfectly (except during the months of April and May where, as we have just seen, the children born in July–September are at a disadvantage). The surge of mortality observed on average at 8 months does not occur at the same age for all children. It occurs, on the contrary, at the same season for all children in the age group 1–13 months, regardless of their precise age. Whatever the season, the mortality rates do not depend on the month of birth of the children: they are, therefore, independent of age. Infant mortality conforms to the ecological, or even economic, rhythms of the seasons rather than to the biological rhythm of increase in age.

We have shown similarly for Abidjan that there are months of high risk (January to March, warm months in the equatorial zone) rather than ages of high risk. In both cases, the children most at risk were those who, at the age of about 8 months, were approaching the season of excess mortality. In

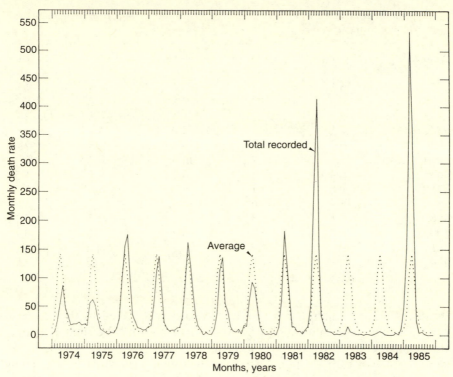

FIG. 4.9. Number of measles deaths recorded by month, Bamako, 1974–1985

Abidjan, knowledge of the date of birth made it possible to follow mortality by month of age beyond 1 year, and to establish an additional finding. After 13 months, mortality by month of age tends to decline. As it occurs on a declining slope, the second peak is weaker, the later it occurs (Fargues, 1986). It seems likely that much the same occurs in Bamako, but we cannot establish that conclusively.

If there were a choice between two recommendations in the area of public health, either systematically to increase the medical surveillance of children at the age of 8 months, or to dissuade parents from conceiving children who will be born in August (or in May in Abidjan), the second would probably be more effective in lowering mortality.

3. Mortality due to Measles

In Bamako, epidemics of measles occur with perfect seasonal regularity, but with variable severity from year to year (Fig. 4.9). We have seen that the

Table 4.4. *Measles death rate (per 1,000) by age at last birthday and calendar year, Bamako, both sexes together*

Year	0 years	1 year	2 years	3 years	4 years
1974	6.1	17.1	10.4	5.8	1.9
1975	6.4	10.2	8.8	4.2	2.1
1976	14.9	33.1	16.4	6.8	4.9
1977	12.1	18.8	12.0	6.3	1.6
1978	9.7	21.3	13.1	6.5	2.6
1979	10.8	17.2	10.5	6.2	2.3
1980	6.4	11.3	6.5	4.2	1.5
1981	9.8	15.1	9.0	5.6	1.9
1982	14.1	25.6	18.9	10.7	3.7
1983	0.5	1.3	0.8	0.2	0.1
1984	0.5	0.9	0.4	0.4	0.1
1985	30.8	14.7	21.2	11.3	4.2
1974–85	10.3	15.7	11.0	5.9	2.3

disadvantage for children born in July/August was linked to the seasonal effect. Is there also an inequality between birth cohorts? We shall first study the average pattern of variations in measles mortality by age. We shall then see how it evolves by birth cohort, and shall finally conclude by discussing the seasonality of this disease.

(*a*) Variations according to age

Measles seems to strike especially hard in the second year of life. The measles mortality rate by year of age calculated for the entire period (Table 4.4, last line) reaches its peak, 15.7 per thousand per year, between 1 and 2 years of age. We have, moreover, confirmed (Fig. 4.4) a well-established phenomenon: measles mortality begins late during the first year of life, and rarely before the age of 6 months. From this fact, we can see that the mortality rate between 0 and 1 year of age is a crude index in that it spreads over the entire year deaths which are in fact concentrated in the last six months of the year. Measles is, therefore, an illness whose progression should be examined month by month.

The computation of an index expressed as the mean number of events per year, irrespective of the length of the age interval concerned ($_am_x$ in column 4 of Table 4.5) leads to the following interesting observation. The frequency of measles deaths increases very rapidly after 6 months to reach its maximum, 22.9 per thousand, at the age of 8 months. From a cross-sectional perspective, measles mortality declines continually after the age of 9 months, and probably throughout the second year. The case fatality rate of

Table 4.5. *Measles life table, both sexes together, Bamako, 1974–1985, and Bandafassi (Senegal), 1975–1983*

Age group (x, x+a)	Bamako, 1974–1985			Bandafassi, 1975–1983		Ratio and rates
	$_aq_x./00$	lx	$_am_x./00$	$_aq_x./00$	lx	
0–6 months	(1.8)			4	10,000	2.2
0–1	0.6	10,000	7.2	—	—	—
1–2	0.1	9,994	1.2	—	—	—
2–3	0.2	9,993	2.4	—	—	—
3–4	0.3	9,991	3.6	—	—	—
4–5	0.3	9,988	3.6	—	—	—
5–6	0.3	9,985	3.6	—	—	—
6–12 months	(6.1)			17	9,960	2.8
6–7	0.8	9,982	9.6	—	—	—
7–8	0.9	9,974	10.8	—	—	—
8–9	1.9	9,965	22.9	—	—	—
9–10	1.7	9,946	20.5	—	—	—
10–11	1.6	9,929	19.4	—	—	—
11–12	1.2	9,913	14.5	—	—	—
1–2 years	15.6	9,901	15.7	31	9,791	2.0
2–3	11.0	9,747	11.0	32.	9,487	2.9
3–4	5.9	9,640	5.9	18	9,183	3.1
4–5	2.3	9,583	2.3	19	9,018	8.3
5–10	2.0	9,561	0.4	25	8,847	12.5
10–15	0.4	9,542	0.1	7	8,626	17.5
15–20	0.3	9,538	0.1	6	8,566	20.0
20–25	0.1	9,535	e	—	—	—
25+	e	9,534	—	—	—	—

Notes: —: Not available.
e: Less than 0.1.
Between 0 and 12 months, rates by months were calculated as: $_1m_x = 12(l_x - l_{x+1})/0.5(l_x + l_{x+1})$.
Source: Pison, 1986, for Bandafassi.

measles is highest, lethal, not between 1 and 2 years of age as one would have thought from rates by year of age, but much earlier. This age pattern is perhaps characteristic of urban areas, where measles vaccination is relatively widespread, but doesn't begin until the eighth month. Anyway, it corroborates an assertion we made earlier, that the older the infant is at the approach of the inevitable yearly measles epidemic, the greater are his chances of survival.

From 3 years of age onwards, measles mortality falls off quite quickly, but it does not disappear completely before the age of 25 years. Overall, if measles were the sole cause of death, a birth cohort of 10,000 new-borns would not have more than 9,534 survivors at the end of the susceptible ages. At birth, therefore, a baby has almost a 5 per cent probability of dying of measles.

This figure is about three times less than the figure recorded for Senegal in the region of Bandafassi (Pison, 1986). As the latter region is a rural zone in an area whose climatic, food, and epidemiological conditions are similar to those in southern Mali, comparison of the two tables clearly brings out the inequal risks of urban and rural dwellers in the face of the disease. From birth to age 2, the probability of dying from measles was about twice as high in the rural region. From the age of 3 onwards, the rural disadvantage increased steadily, so much so that there were 20 deaths in the countryside between the ages of 15 and 20, and only one in the city. This rural disadvantage comes both from better vaccination coverage in the city (there was practically no measles vaccination in Bandafassi at the time when Pison was studying the area), and from the urban–rural differences in the epidemiology of measles (Aaby, in Chapter 14 of this volume).

(b) Change in seasonality between 1974 and 1985

Cases of measles are sufficiently numerous before 5 years of age that rates calculated by year of age and year of death are significant at the 0.0001 level. These rates are presented by calendar year in Table 4.4. The data can also be reconstructed by cohort. We have converted them to rates, and combined them by birth cohort to construct the measles life tables presented in Table 4.6. It will be noted that the birth cohorts presented here actually straddle two years. The column for the cohort of 1974, for example, combines the rates derived from the rate at 0 years in 1974, at 1 year in 1975, and at 2 years in 1976, and so on: therefore the cohort includes children born from 1973 to 1974.

The results thus obtained offer an excellent opportunity to examine the evolution of measles mortality. We see four salient traits:

1. The spikes in the rates (Figs. 4.9 and 4.10) reflect the epidemic nature of measles. They do not show the biennial regularity which would be suggested by the hypothesis of van de Walle (1986), according to which the biennial regularity observed in Bobo-Dioulasso during the years 1981–4 would be general in African cities. On the contrary, one observes only two years without measles, and these were consecutive: 1983 and 1984.
2. Each year, the measles mortality rates follow the same age pattern: in descending order, 1, 2, 0, 3, and 4 years. The curves may be superimposed without ever crossing, with the exception of the rate at 0 years. Let us remember that the curve of this rate owes its intermediate

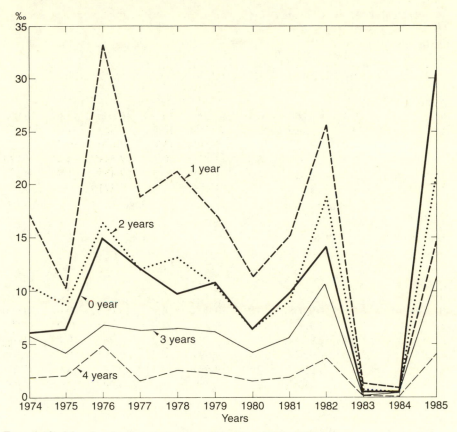

Fᴵɢ. 4.10. Measles death rate by age, Bamako, 1974–1985

position to the manner in which it was calculated. If we had calculated a rate solely on the six months in which the child is actually exposed to measles rather than on the entire first year, that curve would in fact have been situated every year above all other curves.

3. From the two preceding points, it follows that the age pattern of measles varies considerably when cohorts are compared rather than calendar years (Table 4.6). Measles thus presents a variable 'cohort calendar' pattern, which is a result of an epidemic level that varies according to the year, and a relatively constant 'period calendar'. The probability of death by year of age reaches its peak at various times: sometimes at 0 years, for the cohorts born in the 12 months preceding a big epidemic (birth cohort of 1982 and probably of 1985); sometimes at the age of 1 year, for the cohorts born between one and two years before a large epidemic (cohorts of 1975 and 1981), and for the cohorts born when the size of the epidemic doesn't show large annual

Philippe Fargues and Ouaidou Nassour

Table 4.6. *Measles life tables by birth cohort, Bamako, both sexes together*

Birth cohort Age	1974		1975		1976		1977	
	$_1q_x$	l_x	$_1q_x$	l_x	$_1q_x$	l_x	$_1q_x$	l_x
Year(s)								
0	6.1	10,000	6.4	10,000	14.7	10,000	12.0	10,000
1	10.1	9,939	32.6	9,936	18.6	9,853	21.1	9,880
2	16.3	9,839	11.9	9,612	13.0	9,670	10.4	9,672
3	6.3	9,679	6.5	9,498	6.2	9,544	4.2	9,570
4	2.8	9,618	2.3	9,436	1.5	9,485	1.9	9,531
5	—	9,593	—	9,414	—	9,471	—	9,513
$l-l_5$	407		586		529		487	

Birth cohort Age	1978		1979		1980		1981	
	$_1q_x$	l_x	$_1q_x$	l_x	$_1q_x$	l_x	$_1q_x$	l_x
Year(s)								
0	9.7	10,000	10.7	10,000	6.4	10,000	9.8	10,000
1	17.1	9,903	11.2	9,893	15.0	9,936	25.3	9,902
2	6.5	9,734	9.0	9,782	18.7	9,787	0.8	9,651
3	5.6	9,671	10.7	9,694	0.2	9,604	0.4	9,643
4	3.7	9,617	0.1	9,590	0.1	9,602	4.2	9,639
5	—	9,581	—	9,589	—	9,601	—	9,635
$l-l_5$	419		411		399		365	

Birth cohort Age	1982		1983		1984		1985	
	$_1q_x$	l_x	$_1q_x$	l_x	$_1q_x$	l_x	$_1q_x$	l_x
Year(s)								
0	14.0	10,000	0.5	10,000	0.5	10,000	30.3	10,000
1	1.3	9,860	0.9	9,995	14.6	9,995	—	9,697
2	0.4	9,847	21.0	9,986	—	9,849	—	—
3	11.3	9,843	—	9,776	—	—	—	—
4	—	9,732	—	—	—	—	—	—
5	—	—	—	—	—	—	—	—
$l-l_5$	—		—		—		—	

Note: —: Not available.

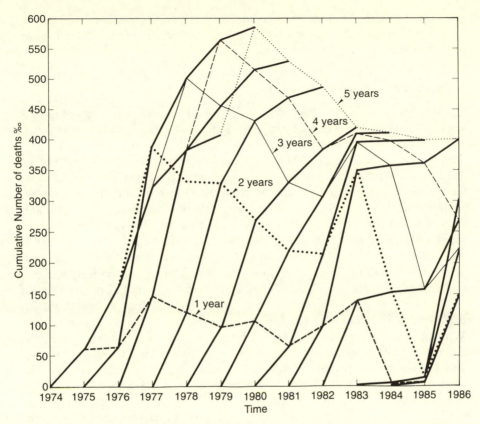

FIG. 4.11. Cumulated life table number of measles deaths by cohort, both sexes together, Bamako, 1974–1985

variations (cohorts of 1976, 1977, and 1978); and sometimes at 2 years, when the two preceding years of life are not marked by serious epidemics (cohorts of 1974, 1980, and 1983).

4. The cumulated number of deaths between 0 and 5 years from the measles mortality tables (1–15 in Table 4.6) is much less unstable than the rates by age which make up this cumulated total (Fig. 4.11). The cohort approach thus reveals a tendency which was hidden in the disorder of cross-sectional fluctuations: from the cohort of 1975 to the cohort of 1981 (the last that can be observed up to the age of 5 years), the partial intensity of measles mortality declines regularly. Despite the quasi-disappearance of the disease during two years (1983 and 1984), only a slow decline shows up, because a process of recuperation was at work: a cohort little marked by measles at the ages where death

imputable to that disease is normally greatest (cohorts 1974, 1979, 1980, 1982) is particularly vulnerable to the next epidemic even if it has reached age 2 in the meantime.

(c) Seasonality of measles mortality

Let us now examine the seasonal variations of measles mortality. Fig. 4.3 gave us some idea of seasonal variation. Fig. 4.9 illustrates these fluctuations from one year to the next. More than any other warm season disease, measles presents a marked (Fig. 4.3) and repetitive (Fig. 4.9) pattern of seasonality. Almost inactive in the period from July to February, it regularly strikes, each year without exception, from the month of March to the month of June, generally reaching its maximum in April, sometimes in March, and sometimes in May. On the other hand, the epidemic attains a very different magnitude every year, which explains the varying size of the peaks in April. 1982 and 1985, two years of serious epidemic, are thus separated by two years in which the epidemic was quite limited although not entirely absent.

As measles receded, the associated causes of death had also regressed in 1983–4, to the point where the probability of dying before age 5 for all causes of death combined ($_5q_0$), had decreased to about 100 per thousand. With the measles epidemic of 1985, diarrhoeal disease and dehydration also came back with a vengeance, causing $_5q_0$ to rise to 158 per thousand for boys and 173 for girls. This shows the extent to which any progress made in the struggle against high death rates remains insecure in Africa.

The brutal resurgence of measles mortality in 1985 has yet to be explained. Two hypotheses have been proffered, between which we will not choose, for lack of epidemiological data. First, vaccination coverage could have dropped in 1985, or the vaccines administered could have accidentally lost their efficacy. In medical circles of the city, it is thought that there had been a break in the 'cold chain', which destroyed many vaccines. But it is equally possible that, despite an anti-measles campaign comparable to previous years, coverage was insufficient to arrest the epidemic. The only data that we have pertain to the year in which the campaign was launched, 1983, where 36 per cent of the children aged between 1 and 2, and 47 per cent of the children aged between 3 and 4 were vaccinated in Bamako (Verschuur and Cornale, 1987). At the outset of the immunization programme in 1983, children 1 year and older had survived the regular epidemics of the previous years. A majority of them had already been immunized by a non-fatal form of the disease. It seems that it sufficed then to vaccinate four in 10 children to arrest the epidemics of the next two years. As a result, the disease was no longer transmitted, and there were birth cohorts in which the non-vaccinated children were not immunized by a benign form of the illness. In 1985, these were the cohorts aged less than 3 years. In the group of high-risk ages, the proportion of immunized children became less than it would have been without the vaccination campaign.

The second explanation permits us to understand why in 1985, unlike all other years, the rate at age 0 was higher than the rates at ages 1 and 2. The transmission of the disease from the older children (aged 2 and 3) to the younger children of less than 1 year, an aggravating factor of the disease (Aaby *et al.*, 1986), would have been particularly frequent in the course of an epidemic in which the older children themselves had little chance of being immunized.

These two explanations have different policy implications for public health. The first would suggest that in order not to be defeated by a resurgence of mortality, the campaign should last several years (more than three years under present circumstances). The second would indicate instead that the campaign should only be undertaken with sufficient coverage (no less than 40 per cent in the case of Bamako), no matter its duration, if the counter-effects of insufficient immunization are to be avoided.

4. Conclusion

In the introduction to this chapter, we raised some questions concerning the permanence of seasonal movements in the mortality of African cities. It is now possible to provide a few answers. First, the cycles of crop production have lost their importance. The successive droughts that hit the Sahel in the period studied left no perceptible trace in the mortality of the population of Bamako. Protected from the uncertainty of local food production, an African capital is, and will always be, protected from the shortages which affect the rural zones.

Preventive medicine can take its course in the cities, and mortality will show a rapid but irregular decline. A sudden resurgence in mortality is observed from time to time, however, as a result of epidemics of infectious diseases. Given that these illnesses always occur at precisely the same time of the year, these epidemics raise the seasonal peak of mortality. This peak flattens in good years, but does not disappear, so that if one considers a period in which favourable and epidemic years alternate, the tendency toward generally lower mortality does not bring in its wake a disappearance of seasonal variations. On the contrary, these epidemics remain sufficiently frequent, by reason of their perfect seasonal regularity, for the month of birth to constitute an important factor of differential mortality among children.

References

Aaby, P., Bukh, J., Hoff, G., Lisse, I. M., and Smits, A. J. (1986), 'Cross-sex Transmission of Infection and Increased Mortality due to Measles', *Review of Infectious Diseases* 8/1: 133–43.

Cantrelle, P. and Ly, V. (1980), 'La Mortalité des enfants en Afrique', in P. M. Boulanger and D. Tabutin (eds.), *La Mortalité des enfants dans le monde et dans l'histoire*, Ordina, Liège, 197–221.

Fargues, P. (1984), 'Âges au décès et niveaux de mortalité: Évaluer le taux d'enregistrement des décès à partir de leur structure par âges: Application à la Tunisie', *Population* 1: 47–76.

—— (1986), 'La Mortalité infantile et juvénile à Abidjan de 1973 à 1983', in *Estimation de la mortalité du jeune enfant (0–5 ans) pour guider les actions de santé dans les pays en développement*, Éditions de l'INSERM 145, Paris, 139–58.

—— and Nassour, O. (1988), *Douze ans de mortalité urbaine au Sahel: Niveaux, tendances, saisons et causes de mortalité à Bamako, 1974–1985*, Travaux et documents 123, INED–PUF, Paris.

Garenne, M. and Fontaine, O. (1990), 'Assessing probable causes of death using a standardized questionnaire: A study in rural Senegal', in J. Vallin, Stan D'Souza, and A. Palloni (eds.), *Measurement and Analysis of Mortality: New Approaches*, Clarendon Press, Oxford, 123–42.

Hill, A. G., Traoré, S. M., and Cluzeau, F. (1986), 'L'Enquête pilote sur la mortalité aux jeunes âges dans cinq maternités de la ville de Bamako, Mali', in *Estimation de la mortalité du jeune enfant (0–5) pour guider les actions de santé dans les pays en développement*, Éditions de l'INSERM 145, Paris, 107–29.

Pison, G. (1986), 'Pourquoi la rougeole tue-t-elle en Afrique? Démographie, structure des familles et létalité de la rougeole', *Biologie des populations*, Colloque national du CNRS, Lyon.

van de Walle, E. (1986), 'Anatomie d'une épidémie de rougeole vue par la lorgnette d'une enquête à passages répétés', in *Estimation de la mortalité du jeune enfant (0–5 ans) pour guider les actions de santé dans les pays en développement*, Éditions de l'INSERM 145, Paris, 419–28.

Verschuur, C. and Cornale, S. (1987), 'Analyse de situation: Femmes et enfants au Mali', Second draft, Bamako.

5 Socio-Economic Factors and Use of Health Services as Determinants of Child Mortality

Cheikh Mbacké and Étienne van de Walle
CERPOD, Bamako, and University of Pennsylvania, Philadelphia

1. Introduction

The factors behind the mortality transition in the Third World continue to be the subject of a lively intellectual debate. Until recently, much of the discussion was based on macro-level information on national income and the budgetary allocation of national resources. In a first stage, the debate was dominated by an optimistic view of the power of medical technology and public health to reduce mortality even in the absence of a broadly based rise in individual incomes (Stolnitz, 1974). In considering the issue, Preston (1975) provided an ingenious demonstration that income effects and technological progress both played a role in the secular rise of expectation of life. By the mid-1970s, the rapid decline in mortality seemed to have spent itself, and views were expressed to the effect that there were no easy technological fixes, and that the stagnation of the world economy would be translated in a slowing down of mortality decline in developing nations (Gwatkin, 1980). This might be particularly applicable in some countries of Africa, where per capita agricultural production and income appear to have declined at times. The interest of scholars has recently focused on the countries which are doing well on the health front, despite their low per capita incomes, either because the equality of income distribution compensates for its low level, or because available public resources are devoted to mortality reducing expenditures such as primary health and education (Caldwell, 1986). Using regional data from Kenya, Mosley (1985) has shown that the increased level of female education accounts for a substantial part of gains in infant and child mortality.

In the last few years, demographers working with the newly available data from the World Fertility Surveys and similar surveys have concentrated on the explanation of micro-level mortality differentials. The most significant set of variables accounting for the variance of child and infant mortality involves parental, and above all, maternal education. The finding that a substantial part of the difference between urban and rural mortality in the surveys, for example, could be explained by the different levels of schooling reached by urban and rural populations, has cast doubt on the effectiveness of medical investments concentrated in cities. The position has been argued cogently by Preston (1985*a*).

Reacting against this interpretation, John Caldwell (1986: 202) has written: 'Demographers may have begun to concentrate too much on maternal education rather than on its larger context.' He suggests that education may be the catalyst that ensures optimum use of existing health facilities. Educated parents ensure their children's survival by using existing services more assiduously than illiterate parents. The dilemma summarized by the phrase 'Is it better to build a school or a hospital?' is a false dilemma: the pre-existence of a school will facilitate the optimum utilization of the hospital. But the absence of adequate health facilities may severely limit the effectiveness of parental efforts in favour of their children.

There are only a few studies which allow the examination of the respective share of income and other personal socio-economic variables, on the one hand, and the access to services, on the other hand, in accounting for the global effect on infant and child mortality. By their nature, World Fertility Survey data are ill suited to decompose the mechanisms through which education and the provision of health services operate on mortality differentials. The mortality information is incidental; it was collected serendipitously with the birth histories, and it is attached (and related in the analysis) to characteristics of the parents that may not have the same time referent as the mortality data. (For example, when a child died, the parents may have been living in a different locality from at the time of the survey.) The measurement of income as such is commonly unsatisfactory in surveys. Finally, the WFS has usually not attempted to collect information on what Mosley and Chen (1984) call the proximate determinants of mortality, including the availability of health services. Hence, the actual mechanism of the relationship between education or income and mortality cannot be studied directly, and must be inferred.

The set of relationships between the classical independent socio-economic variables and infant mortality has been likened to a black box (Mosley and Chen 1984; Akoto 1985). To use Preston's (1985*a*) expression, the impact of education on child mortality has been assimilated to a 'dose-response' mechanism. (In the Sudan, for example, Farah and Preston (1982) suggest that one year of the mother's education resulted in a 3.6 per cent reduction of the mortality rate.) In order to disentangle the mechanisms through which the socio-economic determinants operate on mortality, various frameworks have been designed to guide the analysis of existing data sets. For example, in the analysis of the Malaysia survey, DaVanzo (1984) distinguishes the effects of biological and behavioural variables. In the future, the frameworks should lead to the collection of new data that would be more successful in getting at the direct proximate determinants of mortality.

Until recently, there were very few African surveys which allowed any insights into the determinants of mortality. It is nevertheless in an African context that an attempt was first made to analyse the particular role of female education in bringing about improved chances of child survival. Caldwell (1979) suggested that the children of an educated woman in Ibadan, Nigeria, benefit from her additional prestige and ability to manipulate the familial environment and the medical system for their benefit.

Caldwell's interpretation of his Nigerian data has been largely accepted by those who analyse surveys of the WFS type in Africa. The role played by the direct transmission through education of precise knowledge of disease mechanisms remains unquantified (see Preston, 1985*b*, and the critique by Caldwell, 1986). Male education is usually taken as a proxy for income of the husband (Farah and Preston, 1982). The few surveys that have direct information on income seem to confirm this interpretation. At least in one instance, it has been shown that female income exerts a powerful independent influence on the survival of children (Sulaiman, 1987). The finding may well apply only in situations similar to southern Nigeria, where women and men keep separate budgets, and where mothers are responsible for certain expenditures (food, clothing) in favour of their children.

It should be noted that most of the African surveys analysed for the insights they offer into the determinants of mortality are fertility surveys. Surveys specifically devoted to the study of mortality should cast additional light on the issue. In this respect, the urban surveys of infant and child mortality taken in various cities of francophone Africa using a methodology designed by IFORD, the United Nations Training and Research Center in Yaoundé, Cameroon (which are often called IFORD surveys in short), are of particular interest. The principle behind this type of survey is the follow-up of a cohort of births, born under medical supervision in urban maternity hospitals, until the survivors have reached their second birthday. (For a more complete description, see van de Walle, 1990.)

By their inclusion of many intermediate variables, the IFORD surveys allow a new look at the mechanisms of mortality differentials. Moreover, they control for the urban–rural differentials and in part at least for the differential access to services because they are taken, as it were, within an urban medical system. Thus, *use* of service is conceptually distinct from *access* to service. The longitudinal, multi-round design improves the accuracy of observation. Age reporting, dating of sequential observation, and the collection of causes of death at a time close to death, offer more precise information than that available in retrospective surveys. This allows refinement of the analysis to account for the fact that the mortality risks and the access to facilities are expected to be different for various ages of the child. Most important for our present purpose, the IFORD questionnaires contain information on many proximate determinants of mortality and on the use of services. They include questions on maternal characteristics; use of prenatal and postnatal medical facilities and resort to vaccination; access to sanitation in the home under the form of piped water, electricity, toilet facilities, antimalarial measures; and type of treatment during episodes of disease, including the resort to modern or traditional medicine. At the same time, the surveys make specific reference to a certain number of socio-economic characteristics which were collected at the time of the birth of a particular child or during the period of exposure to mortality. Although they may well represent the best designs we have for the study of the mechanisms behind mortality differentials in urban Africa, the IFORD surveys have a number of liabilities. Because they rely on the periodic resurvey of a poorly identified and highly mobile population, they have been subject to very high attrition, and deficient coverage has probably biased the estimation of mortality downward. Furthermore, as they are cohort studies, a period event such as an epidemic of measles can strongly upset the age pattern of deaths.

The analysis which follows is based upon a survey along the IFORD design, executed in the provincial city of Bobo-Dioulasso between April 1981 and March 1984, by the National Institute of Statistics and Demography of Burkina Faso, with the technical assistance and financial support of the Sahel Institute.

2. The Data

Data in the IFORD survey have been classified under broad categories for the purpose of this article. We borrow heavily from the framework of Mosley and Chen (1984) in classifying the variables as socio-economic background factors, proximate determinants—i.e. child characteristics, biological and behavioural characteristics of the mother—and the dependent variable, mortality. Tables 5.1 to 5.4 include a list of the variables, and we limit ourself here to a few descriptive details.

The socio-economic background variables include a broad estimate of household income. Income is given in CFA francs; in 1982, one CFA franc was roughly equal to $0.0025. Because income data were obtained from the husband in later rounds of the survey, non-response is unfortunately more likely in cases of early death of the child. The survey assumed that unmarried women had no income; they have been classified here in the lowest category of incomes. The level of mothers' schooling is very low. An index for the quality of housing is based on a score combining the result of several questions on the materials of the walls, floors, and ceiling of the house. The source of drinking water could be interpreted either as a proxy for high income, in the same way as the other housing variables, or as a more direct channel for infection, and it could therefore alternatively be classified among the next category of variables.

Among the proximate determinants, two child characteristics deserve comment: the trimester of birth reflects the seasonality of death, particularly because of the measles epidemic of February–March 1982, which only affected children old enough to have lost their maternal immunity (see van de Walle, 1990, for a discussion); and the average number of persons sleeping in the same room as the child provides an index of crowding, with possible implications for the transmission of infections (see Aaby in this volume).

We include information on the use of services among the behavioural characteristics of the mother. The number of prenatal visits, and the date of the first visit are particularly useful, although the date had to be obtained from health documents which could only be consulted at home, during the survey rounds, and were therefore not available in the case of a death in the maternity hospital. The variables indexing postnatal visits and vaccinations during the first year of life of the child (BCG, DPT, or measles vaccine) were used only in analysing mortality differentials during the second year of life. Finally, we use information on mosquito control. The questionnaire stated literally 'means used to prevent malaria', but we suspect that the phrasing of the question used referred to mosquitoes. The most often mentioned method of control was the Chinese mosquito coil, which is not so much meant to kill as to chase away mosquitoes; nets and screens were also mentioned, but use of chemicals such as Nivaquine was almost never reported.

There were a number of biases linked to the study of socio-economic factors affecting mortality. With respect to the dependent variable, death or survival of the child, it is likely that the survey underestimated mortality to some extent, particularly that mortality which occurred very early in life and may have resulted in non-identification of the child in the subsequent survey rounds (Ouaidou and van de Walle, 1987). Mbacké (1986) has shown that mortality of the preceding child is higher for women lost to follow-up than for those who remained under observation; it is likely that these women were also more at risk of losing the index child. The intrinsic difficulty of interviewing women who are at that very moment experiencing the agony of losing a child at birth provides one compelling cause of under-reporting of the information concerning very early deaths. Another series of biases results from the fact that the risk of losses to the survey was undeniably linked to the socio-economic characteristics of the parents, as was mortality itself.

In addition, even when perinatal deaths were identified, the characteristics of the parents were often poorly recorded. In the IFORD methodology, some socio-economic information, particularly that on household income and housing characteristics, was only collected during the follow-up rounds, and is therefore not available for children who died in the first days of life. Table 5.1 presents some statistics on the availability of the indepen-

Table 5.1. *Number and percentage of missing values on selected variables for deceased children from different subsamples*

Variable type and name	Perinatal		Neonatal		Post-neonatal		Second year		Previous child	
	No.	%	No.	%	No.	%	No.	%	No.	%
Socio-economic										
Household income	281	64	161	62	79	23	11	5	140	20
Mother's schooling	116	26	37	14	2	1	1	0	3	0
Type of housing	398	90	138	53	0	0	0	0	69	10
Duration of residence	270	61	83	32	17	5	3	1	36	5
Marital status	103	23	29	11	1	0	0	0	NR	NR
Type drinking water	398	90	138	53	0	0	0	0	69	10
Proximate determinants										
1. Child										
Birth-weight	119	27	29	11	29	8	12	5	41	6
Birth order	33	7	11	4	1	0	0	0	7	1
Plurality	0	0	0	0	0	0	0	0	NR	NR
Sex	18	4	3	1	0	0	0	0	NR	NR
Trimester of birth	0	0	0	0	0	0	0	0	NR	NR
2. Mother										
(*a*) Biological										
Age	83	19	30	12	1	0	0	0	5	1
Outcome previous pregnancy	55	12	19	7	1	0	0	0	NR	NR
(*b*) Behavioural										
No. prenatal visits	104	24	33	13	2	1	1	0	2	0
Date 1st visit	186	42	98	38	50	14	14	6	70	10
Postnatal visits	NR	NR	NR	NR	NR	NR	0	0	NR	NR
Mosquito control	398	90	139	54	0	0	0	0	69	10
Vaccination	NR	NR	NR	NR	NR	NR	0	0	NR	NR
Total number of cases	441	—	258	—	346	—	231	—	717	—

Note: NR = Not relevant.

dent, socio-economic variables in the Bobo-Dioulasso data, in instances where the child died. When the child survived to the end of the two-year period, the information is generally complete. There are losses when the child died, and when it migrated or was lost to follow-up for other reasons. The table shows clearly that one of the major defects of the survey consisted in its coverage of the determinants of neonatal mortality. This is even more true of perinatal mortality, which also includes still births. There are reasons to believe that the problem was not limited to the Bobo-Dioulasso survey, and that other IFORD surveys are similarly affected. Unfortunately, it means for our purposes that any analysis of the determinants of perinatal mortality is severely biased, both because of the selective under-registration of deaths and because of the selective loss of socio-economic information.

It is clear from Table 5.1 that the quantity and quality of the socio-economic information increase as older and older children are considered. Because the impact of socio-economic and service access variables and the structure of mortality determinants change with age of the child (DaVanzo, 1984), it is impossible to generalize from the second year of life to the first, or even from post-neonatal mortality to neonatal or perinatal mortality. We must keep in mind that the reliability of the analyses will vary with successive segments of life.

Some variables cannot be used in the analysis, although an effort had been made to include them in the survey. We exclude them either because the variable seemed to be excessively vulnerable to the omission bias, because it was not exhibiting enough variability in the population to yield significant differentials, or because the analyses involving that variable would have been excessively complex. For example, we left out information about the education and occupation of the husband, since that information was especially likely to be missing from the base questionnaire. On the other hand, women did not report participation in the labour force to an extent that would justify the use of that variable. Similarly, 96 per cent of the women reported that they were using pit latrines as the type of toilet facilities. It is undoubtedly significant for child health that pit latrines are so widespread, the more so because they are unlikely to be used by the very young children observed in the survey. These characteristics are likely to contribute to the high *level* of mortality in Bobo. But they are largely irrelevant when it comes to the study of *differentials*.

There are other factors complicating the interpretation of our findings. The overwhelming majority of children in the survey were born either in modern maternity clinics or with the assistance of certified midwives who refer their patients to the hospital in case of a problem. Because of the selective use of modern facilities by women at risk of losing their child, and the under-reporting of births at home, data on the place of delivery cannot be trusted to show the benefit of modern conditions of delivery for the population. Most infants had been injected at birth with tetanus antitoxins (a procedure which in much of French-speaking Africa replaces vaccination of the pregnant mother), and tetanus had almost no incidence in the survey population; inoculation against the disease is therefore not a factor explaining differentials in mortality.

The present study can only skim the rich information of the survey, because the analysis of sequential data is complex, and we cannot do justice to it in a short paper. This is a report on research in progress, not a definitive assessment.

3. Bivariate Relationships

The results presented in Tables 5.2, 5.3, and 5.4, for socio-economic factors and proximate determinants (child and mother's characteristics) respectively, apply to successive age categories of the children. Death rates are obtained by relating the number of deaths to the number of children alive *at the beginning* of the period who remained under observation to the end, or died. There is some inaccuracy in using that denominator, because some children may be lost through other causes than death, most of all through migration, in the course of the period; but the results provide a first look at mortality differentials.

In each category of determinants, the highest death rates correspond to the 'unknown' category. This is a telling indication of the bias already noted, i.e. that death of the child was often a reason for not collecting information on characteristics.

The differentials for known values of the characteristics are often quite marked. In general, the socio-economic variables (income, mother's education, type of housing) have a clear effect on mortality at all ages (Table 5.2). The proportions of women with at least secondary schooling are small, and the educated women are younger than other mothers. The increased risks to the children of primiparous women hide the impact of education on mortality. Characteristics of the child (birth-weight, birth order, and plurality), affect the chances of survival in ways that are generally acknowledged in the literature (Table 5.3). The influence of the biological and behavioural characteristics of the mother also conforms to expectations (Table 5.4). The effect of the earliness of the first prenatal visits, and of the frequency of subsequent ones, is quite striking.

The socio-economic variables influenced the survival of the previous child in similar ways (Table 5.5). The effect of prenatal visits seems to be limited to the index child, and disappears for the previous child. This suggests that prenatal care has an effect in itself, and not through other factors that are collinear. It is interesting that the loss of a previous child does not seem to influence behaviour in the direction of increased use of health facilities.

Table 5.2. *Number of children (C), number of deaths (D), and proportion deceased (d) in selected subsamples: Socio-economic variables*

Variable type and name	Neonatal			Post-neonatal			Second year		
	C	D	d	C	D	d	C	D	d
Household income									
Unknown	469	161	0.343	308	79	0.256	229	11	0.048
<20,000/not married	1,262	71	0.056	1,191	76	0.064	1,115	54	0.048
20–50,000 CFA	3,827	21	0.005	3,806	158	0.042	3,648	148	0.041
Above 50,000	1,119	5	0.004	1,114	33	0.030	1,081	18	0.017
Mother's schooling									
Unknown	60	37	0.617	23	2	0.087	21	1	0.048
No schooling	5,047	175	0.035	4,872	265	0.054	4,607	182	0.040
Primary	1,190	36	0.030	1,154	55	0.048	1,099	42	0.038
Secondary +	380	10	0.026	370	24	0.065	346	6	0.017
Type of housing									
Unknown	138	138	1.000	—	—	—	—	—	—
Traditional	1,925	45	0.023	1,880	138	0.073	1,742	79	0.045
Semi-modern	3,325	55	0.017	3,270	146	0.045	3,124	119	0.038
Modern	1,289	20	0.016	1,269	62	0.049	1,207	33	0.027
Duration of residence									
Unknown	149	83	0.557	66	17	0.258	49	3	0.061
Born in Bobo	2,014	51	0.025	1,963	93	0.047	1,870	81	0.043
Less than 5 yrs.	1,657	57	0.034	1,600	103	0.064	1,497	62	0.041
5 years or more	2,857	67	0.023	2,790	133	0.048	2,657	85	0.032
Marital status									
Unknown	34	29	0.853	5	1	0.200	4	0	0.000
Not in union	572	38	0.066	534	41	0.077	493	26	0.053
Married	6,071	191	0.031	5,880	304	0.052	5,576	205	0.037
Type of water									
Unknown	138	138	1.000						
Piped water	4,309	69	0.016	4,240	205	0.048	4,035	136	0.034
Well or other	2,230	51	0.023	2,179	141	0.065	2038	95	0.047
Total Cases	6,677	258	0.039	6,419	346	0.054	6,073	231	0.038

Table 5.3. *Number of children (C), number of deaths (D), and proportion deceased (d) in selected subsamples: Child characteristics*

Variable type and name	Neonatal			Post-neonatal			Second year		
	C	D	d	C	D	d	C	D	d
Birth-weight (g.)									
Unknown	588	29	0.049	559	29	0.052	530	12	0.023
Less than 2,500	828	142	0.171	684	65	0.095	619	29	0.047
2,500 to 2,999	2,349	55	0.023	2,294	142	0.062	2,152	97	0.045
3,000 or more	2,914	32	0.011	2,882	110	0.038	2,772	93	0.034
Birth order									
Unknown	19	11	0.579	8	1	0.125	7	0	0.000
First born	1,401	99	0.071	1,302	100	0.077	1,202	58	0.048
Second to fifth	3,437	88	0.026	3,349	182	0.054	3,167	126	0.040
Sixth and above	1,820	60	0.033	1,760	63	0.036	1,697	47	0.028
Plurality									
Single birth	6,462	213	0.033	6,249	319	0.051	5,930	223	0.038
Multiple	215	45	0.209	170	27	0.159	143	8	0.056
Sex									
Unknown	3	3	1.000						
Male	3,294	150	0.046	3,144	171	0.054	2,973	107	0.036
Female	3,380	105	0.031	3,275	175	0.053	3,100	124	0.040
Trimester of birth									
April–June	1,501	47	0.031	1,454	114	0.078	1,340	55	0.041
July–September	1,573	70	0.045	1,503	97	0.065	1,406	41	0.029
October–December	1,800	85	0.047	1,715	70	0.041	1,645	57	0.035
January–March	1,803	56	0.031	1,747	65	0.037	1,682	78	0.046
Room density									
Unknown	172	168	0.977	4	4	1.000	—		—
<4 persons	4,183	60	0.014	4,123	213	0.052	3,910	152	0.039
4 or more	2,322	30	0.013	2,292	129	0.056	2,163	79	0.037
Total cases	6,677	258	0.039	6,419	346	0.054	6,073	231	0.038

Table 5.4. *Number of children (C), number of deaths (D), and proportion deceased (d) in selected subsamples: Mother's characteristics*

Variable type and name	Neonatal			Post-neonatal			Second year		
	C	D	d	C	D	d	C	D	d
No. prenatal visits									
Unknown	59	33	0.559	26	2	0.077	24	1	0.042
No visit	1,827	87	0.048	1,740	106	0.061	1,634	81	0.050
1 to 2 visits	2,054	87	0.042	1,967	121	0.062	1,846	70	0.038
3 or more visits	2,737	51	0.019	2,686	117	0.044	2,569	79	0.031
Date 1st Visit									
Unknown	570	98	0.172	472	50	0.106	422	14	0.033
No visit	1,830	86	0.047	1,744	107	0.061	1,637	81	0.049
<4 months before	1,079	33	0.031	1,046	58	0.055	988	47	0.048
4–5 m. before	1,819	28	0.015	1,791	80	0.045	1,711	52	0.030
Earlier	1,379	13	0.009	1,366	51	0.037	1,315	37	0.028
Postnatal visits									
None in 1st yr.	NR	NR	NR	NR	NR	NR	3,618	158	0.044
At least 1	NR	NR	NR	NR	NR	NR	2,455	73	0.030
Mosquito control									
Unknown	139	139	1.000	NR	NR	NR	NR	NR	NR
None	1,677	50	0.030	1,627	118	0.073	1,509	83	0.055
Net, insecticide	4,861	69	0.014	4,792	228	0.048	4,564	148	0.032
Vaccination 1st yr.									
Unknown	NR	NR	NR	NR	NR	NR	5	0	0.000
None	NR	NR	NR	NR	NR	NR	1,047	68	0.065
At least 1	NR	NR	NR	NR	NR	NR	5,021	163	0.032

Table 5.4. *(cont.)*

Age group									
Unknown	33	30	0.909	3	1	0.333	2	0	0.000
<20 years	1,426	87	0.061	1,339	97	0.072	1,242	66	0.053
20–34	4,511	120	0.027	4,391	224	0.051	4,167	146	0.035
35 and above	707	21	0.030	686	24	0.035	662	19	0.029
Outcome previous pregnancy									
Unknown	32	19	0.594	13	1	0.077	12	0	0.000
Live born, alive	4,486	105	0.023	4,381	210	0.048	4,171	151	0.036
Foetal loss	831	35	0.042	796	39	0.049	757	23	0.030
No pregnancy	1,328	99	0.075	1,229	96	0.078	1,133	57	0.050
Total cases	6,677	258	0.039	6,419	346	0.054	6,073	231	0.038

Note: NR = Not relevant.

Table 5.5. *Number of births, number of deaths, and proportion deceased (d) among the preceding live births*

Variable type and name		Births	Deaths	d
Income:	Unknown	953	140	0.147
	< 20 or not married	806	110	0.136
	20 to 50,000 CFA	3,406	387	0.114
	Above 50,000	1,011	80	0.079
Schooling:	Unknown	46	3	0.065
	No Schooling	4,834	579	0.120
	Primary	1,032	109	0.106
	Secondary +	264	26	0.098
Housing:	Unknown	460	69	0.150
	Traditional	1,705	227	0.133
	Semi-modern	2,892	311	0.108
	Modern	1,119	110	0.098
Residence:	Unknown	276	36	0.130
	Born in Bobo	1,514	158	0.104
	Less than 5 years	1,494	218	0.146
	5 years or more	2,892	305	0.105
Water	Unknown	460	69	0.150
	Piped	3,780	373	0.099
	Well or other	1,936	275	0.142
Birth-weight:	Unknown	544	41	0.075
	Less than 2,500 g.	605	97	0.160
	2,500 to 2,999	2,061	264	0.128
	3,000 or more	2,966	315	0.106
Birth order:	Unknown	11	7	0.636
	First born	1,376	193	0.140
	Second to fifth	3,403	387	0.114
	Sixth and above	1,386	130	0.094
Age of mother:	Unknown	49	5	0.102
	< 20 years	441	85	0.193
	20–34	4,920	555	0.113
	35 and above	766	72	0.094
Prenatal visits:	Unknown	42	2	0.048
	No visit	1,815	206	0.113
	1 to 2 visits	1,880	230	0.122
	3 or more visits	2,439	279	0.114
1st visit:	Unknown	587	70	0.119
	No visits	1,820	209	0.115
	< 4 months before	936	110	0.118
	4–5 months before	1,618	194	0.120
	Earlier	1,215	134	0.110
Malaria control:	Unknown	460	69	0.150
	None	1,491	180	0.121
	Net, insecticide	4,225	468	0.111
Total number of cases		6,176	717	0.116

Table 5.6. *Income, mother's education, and prenatal visits*

Household income (CFA)	Mother's level of schooling						Total	
	None		Primary		Secondary			
	n	e	n	e	n	e	n	e
Unknown	1.7	20.3	2.3	33.3	3.6	55.6	1.9	24.8
< 20,000 or single	1.4	22.1	1.6	22.9	1.8	19.7	1.5	22.0
20 to 50,000	1.9	29.9	2.3	36.1	2.7	37.2	2.0	31.2
50,000 +	1.9	27.9	2.5	36.3	2.8	42.6	2.2	32.1
Total	1.8	28.2	2.2	33.4	2.5	35.4	1.9	29.6

Notes: n = Mean number of prenatal visits.
  e = Proportion of women seeking prenatal care during 1st trimester.

4. Relationship between Socio-Economic and Proximate Variables

The problem of disentangling the effect of the various proximate and socio-economic variables is linked with the strong association of the relevant variables among themselves. Women belonging to high income households are also likely to be more educated and to use the existing services more effectively. This is illustrated in Table 5.6 and in Table 5.7, which show respectively the use of prenatal facilities, and vaccinations and postnatal visits during the first year of the child's life, by known levels of education and by income. In general, the level of schooling is the more important

Table 5.7. *Income, mother's education, and use of medical services during the first year of life*

Household income (CFA)	Mother's level of schooling						Total	
	None		Primary		Secondary			
	p	v	p	v	p	v	p	v
Unknown	0.29	0.74	0.45	0.92	0.78	1.00	0.34	0.78
< 20,000 or single	0.33	0.74	0.36	0.90	0.42	0.92	0.34	0.80
20 to 50,000	0.41	0.82	0.50	0.88	0.56	0.88	0.42	0.83
50,000 +	0.33	0.81	0.51	0.90	0.65	0.95	0.41	0.85
Total	0.38	0.80	0.47	0.90	0.56	0.92	0.40	0.83

Notes: p = Proportion having a postnatal visit in 1st year.
  v = Proportion vaccinated in 1st year.

Table 5.8. *Income, mother's education, and mosquito control (proportion using fumigations, screens, or nets)*

Household income (CFA)	Mother's level of schooling			Total
	None	Primary	Secondary	
Unknown	0.60	0.82	0.78	0.65
< 20,000 or single	0.65	0.84	0.82	0.71
20 to 50,000	0.72	0.80	0.80	0.74
50,000 +	0.81	0.94	0.97	0.86
Total	0.72	0.84	0.89	0.75

factor in explaining the use of services (or the practice of hygiene, as suggested by Table 5.8 on mosquito control). The inclusion of unmarried women in the low income group is quite disruptive of the relation in Table 5.6. For obvious reasons, young unmarried women are not early and eager visitors of prenatal facilities. In Table 5.7, however, educated women with little or no income are shown to use health facilities more assiduously than richer women without education.

5. Multivariate Models

There are too many missing cases on crucial items of information, and the possibility of bias is too great, to use the first month of life in studies of the determinants of mortality. More complex analyses of the data must be limited to post-neonatal mortality and to the mortality of the second year of life. The form of the dependent variable (a child either survives or dies in the period, and deaths are relatively rare events) suggests the use of logistic regressions as the best methodology. The strategy followed is to present three equations for each dependent variable. The first equation is limited to socio-economic variables; the second to proximate determinants; and the third includes all the variables. The list of variables, with indication of their type and of the reference category, appears in Table 5.9. The results of the regressions are in Tables 5.10 and 5.11. Some variables that cluttered the regressions have been eliminated: e.g. age and marital status, because they are collinear with parity; and water supply, because it had no independent effect in the multivariate models.

Post-neonatal mortality seems to be strongly influenced by the income variable and by the quality of housing (Table 5.10). Comparing the first and the second equation suggests that the effects of income on mortality operate through the proximate determinants, perhaps because the richer households

Table 5.9. *Variables used in regressions*

Variable name	Description
Household income	
INCOME N.A.	Unknown
Reference category	< 20,000 or not married
MEDIUM INCOME	20–50,000 CFA
HIGH INCOME	Above 50,000 CFA
Mother's schooling	
Reference Category	No schooling
PRIMARY	Primary
SECONDARY	Secondary +
Type of housing	
Reference category	Traditional
SEMI-MODERN	Semi-modern
MODERN HOME	Modern
Duration of residence	
Reference category	Born in Bobo
RECENT MIGRANT	Less than 5 years
OLD MIGRANT	5 years or more
Birth-weight	
Reference category	Less than 2,500 grams
MEDIUM WEIGHT	2,500 to 2,999
HIGH WEIGHT	3,000 or more
PLURALITY	
SEX	
Trimester of birth	
Reference category	April–June
JULY-SEPT.	July–September
OCT.–DEC.	October–December
JAN.–MAR.	January–March
PARITY[a]	No. of previous births
ROOM DENSITY[a]	Persons sharing room with child
MALARIA CONTROL	Mosquito control
NO. PREVIOUS VISITS	No. of prenatal visits
Date 1st prenatal visit	
1st VISIT N.A.	Date unknown
Reference category	No visits
1st VISIT 1–3m.	< 4 months before
1st VISIT 4–5m.	4–5 months before
EARLIER DATE	Earlier
VISITS YEAR 1	Postnatal visits in 1st year
VACCINATION YEAR 1	Vaccination in 1st year

[a] Numerical variable (all others are dummy variables).

Table 5.10. *Results of logistic regression: Post-neonatal period*

Variable	Equation 1		Equation 2		Equation 3	
	β	p value	β	p value	β	p value
INCOME N.A.	1.6647[a]	0.0000	NI	NI	1.6426[a]	0.0000
MEDIUM INCOME	-0.3801[b]	0.0116	NI	NI	-0.2154	0.1927
HIGH INCOME	-0.6146[a]	0.0065	NI	NI	-0.2292	0.3446
PRIMARY	-0.0545	0.7408	NI	NI	0.0076	0.9654
SECONDARY	0.3589	0.1327	NI	NI	0.2596	0.3275
SEMI-MODERN	-0.5084[a]	0.0001	NI	NI	-0.5143[a]	0.0003
MODERN HOME	-0.4010[b]	0.0231	NI	NI	-0.3633[c]	0.0550
RECENT MIGRANT	0.2993[c]	0.0592	NI	NI	0.3191[c]	0.0531
OLD MIGRANT	0.0803	0.5819	NI	NI	0.1994	0.2192
MEDIUM WEIGHT	NI	NI	-0.2456	0.1565	-0.1757	0.3343
HIGH WEIGHT	NI	NI	-0.7199[a]	0.0001	-0.6324[a]	0.0011
PLURALITY	NI	NI	1.1074[a]	0.0000	1.3195[a]	0.0000
SEX	NI	NI	-0.0709	0.5521	-0.1669	0.1803
JULY–SEPT.	NI	NI	-0.1833	0.2340	0.01274	0.4436
OCT.–DEC.	NI	NI	-0.8268[a]	0.0000	-0.5022[a]	0.0066
JAN.–MAR.	NI	NI	-0.8273[a]	0.0000	-0.4755[b]	0.0103
PARITY	NI	NI	-0.0971[a]	0.0003	-0.1023[a]	0.0009
ROOM DENSITY	NI	NI	0.0511	0.3555	0.0646	0.2702

Table 5.10. (cont.)

Variable	Equation 1		Equation 2		Equation 3	
	β	p value	β	p value	β	p value
MALARIA CONTROL	NI	NI	-0.4647^a	0.0002	-0.3136^b	0.0198
NO. PREVIOUS VISITS	NI	NI	-0.1649^b	0.0319	-0.1690^b	0.0345
1st VISIT N.A.	NI	NI	0.9428^a	0.0005	0.9296^a	0.0011
1st VISIT 1–3m.	NI	NI	0.1332	0.5595	0.1325	0.5762
1st VISIT 4–5m.	NI	NI	0.1062	0.6755	0.1637	0.5351
EARLIER DATE	NI	NI	0.1753	0.5485	0.3062	0.3128
MODEL χ square	168.62		144.17		251.81	
% Reduction in χ sq.	93.5		94.1		89.3	

NI: Not included.
[a] Significant at the 0.01 level.
[b] Significant at the 0.05 level.
[c] Significant at the 0.10 level.

Table 5.11. *Results of logistic regression: Second year*

Variable	Equation 1		Equation 2		Equation 3	
	β	p value	β	p value	β	p value
INCOME N.A.	−0.0182	0.9591	NI	NI	0.1131	0.7622
MEDIUM INCOME	−0.1966	0.2391	NI	NI	0.0555	0.7597
HIGH INCOME	−0.9675[a]	0.0007	NI	NI	−0.6159[b]	0.0443
PRIMARY	−0.0198	0.9130	NI	NI	0.0745	0.6939
SECONDARY	−0.7411[c]	0.0822	NI	NI	−0.5509	0.2030
SEMI-MODERN	−0.0613	0.6870	NI	NI	0.0202	0.8995
MODERN HOME	−0.1794	0.4183	NI	NI	−0.0816	0.7240
RECENT MIGRANT	−0.0435	0.8052	NI	NI	−0.0949	0.6068
OLD MIGRANT	−0.2929[c]	0.0735	NI	NI	−0.1310	0.4562
MEDIUM WEIGHT	NI	NI	0.1131	0.6255	0.1358	0.5653
HIGH WEIGHT	NI	NI	−0.1054	0.6574	−0.0505	0.8349
PLURALITY	NI	NI	0.5931	0.1437	0.6787[c]	0.0966
SEX	NI	NI	0.0883	0.5297	0.0613	0.6659
JULY–SEPT.	NI	NI	−0.4619[b]	0.0346	−0.4211[c]	0.0590
OCT.–DEC.	NI	NI	−0.3439[c]	0.0860	−0.3441[c]	0.0965
JAN.–MAR.	NI	NI	0.0530	0.7734	0.0458	0.8107
PARITY	NI	NI	−0.0984[a]	0.0019	−0.0909[a]	0.0093
ROOM DENSITY	NI	NI	0.0613	0.3496	0.0387	0.5691
MALARIA CONTROL	NI	NI	−0.5114[a]	0.0005	−0.4592[a]	0.0024
VISIT YEAR 1	NI	NI	−0.1134	0.4794	−0.0829	0.6124
VACCINATION YEAR 1	NI	NI	−0.6413[a]	0.0001	−0.6370[a]	0.0002
MODEL χ square	28.83		59.24		69.28	
% Reduction in χ sq.	98.5		96.8		96.2	

NI: Not included.
[a] Significant at the 0.01 level.
[b] Significant at the 0.05 level.
[c] Significant at the 0.10 level.

have better access to medical resource; quality of housing, which is in part a proxy for income, retains an effect of its own after the available intermediate variables are controlled for. The effect of maternal education is not significant. Among the proximate determinants, birth-weight, twinship, and parity have expected effects on survival; the variables reflecting the use of prenatal services are significant, as is malaria control. There are strong seasonal effects, reflecting the visitation of an epidemic of measles during the survey. Unfortunately, data quality problems are still present: the non-availability of data on income and on the date of the first visit are strongly related to mortality, but the causation is probably in the wrong direction: data are missing *because* the child died.

The mortality of the second year is not directly related to the housing variables, but the higher levels of income retain an effect even after controlling for variables denoting access to medical services (Table 5.11). Vaccination is the service variable that emerges as most important; postnatal visits to MCH units do not seem to confer a survival advantage. Malaria control once again appears to make a significant difference to mortality. It is worth noting that some variables fail to reach significance, particularly the mother's education and the crowding index.

6. Discussion

The first surprise in our results is the poor performance of maternal education as an explanatory variable, once additional factors such as the quality of housing, income, and the use of services have been included in the regressions. The finding should be confirmed in other surveys, where more women are educated at higher levels. A provisional conclusion is that the effect of education on mortality in this urban environment, which is evident in the bivariate analysis, is achieved through the access to higher incomes and better medical services. This was Caldwell's (1986) interpretation, and it contradicts those results from World Fertility Surveys that seemed to suggest that maternal education could drastically reduce mortality even in the absence of health facilities and investment in sanitation. This conclusion obviously needs confirmation in other surveys.

Other attractive research hypotheses also fail to receive confirmation in the limited tests that are possible here: the quality of water and the density of bedroom occupation show no impact on mortality. It is possible that the effect of crowding (discussed by Aaby elsewhere in this volume) is better captured by parity (a variable that remains significant throughout) than our rather inadequate index of the average number of persons sleeping in the same room as the index child.

The most startling new finding is the persistent effect, at all ages of the children considered here, of mosquito control. All our tests failed to indicate that the relation between mosquito control and mortality could be attributed to collinearity with other variables in the survey. It is tempting to conclude that the use of mosquito nets and screens, and perhaps above all, of fumigations (the Chinese mosquito coil), has a marked effect on malaria. The coil has been shown to be effective against malaria vectors under controlled conditions (Charlwood and Jolley, 1984). That a reduction of the incidence of malaria would decrease both post-neonatal and second-year mortality, seems well established (McGregor, 1982); but there are too few malaria deaths reported, and the quality of the diagnosis for that cause is too uncertain, to test the connection between mosquito control and malaria mortality directly.

A new data set is always exciting, in that it permits verification of old hypotheses and a look at new and untested variables. In contrast with WFS or DHS, the IFORD surveys provide direct information on the proximate determinants of mortality. As such, they will provide fuel for the old debates, but they can only be a stage on the road to the explanation of mortality differentials among children in Africa. Future surveys should build on their strengths and try to remedy their weaknesses, particularly in the collection of data on very early death.

References

Akoto, E. M. (1985), *Mortalité infantile et juvénile en Afrique. Niveaux et caractéristiques, causes et déterminants*, Département de démographie, Université Catholique de Louvain. Ciaco Editeur, Louvain-la-Neuve.

Caldwell, J. C. (1979), 'Education as a factor in mortality decline: An examination of Nigerian data', *Population Studies* 33/3: 395–413.

—— (1986), 'Routes to low mortality', *Population and Development Review* 12/2: 171–220.

Charlwood, J. D. and Jolley, D. (1984), 'The coil works (against mosquitoes in Papua New Guinea)', *Transactions of the Royal Society of Tropical Medicine and Hygiene* 78: 678.

DaVanzo, J. (1984), 'A household survey of child mortality determinants in Malaysia', in W. H. Mosley and L. C. Chen (eds.), *Child Survival: Strategies for Research, supplement to vol. 10 of Population and Development Review* 307–22.

Farah, A. A. and Preston, S. H. (1982), 'Child mortality differentials in Sudan', *Population and Development Review*, 8/2: 365–83.

Gwatkin, D. R. (1980), 'Indications of change in developing country mortality trends: The end of an era?' *Population and Development Review* 6/4: 615–44.

McGregor, I. A. (1982), 'Malaria: Nutritional implications', *Review of Infectious Diseases* 4: 4.

Mbacké, C. (1986), 'Estimating Child Mortality from Retrospective Reports by Mothers at Time of a New Birth: The Case of the EMIS Surveys', Ph.D diss., University of Pennsylvania.

Mosley, W. H. (1984), 'Child survival: Research and policy', in W. H. Mosley and

L. C. Chen (eds.), *Child Survival: Strategies for Research*, supplement to vol. 10 of *Population and Development Review*, 3–23.

—— (1985), 'Les Soins de santé primaires peuvent-ils réduire la mortalité infantile? Bilan critique de quelques programmes africains et asiatiques', in J. Vallin and A. Lopez (eds.), *La Lutte contre la mort: Influence des politiques sociales et des politiques de santé sur l'évolution de la mortalité*, Travaux et documents 108, INED–PUF, Paris, 101–36.

Ouaidou, N. and van de Walle, E. (1987), 'Réflexions méthodologiques sur une enquête à passages répétés: L'EMIS de Bobo-Dioulasso', *Population* 42/2: 249–66.

Preston, S. H. (1975), 'The changing relation between mortality and level of economic development', *Population Studies* 29/2: 231–48.

—— (1985*a*), 'Mortality in childhood: Lessons from WFS', in J. Cleland and J. Hobcraft (eds.), *Reproductive Change in Developing Countries*, Oxford University Press, 253–72.

—— (1985*b*), 'Resources, knowledge and child mortality: A comparison of the US in the late nineteenth century and developing countries today', in IUSSP, *International Population Conference*, Florence.

Stolnitz, G. J. (1974), 'International mortality trends: Some main trends and implications', in United Nations, *The Population Debate: Dimensions and Perspectives*, vol. 2, pp. 151–9, Papers of the World Population Conference, Bucharest, 1974.

Sulaiman, I. L. (1987), 'Mother's Income and Child Mortality in Southern Nigeria', African Demography Working Paper 15, Population Studies Center, University of Pennsylvania.

van de Walle, E. (1990), 'The IFORD surveys', in J. Vallin, Stan D'Souza, and A. Palloni (eds.), *Measurement and Analysis of Mortality: New Approaches*, Clarendon Press, Oxford, 35–47.

6 Impact of Child Care and Disease Treatment on Infant Mortality

Bamikale J. Feyisetan and Lawrence A. Adeokun
Obafemi Awolowo University, Ile-Ife

1. Introduction

The general knowledge passed on in health promotion programmes, that the death of infants and children can be prevented, often does not appear to influence the behaviour of mothers in traditional societies. It cannot be argued that poverty prevents the adoption of advocated preventive measures, which are often simple and well within the reach of the poorest of the poor. The explanation of the gap between knowledge and behaviour must rather be sought in the social and cultural determinants of behaviour in such matters as child care and diseases treatment.

Specifically, this chapter examines the relationship between some child care and disease control variables and the likelihood of infant mortality being experienced by a sample of Yoruba mothers of different socio-economic background. The variables of child care considered are the adequacy of antenatal care, the place of confinement, and the adequacy of postnatal care. To these aspects have been added some measures of the quality of the illness control behaviour of mothers as they assess the risks, treatment, and expectations of recovery of their children from some selected infant and childhood diseases. The mothers were asked to provide information on their knowledge of causation of four common communicable or immunizable diseases. They were also asked to evaluate the chances of those conditions being prevented and to identify the appropriate treatment for each of the conditions.

Diarrhoea, measles, fever, and convulsion have been chosen as the four diseases of interest because they are the most frequently cited by mothers and the most culturally relevant to the study. These are conditions about which precise traditional health beliefs exist which would be expected to elicit some loyalty in health care seeking behaviour. That loyalty, of course, depends on the extent to which the traditionalism of the mothers has been eroded by contact with modern maternal and child welfare education and practices. In addition, these conditions have been identified by national health policy in Nigeria as deserving of special attention within the context of child survival strategies recommended by the World Health Organization.

The remainder of the chapter will be a discussion of studies of responses to infant and childhood diseases in high mortality societies, followed by a description of the source of the data and an exposition of the principal method of analysis. The major findings of the analysis are discussed and the main policy and primary health system implications are briefly highlighted in the concluding section.

2. The Literature

It has been noted that young children in tropical countries generally tend to suffer from several diseases at one time. It is the synergism between malnutrition and infection which appears to be largely responsible for the particular form of the curve of mortality in children under 6 that is characteristic of tropical Africa (Newman, 1979). This high probability of multiple disease episodes and the interaction between these episodes and malnutrition makes the measurement of the separate effects of malnutrition difficult. Malnutrition can cause and be caused by illness. Bradley and Keymer (1984) noted, with reference to the works of Crompton and Nesheim (1982) and Scrimshaw *et al.* (1968), that parasitism and nutrition are inextricably linked for at least two reasons. First, many parasites are acquired as a direct result of the feeding behaviour of the host, and second, the host provides all the nutrients for the parasites it harbours. With respect to the link between nutrition and infection, it has been demonstrated that malnutrition impairs the body's defence mechanisms (Chandra, 1981; Suskind, 1977). Thus a malnourished child becomes more susceptible to infectious disease agents and is less able to combat infection successfully. Once infected, the child becomes more malnourished as a result of increased nutritional requirements to combat infection, loss of appetite, and the inability to assimilate the food consumed.

The whole idea of synergism between malnutrition and infection and of the possible effect of such synergism on child morbidity and mortality has been extensively discussed (see for instance, Ascoli *et al.*, 1967; Gordon, 1976; Gordon *et al.*, 1965; Koster *et al.*, 1981; McGregor, 1964; McGregor *et al.*, 1983; MacKay, 1974; Martorell and Ho, 1984; Mata, 1975; Morley, 1973; Solomons and Keusch, 1981; Tomkins, 1981). The coexistence of other infections that aggravate the effect of a particular infection, especially measles, has been similarly acknowledged (Koster *et al.*, 1981).

The most common and the greatest killers of children among all the infections and parasitic diseases that have been identified in West Africa are malaria, diarrhoea, measles, neonatal tetanus, whooping cough (pertussis), tuberculosis, and bronchopneumonia (Animashaun, 1977; Ayeni and

Oduntan, 1980; Baxter-Grillo and Leshi, 1964; McGregor, 1964; McGregor and Williams, 1979; McGregor *et al.*, 1970; Morley and MacWilliam, 1961; Morley *et al.*, 1963, 1966, 1968; Ogunlesi, 1961; Wilkinson, 1969). The ages at which children become susceptible to the disease agents and the relative contribution of each disease to child mortality are little known (Garenne, 1981). McGregor and Williams (1979) have noted, however, that measles and whooping cough often appear as major killers during epidemics, but can remain virtually non-existent for many years.

One noteworthy consequence of research into child mortality in less developed countries has been the identification of the major killer diseases and the design of global measures for their management and control. For instance, neonatal tetanus, whooping cough, and measles are preventable through immunization and it has been estimated that three to four million annual deaths can be eliminated by such a measure. In addition, many respiratory deaths can be prevented through low-cost drug therapy (Foster, 1984). While these claims are basically valid, there remains the overall question of the effectiveness of programmes for child survival and the concern that children saved by these programmes can and do die from other causes. However, it is valid to ask why children from less developed countries still die in large numbers from apparently preventable causes. The answer lies partly in the belief systems of the people about diseases. Unless people have a clear conception of the causes of ill health and are convinced about the efficacy of the control or treatment of the condition, the simplicity of available treatment regimes or the relative accessibility of such treatment will have limited impact on the reduction of morbidity and mortality.

Clearly, where conflicting views are held about the causes of an ailment, loyalties can be divided as to which is the appropriate treatment or preventive regime. These are issues central to the understanding of the social and economic differentials which are frequently observed in the levels of infant and childhood mortality in traditional and transitional societies. For example, in a study of differentials in medical beliefs conducted in Ibadan, Nigeria, Maclean (1974) observed that the quality of treatment received in the hospital was a function of the level of education of either the patient or, in the case of children, of the patient's parents, even though the service was free of charge. He attributed this situation not to favouritism but to better and, perhaps, more rational diagnosis of diseases by the more educated patients or parents. Also in a study conducted in Ile-Ife, the degree of rationality with respect to the aetiology of measles was found to vary with mother's level of education and occupational status (Odebiyi and Ekong, 1982*a* and 1982*b*).

For the purpose of the present study, parents' perceptions of disease aetiology are categorized as either rational (adequate) or fatalistic (inadequate). Perceptions are assumed rational and adequate if they indicate natural causes that correspond to scientific categories, and are assumed fatalistic if they do not correspond, or have mythological underpinnings (Foster, 1984; Black, 1984; Bradley and Keymer, 1984). Ideas about preventive measures are classified as either adequate or inadequate depending on whether they conform to scientific recommendations. Therapeutic methods are categorized as modern if responses refer to Western medical systems and traditional if responses refer to indigenous ones.

What we have attempted in this paper is to bring into focus variations in perceptions of disease aetiology, in the understanding of preventive measures, and in health care seeking behaviour, with a view to examining how these variations relate to child survival. It has been impossible to treat all the identified diseases collectively with respect to these dimensions of disease control. Given the predominantly low level of education of the respondents, it was not practicable to assume a high degree of accuracy of diagnosis of some ailments, and to rely on their separation of the effects of the ultimate causes of mortality. It is to be borne in mind that while the dependent variable is mortality from all causes, the independent variables attempt to simplify the measurement of behaviour by asking for behavioural information disease by disease. Although this approach weakens the strength of the explanation, it avoids confusing the respondents and allows some exploration of the vital relation between people's understanding of disease aetiology, prevention, and cure, on the one hand, and infant mortality on the other.

It is also expected that people's conceptions of disease aetiology and their choice of preventive or therapeutic methods will be highly correlated. There may, however, be occasions when they are not. For example, an individual who attributes a disease to supernatural forces may seek modern medical treatment while another individual with a rational perception of disease agents may seek a traditional cure if, in his opinion, modern medical treatments have failed to achieve his ends.

3. Source of Data

This study is based on information on live births and deaths collected in a baseline survey carried out in selected towns and villages in 20 of the 24 Local Government Areas of Oyo State, Nigeria, in preparation for primary health care projects. The live births and infant deaths were those that occurred within the six years preceding the survey's date, May 1987. These data were collected through a three-part questionnaire administered in follow-up home visits.

The first part of the questionnaire dealt with some socio-economic characteristics and a segment of the reproductive history of 3,000 married women in their reproductive ages. The second and third parts are of great importance to this study. The second part concentrated on each pregnancy within the previous six-year period. Information collected on each pregnancy related to outcome, year of delivery, place of delivery, attendance at delivery, place of antenatal care, type of postnatal care, survival of the child at the time of the survey, and age at death if the child was not alive. The purpose of concentrating on the six-year time frame was partly to aid memory of events and partly to reduce the chances of current perception of disease management tainting the interpretation of past events. Hence, the six-year time frame incorporated the period of the intensification of maternal and child welfare programmes upon which the appropriate learning experiences should have been based and from which any benefit to child survival should have been derived.

The third part of the questionnaire concerned the mother's knowledge of diseases. The respondents were asked to mention the childhood diseases common in their areas. In addition they were asked to state the cause, the means of prevention, and the cure for each of the diseases. In their responses, the four most frequently cited diseases were fever, measles, diarrhoea, and convulsions. These four categories are not equally well defined, and not necessarily always exclusive. Measles and diarrhoea are well recognized, but fever and convulsions are symptoms rather than diseases. Fevers are often, but not always, caused by malaria. Some convulsions may be attributable to cerebral malaria or to other causes, but convulsions followed by death within the first 10 days of life may be more commonly ascribed to tetanus. The distinction is not clear in the local phraseology or perception of the conditions.

4. Statistical Model

The principal tool of analysis is the ordinary least squares regression model. In estimating the parameters of the equations that examine the impact of child care and disease control variables on infant mortality, some maternal attributes—age, education, and occupation—are controlled.

Four sets of equations are estimated. The first equation relates infant mortality to child care variables such as provision of antenatal care, quality of place of delivery, and provision of postnatal medical care. The last three equations relate infant mortality to the respondents' perceptions of disease aetiology, prevention, and cure respectively.

The independent variables are dummy variables that assume the value one or zero. The general equation of the probability of infant death is specified as

$$P_{ij} = a_0 + \Sigma^m_{i=1} \Sigma^{g-1}_{j=1} b_j X_{ji} + E_{ij}$$

where

P_{ij} is the probability of infant death among women in group j of variable i;
a_0 is the intercept;
b_j is the regression coefficient;

X_{ji} is the jth category of independent variable i; $i = 1, 2, \ldots, m$; $j = 1$, 2, $\ldots$, $g - 1$ (g is the number of categories of each independent variable);
E_{ij} is the error term.

One category of each of the binary variables has been omitted in the estimation of the parameters of the equation. This is to avoid having a singular matrix that would yield no unique solution for the normal equations when, with the inclusion of a constant term, all dummies corresponding to every level of an independent variable are included. And although the dependent variables are dichotomous in nature, we have avoided the major problem associated with the use of the ordinary least squares regression approach by treating all our independent variables as binary variables.

Estimates of the parameters of the equations are presented in Tables 6.1

Table 6.1. *Ordinary least squares regression results relating child-care variables and maternal characteristics to infant mortality*

Coefficients of:	
1. *Maternal antenatal immunization status*	
Received	−0.0661[a]
Did not receive	RC
2. *Provision of postnatal medical care to baby*	
Yes	0.0007
No	RC
3. *Place of delivery*	
Government clinic	−0.3012[a]
Private clinic/TBA	−0.2789[a]
Religious home	−0.3096[a]
Own house/relative's house	RC
4. *Maternal age*	
15–24	RC
25–34	−0.0111
35–44	−0.0323
45 and above	0.1376[a]
5. *Mother's education*	
No schooling	RC
Primary	0.0031
Secondary	0.0073
University	−0.0114
Others (not stated)	0.0794[a]
Intercept	0.3778
R. square	0.0422

[a] Significant at the 5 per cent level.

to 6.4. The intercept is the standard case defined by women in the excluded category for each factor. The *b* coefficients then represent the differences between the probabilities of experiencing infant death among women in the indicated levels of the factors and those of their counterparts in the excluded categories. The excluded categories are depicted as RC (reference category) in the tables.

5. Results

The least squares estimates of the probabilities of infant death according to identified child care variables and maternal attributes are shown in Table 6.1. The available child care variables whose impact on infant mortality were examined include antenatal inoculation, postnatal medical care, and place of delivery.

Estimates in panel 1 of Table 6.1 show that mothers who received antenatal inoculation are less likely to experience infant death than their counterparts who did not. It has been noted that tetanus immunization of mothers, the last dose of which is taken at least one month prior to delivery, is very effective in preventing neonatal tetanus. Thus, lack of tetanus immunization is a significant risk factor for neonatal tetanus in the infant (Foster, 1984). Our result may, therefore, be reflecting the advantage of tetanus immunization. The estimate in panel 2 does not, however, indicate a significant difference between the infant mortality experience of mothers who had postnatal modern medical care for their children and mothers who did not. It should be emphasized here that the existence of postnatal medical care can reflect two things: whether or not children were vaccinated against major childhood diseases, and whether or not sick children were treated at an hospital. In the present data, postnatal care appears to be more a measure of the former than of the latter.

The regression coefficients in panel 3 demonstrate a strikingly significant dichotomy between the mortality of infants delivered at home and that of their counterparts delivered outside of the home. Mortality among infants delivered outside of the home did not differ significantly according to place of delivery. The estimates indicate higher mortality among infants born at home. Although deliveries at home have been noted to carry a higher risk of neonatal tetanus probably because instruments used to cut the umbilical cord are not adequately sterilized (Foster, 1984), other factors, especially those associated with sanitation, must be responsible for the higher infant mortality among children born at home since we already controlled for immunization against tetanus.

The estimates in panel 4 of the table portray differences in infant mortality risks according to maternal age (at the time of survey rather than at the birth of their children). Contrary to earlier findings (Feyisetan, 1985;

Feyisetan *et al.*, 1987), mothers below the age of 45 had experienced lower probability of infant death than mothers over 45. And although women aged 15–24 are expected to have higher than average mortality because the group contains a majority of the primiparae, our results show no significant differences between the infant mortality experience of this group of mothers and that of mothers between 25 and 44. This finding is consistent with the fact that the study was conducted in a state that is experimenting, on a large scale, with the primary health care system and that this programme is likely to gain wider acceptance among younger women. Moreover, younger women are more likely, and older women less likely, to have their births of the last six years at a time close to the survey and to have benefited from recent programmes.

Finally, estimates in panel 5 of Table 6.1 depict no significant differences in the infant mortality experience of mothers of different educational backgrounds, perhaps because the effect of education operates through the other variables already included in the table, and educated mothers are more likely to use the available medical services.

It was noted at the beginning of this chapter that the choice of preventive or curative measures for any disease is likely to be a function of the individual's conceptions of disease aetiology. In addition, perceptions about disease cause could affect the timeliness of diagnosis and treatment. The probability of seeking adequate therapeutic measures depends largely on the perception of disease cause. An attempt was therefore made to examine differentials in infant mortality according to variations in perceptions of the causes of the four most cited childhood diseases—measles, diarrhoea, fever, and convulsions.

Estimates in the first four panels of Table 6.2 show how infant mortality relates to variations in perceptions of causes of the four childhood diseases, while maternal and child care variables are held constant. The estimates show that while rational and adequate perceptions of the causes of measles and diarrhoea are associated with increased child survival, such perceptions about causes of fever and convulsions do not have a significant impact on child survival. Viewed against the conceptual problems which exist for mothers in making a distinction between the various types of fevers and convulsions, the weakness of the relations is understandable.

An examination of variations in infant mortality according to variations in ideas about preventive measures against the identified childhood diseases was also undertaken. The results are presented in panels 1 to 4 of Table 6.3. The estimates show that adequate ideas about preventive measures had no significant effect on child survival. The result tends to suggest that prevention is not usually being embarked upon though adequate preventive measures are known. It is possible that the financial burden of some preventive measures is a major reason why many families have not utilized them. For instance, the prevention of diarrhoea (which may imply con-

Table 6.2. *Ordinary least squares regression results relating perceptions of disease aetiology to infant mortality*

Coefficients of:	
1. *Aetiology of measles*	
Rational (Adequate)	−0.0389[a]
Fatalistic (Inadequate)	RC
2. *Aetiology of diarrhoea*	
Rational (Adequate)	−0.0297[a]
Fatalistic (Inadequate)	RC
3. *Aetiology of fever*	
Rational (Adequate)	0.0168
Fatalistic (Inadequate)	RC
4. *Aetiology of convulsions*	
Rational (Adequate)	0.0248
Fatalistic (Inadequate)	RC
5. *Maternal antenatal immunization status*	
Received	−0.1007[a]
Did not receive	RC
6. *Provision of postnatal medical care to baby*	
Yes	−0.0321[a]
No	RC
7. *Maternal age*	
15–24	RC
25–34	−0.0212
35–44	−0.0293
45 and above	0.1311[a]
8. *Mother's education*	
No schooling	RC
Primary	−0.0013
Secondary	−0.0044
University	−0.0356
Other (not stated)	0.0575
Intercept	0.1663
R. Square	0.0228

[a] Significant at the 5 per cent level.

tinuous adequate preparation of weaning food and boiling of drinking water) involves financial resources which many families may not have.

The influence of indicated therapeutic methods on infant mortality was also investigated. This investigation was based on the assumption that child survival chances depend on the adequacy of the method of treating a particular infant and childhood disease. While traditional medicine may be

Table 6.3. *Ordinary least squares regression results relating adequacy of respondents' ideas about prevention of diseases to infant mortality*

	Coefficients of:
1. *Adequacy of ideas for preventing measles*	
Adequate	−0.0274
Inadequate	RC
2. *Adequacy of ideas for preventing diarrhoea*	
Adequate	0.0211
Inadequate	RC
3. *Adequacy of ideas for preventing fever*	
Adequate	−0.0084
Inadequate	RC
4. *Adequacy of ideas for preventing convulsions*	
Adequate	−0.0023
Inadequate	RC
5. *Maternal antenatal immunization status*	
Received	−0.0960[a]
Did not receive	RC
6. *Provision of postnatal medical care to baby*	
Yes	−0.0341
No	RC
7. *Maternal age*	
15–24	RC
25–34	−0.0161
35–44	−0.0274
45 and above	0.1350[a]
8. *Mother's education*	
No schooling	RC
Primary	−0.0018
Secondary	−0.0080
University	−0.0290
Other (not stated)	0.0464
Intercept	0.1612
R. Square	0.0217

[a] Significant at the 5 per cent level.

as effective as modern medicine in treating certain diseases, this may not be the case for some other diseases.

The first four panels of Table 6.4 depict how variations in the suggested method of treating each of the four identified childhood diseases translate to differentials in probabilities of infant death. The estimates indicate that, for measles and diarrhoea, preference for modern medical treatment is associated with increased child survival chances. For fever and convulsions, the

Table 6.4. *Ordinary least squares regression results relating therapeutic measures to infant mortality*

Coefficients of:	
1. *Therapeutic measures for measles*	
Modern medical	−0.0235[a]
Traditional	RC
2. *Therapeutic measures for diarrhoea*	
Modern medical	−0.0294[a]
Traditional	RC
3. *Therapeutic measures for malaria*	
Modern medical	0.0102
Traditional	RC
4. *Therapeutic measures for convulsions*	
Modern medical	0.0031
Traditional	RC
5. *Maternal antenatal immunization status*	
Received	−0.0960[a]
Did not receive	RC
6. *Provision of postnatal medical care to baby*	
Yes	−0.0272[a]
No	RC
7. *Maternal age*	
15–24	RC
25–34	−0.0100
35–44	−0.0251
45 and above	0.1319[a]
8. *Mother's education*	
No schooling	RC
Primary	−0.0049
Secondary	−0.0114
University	−0.0340
Others (not stated)	0.0520
Intercept	0.1697
R. Square	0.0230

[a] Significant at the 5 per cent level.

findings indicate that mothers who preferred traditional therapeutic methods had no significant comparative disadvantage over those preferring modern medical treatment. The result may not be surprising since fever and convulsions are not well-defined diseases. It should be noted in this respect that the treatment of malaria by traditional medicine has gained a wide acceptance among literates and illiterates alike, who believe it is as effective as modern medicine.

6. Conclusion

In the preceding analysis, we have drawn attention to some factors that may prevent an effective translation of modern medical knowledge into action for the purpose of reducing infant and child mortality. We also drew attention to the possibility of linking anthropological materials with appropriate statistical techniques, in order to throw light on the relationship between perception of disease aetiology and health seeking behaviour. The analysis demonstrates the existence of some variations in both people's conception of disease aetiology and in their ideas about disease management (preventive and curative measures), as well as the impact of those variations on the survival chances of children in Nigeria.

The four childhood diseases most frequently identified by people in the survey area are measles, fever, diarrhoea, and convulsions. There is no doubt that greater precision in the conceptualization of diseases by the population will, in itself, assist the learning of how to control the diseases. This precision will facilitate the robustness of the estimation of parameters of the equations that relate infant mortality to the child care and disease management variables.

In addition to disease management variables, we also examined the impact of some child care variables—antenatal inoculation, postnatal modern medical care, and place of delivery—on infant mortality. In the process of estimating the parameters of the equations that relate mortality to care and treatment variables, the effects of some maternal characteristics were controlled. The analysis shows that pre-birth inoculation, postnatal modern medical care, and delivery outside the home environment enhance child survival. With respect to disease management variables, modern medical perceptions of disease aetiology enhance child survival probably because such perceptions condition the kind of medical treatments that parents seek for their children when they are ill. The fact that mothers who sought modern medical treatment for measles and diarrhoea experienced lower rates of infant mortality lends credibility to this line of reasoning.

The study raises some fundamental issues about information, education, and communication. First, there is a need to understand people's perceptions of disease aetiology. The more carefully the gap between knowledge and behaviour is understood, the easier it will be for appropriate promotional programmes to be designed. This would help a lot in the effort to make people identify with and use such programmes. Campaigns aimed at changing perceptions are necessary for diseases, such as measles, which are assumed (especially by illiterate mothers) to be caused by supernatural powers (Odebiyi and Ekong, 1982*a*). The fundamental principles of the germ theory of disease are clearly not communicated by programmes which focus on specific priority diseases without attempting a general improvement in the ability of mothers to conceptualize the relationship between disease agents and the preventive or treatment regimes recommended. The thrust of promotive programmes can even reinforce the magical views of some parents so that the modern medical system is seen as a higher order of the supernatural.

Secondly, once the perception hurdle has been cleared, the findings suggest the need to encourage women to have their deliveries in clinics where well-trained personnel can attend to them. The improved quality of personnel and equipment which the modern setting permits will be apparent to the mothers. At the preventive level, it should not be difficult for mothers to understand that adequately sterilized instruments used to cut the umbilical cords of their babies will minimize susceptibility to infection, and that prebirth immunization against tetanus will be a vital insurance of survival of the infant. Once intervention programmes become understood by the public, knowledge will prompt action and the effectiveness of policy will increase.

Thirdly, more research is needed into the social and behavioural aspects of the traditional management of various diseases. The purpose will be to increase understanding of the basis upon which expectations of outcome of treatment are built. Another aim will be to use familiar analogues from the traditional treatment regimes in teaching modern medical concepts without the risk of validating unacceptable traditional practices. Such research will serve as input into the planning and implementation of any collaboration between traditional and modern health care systems.

References

Animashaun, A. (1977), 'Measles and blindness in Nigerian children', *Nigerian Journal of Paediatrics* 4/1: 10–13.

Ascoli, W., Guzman, M. A., Scrimshaw, N. S., and Gordon, J. E. (1967), 'Nutrition and infection field study in Guatemalan villages, 1954–1964: IV. Deaths of infants and preschool children', *Archives of Environmental Child Health* 15: 439–49.

Ayeni, O. and Oduntan, S. O. (1980), 'Infant mortality rates and trends in Nigerian rural populations', *Journal of Tropical Pediatrics and Environmental Child Health* 26/1: 7–10.

Baxter-Grillo, D. L. and Leshi, F. E. A. (1964), 'Factors influencing the occurrence of neonatal tetanus in Ibadan', *West African Medical Journal* 13.

Black, R. E. (1984), 'Diarrheal diseases and child morbidity and mortality', in supplement to vol. 10 of *Population and Development Review*, 141–61.

Bradley, D. J. and Keymer, A. (1984), 'Parasitic diseases: Measurement and mortality impact', in supplement to vol. 10 of *Population and Development Review*, 163–87.

Chandra, R. K. (1981), 'Immunodeficiency in under-nutrition and overnutrition', *Nutrition Review* 39: 225–31.

Crompton, D. W. T. and Nesheim, M. C. (1982), 'Nutritional science and parasitology: A case for collaboration', *Bioscience* 32: 677–80.

Feyisetan, B. J. (1985), 'Environmental sanitation and infant mortality: A study of relationships in Ile-Ife, Nigeria', *Studies in Third World Societies* 34: 235–63.

—— Togunde, O., and Bankole, A. (1987), 'Infant mortality in Ile-Ife, Nigeria: An examination of the impact of maternal occupation and father's income', *Demography India* 16/2: 165–76.

Foster, S. O. (1984), 'Immunizable and respiratory diseases and child mortality', in supplement to vol. 10 of *Population and Development Review*, 119–40.

Garenne, M. (1981), 'The Age Pattern of Infant and Child Mortality in Ngayokheme (Rural West Africa)', African Demography Working Paper 9, Population Studies Center, University of Pennsylvania.

Gordon, J. E. (1976), 'Synergism of malnutrition and infectious disease', in G. H. Beaton and J. M. Bengoa (eds.), *Preventive Medicine*, WHO, Geneva, 193–209.

—— Jansen, A. A. J., and Ascoli, W. (1965), 'Measles in rural Guatemala', *Journal of Pediatrics* 66: 779–86.

Koster, F. T., Curlin, G. C., Aziz, K. M. A., and Hague, A. (1981), 'Synergistic impact of measles and diarrhoea on nutrition and mortality in Bangladesh', *Bulletin of the World Health Organization* 59: 901–8.

McGregor, I. A. (1964), 'Measles and child mortality in the Gambia', *West African Medical Journal* 13: 251–7.

—— and Williams, K. (1979), 'Mortality in a Rural West African Village (Keneba) with Special Reference to Deaths occurring in the first five years of life', mimeo.

—— Willson, M. E., and Billewicz, W. Z. (1983), 'Malaria infection of the placenta in the Gambia, West Africa: Its incidence and relationship to still birth, birth weight and placenta weight', *Transactions of the Royal Society of Tropical Medicine and Hygiene* 77: 232–44.

—— Rahman, A. K., Thompson, H. M., Billewicz, W. Z., and Thompson, B. (1970), 'The health of young children in a West African Gambia Village', *Transactions of the Royal Society of Tropical Medicine and Hygiene* 64/1: 48–77.

Mackay, D. M. (1974), 'The effect of civil war on the health of a rural community in Bangladesh', *Journal of Tropical Medicine and Hygiene* 77/6: 120–7.

Maclean, U. (1974), *Magical Medicine: A Nigerian Case Study*, Penguin, London.

Martorell, R. and Ho, T. J. (1984), 'Malnutrition, morbidity and mortality', in supplement to vol. 10 of *Population and Development Review*, 49–68.

Mata, L. J. (1975), 'Malnutrition–infection interactions in the Tropics', *American Journal of Tropical Medicine and Hygiene* 24: 564–74.

Morley, D. (1973), *Paediatric Priorities in the Developing World*, Butterworths, London.

—— and MacWilliam (1961), 'Measles in a Nigerian community', *West African Medical Journal* 10: 124.

—— Bickenell, J., and Woodland, M. (1968), 'Factors influencing the growth and nutritional status of infants and young children in a Nigerian village', *Transactions of the Royal Society of Tropical Medicine and Hygiene* 62/2: 164–99.

—— Woodland, M., and Martin, W. J. (1963), 'Measles in Nigerian children', *Journal of Hygiene* 61: 115–34.

—— —— —— (1966), 'Whooping cough in Nigerian children', *Tropical and Geographical Medicine*, 169–82.

Newman J. S. (1979), 'Nutrition, disease and mortality in young children', *Population Dynamics, Fertility and Mortality in Africa*, Proceedings of the Expert Group

Meeting on Fertility and Mortality Levels and Trends in Africa and their Policy Implication, 513–26.

Odebiyi, A. I. and Ekong, S. C. (1982*a*), 'Concept of causation and treatment in the Yoruba medical system: The special case of measles and diarrhoea', *Rural Africana* 14: 49–59.

—— —— (1982*b*), 'Mothers' concept of measles and attitudes towards the measles vaccine in Ile-Ife, Nigeria', *Journal of Epidemiology and Community Health* 36/3: 209–13.

Ogunlesi, T. O. (1961), 'Respiratory infections in pre-school child: A review of 435 cases admitted to Adeoyo Hospital, Ibadan', *West African Medical Journal* 10: 231.

Scrimshaw, N. S., Taylor, C. E., and Gordon, J. E. (1968), *Interactions of Nutrition and Infection*, WHO Monograph Series, 57.

Solomons, N. W. and Keusch, G. T. (1981), 'Nutritional implications of parasitic infections', *Nutritional Reviews* 39: 149–61.

Suskind, R. M. (ed.) (1977), *Malnutrition and the Immune Response*, Raven Press, New York.

Tomkins, A. (1981), 'Nutritional status and severity of diarrhoea among pre-school children in rural Nigeria', *Lancet*, 18 Apr., 860–2.

Wilkinson, J. L. (1969), 'Children in hospitals in Sierra Leone: A survey of 10,000 admissions', *Transactions of the Royal Society of Tropical Medicine and Hygiene* 63/2: 263–9.

7 The Two Most Dangerous Days of Life: A Study of Neonatal Tetanus in Senegal (Niakhar)

Odile Leroy and Michel Garenne
ORSTOM, Dakar

1. Introduction

Neonatal mortality remains, in developing countries, a serious public health problem. Neonatal mortality can reach a level of nearly 100 deaths for every thousand live births, varying by country and urban or rural area. The analysis of the causes of neonatal death brings out the major role played by neonatal tetanus, which alone can account for as much as 72 per cent of all deaths between birth and 28 days (in India). More often tetanus accounts for about half of all neonatal deaths (see Table 7.1). These rates are very different from the neonatal mortality due to tetanus in nineteenth-century Europe. McKeown (1976) suggests that neonatal tetanus was a minor cause of death, but we lack quantitative data to verify this assertion and some instances of high mortality due to neonatal tetanus have been noted in historical Europe, as, for example, on the island of St Kilda (Steel, 1975). Few in-depth studies of neonatal tetanus have been carried out in areas covered by demographic surveillance systems. In Matlab, Rahman *et al.* (1982) found levels of 69 per 1,000 live births, but these data need to be interpreted cautiously, because only those deaths described by the mother as 'alga, dhanustoukar or takuria' were counted.

Neonatal tetanus is characterized by a very high case–fatality ratio and even under optimal treatment conditions, it is unlikely at the present time that the case–fatality level could be reduced much below 50 per cent (Diop-Mar and Sow, 1975). The case–fatality rates most commonly cited are over 80 per cent (Schaaf, 1968) and they probably reach 100 per cent in the absence of medical intervention. This situation is the more regrettable because neonatal tetanus can be easily avoided, by vaccinating women who are at the reproductive ages and by improving aseptic conditions at the time of delivery, as Berggren showed in Haiti (Table 7.2).

This chapter was translated by Mark Hereward.

Table 7.1. *Neonatal mortality, overall and from tetanus*

Country 1978–87	Neonatal deaths per 100 births		% due to tetanus
	Overall	From tetanus	
Africa			
Burundi	—	8	—
Cameroon	—	7	—
Ethiopia	8	5	63
Gambia	—	11	—
Ivory coast	34	18	51
Kenya	16	11	69
Lesotho	—	4	—
Malawi	29	12	41
Somalia	91	21	33
Sudan	29	9	32
Togo	11	6	52
Uganda	38	15	40
Zaïre	—	9	—
Zimbabwe	10	4	39
Asia			
Bangladesh	48	27	56
Bhutan	19	13	67
India (rural)	19–93	5–67	16–72
India (urban)	5–26	0–15	0–59
Indonesia (rural)	21	11	51
Indonesia (urban)	17	7	40
Nepal	37	15	39
Pakistan	52	31	60
Philippines	13	6	48
Thailand	21	5	23
South Yemen	19	4	20
North Yemen	31	3	8

Source: WHO, EPI/GAG/87/WP. 11.

There are few data on the respective impacts of these two strategies and their costs and benefits. The impact of care at the time of delivery is a function of its quality. The improvement of obstetric practices and care of the new-born explain the reduction of neonatal mortality due to tetanus in the United States from 64 per thousand in 1900 to one per 100,000 in 1961–4 (Stanfield and Galazka, 1984). As for the vaccination of pregnant women, it requires a strict timetable to be effective (Chen *et al.*, 1983).

In the absence of sanitary measures in the modern sense of the term, i.e. aseptic delivery and vaccination of the mother, tetanus occupies a variable

Table 7.2. *Changes in neonatal mortality from tetanus in Haiti as a result of health interventions*

Period	Nature of intervention	Neonatal mortality from tetanus, per 1,000 live births
1940–48	Before instruction of traditional midwives	262.2
1949–55	Programme of instruction of traditional midwives	220.5
1956–62	Hospital care available; training of auxiliary health workers	136.9
1963–66	Immunization of pregnant women in clinics	78.5
1967–68	Immunization of women on market-places by hospital team	35
1969–70	Immunization of persons identified in home visits by social workers	5
1971–72	Follow-up of out-clinic patients by hospital team	0

Source: Berggren *et al.*, 1983.

role in mortality. A number of epidemiological studies carried out at the beginning of this century established the roles of different epidemiological factors of tetanus (Prévot, 1967). The factors which recurred consistently in the different studies were soil and climate, which determine the presence of the bacterium, and the higher incidence among males, which could reflect either greater exposure to risk, or weaker immunity (Stanfield and Galazka, 1984).

2. The Germ and its Toxin[1]

Tetanus is a non-immunizing toxi-infection caused by a totally anaerobic bacillus, *Clostridium Tetani*, also called Nicolaier's bacillus. It is found either in the resistant form, as a spore, or in the vegetative form, which gives tetanus. The spore can survive many years of darkness and can withstand antiseptics and boiling but is destroyed by sunlight. The vegetative form can be destroyed by heat and antiseptics.

Spores are found in the soil, in earth fertilized by dung, in dust in houses or on the street, and in the faeces of animals (horses and sheep). In humans, they are present in the intestines, on the skin, and occasionally in saliva.

When conditions are favourable, the spore germinates, and the 'vegetative' form arises, which alone produces the toxins. Tetanus infection is a

[1] In this section, we follow Prévot, 1967.

local event that involves the whole body because of the absorption of this toxin which is secreted at the point of entry. It is the diffusion of the exotoxin which gives the tetanus bacillus its pathogenic power.

Three conditions are necessary for the development of tetanus in humans, and they are the presence of tetanus spores in the environment, their penetration into the tissues, and favourable conditions for their development, such as the inhibition of white blood cells (e.g. by cold), and strict anaerobic conditions. These conditions are favoured by microbial connections with common fever-producers such as *Bacillus subtilis*, *Clostridium asporogenes*, the pyocyanic bacillus, or *Welchia perfringens*, by the presence of a foreign body, or by dead tissue, ischaemia. It is possible that some non-pathogenic spores of anaerobic bacteria may exert an anti- or pro-biotic effect upon *Cl. tetani*, and this would explain differences in regional distribution.

3. The Epidemiological Picture

There are many ways a new-born can be infected with tetanus, but in general the point of entry is the umbilical cord, as a result of non-aseptic practices at the delivery, whether by actual contact of the cord with the soil when the delivery is carried out on the ground, by the cutting or tying of the umbilical cord with dirty materials, or by the use of traditional substances for dressing the wound. Less commonly, early circumcision of the boys, piercing of the girls' ears, anti-tubercular vaccinations infected by the application of traditional dressings, and ritual or therapeutic scarring may be to blame (Stanfield and Galazka, 1984).

It is only recently that the statistical importance of neonatal tetanus in the world has been realized. In 1972, Miller estimated the mortality rates for neonatal tetanus at one quarter or even one half of the mortality from tetanus for all ages combined. A few years later Bytchenko caused a stir by estimating that 600,000 new-borns died of neonatal tetanus in the world every year. In 1984, Stanfield and Galazka estimated that tetanus was globally responsible for half the neonatal mortality, which would be close to one million deaths per year.

The greater part of the data presently available on neonatal tetanus in developing countries was collected between 1978 and 1983 in standardized surveys carried out in rural and urban zones with cluster sampling under the aegis of the World Health Organization. Neonatal mortality due to tetanus varies from three per thousand live births in the Republic of Yemen to 67 per thousand in the rural areas of the state of Uttar Pradesh in India (Table 7.1). The difference in levels can be explained by variations in the immunization status of the population, and in particular of women of reproductive age, and by difference in the standards of hygiene and the quality of care in delivering and caring for the new-born. The rural or urban character of the study population plays a role because of the essentially soil-bound character of the tetanus bacillus, i.e. the risk of infection diminishes as the frequency of contact with the soil decreases. The ecology of the bacillus could also be involved, because it is not a germ that is found everywhere, and its geographical distribution is erratic. It is known to be more common in clay-chalk and alkaline soils, in humid and fertile agricultural areas, and in hot climates (Prévot, 1967).

Lastly, it must be noted that the quality of data collection could lead to error. Conventional reporting systems barely record 2 to 5 per cent of the number of cases estimated by means of surveys taken in the community (Stanfield and Galazka, 1984). Under-reporting can occur at the level of the family unit, where there may exist a certain reluctance to declare a death, and even more so if it occurs before the naming ceremony which signifies the entry of the new-born as an individual into the community. Neonatal tetanus is generally well identified as a category of disease, although it is often interpreted as magical. The supernatural connotations of tetanus help explain the persistence of the taboo on the woman and child during the first week after delivery, and the concealing, frequent in Africa, of all events during this period.

At the level of vital registration, the deaths of new-borns are badly registered, because they often take place before the birth is reported; when deaths are registered, few causes are notified, even though the diagnosis of tetanus is easy. At the level of health services, the statistics are almost invariably deficient, and often only take into account cases within hospitals, which account for a small proportion of cases of neonatal tetanus.

Finally, under-reporting can occur because the state is not concerned by neonatal tetanus. It is an endemic disease which does not attract the attention of decision-makers in the way that great epidemics do. There is no immediate economic benefit from the prevention of tetanus, as the cost of this disease is essentially borne by the mother. The amount of money spent on prevention would far outstrip the amount now devoted to treatment, especially in the rural areas where no, or virtually no, money is spent because there is no method of treatment (Bytchenko *et al.*, 1975).

With respect to the epidemiology of neonatal tetanus, it must be noted that the age pattern is very unusual because more than 90 per cent of the deaths from that cause occur in the first two weeks of life. The average age of onset is between the third and seventh day of life, and the average age at death is between the seventh and the tenth day. On the other hand, the incidence by sex varies widely from one country and one source of data to another even though there is an excess male mortality that remains unexplained (Table 7.3).

There remain many hazy areas in our knowledge of the relation between the epidemiology of tetanus and neonatal mortality. Given that spores of the

Table 7.3. *Distribution of neonatal deaths from tetanus, by sex, selected countries*

Country	Period of observation	Male deaths/female deaths
Columbia	1961–6	0.9
Egypt	1981	2.6
Ivory Coast	1981–2	1.1
Pakistan	1981	1.6
rural areas		1.3
urban areas		2.3
Sudan	1981	1.4

Source: Stanfield and Galazka, 1984.

bacillus are present everywhere, why does only a small proportion of new-borns develop tetanus, with poor hygiene conditions, where all of them seem exposed to the same risk? What explains the differences by region, sex, or season? Is there a dose-specific effect, or a threshold level of infection that triggers the disease? Or is it a purely random phenomenon?

To answer these questions, we can consider some ecological and immu-nological factors. Concerning the ecology of the bacillus, Alihounou (1970) found a higher incidence of tetanus in Senegal during the rainy season. Ebisawa and Kurata (1985) showed that heavy rains could have a 'wash-out' effect on the bacillus, and demonstrated that the number of tetanus spores found in an injury was a decisive factor in the severity of the illness.

Concerning natural immunity, Veronesi *et al.* (1975) and Veronesi (1985) attempted to demonstrate in animals, that the regular ingestion of spores or toxin of tetanus brings about the development of an immune response. Can one extend this concept of natural immunity to humans, and is the immunity acquired by the mother sufficient to protect the infant at birth? How can the high sex ratio of neonatal tetanus be explained? Is there a difference in immune status by sex?

This chapter attempts to contribute to the elucidation of these problems through a rigorous study of neonatal deaths in a situation of high mortality.

4. The Area of Study

The study was carried out in the ORSTOM population laboratory of Niakhar, Senegal, which is located in the department of Fatick, about 150 kilometres east of Dakar (see Map 7.1). This is the Sahel region of Senegal, in the heart of the peanut-growing country. The climate is hot and dry from November to June, and hot and humid from July to October, the rainy season. The soil is clay-sandy, and more or less permeable from place to

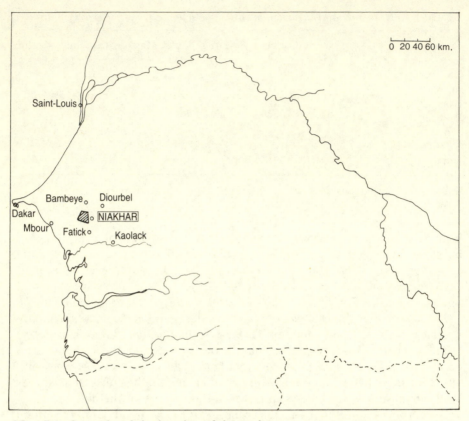

MAP 7.1. Senegal and the location of the study area

place. In the south of the study area, the greenstone soil allows penetration of water and in the north, the deck soil, which has a higher content of clay, retains water better and is more fertile and more favourable to the existence of low-lying flooded areas. The area contained approximately 24,000 people during the period of the survey (1983–6), grouped into 30 villages and hamlets in an area of 230 square kilometres, for a density of 104 people per square kilometre.

This population can be described as a rural society, belonging to the Sereer ethnic group, poorly educated and mostly Muslim, living in small villages. Households are very large, and on average contain 14.0 people per compound. Income levels are very low and are derived in part from growing millet and peanuts, in part from raising cattle, sheep, and goats, and in part from the income of temporary migrants during the dry season.

There are three dispensaries within the area: two public dispensaries in Toucar and Ngayokheme, staffed by state nurses, and a private dispensary in Diohine, staffed by Catholic nuns. The dispensary in Diohine serves a population of about 9,500, that of Toucar about 8,500, and that of Ngayokheme about 6,000. Outside the study area there are four other dispensaries, those of Niakhar, Patar, Ngoye, and Diarere, which might be visited by people from within the area.

Very few anti-tetanus vaccinations were given to pregnant women or women of child-bearing age during the period of study. Only 5 per cent of pregnant women in the study area were said to have been vaccinated during their pregnancy; this, in itself, gives no certainty of the efficacy of this vaccination, in the absence of precise information on its timing. The practice of anti-tetanus sero-prevention of the new-born is more frequent than the vaccination of pregnant women, as 21 per cent of the new-born in the study area had received an anti-tetanus serum. These figures should be treated with caution, since the injection is often delayed until the onset of the first symptoms, when it will not be effective.

5. Survey Method

From March 1983, an inter-disciplinary group of researchers at ORSTOM has observed the population of this area using annual censuses and continuous registration of the principal demographic events: births, deaths, marriages, and migration. This study continued a series of demographic studies in the same region which began in 1962 (Cantrelle, 1969). The method of data collection used since 1983 has been described elsewhere (Garenne, 1984), and so has the method of analysing cause of death by verbal autopsy (Garenne and Fontaine, 1990). For neonatal deaths, a systematic questionnaire is used to gather the case history and to identify the symptoms which led to death. This method permits the imputation of probable cause of death for a small number of illnesses, of which neonatal tetanus is one.

The gathering of data on the probable cause of death was done routinely by a team of interviewers. When a case of neonatal tetanus was suspected, the questionnaire was reviewed by a physician in the field. The questionnaires were analysed independently by two physicians to establish a probable cause of death.

The criteria for imputation were of two sorts: major, obligatory criteria, and minor, discretionary criteria. The following clinical signs were used as major criteria: (*a*) trismus, or lockjaw, where the infant suckled normally after birth and then refused to suckle at the onset of the illness, and had clenched jaws; (*b*) rigidity of the body; (*c*) spasms; (*d*) the age at onset of the illness should be the second day of life or later; the death should occur before the 28th day.

As minor criteria, we used hyper-salivation, constipations, change of colour of the skin, and the absence of fever at the time of the first symptoms. The presence of fever during the course of the illness was considered a sign of severity, and not a criterion of exclusion.

Finally, the diagnosis of the nurse or physician taken from the registers in the dispensaries or hospitals was considered decisive in doubtful cases.

6. Results

The study was carried out over a period of 43 months, and it encompassed all the births in the study area between April 1983 and 31 October 1986. During that period, there were 4,154 live births and 212 neonatal deaths. Tetanus, the most frequent cause, represented close to a third of all neonatal deaths: 66 out of 201 investigated deaths (Table 7.4).

The probability of dying from neonatal tetanus, 16 per thousand live births, turned out to be much higher than was shown by previous figures for Senegal, which were 10 per thousand in rural areas (Debroise and Satge, 1967) and 0.6 per thousand in urban areas (Sow, 1982). This disparity in results is very likely due to the quality of data collection, and to the strong differences between urban and rural areas, rather than to a sudden increase in the prevalence of tetanus. This point underlines the importance of a precise study to gauge the importance of the role of certain diseases in mortality.

7. Factors in Neonatal Mortality due to Tetanus

(*a*) Age at onset and at death

The extreme concentration of neonatal tetanus into certain days of life is the most noteworthy characteristic of its timing in the study area. It occurs essentially during the first two weeks of life, and the deaths are concentrated on days six and seven (Tables 7.5 and 7.6, Fig. 7.1). The average age at onset is 5.2 ± 0.5 days, the average age at death is 7.43 ± 0.62 days, and the median age at death is 6.9 ± 0.38 days. The duration of the illness is very brief, averaging 2.3 ± 0.38 days (Table 7.7). It is remarkable that 69.7 per cent of the deaths occur before the eighth day of life. This extreme concentration in days six and seven gives an unusual shape to the pattern of mortality by age. These are the most dangerous days of life, with an instantaneous mortality rate reaching 2,229 per thousand, three-quarters of which are due to tetanus. Neonatal tetanus is therefore the most deadly disease for humans, probably the only one to produce an instantaneous mortality rate expressed in person-years, greater than one.

Table 7.4. *Neonatal deaths by cause of death and sex, Niakhar, on 4,154 births, April 1983–October 1986*

Cause of death	N	Probability of dying per 1,000 live births	Male deaths/female deaths
Tetanus	66	15.88	1.64 (41/25)
Premature–underweight	64	15.40	1.28 (36/28)
Respiratory system	13	3.12	0.86 (6/7)
Other causes	58	13.96	1.64 (36/22)
No answer	11	2.65	1.20 (6/5)
Total	212	51.00	1.43 (123/87)

Table 7.5. *Neonatal deaths and tetanus cases by age at death, Niakhar*

Age in days	Tetanus			All causes		% tetanus deaths
	Onset	Death	Death rate	Death	Death rate	
0–1	0	0	0.0	40	1.749	0.0
2–3	12	1	0.044	25	1.106	4.0
4–5	27	8	0.356	21	0.935	38.1
6–7	19	37	1.650	50	2.229	74.0
8–9	5	8	0.363	11	0.499	72.7
10–11	1	7	0.318	18	0.818	38.9
12–13	1	2	0.091	7	0.320	28.6
14–20	0	3	0.039	28	0.365	10.7
21–27	0	0	0.0	11	0.145	0.0
Unknown	1	0	—	1	—	—
Total	66	66	0.202	212	0.649	31.1

Table 7.6. *Neonatal mortality for 1,000 live births by cause of death and season, Niakhar, April 1983–October 1986*

Season	All causes	Tetanus	Other causes
Rainy season: August–October	54.25 (69)	22.80 (29)	31.45 (40)
Dry season: Rest of the year	49.62 (143)	12.83 (37)	36.78 (106)
Total	51.00 (212)	15.88 (66)	35.14 (146)
Ratio rainy/dry season	1.093	1.777	0.855

Note: Numbers of deaths are in parentheses.

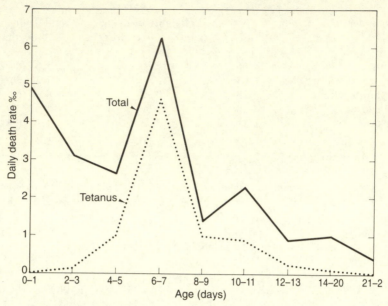

Fɪɢ. 7.1. Neonatal mortality by age in days, Niakhar, 1983–1986

(*b*) Distribution by sex

During the period of study, 41 male and 25 female new-borns died of tetanus, giving a sex ratio of 1.64. The same ratio for neonatal deaths, all causes combined, is 1.43, while the sex ratio at birth during the same period is 1.07 (Table 7.4). It is highly unlikely that families were under-reporting female deaths in the context of this study. Therefore, this confirms the general preponderance of male deaths, both for neonatal mortality in general, and neonatal tetanus in particular, a phenomenon that so far has not received an adequate explanation. In this particular case, it must also be noted that the traditional cutting of the cord is slightly different according to the sex of the new-born, as we shall see later.

(*c*) The seasonal pattern

The analysis of the monthly distribution of neonatal deaths due to tetanus shows a peak during the rainy season, with a lag of one month. A comparison of the seasonality of neonatal tetanus and of other causes of neonatal death, reveals that mortality for all causes is raised by about 10 per cent in the rainy season, but if deaths due to tetanus were excluded, the mortality would be 15 per cent less than expected in the rainy season (Table

Table 7.7. *Deaths from neonatal tetanus, by duration of the disease, Niakhar, births of April 1983 to October 1986*

Duration in days	Number of deaths
1	25
2	18
3	11
4	4
5	4
6	1
7	1
8	1
Unknown	1
Total	66

Table 7.8. *Sex ratio of births and of neonatal deaths by season, Niakhar, April 1983–October 1986*

	Rainy season	Dry season	T	P
All neonatal deaths	1.62 (39/24)	1.29 (84/65)	0.745	0.2280
Tetanus deaths	2.37 (19/8)	1.29 (22/17)	1.150	0.1252
Other deaths	1.25 (29/16)	1.29 (62/48)	−0.085	0.5338
Births	1.08 (667/615)	1.07 (1,499/1,400)	0.191	0.4241

Notes: T: Student's test between proportions male.
  P: Probability (T > 0).
  ( ): Number of male/female.

7.6). In other words, the seasonality of tetanus explains the seasonality of overall neonatal mortality.

The differential in the seasonal distribution of neonatal deaths goes together with an uneven distribution of deaths by sex. Table 7.8 shows a tendency for a higher mortality of males in the rainy season, regardless of cause, but also a much higher sex ratio for tetanus during the rainy season. Because of the small sample, the difference is not statistically significant.

(*d*) The birth environment

The delivery of a child is a stage of initiation in the life of a Sereer wife. She is supposed to give birth alone and in silence, this stoicism being the condition for passing honourably from the status of spouse to that of mother

Table 7.9. *Distribution of mothers by place of delivery*

Place of delivery	Number of mothers
In the hut	92
Behind the hut	102
In front of the hut	19
Among the granaries	9
In the fields	12
In another compound	3
Maternity clinic	10
Hospital	6
Unknown	3
Total	256

(Kalis, 1984). The traditional childbirth practices that we have observed among 256 Sereer wives are particularly favourable for the contamination of the new-born with tetanus, because of the place chosen for the delivery and the method of cutting, tying, and dressing the umbilical cord (Table 7.9). Half the women gave birth in the compound, outside the hut, on the ground. In a third of the cases, this area was regularly travelled by domestic animals (horses, donkeys, goats, sheep, and cattle).

Only 6 per cent of the women gave birth in the village maternity clinic or the regional hospital. In three cases out of four, the mother gave birth unassisted, and the woman who came to 'pick up' the baby did not intervene until after delivery. Only in one case out of every six was the village midwife involved. The umbilical cord was cut half the time with the edge of the stalk from a 'toudouye' reed (*Andropogon gayanus*), a third of the time with a razor blade, and a sixth of the time with scissors by the midwife. The only difference in practice by sex of the new-born involved the ritual of cutting with the toudouye: the stalk is cut in three for daughters and in four for sons, each piece being used in turn.

But whatever the cutting instrument, the woman who was cutting the cord often (two-thirds of the time) used a shard of an earthenware pot or a toudouye reed as a cutting-board. Tying the cord was generally (80 per cent of the cases) done using a little band of cloth cut from the wrapper of the mother, or with a piece of cotton thread spun at home. The dressing for the cord was not aseptic at least half the time. The most diverse substances are used for the dressing, separately or together; in order of frequency we found alcohol, powder of ground earthenware, mentholatum, ashes of burnt packets of sugar, karite butter, and talcum powder. Finally, about a quarter of the new-born received anti-tetanus serum in the first days of life.

The traditional delivery practices in Africa are very different from one ethnic group and one region to another. A more thorough study of the role of each gesture of the Sereer delivery process in neonatal tetanus is being undertaken.

8. Discussion

The study of mortality due to neonatal tetanus raises various questions with regard to interpretation. The first question that arises from the results of this study is about the risk of tetanus. Were all the new-borns in this study exposed to the same risk? Some studies that are under-way try to grapple with this problem. A preliminary analysis of the data observed allows us to put forward several working hypotheses to explain why some of the new-borns escape tetanus.

There could be a strong dose-response effect, and the dose of infection would be a function of the ecology of the bacillus; this would explain the seasonality of the disease. Alternatively, the potential immunity against tetanus could be different for different individuals, and this could account for the fact that male infants consistently have a higher mortality risk. This hypothesis is supported by the data on the interactions between sex and season.

All these hypotheses cannot be confirmed or disproved on the basis of this type of demo-epidemiological investigation.

9. Conclusion

The results of a careful study of causes of death in Senegal show that ecological factors and personal immunity seem to play an important role in neonatal tetanus. Neonatal tetanus accounts for up to three-quarters of the neonatal deaths on certain days of life, or in certain regions. In Senegal, the mortality due to neonatal tetanus is much higher during the rainy season in rural areas, probably because of stronger doses of bacteria picked up by touch ('wash out' of bacteria, moist soil, more contact with earth). Also, mortality from neonatal tetanus is higher for males than females, which suggests an effect due to the immune status. Trivial differences in delivery practices observed among the Sereers do not seem able to account for this differential in mortality by sex.

Despite a large amount of research carried out on the subject, there remain a number of unclear areas in the complex interaction between the ecology and immunity to tetanus.

References

Alihounou, M. E. (1970), 'Le Tétanos en zone tropicale', *L'Enfant en Milieu Tropical* 62: 11.

Berggren, G. G. *et al.* (1983), 'Traditional midwives, tetanus immunization and infant mortality in rural Haiti', *Tropical Doctor* 13: 79–87.

Bytchenko, B. D. *et al.* (1975), 'Panel: Place of tetanus in Public Health', in *Proceedings of the Fourth International Conference on Tetanus*, Dakar, Sénégal, 6–12 Apr. 1975, Fondation Mérieux, Lyon, France, 91–101.

Cantrelle, P. (1969), *Étude démographique dans la région du Sine Saloum (Sénégal). État civil et observation démographique*, Travaux et documents 1, ORSTOM, Paris.

Chen, S. T. *et al.* (1983), 'Timing of antenatal tetanus immunization for effective protection of the neonate', *Bulletin of the World Health Organization* 61/1: 159–65.

Debroise, A. and Satge, P. (1967), 'A propos de 230 cas de tétanos ombilical observés à Dakar', *Annales de Pédiatrie* 43, 14/15: 192–209.

Diop-Mar, I. and Sow, A. (1975), 'Traitement simplifié du tétanos en l'absence de soins intensifs', in *Proceedings of the Fourth International Conference on Tetanus*, Dakar, Senegal, 6–12 Apr. 1975, Fondation Mérieux, Lyon, France, 583–606.

Ebisawa, I. and Kurata, M. (1985), 'A quantitative study of *C. tetani* in the earth', in *Proceedings of the Seventh International Conference on Tetanus*, Copanello, Italy, 10–15 Sept. 1984, Gangemi, Rome, 7–10.

Garenne, M. (1984), 'The concept of follow-up survey and its application for data collection: Example of using a computerized questionnaire for improving the recording of early deaths in rural Senegal (Niakhar)', Paper presented at the IUSSP Seminar on Micro-approaches to Demographic Research, Canberra, 3–7 Sept. 1984.

—— and Fontaine, O. (1990), 'Assessing probable causes of death using a standardized questionnaire: A study in rural Senegal', in J. Vallin, Stan D'Souza, and A. Palloni (eds.), *Measurement and Analysis of Mortality: New Approaches*, Clarendon Press, Oxford, 123–42.

Kalis, M. (1984), 'La Mère et le nouveau-né dans la société traditionnelle wolof: De la conception au *bootlu*, rituel de portage au dos', Thèse de Diplôme d'Étude Approfondie d'Ethnologie, Institut d'Ethnologie de Strasbourg.

McKeown, T. (1976), *The Modern Rise of Population*, Academic Press, New York and San Francisco.

Miller, J. K. (1972), 'The prevention of neonatal tetanus by maternal immunization', *Journal of Tropical Pediatrics*, 18: 159–67.

Prévot, A. R. (1967), *Les Bactéries anaérobies*, Dunod, Paris, 1323–81.

Rahman, M. *et al.* (1982), 'Use of tetanus toxoid for the prevention of neonatal tetanus, 2. Immunization acceptance among pregnant women in rural Bangladesh', *Bulletin of the World Health Organization* 60: 269–77.

Schaaf, B. (1968), Le Tétanos à Dakar', Thèse Médecine, Nancy.

Sow, A. R. (1982), 'Tétanos néonatal à Dakar: Nouvelles données', *L'Afrique Médicale* 21/196: 13–22.

Stanfield, J. P. and Galazka, A. (1984), 'Neonatal tetanus in the world today', *Bulletin of the World Health Organization* 62/4: 647–69.

Steel, T. (1975) The Life and Death of St. Kilda. Fontana Books, London.

Veronesi, R. (1985), 'Naturally acquired tetanus immunity: Still a controversial theme?', in *Proceedings of the Seventh International Conference on Tetanus*, Copanello, Italy, 10–15 Sept. 1984, Gangemi, Rome, 365–72.

—— *et al.* (1975), 'Naturally acquired tetanus immunity: Further evidences in humans and animals', in *Proceedings of the Fourth International Conference on Tetanus*, Dakar, Senegal, 6–12 Apr. 1975, Fondation Mérieux, Lyon, France, 613–26.

8 Morbidity and Mortality from Diarrhoeal Diseases in Children under Age Five in Sub-Saharan Africa

Jeroen K. van Ginneken and Anton W. Teunissen
Netherlands Institute of Preventive Health Care, TNO, Leiden and Regional
Office of Public Health, Dordrecht

1. Introduction

Diarrhoeal or infectious intestinal diseases are an important health problem in developing countries. A recent World Health Organization study
estimated that 4.6 million children under 5 die each year due to this group of
diseases and that 1.2 million of these deaths occur in Africa (Snyder and
Merson, 1982). The root cause of diarrhoeal morbidity and mortality is
poverty. Both exposure and response to this disease are heavily influenced
by economic, environmental, and social factors. Children from poor families
live in household environments which are often characterized by limited and
contaminated water supplies, inadequate disposal of faeces, and unhygienic
preparation and storage of food. A major objective of this paper is to
summarize what is known from past studies about these causes and the
mortality consequences.

Diarrhoeal diseases have been studied in various disciplines. Demographers and epidemiologists have studied this group of diseases using
cause of death statistics. The aetiology and epidemiology of these diseases
have been the topic of investigations by microbiologists, epidemiologists,
paediatricians, and nutritionists. Social and cultural aspects of these diseases
have been examined by sociologists and anthropologists.

This chapter will summarize research that has been undertaken in sub-
Saharan countries on a number of aspects. In the next section clinical and
related aspects (i.e. aetiology and transmission) will be described. The logic
behind this is that if one wants to know more about the causes and consequences of diarrhoeal disease, one needs to know more about the disease
itself. Sections 3 and 4 will summarize demographic and epidemiological
studies on mortality levels and patterns due to diarrhoea and on its incidence and prevalence. In section 5, attention will be paid to seasonal
influences on mortality and morbidity. In sections 6 and 7, results of studies

on three groups of factors which influence diarrhoeal morbidity and mortality are summarized: socio-economic factors, environmental hygiene, and nutrition. In section 8 we shall focus on an entirely different aspect, namely the beliefs and practices of mothers and indigenous health care providers studied from an anthropological angle. Conclusions will be drawn in a last section.

With respect to the epidemiological aspects, we shall focus on longitudinal, population-based studies, which have been conducted in a number of places in Africa. The most important of these are the Kirkos study in Ethiopia (Frey and Wall, 1979), the Keneba study in the Gambia (Rowland, 1983), the Machakos Project in Kenya (van Ginneken and Muller, 1984), the Malumfashi study in Nigeria (Tomkins, 1981), the Ngayokheme study in Senegal (Cantrelle *et al.*, 1986), and the Bakau study in the Gambia (Pickering, 1985). All of these studies are named after the places where they were carried out. The Machakos Project took place in a rural area of Machakos District. A more appropriate name would thus have been the Matungulu/Mbiuni study. The project is, however, known as the Machakos Project and this name will be retained here. All studies took place in rural areas with the exception of the Kirkos and Bakau studies. Details of these projects are found in the references mentioned above.

This review will be limited to risk factors broadly defined; there is no discussion of the impact of various interventions aimed at lowering morbidity and mortality from diarrhoeal diseases such as oral rehydration therapy (ORT), use of curative health services, installation of piped water supplies, and immunization.

A number of important epidemiological studies of diarrhoea have been conducted in regions other than Africa, in particular in the Punjab, India, in Bangladesh (by the International Centre for Diarrhoeal Disease Research), and in Guatemala. These studies will not be considered in this review.

2. Clinical Aspects

The terms 'diarrhoeal or intestinal infectious diseases' encompass a wide range of diseases, including cholera, typhoid fevers, food poisoning, salmonella infections, shigellosis, amoebiasis, and intestinal infections caused by unspecified organisms. The infection may be caused by bacteria, viruses, parasites, or a combination of these. These multiply in the intestines and produce toxins which disrupt the normal functioning of the intestines and lead to a decrease in the absorption of fluids and nutrients into the bloodstream. Instead, there is removal of fluids and nutrients from the body. All of these diseases can strike children under 5, but the focus of this paper will not be on diseases which show typical epidemic patterns such as cholera and typhoid fever. The emphasis will be on the diarrhoea which is associated with the weaning period, 'the time during which breastfeeding is continuing, but other foods are being added, including also the period of three months immediately after discontinuing breastfeeding' (Morley, 1973: 171). This type of diarrhoea is often referred to as weanling diarrhoea or acute diarrhoeal disease.

Diarrhoeal diseases in childhood are mainly caused by three types of micro-organisms: bacterial pathogens such as *Escherichia coli* and *Shigella dysenteriae*; viral types of diarrhoea caused in particular by rotavirus; and finally, parasitic agents of diarrhoea, in particular *Entamoeba histolytica* and *Gardia Lamblia*. It is likely that of the various pathogens, *E. coli*, *Shigella*, and rotavirus are the most common. The presence of these pathogenic micro-organisms can be determined by means of bacteriological and virological tests of stool specimens or from serological tests of blood specimens (in the case of rotavirus). Such tests are usually conducted in hospitals and the results of such microbiological studies have been reported in a number of African countries, including the Gambia, Kenya, Ethiopia, the Central African Republic, Zaïre, and South Africa.

It is not the purpose of this chapter to review these studies, but a few points are important to keep in mind. In the first place, such studies are difficult to conduct and the isolation rates of pathogenic agents achieved are in general low. An implication of the usually low isolation rates found is that little is known about the relative importance and contribution of the various pathogenic agents as causes of diarrhoea in the different regions and countries in Africa. An exception to studies with low isolation rates is a hospital-based study in Nairobi where it was possible to isolate rotavirus in 41 per cent of children hospitalized with diarrhoea, *E. coli* in 18 per cent of cases, and *Shigella* in 11 per cent of cases (Mutanda, 1980).

Secondly, from studies conducted in countries outside Africa it is known that infection by the different pathogenic agents may have somewhat different consequences. In a study in Bangladesh it was found that dehydration was more common in children with diarrhoea from rotavirus and *E. coli* than in children with other or unknown aetiology (Black, 1984). *Shigella* was most often associated with prolonged or chronic (longer than three weeks) diarrhoea; and of all types of diarrhoea it had the strongest negative effect on the growth of children. More than the other pathogens, *Shigella* contributed to malnutrition (Black, 1984: 145). The various pathogens may also have these different effects in African countries.

In the third place, the pattern of transmission varies according to the type of pathogenic agent involved. *E. coli* infection spreads primarily by means of contaminated food and water. These bacteria may be found in large quantities in food; in particular, weaning food contaminated by impure water, unclean utensils, and the unhygienic handling of food. Rotavirus and *Shigella* are usually transmitted by direct person-to-person contact (hand-to-mouth), or by contact with contaminated objects: these two pathogens are infectious in relatively small doses. *Shigella* infections can in addition be transmitted by contaminated food or water (Black, 1984).

In a number of cases, it is not possible to identify the different microorganisms which cause diarrhoeal diseases and, for purposes of treatment, this is in many of these cases not necessary. Diarrhoeal diseases are thus commonly defined by the symptoms they exhibit. These symptoms are defined as 'an increase in the frequency and fluidity of bowel movements relative to the usual pattern of each individual' (Black, 1984).

From the clinical point of view an important distinction is made according to the severity of the disease: three broad groups can roughly be distinguished (Morley, 1973). The first group is the least severe type and is very common in children under 5. There is mild discomfort lasting one to two days with passing of loose and watery stools, but no serious morbidity and the symptoms disappear spontaneously. Various circumstances may lead to this condition, and it is quite possible that none of the above-mentioned pathogens is involved.

The second and third types are much less common, but are much more severe. In the second type the onset of the disease is rapid with liquid or semi-liquid stools occurring from three to 20 times a day. Some children have blood or mucus in their stools, and this means a loss of valuable proteins. Low-grade fever is usual as well as intestinal cramps. The disease is often accompanied by the onset of respiratory tract infection. The third type is also severe and often occurs in malnourished children. In such cases diarrhoea is chronic, lasting on and off for a month or more.

Malnutrition and diarrhoea operate together. Malnutrition diminishes immunity to many common organisms and thereby weakens the resistance to disease. At the same time, a consequence of diarrhoea is that the child eats less and absorbs less of the food which is eaten due to the effect of diarrhoea itself. Therefore, the disease leads to a deterioration of nutritional status (Chen, 1983).

The main danger of both types of severe diarrhoea is that they lead to dehydration. A result of the infection is malabsorption of water, sugars, electrolytes, minerals, and other nutrients. The first symptoms of dehydration appear after fluid loss equivalent to 5 per cent of body weight. Loss of fluids and electrolytes reaching 10 per cent leads to malfunctioning of vital organs culminating eventually in death. It is thus vitally important to reverse the process of dehydration and this is accomplished by means of rehydration therapy. Rehydration therapy is thus not aimed at curing the infection but primarily at restoring basic vital functions. At the same time the sick child is able to build up natural immunity against the pathogenic organisms. This is the most important step in curing the infection and in preventing further attacks.

Jeroen K. van Ginneken and Anton W. Teunissen

Table 8.1. *Mortality of children under 5 by cause of death, Machakos Project, Kenya, 1975–1978*

Cause of death	Below 1		Age 1–4		Below 5	
	N	Rate per 1,000 live births	N	Rate per 1,000 population	N	Rate per 1,000 live births[a]
Intestinal infectious diseases	52	11.2	14	0.9	66	14.8
Measles	15	3.2	33	2.1	48	11.7
Malaria	4	0.9	10	0.6	14	3.5
Other infectious diseases	4	0.9	9	0.6	13	3.2
Nutritional deficiencies	4	0.9	17	1.1	21	5.3
Pneumonia	53	11.5	13	0.8	66	14.9
Congenital anomalies	12	2.6	—	—	12	2.6
Birth trauma, difficult labour	31	6.7	—	—	31	6.7
Other perinatal problems	44	9.5	—	—	44	9.5
Accidents (burns)	1	0.2	3	0.2	4	1.0
Unknown	10	2.2	9	0.6	19	4.5
Total	230	49.7	108	7.0	338	77.7

[a] Calculated by multiplying the 1–4-year-old death rate by a factor of 4 and adding the infant mortality rate.

Source: Omondi-Odhiambo *et al.*, 1987.

Table 8.2. *Mortality of children under 5 by cause of death and sex, Machakos Project, Kenya*

Cause of Death	Male		Female	
	N	Rate per 1,000 live births	N	Rate per 1,000 live births
Intestinal infectious disorders	36	15.9	30	13.7
Measles	29	14.2	19	9.3
Malaria	9	4.5	5	2.4
Other infectious diseases	6	3.0	7	3.3
Nutritional deficiencies	7	3.5	14	7.1
Pneumonia	32	14.1	34	15.5
Congenital anomalies	4	1.7	8	3.5
Birth trauma, difficult labour	20	8.5	11	4.8
Other perinatal problems	30	12.7	14	6.2
Accidents (burns)	4	2.0	—	—
Unknown	10	4.8	9	4.1
Total	187	85.1	151	70.0

Source: See Table 8.1.

3. Mortality Levels and Patterns

(a) The Machakos study, Kenya

Table 8.1 shows that in the Machakos Project area mortality in the under-5 population was about 78 per thousand live births in 1975–8. Mortality due to diarrhoeal diseases—here referred to as intestinal infectious diseases— was 14.8 per thousand live births; this means that it is one of the leading causes of death in children below the age of 5.

Mortality from diarrhoeal diseases was higher in the first year of life (11.2 per thousand live births) than in the age group of 1 to 4 years old (0.9 per thousand population or approximately 3.6 per thousand surviving children).

Table 8.2 shows cause of death figures in the Machakos Project by sex. Total mortality of male children below 5 (85 per thousand) was higher than that of female children (70 per thousand), but rates of diarrhoeal mortality were about the same for both sexes (15.9 male deaths per thousand compared to 13.7 female deaths). The various procedures used to collect these data and more results have been reported by Omondi-Odhiambo *et al.* (1987).

More details on total mortality (all causes combined) and on mortality from diarrhoeal diseases by age are provided in Table 8.3. Mortality of all causes combined was highest in the first six months (34.4) and considerably less between six and twelve months (15.9). There were further declines in mortality from the second to the fifth year after birth. The pattern of mortality from diarrhoeal diseases by age is somewhat different from that of all causes combined. The main difference is the increased mortality between the ages of 6 and 12 months, which reaches 6.7 per thousand.

This increase in mortality due to diarrhoea between six and eleven months

Table 8.3. *Total mortality, and mortality due to diarrhoea, of children under 5 by age at death in months, Machakos Project, Kenya, 1975–1978 (mortality rates per 1,000 surviving children at beginning of age interval)*

	<6 m.	6–11	12–23	24–35	36–47	48–59	Total
All causes							
Rate per 1,000 surviving children	34.4	15.9	11.6	7.1	3.7	2.3	73.1
N	159	71	51	31	16	10	338
Diarrhoea							
Rate per 1,000 surviving children	4.8	6.7	1.8	0.2	0.5	0.7	14.3
N	22	30	8	1	2	3	66

after birth is related to the transition from full breast-feeding to the introduction of cows' milk and/or solid foods (for more details see section 7).
The mean age at death from diarrhoea was about 10.5 months and the
median age 7.6 months.

Further details concerning diarrhoeal mortality in the Machakos Project
area are provided in Tables 8.4 and 8.5. Table 8.4 indicates that about 60
per cent of all diarrhoeal deaths of children under 5 years old took place at
home (in 1975–8) and about 40 per cent in the hospital. The median age at
death at home was 8.2 months and in the hospital 7.2 months. Seasonal
variation in mortality from all causes and from diarrhoea is shown in Table
8.5. The number of deaths as a result of diarrhoeal diseases is higher between January and July than during the rest of the year. We shall elaborate
on this topic in section 5.

(b) The Ngayokheme study, Senegal

Mortality levels and patterns in rural Senegal are very different from those
observed in the Machakos area in Kenya. The total under-5 mortality rate in
Ngayokheme was 368 per thousand live births between 1972 and 1981
(Cantrelle *et al.*, 1986). The corresponding rate in Machakos was 78 per
thousand. A more detailed comparison was possible for some causes of
death with respect to deaths occurring between 6 and 36 months. These
causes of death were determined on the basis of information provided by the
family. Reporting of diarrhoea as a cause of death was considered to be
reasonably accurate since it is an easily identifiable disease.

Table 8.6 indicates that in Ngayokheme in the age group 6–17 months,
total mortality was nearly five times as high as in Machakos (114 versus 24
per thousand surviving children) while in the age group 18–35 months
mortality was nearly nine times higher (95 versus 11 per thousand surviving
children). There were also substantial differences in mortality between the
two areas in the age groups 6–17 months and 18–35 months because of
the following causes: diarrhoea, fever and malaria, and 'other diseases'.
Differences between these two areas in mortality from these three groups
of causes are probably larger than indicated in Table 8.6 because in

Table 8.4. *Number of deaths under 5 due to diarrhoea by age at death in months and
by place of death, Machakos Project, Kenya*

	<6m.	6–11	12–17	18–23	24–35	36–47	48–59	Total
Home	10	18	3	1	1	1	2	36
Hospital	9	8	2	2	0	1	1	23
Total	19	26	5	3	1	2	3	59

Table 8.5. *Total number of deaths, and deaths due to diarrhoea, under 5 by month of death, Machakos Project, Kenya*

	Jan.	Feb.	Mar.	Apr.	May	June	July	Aug.	Sept.	Oct.	Nov.	Dec.	Total
All causes	28	24	30	33	40	30	30	27	18	21	32	18	331
Diarrhoea	5	6	6	7	8	6	8	3	2	3	4	1	59

Table 8.6. *Mortality by cause of death in various age groups of children under 5 in rural areas of Senegal and Kenya (mortality rates per 1,000 surviving children at beginning of interval)*

Cause of death	Ngayokheme, Senegal[a] 1972–1981		Machakos, Kenya[b] 1975–1978			
	6–17 months	18–35 months	0–5 months	6–17 months	18–35 months	36–49 months
Diarrhoea	18	21	5	9	1	1
Fever and malaria	22	14	0	2	1	1
Respiratory diseases	13	5	9	5	3	1
Measles	9	18	0	6	3	1
Other diseases	11	13	16	1	3	1
Unknown	40	24	4	2	1	1
Total	114	95	34	24	11	6
N	199	193	159	105	48	26

[a] Adapted from Cantrelle *et al.* (1986), pp. 107 and 111.
[b] Fever is not included in the category 'Fever and malaria'

Ngayokheme, a considerable number of deaths in the category 'cause of death unknown' were also due to diarrhoea, fever and malaria, and other causes.

Another difference with the Machakos area is that in Ngayokheme diarrhoea mortality is already higher in the age group 6–17 months and much higher in the age group 18–35 months. This is probably related to the increased risk to which children are exposed in the weaning period. This period of increased risk occurs later in Ngayokheme than in Machakos due to a prolonged period of breast-feeding (Cantrelle *et al.*, 1986).

Recently a new technique has been developed and tried out to determine the main causes of death with the help of a standardized questionnaire used by field-workers together with assignment of causes of death by a physician (Garenne and Fontaine, 1990). Provisional results show again that diarrhoeal disease was a leading cause of death in children under 5.

(c) Other studies

Roughly similar rates to the total mortality rates of children under 5 in Ngayokheme were observed in Bandafassi, a rural area in eastern Senegal (Pison and Langaney, 1985). Mortality rates in the second and third year in particular remained very high and it is likely that high levels of diarrhoeal diseases are one reason for this. The importance of diarrhoeal disease as a leading cause of death is confirmed in other studies in West Africa. A review of studies by Cantrelle and Ly found diarrhoeal mortality rates for 1–5 years of between 40 and 76 per thousand in several West African countries (Cantrelle and Ly, 1981). Similar results have been found in urban areas of Senegal and Kenya on the basis of analysis of death certificates (Cantrelle *et al.*, 1986; Ewbank *et al.*, 1986). Diarrhoea was also an important cause of death in a study in Brazzaville (Mfoulou, 1986).

4. Morbidity Levels and Patterns

(a) The Machakos study, Kenya

In the Machakos Project the incidence of diarrhoeal disease was determined in two different ways. In the first approach, field-workers asked mothers during fortnightly home visits whether any of their children below 5 years of age had been ill since the previous visit. If the answer was affirmative, information was sought on the occurrence of diarrhoea during this period of two weeks. No enquiries were made about the number of diarrhoeal spells per fortnight. This approach leads to a minimum estimate of incidence of diarrhoea.

In the second approach, data on the occurrence of diarrhoea were obtained

Table 8.7. *Number of episodes of diarrhoea per child per year by age of the child*

Age (months)	Kirkos, Ethiopia[a] 1975	Machakos, Kenya 1974–1977		Lagos, Nigeria[d] 1963–1965
		min.[b]	max.[c]	
0–5		0.9	4.1	1.1
6–11	6.8	1.5	6.4	2.1
12–23		0.9	4.1	1.4
24–35		0.3	1.9	0.7
36–47	4.6			0.5
48–59		0.1	1.0	0.3
5–12 years	1.1	—	—	—
N	216	3900	1300	411

[a] Extrapolated from daily visits in period of 60 days (Frey and Wall, 1977).
[b] Based on two-weekly visits; figures based on only those children who were reported/observed to be ill in interval of 2 weeks (only one spell of diarrhoea per period of 2 weeks) (Leeuwenburg *et al.*, 1984).
[c] Based on two-weekly visits; figures based on all children who were visited (only one spell of diarrhoea per period of 2 weeks) (Leeuwenburg *et al.*, 1984).
[d] Based on home visits at intervals of 2–3 weeks (Rea, 1970).

about *all* children irrespective of whether the mother had reported them ill or not. This leads to what we shall call here the maximum estimate of incidence of diarrhoea. The results of both estimates are shown in Table 8.7. The number of episodes of diarrhoea for the whole below-5 population was 0.6 per year according to the first approach and 2.7 per year according to the second. Regardless of the approach chosen, the same pattern of incidence in the various age groups was observed. In both cases the highest rates were found in the age group 6–11 months. Rates were also high in the first six months of life and during the second year (Leeuwenburg *et al.*, 1984).

Two small-scale studies were also conducted to verify the information obtained with the second approach. In one of these studies field-workers first received training in the examination of stools during their visits and in deciding whether or not these samples should be classified as diarrhoea. Mothers were then asked by field-workers to keep a stool specimen on the day of the next visit by the field-workers when they thought one of their children had diarrhoea. Field-workers inspected these stools during their visits and decided whether or not diarrhoea was involved. On the basis of this and another study it was concluded that there was 15–40 per cent over-reporting of diarrhoea by mothers (Leeuwenburg *et al.*, 1984).

Two conclusions can be drawn from these Machakos studies. One is that results on the incidence of diarrhoea are very much dependent on the way questions on diarrhoea are asked. A second conclusion is that the mothers' definition of what constituted diarrhoea was much wider than the definition used by the investigators. Mothers tended to consider diarrhoea as a common condition among the children under 5, and not necessarily always an illness.

(b) The Kirkos study, Ethiopia

Detailed data on the incidence, duration, and prevalence of diarrhoeal morbidity are available from the Kirkos study in Ethiopia. A study was carried out in 1975 in which 216 children were visited daily by field-workers for a period of 60 days. Figures on the number of episodes from these 60 days of observation were multiplied by six to yield annual figures. Children were recorded as ill or not ill according to the mother's report. A child was considered as having diarrhoea when it had at least four loose stools or one watery or bloody stool per day. It was found that the number of episodes of diarrhoea per year of children below 2 years, between 2 and 5 years old, and between 5 and 12 years was respectively 6.8, 4.6, and 1.1 (see Table 8.7). The mean duration of diarrhoeal episodes in these three age groups was respectively 9.6, 6.9, and 4.3 days and the median in these age groups was 5.7, 3.8, and 3.4. The percentage of time ill with diarrhoea in the three age groups was respectively 17, 8, and 1. These percentages can be recalculated in terms of total time observed ill per year. Children under the age of 2 were estimated to suffer from diarrhoea on average 63 days per year; the corresponding figure for children between 2 and 5 years was 30 days, and for children over the age of 5 it was four days. Figures on incidence multiplied by duration were found to equal prevalence. For example, 6.8 times 9.6 equals 65 days per year ill with diarrhoea (Frey and Wall, 1977).

Comparison of the results obtained in Kirkos with those of Machakos shows a substantially higher number of episodes in the Kirkos study (see Table 8.7). A comparison is also made by Frey and Wall of results from the Kirkos study with those from other population-based studies which have been conducted in a number of developing countries. The morbidity figures in the Kirkos study turn out to be very high (especially in terms of the number of episodes, and less so with respect to duration).

(c) The Keneba study in the Gambia

In the Keneba study figures on percentages of time ill with diarrhoea were based on reports by mothers. Diarrhoea was found to have a clear and unequivocal meaning in the local language. Many stool specimens were collected and seen during this study and it was concluded that the mothers' definitions were usually in accordance with those of the investigators. Diarrhoea morbidity was measured in terms of prevalence, that is, as the percentage of time spent ill in a certain period. Children were followed from birth to about 3 years of age, and they were seen every four to six weeks. It is estimated that percentages of time ill with diarrhoea of children 0–5 months old, 6–12 months old, and 12–17 months old were 9, 20, and 15 respectively (estimated from Fig. 1D in Rowland *et al.*, 1978). The percentage of time ill was even higher in the rainy season (namely 25 per cent of the time for children between 6 and 12 months old).

(*d*) The Malumfashi study, Nigeria

Finally, some figures on the incidence and prevalence of diarrhoea are available from a study conducted in Malumfashi in northern Nigeria. A total of 343 children between 6 and 32 months were visited weekly for a period of three months starting at the beginning of the rainy season. Diarrhoea was recorded if the disease reported corresponded with two locally used words for this disease. The results presented here are extrapolated to a whole year. The number of episodes for children between 6 and 32 months was 5.6 per year and children spent 10.5 per cent of the time ill with diarrhoea (Tomkins, 1981).

In another study carried out in urban Lagos in the early 1960s (Rea, 1970), low rates of incidence of diarrhoea were observed (see Table 8.7). No information was available on the way incidence figures were calculated.

5. Morbidity and Mortality by Season

(*a*) The Ngayokheme study, Senegal

Strong seasonal differences in mortality were observed in rural Senegal. The total death rate between 1972 and 1981 (all causes combined) was about 2.5 times higher in the rainy season than in the dry season for children between 6 and 36 months. The total number of deaths in the three months of the rainy season was only slightly less than the number of deaths in the other nine months. It is plausible that the elevated risk of mortality in the rainy season is to a considerable extent due to malaria and to a lesser extent to diarrhoea (Cantrelle *et al.*, 1986).

Differences in total mortality between the rainy and dry season were also observed in Bandafassi, another area in Senegal. Seasonal differences there were weaker than in Ngayokheme (Pison and Langaney, 1985).

(*b*) The Keneba study in the Gambia

The peak prevalence of diarrhoea in the Gambia largely coincided with the time of peak precipitation. Diarrhoeal prevalence during or shortly after the rainy season was nearly twice as high as during the dry season. Also discovered was the regular occurrence of a smaller epidemic of diarrhoea prevalence in the middle of the dry season. The main rainy season outbreak is probably to a large extent caused by toxin-producing *E. coli* and *Campylobacter* bacteria. It was suggested that rotavirus was an important component of the secondary dry season peak of diarrhoea (Rowland, 1983). The importance of rotavirus in the cool dry winter months was confirmed in a later study carried out in Bakau in the Gambia (Rowland, *et al.*, 1985).

The main rainy season outbreak of diarrhoea was due to a combination of factors, explained by Rowland (1983). The most important of these is a deterioration of environmental hygiene. In Keneba water is provided by a number of wells and there are hardly any sanitation facilities. In particular, small children commonly defecate within the main compound areas and the well areas are not enclosed. Detailed studies showed that the well water was polluted at all times as a result of a mixture of human and animal faecal contamination. In the wells an enormous increase in levels of faecal substances occurs within a week of the onset of the rains. This contaminated water is to some extent responsible for the infection of small children when they consume this well water. Moreover, and more importantly, this well water is used for preparation of weaning foods (see section 7 for more details).

More evidence on the impact of the rains on diarrhoeal morbidity is provided in another series of studies which took place much earlier, in 1962–3, in Keneba. During the rainy season a much higher prevalence of diarrhoea was observed than in the dry season. This was especially true for the group of children between six and 18 months old (McGregor *et al.*, 1970).

(c) The Machakos study, Kenya

Information from the Machakos Project on the number of deaths by month of death has already been shown in Table 8.5. The number of deaths due to diarrhoea was higher between January and July than in the other months of the year. The elevated number of deaths between March and July roughly coincides with the period of the long rains, but there is no increase in deaths in the period of the short rains between roughly the middle of October and the middle of January.

The relationship of seasonality and morbidity due to diarrhoea was also studied over two years. Trends in the incidence of diarrhoea did not correspond with trends in the amount of rain that fell in these two years. The conclusion derived from the Machakos studies is that seasonal patterns of mortality and morbidity of diarrhoea could not be ascribed to seasonal differences in rainfall (Leeuwenburg *et al.*, 1984).

6. Impact of Socio-Economic Status and Environmental Hygiene

(*a*) **The Kirkos study, Ethiopia**

The factors explaining variation in the occurrence of diarrhoea were studied among 390 children under 5 years by means of multivariate analysis. Data on the independent variables were obtained from a cross-sectional survey conducted in the middle of the study which took place in 1972–3. Data on the dependent variable were obtained from disease surveillance using bi-weekly home visits for a period of one year. This dependent variable consisted of four categories: 0 to 5 per cent, 5 to 10 per cent, 10 to 20 per cent, and more than 20 per cent of the time ill with diarrhoea.

Education of the father and mother were important predictors of diarrhoeal morbidity (after controlling for other variables). Parents with more education had children with less diarrhoea than parents with less education. In addition, several indicators of the hygiene and sanitation status of the household were investigated. Families with private pit latrines had children with lower diarrhoeal prevalence than families with children who used shared pit latrines (after controlling for other variables). Families with private taps as their source of water had children with less diarrhoeal prevalence than families with shared taps or a community standpipe (after controlling for other variables). Families with less water consumption (in terms of litres per person) had children with more diarrhoea than families who used more water. Two housing variables related to diarrhoeal morbidity were type of floor and number of household members per room. Children in families with floors consisting of the bare ground had higher diarrhoeal prevalence than those in families with floors of cement, wood, etc. Families who lived in houses with three or more household members per room had children with higher diarrhoeal prevalence than families who lived in houses with fewer than three family members per room (Frey and Wall, 1977 and 1979).

(*b*) **The Bakau study, the Gambia**

Environmental and social factors associated with diarrhoea were studied in an urban area in the Gambia. About 500 children between 6 and 36 months of age were visited weekly for a period of 105 days during the rainy season. Information on the social, economic, and other conditions in the households of these children was available from a cross-sectional survey. It was concluded that none of the social and environmental variables showed a significant relationship with diarrhoea prevalence. It is possible that living conditions in this urban community were better than average and that these were responsible for the relatively low levels of diarrhoea

(Pickering, 1985). Another possibility is that this is a relatively homogeneous community; it could be that families with high and/or low living standards are under-represented.

(c) The Machakos study, Kenya

A multivariate analysis was performed relating a number of indices of socio-economic status to mortality under five and to several causes of death including diarrhoeal diseases. Several indices showed statistically significant relationships with mortality from all causes. All socio-economic variables together also had a statistically significant impact on mortality from diarrhoeal diseases, but this was not the case when they were taken separately (Gemert *et al.*, 1984). In this study it was thus not possible to identify which of the various aspects of socio-economic status influenced diarrhoeal mortality. An unusual form of multivariate analysis was used and it is impossible to say if the same results would have been reached with a different statistical technique.

7. Impact of Nutritional Status, Breast-Feeding, and Food Intake

(a) The Keneba study in the Gambia

Data were collected not only on diarrhoeal morbidity in children between the ages of 0 and 18 months, but also on weight-for-age. From the age of 3 months, weight-for-age as a percentage of the Harvard standard started to fall behind, to about 78 per cent of the standard by age one. Diarrhoeal disease appeared at about three months after birth and increased to a prevalence level of 20 per cent (percentage of time ill with the disease) at one year after birth (Rowland *et al.*, 1978). It is plausible that in general two groups of nutritional factors explain the simultaneous decline in nutritional status and the increase in diarrhoea: the discontinuation of breast-feeding, and patterns of intake of water, cows' milk, and solid foods.

Research on the impact of aspects of breast-feeding (i.e. breast-feeding versus bottle feeding, time of introduction of supplementary food, types of solid foods consumed) on diarrhoeal morbidity and mortality will not be reviewed here. (For such reviews see for example Winikoff, 1980; Feachem and Koblinsky, 1984.)One finding of the Keneba study, however, is relevant in this connection. Infants with higher breast milk intake were given supplementary food later than children with low breast milk intake. The later introduction of solid foods led to a delay in the onset of diarrhoea and episodes of diarrhoea were milder than in children who were introduced early to solid foods (Watkinson, 1981).

A second group of factors explaining the decline in nutritional status and increase in diarrhoea has to do with aspects of food intake. In Keneba it was found that the unsatisfactory quality of weaning foods was a particularly important reason for the increase in diarrhoeal disease. Detailed microbiological studies on weaning foods were carried out and showed high contamination levels of freshly prepared foods. The contamination was introduced by means of well water (as already shown in section 5). Cooking reduced the harmful *E. coli* bacteria, but did not eradicate them. The contamination of prepared food was especially common in the wet season. The custom that food is usually prepared for the child in the early morning and consumed in the course of the day contributed to this contamination. In such a situation massive bacterial overgrowth occurs. It was shown that freshly cooked foods were contaminated in 35 per cent of samples tested and that this percentage increased to 96 per cent eight hours after the cooking (Barrell and Rowland, 1979).

Another adverse factor that plays a role here is that the rainy season is a period of labour-intensive farming usually done by women. Infants are often left behind in the compounds in the care of relatives or older siblings. It is especially in such cases that the child is provided with food cooked by the mother in the early morning. Still another factor that played a role in the pollution of weaning foods is that local cows' milk had been used during their preparation. It was shown that this cows' milk was often stored in a highly unhygienic manner (Rowland, 1983).

(b) The Machakos study, Kenya

Several longitudinal nutritional studies were conducted in the Machakos project (Oomen *et al.*, 1984; van Steenbergen *et al.*, 1984). Information was available on nutritional status (weight-for-age), time of introduction of solid foods, and food intake. Information on these factors by age of the child as well as on incidence of diarrhoea is provided in Table 8.8.

It can be seen that the nutritional status starts to decline at about 6 months of age and that the incidence of diarrhoea starts to increase at about the same time. It was suggested that the contamination of weaning food was a likely reason for this phenomenon (Leeuwenburg *et al.*, 1984). Studies on the bacterial contamination of foods commonly eaten by young children were also conducted. A total of 44 per cent of 214 samples of food consumed by children were contaminated by *E. coli* bacteria and were unsafe for consumption and 12 per cent of the samples were infected by *Staph. aurus*.

This finding makes it plausible that the weaning food given to children was an important cause of the diarrhoeal morbidity. As in the Keneba study, it was found that colonization of bacteria increased with storage time. However, unlike the Keneba study it was found that samples of drink-

Table 8.8. *Nutritional status and incidence of diarrhoea by age of the child in months, Machakos Project, Kenya*

	0–2	3–5	6–8	9–11	12–14	15–17	18–23	24–35
Breast-feeding[a] (%)								
Full BF	100	35	0					
Partial BF	0	65	100	80	85	80	40	30
Total BF	100	100	100	80	85	80	40	30
Energy intake[b] (in kcal)	485	576	712		799		984	1,028
Weight/age[c] (% of Harvard Standard)	98	97	89	87	86	84	82	83
Incidence of Diarrhoea[d]	4.1		6.4		4.1		1.9	

[a] % Breast-feeding at beginning of interval (van Steenbergen *et al.*, 1984. Estimated from Fig. 1).
[b] Breast milk included (van Steenbergen *et al.*, 1984).
[c] Oomen *et al.*, 1984.
[d] Number of episodes per year derived from two-weekly incidence figures (Leeuwenburg *et al.*, 1984).

ing water from wells and open rivers were in general not polluted (van Steenbergen *et al.*, 1983).

(c) The Kirkos study, Ethiopia

In the previous section reference has already been made to the study linking socio-economic status and environmental hygiene to the prevalence of diarrhoea. In the same study data were also collected on nutritional status. Weight-for-age was measured before the series of morbidity observations and expressed in percentages of the Harvard standard. Through multivariate analysis it was shown that nutritional status measured by weight-for-age was one of the most powerful predictors of prevalence of diarrhoea (Frey and Wall, 1979). Information on factors which could explain how nutritional status affects diarrhoea was not available in this study.

(d) The Malumfashi study, Nigeria

In this study nutritional status was determined at the beginning of the period of observation. After the baseline survey, weekly visits were conducted for a period of three months during the rainy season. During these visits, data were collected on the incidence and duration of diarrhoea. The results of the study are shown in Table 8.9.

Table 8.9. *Nutritional status and diarrhoeal morbidity in children 6–32 months old in Malumfashi, Nigeria, 1979*

	No. of episodes per year[a]	% of time ill	N
Weight-for-age			
(% of Harvard standard)			
<75%	6.1	11.3	123
>75%	5.0	8.5	220
Height-for-age			
(% of Harvard standard)			
<90%	5.8	10.8	98
>90%	5.5	7.9	245
Weight-for-height			
(% of Harvard standard)			
<80%	7.6	13.6	41
>80%	5.2	7.6	302
Total	5.6	10.5	343

[a] Extrapolated on basis of 3 months of observation beginning at the start of rainy season.
Source: Tomkins, 1981.

The frequency of diarrhoea was not higher in underweight (<75 per cent weight-for-age of the Harvard standard) or stunted (<90 per cent height-for-age) children than in other children. Those who were wasted (<80 per cent weight-for-height), however, experienced about 47 per cent more episodes of diarrhoea than those who were not wasted. Pre-existing malnutrition affected duration of diarrhoea as follows. Duration was 33 per cent longer in underweight children, 37 per cent longer in stunted children, and 79 per cent longer in wasted children. In general, nutritional status is more strongly related to the duration of diarrhoea than to the number of episodes or attacks. In particular the wasted child (measured in terms of weight-for-height) was at risk for having more frequent and more protracted episodes of diarrhoea (Tomkins, 1981).

8. Beliefs and Practices of Mothers and Traditional Healers

(a) The Swaziland study

Entirely different aspects of diarrhoea than those described in the previous sections were investigated by means of anthropological methods in Swaziland and Kenya. In the Swaziland study, in-depth interviews were held with about 160 indigenous health practitioners on various aspects of traditional beliefs and practices regarding diarrhoea. In addition, a number of mothers were interviewed concerning their perceptions and treatment of diarrhoea. The study was conducted by Green between 1981 and 1983 (Green, 1985).

Swaziland is a country with many traditional healers; they are more easily accessible to the population than clinics and hospitals. Most mothers in Swaziland will first visit a traditional healer for advice and treatment for their children's diarrhoea before going to a Western-type clinic or hospital. Another important fact is that for most Swazi many illnesses are believed to be caused by sorcery, the deliberate use of spells or medicines for harmful purposes. It is in general believed that these non-natural diseases are spread by air, and that water or human faeces are not significant agents of disease transmissions. A relatively small number of diseases such as colds, flu, and simple diarrhoea are regarded as occurring naturally.

The general term for simple diarrhoea is *umshako* and is recognized as the frequent passing of wet, loose stools. This type of illness is typically found in infants and children and is treated with herbs. If the disease episode responds to these herbs within three days, the illness is considered naturally caused. Causes recognized for this type of diarrhoea are bad food, insufficient food, a change of seasons, the eating of unripe fruits, the drinking of spoiled milk, etc. One variety of *umshako* or natural diarrhoea is thought to accompany teething in a baby. The teething is said to cause heat in a

child, and the heat in turn causes diarrhoea. Traditional medicines are
sometimes rubbed on a child's emerging teeth 'to make them grow faster'.
The common practice in many societies of withholding food and fluids
(including breast milk) from a baby suffering from diarrhoea is not followed
here.

If *umshako* does not respond to the usual treatment methods, it is suspected that it might be one of the two more serious childhood diseases. The
first one is *kuhabula* and is regarded as not natural. There are various
symptoms such as a sunken fontanelle and vomiting in addition to frequent
loose stools. None of these signs, however, are thought to be related to
dehydration. Babies become ill with *kuhabula* when they inhale vapours
and fumes or herbal medicines other than those of their own clan. Their
exposure may be accidental or deliberate. When a child exhibits the symptoms of this type of diarrhoea it is generally taken at once to a traditional
healer to be treated. Some healers also give enemas to babies.

The third commonly recognized childhood diarrhoeal illness is *umphezulu*.
A child is believed to be born with this type of disease, which is the result of
the mother's behaviour during pregnancy (e.g. she passed through an area
where lightning had recently struck). When this type of disease is suspected,
most babies are taken to traditional healers to undergo the enema procedure, which contributes to dehydration. Hospital or clinic treatment for
umphezulu is regarded by traditional healers as dangerous and ineffective.

One of the recommendations for health and health education programmes
from this study builds upon the important role of traditional healers in
Swaziland. It is recommended that the government distribute ORT packets
to traditional healers with the aim of letting this type of treatment become
one of the types of therapy provided by traditional healers. The strategy
would be for enemas to be replaced by ORT. A related recommendation is
that health education directed at traditional healers should aim at demon-
strating the harmful effects of practices such as enemas (Green, 1985).

(b) The Machakos study, Kenya

In this Kenyan study, which took place among the Akamba, participant
observation methods were combined with interviews with 250 mothers of
children under five (Maina, 1977; Maina-Ahlberg, 1984). The study dealt
with beliefs and practices regarding both measles and diarrhoea. Here we
shall only discuss the results on diarrhoea. Before presenting these results it
is appropriate to describe briefly one of the several disease classification
systems which exist in Akamba society: these systems were the topic of
another study conducted by van Luyk (1984). One important classification
system is based on the cause of a disease. Diseases are grouped into five
classes, of which only two will be described here: diseases of God or natural
diseases, and diseases caused by witchcraft.

If there are no obvious reasons for disease and death, then the cause is said to be 'natural' (as indicated by the description 'a disease caused by God himself') or not caused by sorcery or witchcraft. Another term for 'diseases of God' is 'natural diseases'. Herbal treatment by knowledgeable persons is sufficient to cure these natural diseases. Diseases that belong in this class include measles, whooping cough, diarrhoea, and the teething problems of small children.

Another group of diseases are those caused by witchcraft. A witch can cause all kinds of misfortunes and many types of diseases, and witchcraft is suspected when a disease does not respond to normal treatment. This could, for example, be the case when the normal treatment of diarrhoea does not lead to its cure.

When a normal cure does not help, people believe that the child has been bewitched. When such a child dies from a common illness (a natural disease), it is said that some witch stole the life of the child. If witchcraft is suspected, the bewitching power has to be taken away before the child can be treated with herbal medicine. The evil power can be taken away by the *munde mue* (traditional medical functionary) (van Luyk, 1984; Ndeti, 1972).

In interviews with the mothers it was established that diarrhoea is classified as one of God's diseases or as a natural disease. It is common during teething, weaning, crawling, and learning to walk. Diarrhoea associated with these stages of development is commonly known as 'teething diarrhoea'. Treatment of teething diarrhoea can involve the cutting of the sides of a child's gum with a sharp tool or rubbing hard until the gum becomes sore, and then applying indigenous herbs. The purpose of this operation is to force the teeth out more quickly and this is believed to remove the cause of teething diarrhoea. In recent times, shop medicine has been replacing herbs.

A second type of natural diarrhoea is identified as 'sickness diarrhoea'. A child who is having diarrhoea which is not associated with teething is believed to suffer from this more serious form of the disease. Sickness diarrhoea is also treated with herbs and increasingly by shop medicine and visits to health centres or hospitals. Frequently practised during episodes of both types of diarrhoea is the withholding of water, milk, or foods. In this study it was stated that about 60 per cent of the mothers withheld milk and water during episodes of diarrhoea (Maina, 1977).

In this community, when diarrhoea occurred, modern medical care alone was used in 63 per cent of all cases, indigenous care alone in only 9 per cent, and modern and indigenous care both in the remaining 28 per cent of the cases. About three-quarters of the modern medical care consisted of visits to health centres or hospitals and about one-quarter consisted in home treatment with shop medicine. With respect to indigenous care, about one-third used the services of a herbalist, one-third the services of a teething expert, and one-third practised self-medication (Maina-Ahlberg, 1984).

9. Summary and Conclusions

In view of the fact that diarrhoeal diseases are an important health problem in Africa (1.2 million deaths under 5 each year) it is appalling to note how little research has been done on their demographic, epidemiological, nutritional, and social and cultural aspects. Only a few longitudinal, population-based studies on the epidemiology of diarrhoeal diseases could be identified in sub-Saharan Africa and likewise only a few anthropological studies dealing specifically with this disease were available. In interpreting the results of these various studies one should take into account that they were conducted in small areas in several African countries; the results achieved with these studies are not representative of whole countries.

In addition to these longitudinal studies, several cross-sectional epidemiological surveys with diarrhoeal diseases as one of the topics of research have been conducted in Ghana, Cameroon, and Kenya. These were not considered here, because they gave relatively little information on diarrhoea among children under 5. Data from the Demographic Health Surveys project which has recently been implemented in a number of countries are not yet available.

Very high rates of diarrhoeal mortality were found in the Ngayokheme study in rural Senegal. Much lower rates were observed in a rural area of Machakos District in Kenya. In both places diarrhoea was the leading or one of the leading causes of death among children below the age of 5. Cause of death data are also available from civil registers in a few countries in West and East Africa and they confirm the importance of diarrhoea as a cause of death.

Seasonal differences in mortality from all causes combined were very marked in the Ngayokheme study. Total mortality in the wet season was 2.5 times higher than in the dry season and the number of deaths under the age of 5 in the three months of the wet season nearly equalled the number of deaths in the remaining nine months. It is likely that strong seasonal differences exist with respect to diarrhoeal diseases as well. No seasonal difference in diarrhoeal mortality could be found in the Machakos study.

More data on cause-specific mortality are urgently needed in the various countries and regions of Africa. One promising possibility is the approach developed in the Ngayokheme study by means of standardized questionnaires used by field-workers together with the assignment of causes of death by a physician (Garenne and Fontaine, 1986). In view of the strong seasonal variation in mortality that was found to exist, it is usually necessary to include both the wet and the dry seasons in the observation period in order to obtain representative figures.

The incidence of diarrhoeal disease (number of episodes per year) was very high in the Kirkos study in Ethiopia and much lower in the Machakos study, especially when the minimum estimate is used. These results make it likely that in Africa wide differences in diarrhoeal morbidity exist. Conclusive evidence for such variation does not exist since it is difficult to compare the results of the several longitudinal studies; the reason is that the operational definitions and measurement procedures used vary considerably. Strong seasonal differences in diarrhoeal morbidity were found in the Keneba study in the Gambia; such seasonal differences could not be identified in the Machakos study.

The determination of levels of diarrhoeal morbidity is very much dependent on the operational definitions and measurement procedures used. Variations in these definitions and procedures were found with respect to the following aspects:

(a) the length of the recall period (e.g. two weeks, one week, day of visit by the field-worker);

(b) the definition of diarrhoea (definitions of the mothers versus specification of, for instance, four or more loose or watery stools per 24 hours);

(c) the counting of only serious cases of diarrhoea versus the counting of the serious cases plus the less serious (mild) cases;

(d) the counting of cases of diarrhoea as such only versus counting of these cases plus those which are associated with diseases such as measles;

(e) the duration of the study period (wet season only, dry season only, or both).

Some studies have measured morbidity in terms of incidence (number of episodes), others in terms of prevalence (percentage of time ill). More emphasis should be placed on the use of prevalence measures (Rowland, 1983).

In two longitudinal studies the impact of two types of factors on diarrhoeal morbidity was determined: socio-economic status and environmental hygiene. In the Kirkos study both factors had a strong impact on the prevalence of diarrhoea; in the Bakau study in the Gambia this was not the case. A reason explaining the impact of these factors in the first but not in the second study could be that the Kirkos study took place in an urban area that was disadvantaged, but still heterogeneous in several ways, while the Bakau study was conducted in a more prosperous and more homogeneous urban area.

Results from several studies were available on the influence of nutritional factors on diarrhoeal morbidity. In the Malumfashi and Kirkos studies it could be shown that nutritional status, measured before the start of the disease surveillance, had an impact on diarrhoeal prevalence. Some results were also available from the Keneba study on the influence of breast-feeding practices on diarrhoeal morbidity. More research was done on the role of the quality of weaning foods. Both in the Keneba and the Machakos studies it was shown that weaning foods were often severely contaminated. These contaminated weaning foods are a very important reason for the increase in diarrhoea in the period following cessation of breast-feeding or after the introduction of water, milk, or solid food, while breast-feeding is continuing.

The two anthropological studies reviewed here used entirely different methods from the studies on socio-economic, environmental, and nutrition factors described above. In contrast to these last types of studies, the aim of anthropological studies is to describe and understand the local culture of health and the patterns of behaviour that are linked to it. An important contribution of both the Swaziland and the Machakos projects was their focus on the existence of harmful practices followed by mothers and traditional healers. Examples of such practices are withholding of water, milk, or food during an episode of diarrhoea, and the giving of enemas as a treatment. Such studies need to be followed by other research including surveys yielding figures on how widespread such practices are and what their influence on health is. The Swaziland study is also a good example of how the results of anthropological research may be used to formulate policy implications for health care and health education programmes.

Prior to the start of demographic and epidemiological projects it would be valuable to do anthropological research on definitions and meanings of local terms used to describe diseases. Such studies would add precision to these demographic or epidemiological studies. There is scope for more anthropological research focusing on topics other than beliefs and practices of mothers and health care providers (Chen, 1986; Fosu, 1981). An example is the influence of mothers' farming duties on child care. The Keneba study noted the influence of mothers' heavy farming duties on child care during the rainy season: it was suggested that farm labour by mothers in that season was one of the reasons for an increase in morbidity from diarrhoea among children. Another topic that would be worth investigating concerns various aspects of the mother's behaviour towards her child and of one child towards another. Such research could have implications for the understanding of transmission of infectious diseases from mother to child or from one child to another.

References

Barrell, R. A. and Rowland, M. G. (1979). 'Infant foods as a potential source of diarrhoeal illness in rural West Africa', *Transactions of the Royal Society of Tropical Medicine and Hygiene* 73/1: 85–90.
Black, R. (1984), 'Diarrheal diseases and child morbidity and mortality', Supplement

to vol. 10 of *Population and Development Review*, 141–61.

Cantrelle, P. and Ly, V. (1981), 'La Mortalité des enfants en Afrique', in P. M. Boulanger and D. Tabutin (eds.), *La Mortalité des enfants dans le monde et dans l'histoire*, Ordina, Liège, 197–221.

—— Diop, I., Garenne, M., Gueye, M., and Sandio, A. (1986), 'The profile of mortality and its determinants in Senegal, 1960–1980', in United Nations, *Determinants of Mortality Changes and Differentials in Developing Countries*, New York, 86–116.

Chen, L. (1983), 'Interactions of diarrhea and malnutrition: Mechanisms and interventions', in L. Chen and N. Scrimshaw (eds.), *Diarrhea and Malnutrition*, Plenum Press, New York, 3–19.

—— (1986), 'Primary health care in developing countries: Overcoming operational, technical and social barriers', *Lancet*, 29 Nov. 1260–5.

Ewbank, D., Henin, R., and Kekovole, J. (1986), 'An integration of demographic and epidemiologic research on mortality in Kenya', in United Nations, *Determinants of Mortality Change and Differentials in Developing Countries*, New York, 33–85.

Feachem, R. and Koblinsky, M. (1984), 'Interventions for the control of diarrhoeal diseases among young children: Promotion of breastfeeding', *Bulletin of the World Health Organization* 62/2: 271–91.

Fosu, G. B. (1981), 'Disease classification in rural Ghana: Framework and implications for health behaviour', *Social Science and Medicine* 15B: 471–82.

Frey, L. and Wall, S. (1977), 'Exploring child health and its ecology: The Kirkos study in Addis Ababa', *Acta Paediatrica Scandinavica*, supplement 267, Stockholm.

—— —— (1979), 'Quantity and variation in morbidity: THAID-analysis of the occurrence of gastroenteritis among Ethiopian children', *International Journal of Epidemiology* 8/4: 313–25.

Garenne, M. and Fontaine, O. (1990), 'Assessing probable causes of death using a standardized questionnaire: A study in rural Senegal', in J. Vallin, Stan D'Souza, and A. Palloni (eds.), *Measurement and Analysis of Mortality: New Approaches*, Clarendon Press, Oxford, 123–42.

Gemert, W., Slooff, R., van Ginneken, J., and Leeuwenburg, J. (1984), 'Household status differentials and childhood mortality', in van Ginneken and Muller (1984), 271–80.

Green, E. (1985), 'Traditional healers, mothers and childhood diarrheal disease in Swaziland: The interface of anthropology and health education', *Social Science and Medicine* 20/3: 277–85.

Leeuwenburg, J., Gemert, W., Muller, A. S., and Patel, S. C. (1984), 'The incidence of diarrhoeal disease', in van Ginneken and Muller (1984), 109–18.

McGregor, I. A., Rahman, A. K., Thompson, A. M., Billewicz, W. Z., and Thompson, B. (1970), 'The health of young children in a West African (Gambian) village', *Transactions of the Royal Society of Tropical Medicine and Hygiene* 64/1: 48–76.

Maina, B. (1977), 'A socio-medical inquiry: Modern and indigenous medical care utilization patterns with respect to measles and acute diarrhoea among the Akamba', MA thesis, University of Nairobi, Kenya.

Maina-Ahlberg, B. (1984), 'Beliefs and practices related to measles and acute diarrhoea', in van Ginneken and Muller (1984), 323–32.

Mfoulou, R. (1986), 'Les Causes de mortalité infantile à Brazzaville', in P. Cantrelle *et al.* (eds.), *Estimation de la mortalité du jeune enfant (0–5 ans) pour guider les actions de santé dans les pays en développement*, Éditions de l'INSERM 145, Paris, 371–84.

Morley, D. (1973), *Paediatric Priorities in the Developing World*, Butterworths, London.

Mutanda, L. (1980), 'Epidemiology of acute gastroenteritis in early childhood in Kenya, III', *East African Medical Journal* 57: 317–26.

Ndeti, K. (1972), *Elements of Akamba Life*, East African Publishing House, Nairobi.

Omondi-Odhiambo, van Ginneken, J. K. and Voorhoeve, A. (1987), 'Age and sex-specific mortality and cause of death in a rural area of Machakos District, Kenya in 1975–1978', *Journal of Biosocial Science* 22: 63–75.

Oomen, H. A., Blankhart, D., and 't Mannetje, W. (1984), 'Growth pattern of pre-school children', in van Ginneken and Muller (1984), 183–96.

Pickering, H. (1985), 'Social and environmental factors associated with diarrhoea and growth in young children: Child health in urban Africa', *Social Science and Medicine*, 21/2: 121–7.

Pison, G. and Langaney, A. (1985), 'The level and age pattern of mortality in Bandafassi (Eastern Senegal): Results from a small-scale and intensive multi-round survey', *Population Studies* 39/3: 387–406.

Rea, J. N. (1970), 'Social and nutritional influences on morbidity: A community study of young children in Lagos', *Proceedings of the Nutrition Society* 29: 223–30.

Rowland, M. G. (1983), 'Epidemiology of childhood diarrhea in the Gambia', in L. Chen and N. Scrimshaw (eds.), *Diarrhea and Malnutrition*, Plenum Press, New York and London, 87–98.

—— Barrell, R. and Whitehead, R. (1978), 'Bacterial contamination in traditional Gambian weaning foods', *Lancet*, 21 Jan., 136–8.

—— Goh, S., Williams, K., Campbell, A., Beards, G., Sanders, R., and Flewett, T. (1985), 'Epidemiological aspects of rotavirus infection in young Gambian children', *Annals of Tropical Paediatrics* 5: 23–8.

Snyder, J. D. and Merson, M. H. (1982), 'The magnitude of the global problem of acute diarrhoeal disease: A review of active surveillance data', *Bulletin of the World Health Organization* 60/4: 605–13.

Tomkins, A. (1981), 'Nutritional status and severity of diarrhoea among pre-school children in rural Nigeria', *Lancet*, 18 Apr. 860–2.

van Ginneken, J. K. and Muller, A. S. (eds.) (1984), *Maternal and Child Health in Rural Kenya: An Epidemiological Study*, Croom Helm, London.

van Luyk, J. N. (1984), 'The utilization of modern and traditional medical care', in van Ginneken and Muller (1984), 231–308.

van Steenbergen, W. M., Kusin, J., and Jansen, A. (1984), 'Food consumption of pre-school children', in van Ginneken and Muller (1984), 167–82.

—— Mossel, D., Kusin, J., and Jansen, A. (1983), 'Machakos project studies XXIII: Bacterial contamination of foods commonly eaten by young children in Machakos, Kenya', *Tropical and Geographical Medicine* 35: 193–7.

Watkinson, M. (1981), 'Delayed onset of weaning diarrhoea associated with high breast milk intake', *Transactions of the Royal Society of Tropical Medicine and Hygiene* 75/3: 432–5.

Winikoff, B. (1980), 'Weaning: Nutrition, morbidity and mortality consequences', in S. H. Preston (ed.), *Biological and Social Aspects of Mortality and the Length of Life*, Ordina, Liège, 113–48.

9 Malaria in Kenya: Prevention, Control, and Impact on Mortality

Dan C. O. Kaseje
Aga Khan Health Service, Kenya

1. Introduction

Human malaria is caused by the four major *Plasmodium* species: *P. falciparum*, *P. vivax*, *P. malariae*, and *P. ovale*. In most parts of the world the prevailing parasite is *P. falciparum*, which causes the most severe form of acute disease that is often fatal depending on the immune status of the host. The parasite is transmitted by various species of the anopheline mosquito from one infected to another susceptible human host. The sporozoite, the infectious form of the parasite, released from mosquito salivary glands, initiates the exoerythrocytic cycle in the liver. Subsequently the developed merzoites invade erythrocytes, and the asexual cycle continues through the course of the infection. A subset of the erythrocytic form of the parasite develops into male and female gametocytes. The gametocytes, when taken up by the female anophele mosquito, develop into sporozoites, which result in disease transmission.

Malaria is one of the major infectious diseases in the world, with acute malaria affecting more than 100 million people each year according to World Health Organization estimates (WHO, 1984). Elimination of malaria world-wide has proved impossible, and thus the current efforts are devoted to the control of malaria (WHO, 1979). Even in the few instances where eradication was attempted, the achievement was only transient. The long-term control strategy must also be carefully planned. The principles involved include the determination of clear objectives based on the local malaria situation; easy access to antimalarials for treatment for every member of the community living in malarious areas, with enough information and education to enhance proper use of chemotherapy; adequate case detection and treatment within a primary health care system; community participation in all antimalarial activities; adequate epidemiological services to support antimalarial activities; adequate referral and technical back-up support systems; and assessment of impact, the results of which are fed back into planning and programme activities.

The control measures to be implemented must be those that can be sustained by the local system indefinitely and they must differ from place to place according to various environmental, socio-economic, and biological factors that determine the stability of malaria transmission.

In this chapter an attempt is made to define various malaria situations, discuss control strategies appropriate for each situation, and summarize results of a study in Saradidi, Kenya, where some of these control strategies have been tried.

2. Malaria Transmission

It has been known for the better part of this century that malaria transmission is related to climatic conditions (Celli, 1900); the name of the disease itself suggests so much. This knowledge was there even before the mode of transmission was worked out and before the disease agent was discovered (Russell *et al.*, 1963). In 1938 Gill defined four climatic zones of malaria in the world. Later Macdonald (1957) distinguished 12 epidemiological malaria zones. During the same period malaria maps were produced in Kenya and Tanzania (Survey Division, 1956*a* and 1956*b*).

Various determinants of malaria transmission have been used to define these zones of malaria: the length of the transmission season, the level of endemicity of parasite prevalence, and the ecological systems that depend heavily on the climatic conditions (Lysenko, 1983). Malariologists have found it necessary to identify, characterize, and delimit malaria situations in order to work out appropriate control strategies. This is done by studying the local variability at the meteorological level in order to improve the effectiveness and efficiency of malaria control (Fontaine, 1985; WHO, 1984).

This effort to identify, characterize, and delimit the malaria situation in different areas has been termed the stratification of malaria. The stratification idea recognizes that the problem of malaria today is complex and is getting ever more complex. The determinants of malaria distribution are no longer simply biological or climatic but also include sociological and economic factors and more recently the response of the malaria parasite (particularly *Plasmodium falciparum*) to treatment.

The determinants could be grouped as follows:

1. *Epidemiological determinants.* Rainfall, temperature, altitude, malaria vectors, prevalence, incidence, and related mortality and morbidity, and their distribution in the population.
2. *Socio-economic determinants.* Demographic patterns (population structure and movement), socio-cultural characteristics of various communities, economic activities and projects (e.g. irrigation and

hydroelectric schemes), housing (where sited and how constructed), and economic activities of individuals (e.g. fishing).

3. *Resource distribution, availability, and effectiveness for malaria control.* Availability of primary health care services and response of the local parasite to available treatment.

It can be seen from these determinants that the malaria strata that may be defined cannot be discrete but must overlap greatly as various factors will exist in varying combinations.

3. Definition of Malaria Strata by Levels of Transmission

Stratum 1. Rural areas with traditional agricultural systems and with stable perennial malaria transmission (e.g. in the forest belt of tropical Africa).

In this stratum the incidence and prevalence of malaria are both very high. Morbidity and mortality are concentrated in children under the age of 5 years, pregnant women (particularly those pregnant for the first time), and visitors from non-malarious areas. The adults are clinically immune but have malaria parasites circulating in their peripheral blood. These are the areas described as holoendemic using the endemicity classification suggested by WHO (1951) at the first conference on malaria in Africa, held in Kampala, Uganda.

Stratum 2. Rural areas with traditional agricultural systems but with stable seasonal malaria transmission.

This is found in savannah areas and is characterized by high prevalence and incidence most of the year but with marked seasonal variations. For this stratum, morbidity tends to be concentrated, to a greater or lesser extent, depending on the level of overlap with the first stratum above, among children under 5 years, pregnant women (particularly those pregnant for the first time), and immigrants from non-malarious areas. These areas are described as hyperendemic (WHO, 1951).

Stratum 3. Arid or semi-arid rural areas with traditional agricultural systems and with unstable transmission due to aridity.

Morbidity and mortality in these areas extend to adults and may vary greatly from year to year. The areas are characterized by recurrent epidemics.

Stratum 4. High altitude rural areas with traditional agricultural systems, unstable malaria transmission, and with recurrent epidemics.

Stratum 5. Populations of nomadic or semi-nomadic pastoralists who may belong to more than one stratum.

They will also tend to experience recurrent epidemics affecting all age groups.

Stratum 6. Modern irrigation schemes that tend to extend and stabilize transmission.

The widespread use of insecticides in agriculture may render the local mosquito vector prone to developing resistance to insecticides that may be used for mosquito control. Migrant labour in the area may influence transmission, incidence, prevalence, morbidity, and mortality. The extent of this influence depends on the place of origin of the migrants and how they are settled in their new settlement areas.

Stratum 7. Temporary development projects, e.g. bridge and other construction works.

Development activities may increase breeding sites and may also bring about migration and migrant labour that may create a unique malaria transmission situation.

Stratum 8. Urban and suburban areas.

Since drug resistance is rapidly developing in sub-Saharan Africa (Onori, 1984), further consideration is now also given to the response of the local parasite (*Plasmodium falciparum*) to chloroquine. An area may therefore be described as (Koznetsov *et al.*, 1986):

fully sensitive to chloroquine;
low-level resistance to chloroquine;
high-level resistance to chloroquine;
high-level resistance to chloroquine and resistance to Fansidar.

While the global malaria situation, which worsened in the period 1973–6, has tended to improve since then, the malaria situation in Africa south of the Sahara has remained either unaffected or has deteriorated. In most of rural Africa, malaria transmission is at its highest, maintained by the most efficient vectors, *Anopheles gambiae*, *An. arabiensis*, and *An. funestus*. Considerable geographical and seasonal variations occur due to altitude, natural drainage or the extent of the dry season (Olsen, 1979), and the socio-cultural and economic factors described above.

4. Malaria Control

The stratification of the malaria situation described above is for the purpose of designing malaria control measures within primary health care which are suitable for each stratum. The choice of a strategy should be made only after evaluating the local epidemiology, socio-economic conditions, and resources available including the state of the development of the health service infrastructure. In this way one can determine not only what is necessary but also what is possible.

Four priority levels have been described by the World Health Organization in the control of malaria and are usually referred to as tactical variants (WHO, 1984).

(*a*) Tactical variant 1

This is the first priority in all malarious situations and its purpose is to control mortality. In primary health care, this refers to making effective chemotherapy available in the community for presumptive treatment of all fever cases. The microscopic confirmation of diagnosis in such circumstances may not be practical or desirable in places which are holoendemic or hyperendemic. The success of such a programme depends on:

- the availability of appropriate antimalarials;
- the availability of competence within the community, e.g. trained Community Health Workers to provide appropriate treatment as soon as possible after a malarial attack;
- the availability of information and education that would enable informed use of antimalarials by the community, families, and individuals;
- adequate technical supervision and referral back-up;
- adequate surveillance systems to monitor the malaria situation and the response of malaria parasites to treatment.

The Saradidi Rural Health Programme in Kenya has demonstrated the feasibility of this tactical variant. Some of the results are summarized in this paper (Kaseje *et al.*, 1987*a* and *b*; Mburu *et al.*, 1987; Spencer *et al.*, 1987*a* and *b*).

(*b*) Tactical variant 2

The purpose of this variant is to control both mortality and morbidity. It has limited impact on controlling prevalence. The goal is achieved through chemotherapy as in tactical variant 1, but also by chemoprophylaxis on the members of the community most at risk. For Strata 1 and 2, chemoprophylaxis is usually limited to the non-immune or relatively non-immune members of the community: visitors from non-malarious areas and pregnant women (mainly first exposed pregnancy). Children under the age of 5 years may no longer be considered target groups for chemoprophylaxis because:

- such a programme is not sustainable indefinitely in most African countries;
- if given for five years, enough chloroquine may be deposited in the tissues to cause toxicity;
- it may hinder the development of immunity against malaria;
- it may accelerate the development of resistance to chloroquine in the local parasite population because of drug pressure.

The chemoprophylaxis to pregnant women remains one of the most important activities in primary health care because it prevents anaemia in pregnancy, it improves the health of the mother, and it prevents low birth-weight and hence reduces perinatal and post-neonatal infant mortality. The women should have full prophylaxis throughout pregnancy to fully benefit from it. The chemoprophylaxis can also be provided by community health workers, traditional birth attendants, and antenatal clinics. The relative ineffectiveness of the community health workers system, working in the village by themselves, was demonstrated at Saradidi (Kaseje *et al.*, 1987*a*). The workers at Saradidi proposed that a monthly regimen given at antenatal clinics might be the best strategy since the weekly supply of chemoprophylaxis to pregnant mothers seemed to place an unmanageable demand on the time of the part-time, fully voluntary workers at Saradidi. The monthly regimen needs to be carefully worked out and must be supported technically and logistically, and should include an effective information and education system.

Thus, for both tactical variants 1 and 2 a strong supporting health service system is necessary to provide referral, supplies, supervision, training, laboratory backing, and detection of resistance.

During epidemics in strata 3, 4, 5, 6, and 7 already described, similar antiparasite activities (chemoprophylaxis and chemotherapy) may be appropriate to limit the mortality and morbidity during transmission periods. It may often be necessary to provide mass treatment, whether weekly, fortnightly, or monthly, according to feasibility on the basis of the available resources. In this case antimalarials should include schizonticidal and gametocytocidal agents (e.g. chloroquine and primaquine), and the drug distribution should be continued until the end of one month after the transmission season. The effectiveness of Community Health Workers in this exercise should be investigated. Their effectiveness will also depend on information, education, and training given both to them and to the rest of the community.

(c) Tactical variant 3

This aims at reducing not only mortality and morbidity by the antiparasitic methods described above, but also prevalence of parasitaemia by interrupting the actual transmission. This variant can be complex, expensive, and dependent on such high levels of supervision and support that it is not commonly found in developing countries. Antivector activities do include individual protection methods which are feasible at the family or community level and should be encouraged in all the strata. These methods may include the use of bed nets (better still if impregnated by insecticides), mosquito repellents, screens in the windows (which is limited to permanent houses), and changing dwelling sites. These individual protection activities are also dependent on socio-economic conditions, information and education, and the availability of supplies.

The most effective antivector method, which is the key to this tactical variant, is insecticide spraying. At present, this is only used in very special circumstances because it is too costly and has too many logistic problems for most developing countries in Africa to handle. It is also heavily dependent on technical expertise. Insecticide application can be by indoor residual spraying (the most common method) or outdoor space spraying.

Whenever this is to be implemented, it is of vital importance to carefully define the roles and responsibilities of the various actors involved. The actors should include the community, individuals, and the health services. This method can be used in strata 2, 4, 6, and 7 during risk of epidemics. If it is in the context of primary health care, then the community should be fully involved in planning, executing, and evaluating the activities. The involvement of the community in antivector operations has been described in Ethiopia, Sudan, Thailand, and Vietnam (WHO, 1969).

Outdoor spraying operations are only effective in urban centres, where they are used to reduce the population of adult infected mosquitoes. The spraying operations should be timed properly to be effective, and this usually demands a special malaria unit for its adequate management.

The control of vector breeding is another commonly used antivector method. Removal of breeding sites around houses and sanitation of living areas should be done by the community following receipt of information and education. In tropical Africa, the adequate reduction of breeding sites is only possible in special circumstances such as in urban areas, irrigation schemes, and in the arid areas (strata 3, 6, 7, and 8). Other methods of source reduction include larviciding and environmental modification. These activities should always be planned into the development projects in malarious or potentially malarious areas.

(d) Tactical variant 4

This is the total eradication of malaria, which is now considered virtually impossible, at least in tropical Africa. This has to do with both antiparasite and antivector activities.

In recent years the approach of integrated vector control has been advanced by Laird and his colleagues (1983). This approach recommends the use of all appropriate technology to bring about an effective degree of vector control. This approach must be based on sound ecological understanding of the environment including the availability and adequacy of health systems (Fontaine, 1987; Fontaine *et al.*, 1976). It is also very important to have a thorough knowledge of breeding sites and mosquito habits. This is the only way to decide the best strategy (Kliger, 1930).

In the context of primary health care, the methods to be applied must be those that are suitable to the community given its competence and resources. Other workers have also stressed the appropriateness of methods not only with regard to what the community can do but also to its sound understanding of vector control (Axtell, 1979; Baudon *et al.*, 1984; Fontaine, 1985). Understanding of vector control implies:

(*a*) a sound understanding of the target vectors;
(*b*) a quantitative analysis of cost and benefits in terms of impact on man and his environment;
(*c*) the possibility of source reductions;
(*d*) that integratable, complementary control measures are possible;
(*e*) a monitoring system to detect impact;
(*f*) the ability to feed the results of monitoring and evaluation back to ongoing antivector or antimalarial activities.

A good vector control effort should reduce the transmission of malaria to levels acceptable to the community. The monitoring system should include surveillance to be able to predict the risk of impending transmission and to assess regularly the vectorial capacity and factors affecting it, such as vector population density, longevity, anthropophilic behaviour, and the length of the sporogenic cycle. The understanding of these elements is vital for the selection of the most suitable integrated vector control methods.

One of the main lessons learned from the attempt to eradicate malaria from the world is the high degree of local variability of the malaria problem not only in its intensity but also in its response to control interventions. The main aim of the epidemiological approach to malaria control is to identify appropriate technologies for malaria control as part of the development of primary health care. The concept of appropriate technology implies its being scientifically sound for the solution of the problem and adapted to the society considering its application in terms of acceptability and affordability. For this reason, a malaria control package must be well suited to the stratum and reflect adequate understanding of all the factors that determine the problem. This includes those factors that would influence the process of implementing control measures and the response of the disease parasites and its vectors to the intervention strategies.

Several studies have been undertaken at Saradidi to determine the malaria situation there and to test the effectiveness of a community-based chemotherapy and chemoprophylaxis programme that has been described above. More specifically, three types of studies were conducted, on (1) malaria transmission; (2) the sensitivity of *Plasmodium falciparum* to chloroquine and other antimalarials; and (3) the effectiveness of community-based chemotherapy and selective chemoprophylaxis.

5. Summary of Studies

(a) Study (1): Malaria transmission

This study correlated the incidence of malaria among children under 6 years with entomological and meteorological data gathered during the same period (January to December 1986).

Every four weeks a cohort of about 47 children aged 6 months to 6 years were enrolled in the study. They were examined at enrolment, when thin and thick blood slides were made and serum samples were obtained for antibody assays. All the children were treated with Fansidar (sulfadoxine/pyrimethamine combination), known to be effective in treating malaria in the area. They were seen daily thereafter for 12 weeks. This was to detect any new illness and ensure that no antimalarial drugs were given to them except within the study. Each time a child was seen for an illness, malaria slides were repeated and they were treated promptly if positive. Other illnesses were treated, but with drugs known not to have an effect on malaria.

Additionally, routine malaria smears were made on the children on weeks 1, 2, 4, 6, 8, and 12 after initial treatment. All the smears were strained with Giemsa, and 200 oil immersion fields were examined independently by two observers. Children who developed recurrent parasitaemia on or before day 28 following treatment were considered to have had a recrudescence and were treated and dropped from the study. The remaining children were checked every two weeks for new parasitaemia and were treated as soon as found positive and dropped from the study. The rest were followed for 12 weeks after their enrolment.

The incidence of new malaria infections was calculated for the periods, after week four, and was expressed as the proportion of children who developed parasitaemia during the two-week period among those who were negative at the beginning of the period.

Concurrent studies were performed on *Anopheles* vectors of malaria in the community. Once a week, six pairs of men collected mosquitoes from one another for half-hourly periods, followed by half an hour of rest each time, from 6 p.m. until 6 a.m. in six houses. The mosquitoes collected were examined the following morning in the laboratory for identification of their species, and dissected for parity. Only three species, *An. gambiae* (*sensu strictu*), *An. arabiensis*, and *An. funestus* were found. The entomological inoculation rate was calculated by multiplying the average number of anopheles collected per man per night and the proportion with sporozoites in their salivary glands.

Maximum and minimum temperatures, relative humidity, and rainfall were recorded at two sites in the community.

(b) Study (2): Sensitivity of malaria parasites to treatment

This study was initiated in 1980 to identify chloroquine-resistant infections in Kenyan residents and to follow changes in resistance patterns throughout time.

Children in nursery and lower primary schools in Saradidi were screened with thick blood smears for malaria infection. Those with 500 or more *P. falciparum* parasites per cubic mm. of blood, without other malaria parasites seen and with a negative Dill Glazko test for 4-aminoquino-lines in the urine, were enrolled into the study. The children were then treated with chloroquine at a total dose of 25 mg. base per kg. of body weight given over three days. In a sample of the children, venous or finger-stick blood was obtained for *in vitro* drug sensitivity testing. Children were seen daily for the first week and again at day 14 after starting treatment, and thick blood smears were made at each visit.

The mean age of the children was 7, with a range of 2 to 13 years. Another study was carried out in the same way to test the sensitivity of malaria parasites to other antimalarials. Similar studies were carried out in other areas of Kenya.

(c) Study (3): Effectiveness of community-based chemotherapy and chemoprophylaxis

The study population of 60,000 was divided into three areas, A, B, and C. Area A received chloroquine treatment at the village level provided by community health workers. Area B received chloroquine for chemotherapy and for chemoprophylaxis for pregnant women also at the village level through the Community Health Workers.

Mortality rates were measured from 1981 to 1987 by prospective registration of vital events as part of a community-based health development programme.

In 1980, there was a total population count and household listing in Saradidi. This information was updated every six months by a trained team that visited every household to enquire about births and deaths during the six months. A specific question was asked to find out those who were born but died between update visits. Interviews and examinations were carried out on samples of the Saradidi population to determine the rate of usage of this malaria control system.

6. Summary of Results

(a) Results of Study (1)

The incidence of *P. falciparum* infections was 0.1 in January, rose to a plateau of 0.65 in April to August, and dropped again to 0.1 in September.

Anopheles biting rates averaged less than one per man per night from one night human-bait collections from January to March. The rate rose to 15 mosquitoes per man per night in May and slowly declined to three mosquitoes per night by August and to less than one by September. Sporozoite rates were about 0.2 in January, fell to 0.01 in April, and began to increase again in May to a peak of 0.3 in August, and then declined again. The entomological rate was 0.2 in January, fell to 0.005 in March, rose to a peak of 1.4 in June, and then fell to 0.01 by September. Little rainfall was recorded from December 1985 to February 1986. The heaviest seasonal rains, which peaked at 10 mm. per day, occurred in April and tapered to 1.5 mm. per day in June. Little rain fell from July to September.

From these results it can be seen that the seasonal patterns of the incidence of *P. falciparum* malaria and the entomological inoculation rate were similar except for the multiple simultaneous *P. falciparum* infections occurring at the peak of the transmission season, which could not be detected.

We concluded that the incidence and hence the transmission of *P. falciparum* malaria was highest in the period of April to August. This increase was preceded by increased rainfall, which peaked in April, and increased numbers of anopheles and higher entomological inoculation rates, all of which rose in early to mid-April, just before the increase in malaria incidence in late April.

Thus the timing and duration of high transmission can be precisely defined from year to year using this method, and appropriate antimalarial actions can be planned and undertaken in communities such as Saradidi to maximize the cost-effectiveness of interventions.

(*b*) Results of Study (2)

This study has demonstrated (1) a decrease in *in vivo* sensitivity of *P. falciparum* in Saradidi from 99 per cent in 1983 to 79 per cent in 1985 and an increase in *in vitro* resistance in Saradidi from 18 per cent in 1983 to 32 per cent in 1987; (2) a greater sensitivity of *P. falciparum* to amodiaquine than to chloroquine both *in vivo* and *in vitro*; (3) the presence of chloroquine-resistant *P. falciparum* (CRPF) in most malarious areas of Kenya; (4) the sensitivity of over 85 per cent of infections to a single dose of pyrimethamine/sulfadoxine (Fansidar).

The response to chloroquine and amodiaquine at day seven in the 1987 study showed that 68 per cent of children given chloroquine cleared their infections, compared with 96 per cent given amodiaquine. These are considered sensitive infections by WHO criteria. Fourteen per cent of children receiving chloroquine cleared their parasites but had a recurrence by day seven, which is classified as R-I resistance. By contrast, only four per cent of amodiaquine recipients had resistance. An additional 18 per cent of children given chloroquine failed to clear their parasites, though they had at least a

Table 9.1. In vivo *sensitivity of* P. falciparum *to chloroquine 25 mg./kg. among schoolchildren in Saradidi, Kenya, 1980–1987*

Year	Number examined	Pattern of resistance, in %			
		Sensitive[a]	R-I[a]	R-II	R-III
1980	125	100	0	0	0
1981	122	122	100	0	0
1983	119	98	2	0	0
1984	222	92	4	3	1
1985	42	79	12	7	2
1986	389	82	13	5	0
1987	72	68	14	18	0

[a] At day 7.

75 per cent decrease in the number of parasites. These are considered R-II resistant infections. There was no R-II resistance in the amodiaquine group. Between 1983 and 1987 the number of children with recurrent or persistent infections increased from 32 to 59 per cent among chloroquine recipients and from 4 to 19 per cent among amodiaquine recipients.

Table 9.1 shows the *in vivo* sensitivity of *P. falciparum* to chloroquine in Saradidi, in studies done in school-age children since 1980. One can see that the level of sensitivity has decreased since 1983, though most of the resistance is at the R-I and R-II levels.

In vitro micro tests were performed by the method of Rieckmann using predosed plates from WHO. Briefly, parasitized blood is diluted 1 to 10 in culture medium, 50 μl is placed into wells containing different concentrations of drug, and the parasites are incubated for 24 hours. Results are read as the concentration of drug needed to inhibit schizont development. *In vitro* tests were attempted with 133 isolates and were successful with 112, or 84 per cent. Table 9.2 shows the number of isolates whose growth was inhibited at each concentration of drug tested. Parasites are considered sensitive if they are inhibited by chloroquine 114 nmol/L or less and by amodiaquine 80 nmol/L or less. As can be seen, only 15 per cent of parasites appeared to be sensitive to chloroquine and 13 per cent to amodiaquine. However, a higher proportion of isolates were not inhibited by higher concentrations of chloroquine, 2 per cent continuing to grow at even the highest concentration tested.

Table 9.3 shows the proportions of isolates from Nyanza Province since 1982 which have been sensitive and resistant to chloroquine. Those tested in 1987 appear to have a much higher proportion resistant. Table 9.4 shows an even more dramatic change with amodiaquine.

In summary, we have observed a modest increase in *in vivo* resistance

Table 9.2. *Minimal inhibitory concentrations (MIC) of chloroquine and amodiaquine in the micro test, at Saradidi, October–November 1987*

MIC nmol/L	Chloroquine		Amodiaquine	
	Number inhibited	Cumulative % inhibited	Number inhibited	Cumulative % inhibited
< 80	9	8	15	13
114	8	15	n.a.	
160	9	23	58	65
320	27	47	27	89
640	28	72	n.a.	
Number tested	112		112	

n.a. Not available.

Table 9.3. In vitro *sensitivity of* P. falciparum *to chloroquine by the micro test, Nyanza Province,*[a] *1982–1987*

Year	Number	Sensitive (%)[b]	Resistant (%)
1982	31	46	54
1983	34	82	18
1984	38	58	43
1985	57	68	32
1986	64	64	36
1987	112	15	85

[a] The Province in which Saradidi is situated.
[b] Schizont development inhibited at concentration greater or equal to 114 nmol/L.

Table 9.4. In vitro *sensitivity of* P. falciparum *to amodiaquine by the micro test, in Saradidi, 1982–1987*

Year	Number	Sensitive (%)[a]	Resistant (%)
1984	37	100	0
1985	57	100	0
1986	73	90	10
1987	112	13	87

[a] Schizont development inhibited at concentration greater or equal to 80 nmol/L.

Table 9.5. *Perinatal mortality rates by area and period, Saradidi*

Area	Pre-intervention[a]		During intervention[b]		Post-intervention[c]	
	No.	Rate	No.	Rate	No.	Rate
A	46	60.4	79	87.6	82	71.1
B	40	81.3	45	79.5	49	78.8
C	49	76.8	73	97.2	82	94.3
All areas	135	71.2	197	88.8	213	80.5

[a] Pre-intervention: 1 May 1981–30 Apr. 1982.
[b] During intervention: 1 Sept. 1982–31 Aug. 1983.
[c] Post-intervention: 1 Sept. 1985–31 Aug. 1986.

among schoolchildren in Saradidi with 32 per cent of infections resistant to chloroquine in 1987. *In vitro* resistance in western Kenya appears to have increased significantly in 1987. These findings will have implications for mortality in this community which should be anticipated and an appropriate intervention should be undertaken.

(c) Results of Study (3)

Vital rates. Crude death rates were 13.1 per thousand in the year before intervention (May 1981 to April 1982) and 12.3 during intervention (September 1982 to August 1983). The neonatal mortality rate increased from 36.8 per 1,000 live births pre-intervention to 49.1 during intervention. This could be a result of improved reporting. There was a slight decline in post-neonatal (1–12 months) mortality (72.8 to 67.0 and 70.1 per thousand) and a significant drop in early childhood mortality (25.2 to 18.2) during the intervention period. Measles accounted for 35.7 per cent of the reported deaths in infants 1 to 12 months of age and for 40.9 per cent of deaths in children 1 to 4 years old. Table 9.5 summarizes information on the perinatal mortality rate, which has remained consistently high during the study period. This may reflect, in part, the failure of community health workers to provide pregnant women with adequate chemoprophylactic drugs. Infant mortality, however, dropped steadily during the drugs intervention period, and remained low after. There was no obvious impact on mortality rates attributed to the drugs-based malaria control activities as these rates did not differ significantly in the three areas A, B, and C (see Table 9.6). One of the surveys in the area showed that persons thought to be too ill were generally not taken to the community health workers but to other sources, the reason being that the workers had only one type of drug.

There was little change in reported malaria-specific mortality rates in infants and young children. Both pre-intervention and during intervention infants were significantly more likely to have died without medical consultation than children aged 1 to 4 years. However, 79.2 per cent of 284 infants and 90.7 per cent of 193 children died in spite of having consulted a health worker prior to death.

The fact that the infants and young children died in spite of receiving medical attention indicates both the inadequacy of curative medical services in this high mortality setting, and the necessity of promoting preventive health measures. The reports of the community health workers on chloroquine distribution show that utilization among some of the high-risk groups, such as children, was not as high as expected.

The study shows that to affect mortality in an area such as Saradidi, an integrated comprehensive approach will achieve the best results. The major killers, measles, diarrhoea and vomiting, acute respiratory infections,

Table 9.6. *Infant mortality rate by area and period, Saradidi*

Area	Pre-intervention		During intervention		Post-intervention	
	No.	Rate[a]	No.	Rate[a]	No.	Rate[a]
A	128	168	104	115	115	99.7
B	79	160.6	52	91.9	66	106.3
C	101	158	78	103.9	96	110.1
All areas	308	162.5	234	105.5	277	104.6

[a] IMR = No. of deaths of children under the age of 1 year during the period per 1,000 live births in the same period.

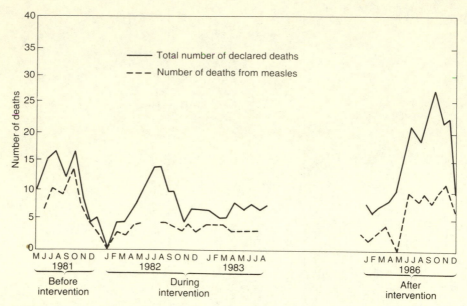

Figure 9.1. *Evolution of the total number of deaths and deaths from measles in Saradidi, Kenya*

malaria, and malnutrition, are all interrelated. Intervening against only one will not have much effect. The integrated primary health care intervention brought down the mortality rate in all the three areas and the additional intervention by chemotherapy at the village level by community health workers failed to significantly lower mortality.

Use of chemoprophylaxis by pregnant women. Only 29 per cent of 357 pregnant women seen in antenatal clinics from 1983 to 1984 were on chemoprophylaxis (see Table 9.7). One hundred and seven pregnant women from 22 villages were interviewed in June 1984 to determine the reasons for not using antimalarial drugs. For the 92 women who had been pregnant before, the last pregnancy had resulted in a live birth for 81 women (88 per cent), a still birth for nine (10 per cent) and a miscarriage for two; 15 women had one still birth or miscarriage at some time, five twice, and one woman four times. Malaria was the most frequently mentioned cause of the last still birth or miscarriage (see Table 9.8). The major reason for not using chemoprophylaxis was lack of awareness that the service was available (see Table 9.9).

The results suggest that the Saradidi programme has not been effective in providing malaria chemoprophylaxis to pregnant women even though malaria is perceived as an important cause of abortions and still births.

Table 9.7. *Proportion of pregnant women from Area A taking malaria chemoprophylaxis by age, Saradidi, 1983–1984*

Age in years	Number of women	% taking chemoprophylaxis
Less than 20	127	16.5
20–29	144	32.6
30–39	75	45.3
40 and more	7	28.6
Unknown	4	0
Total	357	29.1

Note: χ square = 19.1, df = 2, $p < 0.0005$.
 (Computation excludes those of unknown ages, and includes women 40 and above with those 30–39.)

Table 9.8. *Event preceding last non-live birth in 21 pregnant women with a history of previous still birth or abortion, Saradidi, 1984*

Event	Number of women
Malaria	6
Pain then bleeding	5
Fever and headache	2
Fatigue or accident	2
Other or no symptoms	4
Did not recall	2

Table 9.9. *Reasons given by 107 pregnant women for not receiving malaria chemoprophylaxis from community health workers, Saradidi, 1984*

Reason	% of women
Unaware of service	53.3
Chloroquine causes itching	10.3
CHW had no drug	8.4
CHW had not advised her to take	8.4
Not sick	7.5
'Lazy'	6.5
Not prescribed by clinic so afraid to 'mix' medicines	3.7
Chloroquine bad for pregnancy	1.9

Most pregnant women interviewed were not taking chloroquine for logistical or organizational reasons. The responses elicited suggested problems in training and communication. Asking community health workers to give malaria chemoprophylaxis to pregnant women in addition to their other responsibilities was perhaps too difficult for many of them. Providing chemoprophylaxis in antenatal clinics may be more effective. This is being investigated at the moment.

Use of chloroquine for treatment.   In May 1982, a community-based malaria control programme was initiated in 36 villages in Saradidi. Treatment of malaria was provided free of charge in each village by the volunteer. Previous surveys done in the area had identified the major sources of medicine for malaria to be shops, Ministry of Health facilities (two dispensaries), and a missionary hospital. Since the pattern of utilization of treatment in the village would determine the effect on health, it was important to know if people were in fact obtaining treatment from the community health workers or were continuing to use alternative sources.

In June 1983, ten of the then 36 villages were randomly chosen; from these ten villages, 100 households were randomly selected and 222 people 10 years of age or more were interviewed. The situation was as follows: 113 (50.9 per cent) had a history of malaria in the previous two weeks and 82 (72.6 per cent) of these 113 had taken medicine for malaria during that period. Of these 82, 51.2 per cent had obtained the drug from community health workers, 28 per cent had purchased it from a shop, 12.2 per cent from a health facility, 4.9 per cent from family members, and 3.7 per cent from a private practitioner or a shop outside Saradidi. Reasons given for not obtaining treatment from the community health worker were that he was not at home when needed (35 per cent); he had no drugs in the home; he was 'no good' (7.5 per cent); and that it was more 'convenient' to go elsewhere (5 per cent). Similar results were obtained from mothers for 103 children aged 0 to 9 years in these households; 67 (65.0 per cent) children had a history of malaria ·in the previous two weeks and 59 of these 67 children had received antimalarial treatment. The community health worker was the principal source of treatment (50.8 per cent of 59); the major reasons for not obtaining treatment from the CHW was that the CHW was not at home (23.3 per cent of 30), the CHW had no drug (13.3 per cent), or the patient was too sick (20 per cent). It is clear that the community-based programme was the main source of antimalarial treatment in Saradidi. Drug consumption was high in both adults and children, perhaps because the survey was done during the season of peak malaria transmission. The main reason for failure to obtain treatment from the community health worker were logistical or organizational.

Another survey was carried out in December 1986 and January 1987 (i.e. the post-intervention period) to determine the sources of antimalarial drugs and what was felt to be the best source of such drugs. People obtained these from mission or government clinics (29 per cent), the Saradidi clinic (27 per cent), community health workers (24 per cent), and local shops (7 per cent). So the project set-up (community health workers and clinic) provided nearly 50 per cent of the antimalarials. Local shops had gone far down as a source of drugs, even when free antimalarials were no longer provided at the village level.

The best sources of medicine for malaria were felt to be the Saradidi clinic (33 per cent), missions or government clinics (31 per cent), and community health workers (23 per cent). Once again the project set-up was the best source for 56 per cent of the people.

The community determined where to go on the basis of the quality of the source in its effectiveness in treating malaria (40 per cent), distance (33 per cent), and cost (5 per cent).

Effect on parasitaemia and parasite levels. To determine the effects of chloroquine phosphate (300 mg. base weekly), chemoprophylaxis for malaria provided by volunteer village health workers to pregnant women attending antenatal clinics in Saradidi, was examined each month. Parasitaemia, haemoglobin levels, and the presence of urinary 4-aminoquinolines were determined at each visit. The age composition and parity of women taking chemoprophylaxis were not significantly different from those of the other women.

A total of 104 (20.1 per cent) of 357 pregnant women from 23 villages where chemoprophylaxis was provided by community health workers said they were taking it. Women 30 to 44 years of age (43.9 per cent of 82) were more often taking prophylaxis than younger women (25.1 per cent of 271) ($p < .0005$).

An additional 573 pregnant women to whom regular chemoprophylaxis was not provided from 33 control villages were also examined at least once. When compared with those from women not taking prophylaxis, blood samples from pregnant women on antimalarial prophylaxis had lower parasite rates (17.7 per cent of 265 compared with 26.2 per cent of 17,000, $p < .0005$), higher haemoglobin levels (59.1 per cent of 127 were > 10.0 g./1 compared with 49.7 per cent of 1,111, $p < .05$), and higher mean haemoglobin level (9.95 g./100 ml. compared with 9.62, $p < .019$), and urine samples were more often positive 4-aminoquinolines (15.7 per cent of 255 compared with 8.3 per cent of 1,656, $p < .0005$). For women with two or more parasitologic samples, 69.6 per cent of 79 pregnant women on prophylaxis had no parasites found on any visit compared with 51.6 per cent of 516 women not on chemoprophylaxis ($p < .005$) (see Tables 9.10 and 9.11).

Parasitaemia rates in samples from 317 infants were high (37.3 per cent of 1,047). Infection was present in 2.3 per cent of 43 samples from infants less

Table 9.10. *Relationship of anti-malarial chemoprophylaxis and proportion of pregnant women with 2 or more parasitologic samples where all samples were negative for parasites, Saradidi, 1983–1984*

	Number of women with 2 or more parasitologic samples	% of women with all samples negative
Chemoprophylaxis	79	69.6
No chemoprophylaxis	516	51.6

Note: χ square = 10.66, df = 1, $p < 0.005$.

Table 9.11. *Relationship between haemoglobin level and anti-malarial chemoprophylaxis in pregnant women, Saradidi, 1983–1984*

Haemoglobin level (grams/100ml.)	Yes (%)	No (%)
5 to 7.4	0.8	6.0
7.5 to 9.9	40.2	44.3
10.0 to 13.5	59.1	49.7
Total number samples	127	1111

Note: χ square = 6.730, df = 2, $p < 0.05$.

than 1 month old and by 4 months of age, 49.3 per cent of 135 samples were positive. Although samples from infants whose mothers said they were taking chemoprophylaxis had a lower prevalence of parasitaemia (32.6 per cent of 190) than those from the other infants (38.4 per cent of 857), the difference was not statistically significant.

Community-based delivery of antimalarial chemoprophylaxis by Community Health Workers appeared to be successful in reducing parasitaemia and increasing haemoglobin levels, but antenatal clinics may be a better way of providing chemoprophylaxis to pregnant women. The additional responsibility may be too much for Community Health Workers. At the clinic, chemoprophylaxis can be presented as part of comprehensive antenatal care. After delivery, care can then be extended to the infant.

A study using the antenatal clinic to provide chemoprophylaxis is currently being done. There is evidence to support the belief that this is a better way of providing and ensuring compliance. Preliminary results among the primigravidae also indicate that the health of the mother and the outcome of the pregnancy are greatly improved by this method.

Chloroquine phosphate was made available in Saradidi both for chemo-therapy and chemoprophylaxis. Utilization rates for chemotherapy were high, especially among women of child-bearing ages. This in turn led to relatively low utilization among children under 5 years of age, who should have used more.

The community also proved that it was able to diagnose malaria quite accurately and seek treatment for it. The Saradidi community has demon-strated that community-based chemotherapy can work, that the Community Health Workers can diagnose malaria, dispense chloroquine, and keep records properly.

Through the community-based system, treatment is within easy reach especially for children. However, the process of malaria as a disease in a child is so rapid that an intervention based on chemotherapy alone does not seem to reduce that mortality which is directly attributed to malaria. This could be due to the fact that when patients are seriously ill, they do not usually go to the community health worker, and this lengthens the time before they receive treatment. For these reasons we were unable to show in Saradidi that chemotherapy through the community health workers would reduce mortality, as mortality declines were experienced in all three areas A, B, and C.

7. The Scale of Malaria Mortality

There are three main ways of attempting to measure mortality due to a disease such as malaria; from clinical records as to the cause of death, from observing the rise in mortality during malaria epidemics and determining the fall in mortality when malaria is brought under control, and by attempting a verbal autopsy following deaths in a study population. Molineaux (1985) has reviewed some examples of consequences of malaria mortality which involved calculating the mortality necessary to maintain the observed level of the sickling gene in a balanced polymorphism.

The scarcity of post-mortem series means that what is usually viewed as the best possible source of accurate data is not useful for assessing malarial mortality in Africa. Clinical records of cause of death are equally unsatis-factory in most of Africa as most people die outside the hospitals. Add to this the scarcity of laboratory facilities in many peripheral care centres (meaning that most diagnoses of malaria are not definitive) and then hos-pital data and even death certificates become poor guides to malaria prob-lems in the community. Nevertheless, it is the case that malaria is the commonest cause of admission and of death in children under 5 years of age in most of tropical Africa. Perhaps the most informative picture for Kenya comes by comparing the mortality rates of the least and most malarious districts. The most malarious districts have much higher mortality rates than

Table 9.12. *Reduction of infant mortality in various studies in Africa*

Study Area	Infant mortality rate	
	Before intervention	At end of intervention
Kisumu (Kenya)	157	93
Saradidi (Kenya)	162.5	106
Garki (Nigeria)	255	76

the least malarious ones. The mortality rate under 2 years in the highly malarious districts was found to be consistently double that seen in less malarious districts, even when other factors such as the mothers' education were taken into account.

The best African data on malarial mortality derive from local field research projects that have attempted to stop malaria transmissions, usually by means of residual insecticides combined with chemotherapy and chemoprophylaxis (see Table 9.12). Of particular interest are the Kisumu Fenitrothion Project, 1973 to 1976, and the Garki Project, 1971 to 1974. The Kisumu study in western Kenya used Fenitrothion to achieve a 96 per cent reduction in malaria transmission. This was accompanied by a fall in the infant mortality rate, from 157 to 93 per thousand. The malaria effect was greatest between 3 and 10 months of age.

The second study was in the Garki area of northern Nigeria between 1971 and 1973, with extremely intense seasonal malaria transmission (Molineaux and Gramiccia, 1980). Intervention was by residual insecticide spraying with propoxur, backed up by mass drug administration for part of the area, which had a very substantial effect in reducing transmission. Infants were not given drugs unless and until they were found to be infected. The most dramatic finding was a large fall in the infant mortality rate from 255 to 76 per thousand. Comparable unprotected villages had an infant mortality rate greater by 80 and 90 points during the two intervention years. The death rate of children aged 1–4 years was less than half that in unprotected villages, as was the crude death rate. Moreover, in the absence of protection there was a close seasonal parallel between the infant mortality rate and the rate of conversion of infants to parasite positivity, with the infant mortality rate about 10 per cent of this measure of incidence. Under protection, the infant mortality rate both fell and lost its seasonal peaks.

In Senegal, the first of three chemotherapy/chemoprophylaxis trials (Garenne et al., 1985) showed a marked fall in the mortality of those aged 6 to 35 months, which was halved, but no effect on older or younger children. Moreover, there was a large fall in the diagnosis 'fever and malaria' in the stated causes of death. As this was rather precisely matched by a rise in the 'miscellaneous or not known' category, Carnevale and Vaugelade (1987) have some doubts about this interpretation.

Subsequent studies in the Congo at Kinkala, and in Bobo-Dioulasso (Burkina Faso) by Baudon *et al.* (1984) showed very little effect of intense chemoprophylaxis and chemotherapy upon mortality. This was also our own finding in Saradidi, where community-based chemotherapy did not seem to have an added effect on mortality as there was no significant difference between villages with and villages without community-based chemotherapy.

Molineaux (1985), in an exceptionally careful and imaginative analysis of the data on malaria mortality, confronts two problems. The first is the much greater reduction in mortality observed after malaria control operations than the fall in deaths ascribed specifically to malaria would suggest. The reason for this has not been fully worked out. Even in Kisumu, where malaria is holoendemic, the crude death rate after insecticide spraying fell more than could he accounted for by infant and early childhood mortality decreases. Experimental work on interaction of other infections with malaria in laboratory animals is consistent with a synergistic effect on mortality under some circumstances. The scale of this has not been precisely assessed although the data available suggest its relevance.

A converse effect appears to prevail in two West African studies, where the removal or massive reduction in deaths from malaria has led to a much smaller fall than expected in infant and young child mortality. This was seen in Garki, Nigeria, where malaria control removed the seasonal peaks of malaria deaths but mortality remained high overall, and in the Gambia, when a measles epidemic shifted the peak season of infant mortality from malaria without massive effects on total mortality. The possible hypothesis to explain these results is that of competing risks: a certain number of children are postulated as likely to die anyway, possibly with low birthweights and for other ultimate reasons, and the immediate cause of death may be malaria if present, and some other infection if malaria is absent. Malaria, measles, and diarrhoea and vomiting are sufficient causes and only one of them is necessary. Thus deaths averted by malaria control are not equal in number to deaths due to malaria.

The studies are all compatible with the incidence of heavy infant and childhood mortality in areas of uncontrolled holoendemic malaria, greatly reduced by control of the transmission of malaria while access to chemotherapy through Community Health Workers alone does not seem sufficient to cause significant mortality decline.

The control of transmission such as was undertaken in Kisumu (Kenya) and Garki (Nigeria) was found to be too expensive and complicated for most African governments to run on an ongoing basis indefinitely. For this reason, the only feasible approach to malaria control is chemotherapy and selective chemoprophylaxis within a comprehensive integrated primary health care programme. Technical back-up should be a necessary part of this approach.

References

Axtell, R. F. (1979), 'Principles of integrated pest management (IPM)', *Mosquito News* 39: 709–18.

Baudon, D., Roux, J., Carnevale, P., Vaugelade, J., Boudin, Ch., Chaize, J., Rey, J. L., Meyran, M. B., and Brandicourt, O. (1984), 'Étude de deux stratégies de contrôle des paludismes, la chimiothérapie systématique des accès fébriles et la chimioprophylaxie hebdomadaire dans 12 villages de Haute-Volta, en zone de savane et zone rizicole de 1980 à 1982', Document technique OCCGE, Organisation de Coordination et de Coopération pour la Lutte contre les Grandes Endémies, no. 8450.

Carnevale, P. and Vaugelade, J. (1987), 'Paludisme, morbidité palustre et mortalité infantile et juvénile en Afrique sub-Saharienne', WHO/MAL/87.1036.

Celli, A. (1900), *Die Malaria nach den neuesten Forschungen*, Urban and Schwarzenbierg, Berlin and Vienna.

Fontaine, R. E. (1985), 'Integrated vector control and selection measures suitable for specific epidemiological conditions', unpublished paper presented at a WHO informal consultation on stratification for planning antimalaria action, Moscow, 3–7 June.

—— (1987), 'Integrated vector control and selection of measures suitable for specific epidemiological conditions', WHO/MAL/87.1034.

—— Pill, J., Payne, D., Pradhan, G. D., Joshi, G., and Pearson, J. A. (1976), 'Evaluation of fenitrothione (OM 543) for malaria control in a large-scale epidemiological trial, Kisumu', WHO/VBC/76.645.

Garenne, M., Cantrelle, P., and Diop, I. L. (1985), 'Le Cas du Sénégal (1960–80)', in J. Vallin and A. Lopez (eds.), *La Lutte contre la mort*, Travaux et documents 108, INED–PUF, Paris, 307–30.

Gill, G. (1938), *The Seasonal Periodicity of Malaria and Mechanism of the Epidemic Wave*, J. and A. Churchill, London.

Kaseje, D. C. O., Sempebwa, E. K. N., and Spencer, H. C. (1987a), 'Malaria chemoprophylaxis to pregnant women by community health workers in Saradidi, Kenya', *Annals of Tropical Medicine and Parasitology* 81, supplement 1.

—— —— —— (1987b), 'Usage of community-based chloroquine treatment for malaria in Saradidi, Kenya', *Annals of Tropical Medicine and Parasitology* 81, supplement 1.

Kliger, I. J. (1930), *The Epidemiology and Control of Malaria in Palestine*, University of Chicago Press, Chicago.

Koznetsov, R. L., Molineaux, L., and Beales, P. F. (1986), 'Stratification of malaria situations in tropical Africa for the development of malaria control within primary health care strategy', WHO/MAL/86.1028.

Laird, M. and Miles, J. W. (1983), *Integrated Mosquito Control Methodologies 1*, Academic Press, New York.

Lysenko, A. Y. (1983), 'Malariological stratifications: Its principles, methods, and practical application', in *Malaria Control by Ecologically Safe Methods: Collection of Teaching Aids for International Training Course*, vol. 1, Centre of International Projections, Moscow, 48–60.

Macdonald, G. (1957), *The Epidemiology and Control of Malaria*, Oxford University Press, London.

Mburu, F. M., Spencer, H. C., and Kaseje, D. C. O. (1987), 'Changes in sources of treatment occurring after inception of a community-based malaria control program in Saradidi, Kenya', *Annals of Tropical Medicine and Parasitology* 81, supplement 1.

Molineaux, L. (1985), 'La Lutte contre les maladies parasitaires: Le Problème du paludisme, notamment en Afrique', in J. Vallin and A. Lopez (eds.), *La Lutte contre la mort*, Travaux et documents 108, INED–PUF, Paris, 111–40.

—— and Gramiccia, G. (1980), *The Garki Project: Research on the Epidemiology and Control of Malaria in the Sudan Savanna of West Africa*, WHO, Geneva.

Olsen, J. K. (1979), 'Application of the concept of integrated pest management (IPM) to mosquito control programmes', *Mosquito News* 39: 718–23.

Onori, E. (1984), 'The problem of *Plasmodium falciparum* drug resistance in Africa south of the Sahara', *Bulletin of the World Health Organization* 62, supplement, 55–62.

Russell, P. F., West, L. S., and Manwell, R. D. (1963), *Practical Malariology*, 2nd edn., Oxford University Press, London.

Spencer, H. C., Kaseje, D. C. O., Roberts, J. M., and Huong, A. Y. (1987a), 'Consumption of chloroquine phosphate provided for treatment of malaria by volunteer village health workers in Saradidi, Kenya', *Annals of Tropical Medicine and Parasitology* 81, supplement 1.

—— —— Sempebwa, E. K. N., Huong, A. Y., and Roberts, J. M. (1987b), 'Malaria chemoprophylaxis to pregnant women by community health workers in Saradidi, Kenya', *Annals of Tropical Medicine and Parasitology* 81, supplement 1.

Survey Division (1956a), *Atlas of Kenya*, 1st edn., Malaria map 1:3,000,000, Department of Lands and Surveys, Nairobi.

—— (1956b), *Atlas of Tanganyika, East Africa*, 3rd edn., Malaria map 1:3,000,000, Department of Lands and Surveys, Dar es Salaam.

WHO (1951), Malaria conference in equatorial Africa (Kampala, Uganda, 1950), *Technical Report series* 38: 63.

—— (1969), *Twenty-Second World Health Assembly*, Part 1, Resolutions and decisions, WHO Official Records 176.

—— (1979), *Technical Report Series* 640.

—— (1984), *Statistical Quarterly* 37: 130.

10 Mortality Differences in Childhood by Sex in Sub-Saharan Africa

Kuakuvi Gbenyon and Thérèse Locoh
Unité de Recherche Démographique, Lomé, and Institut National d'Études Démographiques, Paris

1. Introduction

Equality in rights and opportunities for men and women has become a theme of speeches and a primary objective in today's world. Meanwhile, death arbitrarily denies this legitimate aspiration and continues to discriminate against the stronger sex.

As duration of life has increased in the countries with the greatest health improvements, the inequalities in life expectancy between men and women have persisted or increased (Vallin, 1983). These privileged countries had in the past not only an excess maternal mortality linked to the risks of pregnancies and childbirth, but also an excess female mortality in childhood due to the differential attitudes of parents towards their young children. Tabutin (1978) has shown, for example, that France had higher female mortality between the ages of 5 and 14 until around 1930, probably on account of less concern for the care of sick girls. In all countries where a secular decline of mortality has occurred, however, the trend has been accompanied by an increase in the sex ratio of child deaths. It would seem that girls have benefited more than boys from the gains achieved.

In high mortality countries, particularly in the Near and Middle East, recent studies have extensively documented the existence of excess female mortality in childhood as a reflection of the discriminatory attitude of parents towards girls. This discrimination has been observed in the countries of the Indian subcontinent, particularly in Bangladesh (Chen *et al.*, 1981) and India (Das Gupta, 1987). In rural Bangladesh (Matlab Project), the mortality of girls between 1 and 5 is more than 50 per cent higher than that of boys. This is apparently linked to the uneven distribution of food and the unequal care given to sick children. In diarrhoea cases, the use of health centres is 66 per cent higher for male children, even though the incidence of diarrhoea is nearly identical for both sexes.

In several Muslim countries of the Mediterranean periphery where the preference for boys is a very pronounced cultural norm, excess female mortality in childhood is also observed (Suchindran and Adlakha, 1985; Haffad, 1984; Vallin, 1983). According to the World Fertility Survey, significant mortality differences between the sexes occur from 1 to 5 in Egypt, and to a lesser degree in Tunisia, Syria, and Turkey. In Algeria, Vallin (1983) has found evidence of excess female mortality from the third month of life into adulthood.

What about sub-Saharan Africa? The fight against death in childhood has made marked progress in the last twenty years, as indicated by the World Fertility Surveys, but mortality remains at a very high level, especially in the poorer regions. Islam is widespread in certain countries, particularly in West Africa, and a relative inferiority of the status of women is obvious in a number of countries. Does infant mortality reveal the impact of gender inequality, and what accounts for it?

2. Available Data on Sex Differences in Mortality

When measuring demographic phenomena in Africa, it is always necessary to think about the reliability of the data. In our investigation of differences in mortality by sex, we shall use a widely available index: the ratio between male and female mortality rates, often improperly called 'the sex ratio of deaths' (Akoto, 1985; Haffad, 1984). We shall essentially use two indices: SRI, the ratio between male and female infant mortality rates ($_1q_0$), and SRC, the ratio between child mortality rates (i.e. between 1 and 4 years, $_4q_1$). These indices, which we will call the sex ratios of death rates, are defined as follows:

$$\text{SRI} = (_1q_0{}^M/_1q_0{}^F)\ 100$$
$$\text{SRC} = (_4q_1{}^M/_4q_1{}^F)\ 100.$$

The rates at these ages are available for a fairly large number of countries. In the last ten years, World Fertility Surveys (taken in 10 countries of sub-Saharan Africa) have markedly increased our knowledge of mortality trends between the ages 0 and 5. Data about ages 5 to 15 are less often available, and are derived from relatively less reliable census data. It is therefore essentially on ages 0 to 4 that we have been able to collect usable data. We have limited ourselves to the period 1969–83. As a result, we cannot cover all the countries of sub-Saharan Africa, and West Africa is better represented than the other sub-regions.

The data can be grouped according to the way they were collected. Those in the first categories cover whole countries, but suffer from the imprecision inherent in censuses and national surveys. The other types—urban surveys and surveys in rural areas—give more localized information but with a much narrower margin of error. We have thus distinguished three groups of data sources.

(*a*) **Census and national surveys**

Most of the results from censuses have been obtained by adjusting the reported information with the help of model life tables (Brass African standard table, model tables from Coale and Demeny). We have used only those censuses where the computations could be made separately by sex. We have also included in this group data from ten World Fertility Surveys in sub-Saharan Africa, as they give estimates of infant and child mortality at the national level (Table 10.1(*a*)).

(*b*) **Urban statistics**

Most of these are recent and have been collected in a few capitals either through vital registration (Abidjan) or from registers of burial permits in the cities where special regulations ensure a good coverage of deaths (Bamako and Brazzaville). These sources give relatively accurate information on the recent levels and trends of childhood mortality (Fargues, 1986; Fargues and Nassour, 1988; Antoine and Herry, 1984; Duboz, 1984) (Table 10.1(*b*)).

(*c*) **Rural surveys**

A few 'population laboratories' provide the third category of data. These are often of remarkable quality because of the quasi-continuous methods of observation that have been used. This is the case in the surveys of Senegal (Garenne, 1981; Pison and Langaney, 1985), the Mossi region in Burkina Faso (Livenais, 1984), and the Dayes plateau of Togo (Vimard, 1984) (Table 10.1(*c*)). The Malian survey cited in Table 10.1(*c*) (Hill, 1986) is of a different type: a one-round survey that collected maternity histories.

Before we can use the results obtained from these three sources, we must ask whether the collection of data on the deaths does not suffer from a systematic bias. If, for one reason or another, there is under-reporting of deaths of either sex, then all comparisons of mortality between males and females will be distorted. Several authors have raised this issue. Morah (1985) estimates that there may be an under-reporting of the less valued sex in Nigeria (and therefore an under-reporting of female deaths). On the other hand, Sombo (1985) suspects an under-reporting of male deaths in the Ivory Coast on the basis of the World Fertility Survey,. The sex ratios of births declared by mothers, classified by number of years elapsed since the birth, do not seem to indicate any differential under-reporting of females, which would essentially be an under-reporting of deceased girls (Akoto, 1985). We have therefore not found consistent results confirming the hypothesis of a systematic bias in the reporting of deaths according to sex. In spite of certain irregularities in the series of observed sex ratios, there is no evidence of an increase in the under-reporting of female deaths as a function of the age of the mothers, except in Mauritania (Table 10.2).

Table 10.1. (a) *Mortality under 5 years by sex in sub-Saharan Africa: $1q_0$ and $4q_1$ per 1,000, and ratios SRI and SRC, data from censuses and national surveys*

Country	Source and date	$1q_0$			$4q_1$			Reference
		Males	Females	SRI	Males	Females	SRC	
North Africa								
Sudan (North)	WFS 1979	84	75	112	70	78	97	Rutstein, 1983–4
West Africa								
Benin	WFS 1981–2	118	97	122	110	107	103	Rutstein, 1983–4
Gambia	Census, 1973	230	204	113	172	143	120	
Ghana	Census, 1971	130	111	117	65	58	112	Singh et al., 1985
Ivory Coast	WFS 1981–2	126	99	128	71	62	115	Rutstein, 1983–4
	Survey, 1978–9	161	126	128	90	89	101	Antoine and Herry, 1984
Liberia	Census, 1970	149	135	110	69	70	98	United Nations, 1980
Mali	Census, 1976	130	111	117	158	149	106	Akoto, 1985
Mauritania	WFS 1981–2	98	82	120	112	120	93	Rutstein, 1983–4
Nigeria	WFS 1980–2	99	81	123	79	89	89	Rutstein, 1983–4
Senegal	WFS 1978	120	103	116	175	164	107	Rutstein, 1983–4
Togo	Census, 1970–1	97	87	111	149	137	109	Gbenyon, 1985
East Africa								
Kenya	WFS 1977–8	89	84	106	60	61	98	Rutstein, 1983–4
	Census, 1979	89	81	110	96	96	100	Ewbank et al., 1986
Malawi	Census, 1977	190	162	117	149	143	104	Malawi, 1984
Mozambique	Census, 1970	177	168	105	98	110	89	Akoto, 1985
Rwanda	Survey, 1983	107	96	112	101	109	93	Rwanda, 1983
	Census, 1970	135	120	112	139	157	92	
Zambia	Census, 1980	100	94	106	75	69	109	Zambia, 1980
Zimbabwe	Census, 1982	102	91	112	117	100	117	
Central Africa								
Cameroon	Census, 1976	146	116	126	78	79	99	Akoto, 1985
	WFS, 1978	115	96	120	96	104	92	Rutstein, 1983–4
South Africa								
RSA, Bantus	Census, 1970	165	147	112	61	59	101	Akoto, 1985
Lesotho	WFS, 1977–8	127	123	106	61	48	126	Rutstein, 1983–4

Table 10.1. (*b*) *Mortality under 5 years by sex in sub-Saharan Africa:* $1q_0$ *and* $4q_1$ *per 1,000, and ratios SRI and SRC, data from urban surveys*

Country	Source and date	$1q_0$			$4q_1$			Reference
		Males	Females	SRI	Males	Females	SRC	
West Africa								
Ivory Coast								
Abidjan	Multiround survey, 1978–9							
	Direct estimate	93	75	124	67	68	98	Antoine and Herry, 1984
	Indirect estimate	102	93	110	93	95	98	Antoine and Herry, 1984
Abidjan	Vital registration							
	1974–8	65	56	116	49	50	98	Fargues, 1986
	1979–83	43	33	130	26	25	104	Fargues, 1986
Mali								
Bamako	Service of Hygiene 1974–85	83	91	91	75	91	83	Fargues and Nassour, 1988
Togo								
Lomé	Survey, 1974–83	48	30	160	54	52	104	Non-published data
	Survey, 1979–80	44	34	129	—	—	—	Togo, 1986
Senegal								
Dakar-Pikine	Survey, 1986	68	49	133	68	70	97	Antoine and Diouf, 1986
Central Africa								
Cameroon								
Yaoundé	Survey, 1978–9	54	56	97	—	—	—	Ngatchou, 1987
Congo								
Brazzaville	Vital registration, 1974–5	65	63	103	66	68	97	Duboz, 1984

Table 10.1. (c) *Mortality under 5 years by sex in sub-Saharan Africa: $1q_0$ and $4q_1$ per 1,000, and ratios SRI and SRC, data from rural surveys*

Country	Area and date	$1q_0$ Males	$1q_0$ Females	SRI	$4q_1$ Males	$4q_1$ Females	SRC	Reference
Burkina Faso	Kongoussi, 1954–74	127	117	108	147	154	95	Livenais, 1984
Gambia	Keneba, 1951–75	251	246	102	104	107	97	Billewicz and McGregor, 1981
	Farafeni, 1981	157	127	124	48	38	126	Greenwood et al., 1987
Kenya	Machakos, 1975–8	53	50	106	—	—	—	van Ginneken and Muller, 1984
Mali	Fulani, Seno-Mango, 1981–2	152	150	101	187	219	79	Hill, 1985
	Delta	237	206	115	356	355	100	Hill, 1985
Senegal	Ngayokheme, 1963–73	228	202	113	339	319	106	Garenne, 1981
	Bandafassi, 1970–83	211	207	102	261	275	95	Pison and Langaney, 185
Togo	Dayes, 1965–9	69	68	101	47	45	104	Vimard, 1984

Table 10.2. *Sex ratio at birth according to age of mothers at survey, selected countries*

Age	Total	Cameroon, WFS 1978		Ivory Coast, WFS 1981–2	Lesotho, WFS 1978	Mauritania, WFS 1981–2	Rwanda Survey 1983	N. Sudan, WFS 1979	Zambia Census 1982	Zimbabwe Census 1982
		Rural	Urban							
15–19	108	108	100	—	105	—	104	114	103	103
20–24	105	103	109	107	103	116	98	111	101	100
25–29	103	102	105	105	103	104	93	105	101	100
30–34	105	105	104	102	103	102	110	104	101	101
35–39	104	104	105	98	101	123	102	108	101	101
40–44	102	102	104	87	102	93	102	104	102	104
45–49	106	106	100	92	103	142	103	104	102	104
50–54	102	103	97	—	—	—	—	102	—	102

3. Recent Data on Differential Mortality by Sex

(*a*) Infant mortality

During the first year of life boys almost always have higher mortality than girls. The sex ratio of death rates exceeds 100 in most countries of the world. The distinction between the neonatal (0–30 days) and the post-neonatal (1 month to 1 year) period becomes important. The first days after birth are most unfavourable for boys. Afterwards, the risks are more even, and in some countries where discrimination exists against girls, excess mortality has even been observed from 3 or 4 months onwards. This is the case in Algeria for example (Vallin, 1983). In sub-Saharan Africa, such excess mortality is noted by Fargues and Nassour (1988) for the city of Bamako. This is the only instance where the available data show excess female mortality for the entire first year of life (SRI < 100). The results of World Fertility Surveys in ten African countries and the Rwanda Survey confirm that excess male mortality in the first year is most typical of the neonatal period (Table 10.3). Kenya even exhibits excess female mortality in the post-neonatal period.

Among the nation-wide results (Table 10.1(*a*) and Fig. 10.1), the sex ratio of death rates for the first year of life fluctuates between 100 and 128. There is no obvious way to geographically group the differential mortality indices by level (Fig. 10.2).

Among the statistics for capital cities, those for Bamako, as already noted, are the exception to the rule of excess male mortality. The results for Yaoundé (SRI = 97) were drawn from a sample, and the difference between boys and girls is not statistically significant (Dackam-Ngatchou, 1987).

Table 10.3. *Sex ratio of probabilities of dying before age 1, neonatal and post-neonatal mortality*

Country	Neonatal	Post-neonatal	$_1q_0$
Benin, 1981–2	142	107	122
Cameroon, 1978	136	109	120
Ghana, 1979	142	117	130
Ivory Coast, 1981–2	143	114	128
Nigeria, 1980–2	125	120	123
Mauritania, 1981	118	121	120
Senegal, 1978	137	112	116
Kenya, 1977–8	138	88	106
Lesotho, 1977	104	107	106
Rwanda, 1983	118	116	117
N. Sudan, 1979	110	116	113

Source: Rutstein, 1984, for WFS countries; Rwanda, 1983.

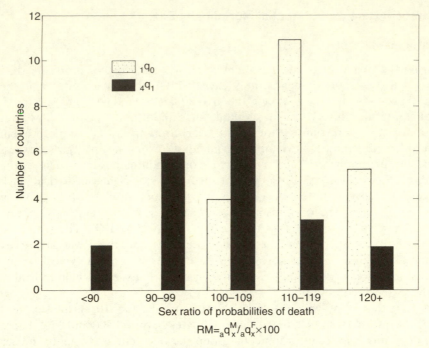

FIG. 10.1. Sex ratios of the probabilities of dying under 1 year and from 1 to 4, twenty countries of sub-Saharan Africa, 1969–1983

The intensive surveys in rural areas often give lower values for the sex ratio of death rates than the national surveys. This suggests that there could be a hidden excess mortality of males after the neonatal period.

(*b*) Child mortality (1 to 4 years)

Certain developing countries that have already been mentioned have excess female mortality at ages 1 to 4. Several writers have traced the excess back to different attitudes of adults toward male and female children (Sombo and Tabutin, 1985; Chen *et al.*, 1981).

This time in the life of African children is characterized by much higher mortality than in other continents; at least, this is the case in West Africa, where several studies have shown that overall child mortality is dominated by the high share of deaths between one and four (Cantrelle, 1980; Garenne, 1981; Pison and Langaney, 1985). Deaths at those ages are mainly due to parasitic and infectious diseases (mostly malaria and diarrhoea), to respiratory infections, and to measles, but these diseases can be aggravated by malnutrition. Although these causes of death are largely dependent on environment conditions, the attitudes of adults who look after children also play an important role: everyday hygiene, child feeding, use of health

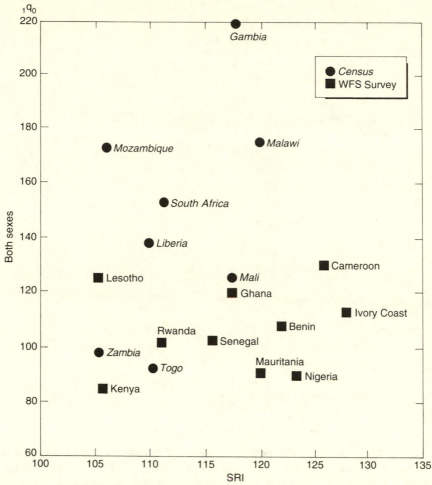

FIG. 10.2. Infant mortality, both sexes together, by the sex ratio SRI of the probabilities of dying, surveys and censuses of sub-Saharan Africa, 1969–1983

centres and hospitals in case of sickness. The results, however, do not lead to an unambiguous conclusion as to variations in practice by sex of the child. What stands out is that, with the exception of Bamako, the mortality differences between boys and girls are mostly absent or insignificant.

It is true that national surveys and censuses indicate that several nations have a sex ratio of the death rate (SRC) below 100. But these results include those for the World Fertility Survey of North Sudan, Mauritania, Nigeria, Kenya, Rwanda,[1] and Cameroon, which were based on samples (Figs. 10.1

[1] Although the 1983 Survey of Rwanda was not, strictly speaking, part of the series of World Fertility Surveys, it was carried out with similar sampling techniques and a similar questionnaire.

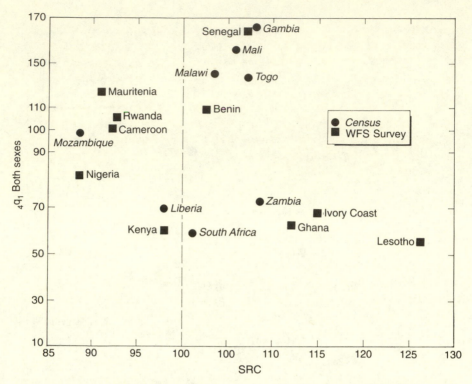

FIG. 10.3. Child mortality, both sexes together, by the sex ratio SRC of the probabilities of dying, surveys and censuses of sub-Saharan Africa, 1969–1983

and 10.3). We tested for the significance of mortality differences; in all cases, the differences were not significant (at the .05 confidence level), either for the time just prior to the survey, or for the preceding 10 to 14 years. For three countries, however, the results of the censuses (1970 for Rwanda, 1976 for Cameroon, and 1979 for Kenya) confirm those of the World Fertility Survey: the SRC index is below or equal to 100, at 92 in Rwanda, 99 in Cameroon, and 100 in Kenya. This leaves Liberia and Mozambique, which had SRC indices below 100 in the 1970 censuses, suggesting excess female mortality.

To summarize the results of the national statistics, we have five countries where at face value, the census indicates a higher mortality of girls from 1 to 4 years, and 15 countries where the differences in mortality by sex are not significant. Excess male mortality disappears almost everywhere after the first year of life.

No geographic grouping by level of the sex ratio of death rates in childhood appears satisfactory. Because the coverage of the available statistics is incomplete, an attempt of this kind is difficult to make. The lowest SRC ratios are found far west (Mauritania, 93), as well as east (Mozambique, 89), and along the Gulf of Benin (Nigeria, 89). The highest SRC ratios, which indicate a more favourable situation for girls, are found in Gambia (120), Ivory Coast (115), and Ghana (112), and also in Zimbabwe (117), Zambia (109), and Lesotho (126).

The urban statistics provide rather surprising results. In these locations where mortality has been drastically lowered, one would expect to find SRC indices of differential mortality revealing a more favourable situation for girls. But the SRC indices are less than 100, except in Abidjan for the period 1979–83 (104) and in Lomé (104). In Abidjan, three sets of results obtained by different methods of data collection and estimation indicate a small excess female mortality between one and four years (Fargues, 1986; Antoine and Herry, 1984). Finally, the statistics from intensive surveys in rural areas, where mortality levels are very high (except in Togo), also give SRC indices close to 100. The SRC index for the Fulani of Seno-Mango is particularly low, but the $_4q_1$ are not significantly different by sex.

Childhood mortality is a particularly substantial part of the overall mortality of sub-Saharan Africa. At that age, mortality risks depend on the environment as well as on parents' attitudes towards nutrition, hygiene, and care of the sick. A review of the available data leads one to conclude that, with certain exceptions, Bamako (1987), Liberia (1970), and Mozambique (1970), there is an absence of significant difference in childhood mortality between boys and girls. This conclusion is the more remarkable because it prevails at the highest as well as at the lowest levels of mortality, in contrast to what has been observed elsewhere.

(c) Mortality between 5 and 10 years

Data on this age group are scarce. Table 10.4 presents a few mortality rates between 5 and 10 ($_5q_5$). For the countries shown, the sex ratio of death rates appears to indicate that females have a better chance of surviving than males, but these results must be used with caution.

4. Mortality Level and Variations in the Sex Ratio of Death Rates: Comparisons between Countries and Between Regions

Rustein (1984) concludes from the results of the World Fertility Survey that the SRI index rises as the level of mortality declines. The relationship is less clear for ages 1 to 4, where female mortality often exceeds male mortality. For sub-Saharan Africa, the 20 available national figures do not permit conclusions that there is any relationship between the level of mortality and the indices of differential mortality. This is apparent from Fig. 10.2 and

Table 10.4. *Probability of dying between 5 and 10 years*

Country	Male $_5q_5$	Female $_5q_5$	Ratio male/female
Ivory Coast			
Abidjan, 1974–8	10.8	9.5	114
Abidjan, 1979–83	8.0	5.7	140
Liberia			
Census, 1971	37	30	123
Malawi			
Census, 1977	62.5	61.6	101
Togo			
Census, 1970–1	66	57	116
Zambia			
Census, 1980	35	32	109

Sources: See Tables 10.1 (*a*) and 10.1 (*b*).

10.3. As far as infant mortality is concerned, classifying the countries in three groups by level of mortality does not bring out any differences in the level of the SRI indices (Table 10.5).

As for child mortality, the average SRC index is lower at an intermediate level of mortality ($_4q_1$ between 80 and 110 per thousand). Here too, excess male mortality is not observed to increase with the decrease of mortality. It is true that none of the countries with the highest mortality (Senegal,

Table 10.5. *Sex ratios of death rates, SRI and SCR, by mortality level, national censuses and surveys*

Mortality level	Average sex ratio	Number of countries
Infant mortality, $_1q_0$		
Less than 100 per 1,000	117	7
100 to 129 per 1,000	117	8
130 per 1,000 or more	114	7
Total	116	22
Child mortality, $_4q_1$		
Less than 80 per 1,000	106	9
80 to 109 per 1,000	99	7
110 per 1,000 or more	104	6
Total	103	22

Table 10.6. *Sex ratio of child mortality rates for selected countries in various types of sources*

Type of source	Ivory Coast	Mali	Senegal	Togo
National surveys				
WFS	115	—	107	—
Multi-round	101	—	—	—
Census	—	106	—	109
Urban sources				
Vital registration	98	83	—	—
	104			
Survey	98	—	97	104
Rural surveys	—	79	106	104
		100	95	

Sources: See Tables 10.1 (*a*), 10.1 (*b*), and 10.1 (*c*).

Gambia, Mali, Malawi, Togo) has high SRC indices, but countries with a child mortality rate of less than 80 per thousand show no systematic relation with SRC indices. The progressive increase of the SRC index which occurs, in general, when mortality levels decline in a country, is not observed when one compares different sub-Saharan African countries at different levels of mortality.

The comparison of data from a few capitals with corresponding national statistics leads to the same conclusion. Three cities (Bamako, Brazzaville, and Yaoundé) do not show that usual excess male mortality before the age of 1 year. Male mortality in Bamako and in Yaoundé is slightly lower than that revealed for Mali and Cameroon by their respective censuses, and this might indicate excess female mortality in the post-neonatal period.

The comparison between the capital and the whole country is most surprising for ages 1 to 4. Contrary to expectations, although the mortality of children is relatively low in the capital, excess male mortality is everywhere less marked than in the whole country. Table 10.6 compares the SRC ratios for the three sources of data which we treat separately: national censuses and surveys, urban statistics, and intensive rural surveys. National data reflect higher excess male mortality than appears either in the capitals or in the rural surveys. Does the fault lie with the quality of national data collection systems, where biases in the reporting of death by sex would give a false advantage to females? Must the quality of urban statistics be questioned?

Most of the urban and rural statistics which we have used have been collected with great care and offer a degree of precision uncommon for sub-

Table 10.7. *Decline in infant and child mortality, by sex, per cent*

(*a*) World fertility surveys

Country, 10–4 to 0–4 yrs. before survey	$_1q_0$		$_4q_1$	
	Males	Females	Males	Females
Benin, 1981–2	25	33	28	20
Cameroon, 1978	11	47	39	11
Ghana, 1979	20	20	37	32
Ivory Coast, 1980–2	43	47	54	67
Kenya, 1977–8	18	15	25	18
Lesotho, 1977	14	20	2	22
Mauritania, 1981–2	−6	−18	−19	−20
Senegal, 1978	9	3	17	16

(*b*) Other sources

Country	Period	$_1q_0$		$_4q_1$	
		Males	Females	Males	Females
Abidjan	1974–8 to 1979–83	34	40	47	50
Bamako	1974 to 1985	33	21	44	41
Dayes	1950–64 to 1965–9	64	28	55	55
Cameroon	1964 to 1976	−4	11	50	43
Kongoussi	1950–4 to 1965–9	60	48	63	67

Sources: See Tables 10.1 (*a*), 10.1 (*b*), and 10 (*c*); for Cameroon, computed from the censuses.

Saharan Africa. And most of them, at the highest (Mali and rural Senegal)[2] as well as at the lowest levels of mortality (Abidjan, Lomé), show no disadvantage for boys; the exceptions suggests slight excess female mortality (Abidjan, Dakar) or a very marked excess (Bamako).

5. Time Trends in Differential Mortality by Sex

In the World Fertility Surveys, it is possible to compare mortality levels for each country at various times prior to the survey. Because of unreliable reporting and forward or backward shift of birth dates, these results must

---

[2] According to the write-up of survey results, the rural surveys, which are mostly multi-round, reflect no difference, or small differences, between boys and girls before the age of 1; the differences are not statistically significant (at the .05 level), at 1 to 4 years.

be examined with caution. The more one goes back in time, the more questionable the quality of the information. We limit ourselves here to trends in the SRI and SRC indices between the period of 10–14 years and of 0–4 years before the survey. The results do not agree for the two age groups that we have considered. In the first year of life, the decline seemed to be faster for females except in Kenya and Senegal (Table 10.7 and Fig. 10.4 (*a*)), whereas between 1 and 4, the gains were more substantial for boys than for girls, except in Lesotho and the Ivory Coast. Mauritania showed an increase in mortality during the period; this deterioration of the situation affected both sexes. In the Sudan (not shown), however, it affected only girls, whose death rate for the first year increased by 13 per cent in ten years, and whose death rate for ages 1 to 4 years increased by 22 per cent. In the meantime, the mortality of boys at the same ages continued to fall.

Several surveys and estimates from the urban vital registration also provide trend data on infant and child mortality by sex. These are shown in Table 10.7. In general the results, which cover a period of about ten years, reflect the same trend as the World Fertility Surveys for 1 to 4-year-olds: a faster decline of male mortality at very different levels of mortality (Figs. 10.4 (*a*) and 10.4 (*b*)). The rapid decrease of mortality in the Ivory Coast, including Abidjan, benefited girls a little more than boys, before as well as after one year of age.

6. Discussion

These observations suggest more questions than firm answers. Of course, it is not surprising that the patterns of differential mortality in childhood are not identical in all countries and regions for which we have statistics. But the levels of infant mortality between countries vary by a factor of three. The recent trends range from Mauritania—where there has been an increase rather than a decrease—to the Ivory Coast where the decrease has been in the order of 50 per cent in ten years. The differential mortality between boys and girls places together two countries as geographically and culturally removed as Mauritania and Mozambique, which are characterized by excess female mortality between ages one and four, or as the Ivory Coast and Zimbabwe, which appear to have excess male mortality at the same ages.

Nevertheless, the analysis of the available data for sub-Saharan Africa and the comparison with other world regions permit us to draw some overall conclusions on the differences in mortality between boys and girls before the age of 5.

1. As in other parts of the world, most of the results attest to the existence of excess male mortality during the first year of life, essentially because of the lower resistance of boys during the neonatal period

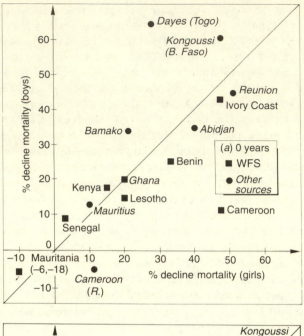

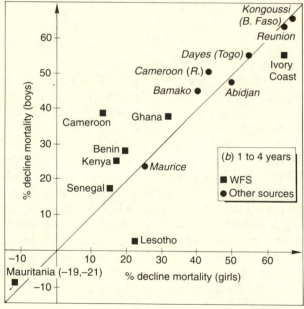

FIG. 10.4. (*a*) Decline in infant mortality by sex, in approximately ten years. (*b*) Decline in child mortality by sex, in approximately ten years

(endogenous mortality). The results for Bamako (Fargues and Nassour, 1988) are an exception to this general rule, and indicate excess female mortality in the post-neonatal period.

2. Among young children (1 to 4-year-olds), there is nowhere in sub-Saharan Africa the high excess female mortality that has been seen in Bangladesh, where the difference reaches 50 per cent (Chen *et al.*, 1981). Most observations, including the most reliable (multi-round surveys), conclude that there are no significant differences in mortality by sex. The exceptions are Bamako and five countries (Cameroon, Liberia, Mozambique, Rwanda, and Kenya) where the census data suggest a certain degree of discrimination against females after infancy.

3. The comparison of mortality levels, both within and between countries, does not reveal a clear tendency in favour of girls in the countries or regions of lower mortality, as is generally observed in other regions of the world. Should we go further and suggest that excess male infant and child mortality (up to age 5) is the biologically 'normal' situation, since it is observed in countries of very low mortality, and that an absence of difference in itself suggests an unfavourable treatment of females? At levels of mortality comparable to those of sub-Saharan Africa, the old life tables available for other regions show that death rates between 1 and 4 were also approximately equal. It is possible that these old tables were also incorporating behavioural factors unfavourable to female children. But on the whole, we believe that the absence of differences in mortality levels in Africa is not sufficient evidence to infer a hidden excess mortality of girls.

4. In the countries where it can be measured, the relationship between the sex ratio of death rates and mortality trends is different for the two age groups considered. The survival gains are a little more rapid for girls in the first year of life, and they are more rapid for boys between 1 and 4 years.

5. Certain countries, where excess post-infantile female mortality is observed, have predominantly Muslim populations (for example, Mauritania, where as noted, the differences are not statistically significant by sex, or Bamako). This raises the issue of a possible relationship between Islam and the status of young girls, as in North Africa and the Near East. There are, however, some non-Islamic countries where an unfavourable situation for girls prevails, and at least one country, Senegal, where the culture is strongly permeated by Islam, and where this gender inequality in death rates does not appear. Islam certainly plays a role in determining the status of women where it is widely present, but its influence alone cannot explain the variations in the sex ratio of deaths in childhood in sub-Saharan Africa. There is no significant correlation between these ratios and the proportion of Muslims in the country.

There are several reasons to question the assumption that children of both sexes in African societies are equal in the face of death. Excess female mortality is sometimes observed after the neonatal period, a period normally less favourable to male survival. In most surveys, the differences between the sexes are of little significance. And finally, it is observed that in Africa, recent declines in mortality between ages 1 and 4 have often benefited boys more than girls. National results may well hide the diversity of ethnic groups, regions, and social classes, observed in the cities. The more or less rapid decline of mortality in sub-Saharan Africa has been accompanied by an increase of inequality as regards access to the means of improving health and hygiene.

In situations of very high mortality, discrimination between male and female children would probably be manifested in the care of sick children and in the allocation of food. We have found only one reference to a poorer diet for girls. Loutan (1985) mentions that among the Fulani of Mali, young girls receive less milk than young boys; even here, the opposite is true between 5 and 10 years. Ewbank *et al.* (1986) have noted the results of a nutrition survey in Kenya (1977–8) which concluded that the nutritional status of boys and girls were similar. In many African societies there are inequalities in the access to food between men and women, on the one hand, and between adults and children, on the other. But because small children of both sexes eat together from a common source of food, there is little room for discrimination.

With respect to the care of adults for their children, particularly when they are sick, it would appear that the primary goal is to safeguard *all* children. After all, girls and boys all represent a promise of prosperity for the lineage; both sexes are soon actively committed to production. In patrilineal societies, the girls will leave their original lineage, but the latter will receive various compensations including bridewealth, which is almost universal in Africa as a guarantee of the union.[3] Moreover, a number of African societies are matrilineal systems, where children belong to the maternal lineage. The lineage survives and grows through its daughters, and it is not clear why the survival of girls would be less valued than that of boys.

Results from the cities (Abidjan, Bamako, Brazzaville) give another picture. Here, relatively low levels of mortality are nevertheless associated either with obvious (in Bamako), or possible (in Abidjan or Brazzaville) excess female mortality. This suggests that the urban setting increases the share of mortality decline which is due to health expenditures (drug purchases, consultations, stays in a hospital), thereby also increasing the opportunity for discrimination against female children.

---

[3] In India, the dowry system, where the bride's family gives money to the groom's, is generally considered to be one of the factors that leads to discrimination against female infants.

When a market economy replaces the subsistence economy, there are new expenses for children, in the provision of schooling and health care, for instance. Hence choices must be made about the distribution of scarce resources in the household to satisfy new needs. The case of schooling is obvious: everywhere in Africa boys are more educated than girls. Several studies of hospital patients by sex of child indicate that choices are also made in the area of health. In Togo (Locoh, 1987) the frequency of visits to free clinics is identical for girls and boys between 1 and 4, but 60 per cent of child patients in Lomé hospitals are boys, and only 40 per cent girls; in addition, the case fatality ratio is significantly higher for girls (12 per cent) than for boys (9 per cent). Similar results were found in a hospital in Dakar (Lallement and Teyssier, 1988), and at Serabu hospital in Sierra Leone (see Chapter 12 by Bledsoe and Brandon). In Lomé we were able to demonstrate the relationship between the economic status of the father and the sex ratio of child patients in hospitals. The fathers with low socio-economic status had the most lopsided sex ratios in favour of boys.

Finally, sex differences in mortality may originate in part in the behaviour taught to children, rather than in true discrimination of adults towards them: boys may be encouraged to experiment, and be left free to escape the compound and the control of adults. The work of Aaby (see Chapter 14 in this volume) opens up new perspectives on the role of crowding in the transmission of infectious disease. The children who contract secondary cases of measles by infection in the house will be more seriously affected than those who contract it through random encounters outside the home. In societies where boys go out more than girls, the latter could contract more serious or even fatal cases of measles. Fargues and Nassour's (1988) results for Bamako appear to confirm this hypothesis. It is likely, however, that the mechanism would not operate where women are accustomed to move freely with their last-born child on their back. Boys and girls then would have equal chances to leave the home and to contract 'primary' measles.

Child mortality in sub-Saharan Africa appears to fall between extremes. It shows neither the rather high excess male mortality of Europe and other countries with low mortality (attributed to a specific weakness of the male sex and to the more accident-prone behaviour of boys), nor the very pronounced excess female mortality of some countries in the Near and Middle East or the Indian subcontinent (explained by a complex of discriminatory attitudes towards the female sex). A large variety of situations is observed. When mortality is very high the risks are comparable for each sex, but as it declines the situation becomes more diverse. In certain regions, despite a noticeable improvement in health conditions, the excess mortality of females appears or maintains itself as a result of a particular cultural context (Mauritania, Bamako), or because the growing cost of health care imposes choices which are often made in favour of boys.

Trying to provide an overview of sub-Saharan Africa is necessarily a reductionist undertaking. Differences in mortality by sex are linked, on the one hand, to the level of mortality in the region, and on the other hand, to a combination of socio-cultural factors which determine the status of women and, in time, modify the behaviour of adults towards female children. This has been shown for other cultures (Das Gupta, 1987). There is not one but several child mortality differentials in sub-Saharan Africa.

References

Akoto, E. A. (1985), *Mortalité infantile et juvénile en Afrique: Niveaux et caractéristiques, causes et déterminants*, CIACO, Louvain-la-Neuve.

Antoine, P. and Diouf, P. D. (1986), 'Indicateurs de mortalité et conditions socio-économiques en millieu urbain: Premiers résultats d'une enquête menée à Pikine', mimeo.

—— and Herry, F. (1984), 'Mortalité infantile et juvénile à Abidjan (1978–1979)', *Cahiers ORSTOM*, Sciences Humaines 20/2: 141–55.

Billewicz, W. Z. and McGregor, I. A. (1981), 'The demography of two West African villages, 1971–75', *Journal of Biosocial Science* 13: 219–40.

Cantrelle, P. and Ly, V. (1980), 'La Mortalité des enfants en Afrique', in D. Tabutin and P. M. Boulanger (eds.), *La Mortalité des enfants dans le monde et dans l'histoire*, Ordina, Liège, 197–221.

Chen, L. C., Huq, E., and D'Souza, S. (1981), 'Sex bias in the family allocation of food and health care in rural Bangladesh', *Population and Development Review* 7/1: 55–70.

Dackam-Ngatchou, R. (1987), 'Causes et déterminants de la mortalité des enfants de moins de 5 ans en Afrique Tropicale', Doctorate thesis, University of Paris I.

Das Gupta, M. (1987), 'Selective discrimination against female children in rural Punjab, India', *Population and Development Review* 13/1: 77–100.

Duboz, P. (1984), 'Mortalité et morbidité infantile et juvénile en République Populaire du Congo', *Cahiers ORSTOM*, Sciences Humaines 20/2.

Ewbank, D., Henin, R., and Kekovole, J. (1986), 'An integration of demographic and epidemiologic research on mortality in Kenya', in United Nations, *Determinants of Mortality Change and Differentials in Developing Countries*, New York, 33–85.

Fargues, P. (1986), 'La Mortalité infantile et juvénile à Abidjan de 1973 à 1983', in Séminaire INSERM, *Estimation de la mortalité du jeune enfant (0–5 ans) pour guider les actions de santé dans les pays en dévelopment*, Éditions de l'INSERM, 145, Paris, 139–58.

—— and Nassour, O. (1988), *Douze ans de mortalité urbaine au Sahel: Ages, saisons et causes de décés à Bamako, de 1974 à 1985*, Travaux et documents 123, INED-PUF, Paris.

Garenne, M. (1981), 'The Age Pattern of Infant and Child Mortality in Ngayokheme (Rural West Africa)', African Demography Working Paper 9, University of Pennsylvania.

Gbenyon, J. (1985), 'Pour une mesure indirecte de la mortalité: La Méthode de

Courbage-Farges, adaptation ou inadaptation', *Études Togolaise de Population* 9, Unité de Recherche Démographique, University of Benin.

Greenwood, B. M. *et al.* (1987), 'Deaths in infancy and early childhood in a well-vaccinated, rural, west African population', *Annals of Tropical Pediatrics* 7: 91–9.

Haffad, T. (1984), 'Les différences de mortalité selon le sexe et leurs conséquences', Doctorate thesis, EHESS, Paris.

Hill, A. G. (1985), *Population, Health and Nutrition in the Sahel*, KPI, London.

Lallement, A. M. and Teyssier, J. (1988), 'Étude sur le morbidité et la mortalité dans un service de pédiatrie à Dakar, Sénégal', *Population* 43/1: 212–5.

Livenais, P. (1984), 'Déclin de la mortalité dans l'enfance et stabilité de la fécondité dans une zone rurale Mossi', *Cahiers ORSTOM*, Sciences Humaines 20/2.

Locoh, T. (1987), 'La Répartition par sexe des enfants hospitalisés à Lomé (Togo)', *Population* 42/3: 549–57.

Loutan, L. (1985), 'Nutrition amongst a group of Woodabe (Fulani Bororo) pastoralists in Niger', in A. Hill (ed.), *Population Health and Nutrition in the Sahel*, KPI, London.

Malawi Government (1984), *Malawi Population Census 1977*, Analytical Report, vol. II.

Morah, B. C. (1985), 'Evaluation of the Nigeria Fertility Survey (1981)', WFS Scientific Reports 32, ISI, Voorburg.

Pison, G. and Langaney, A. (1985), 'The level and age pattern of mortality in Bandafassi (Eastern Senegal): Results from a small-scale and intensive multi-round survey', *Population Studies* 39/3: 387–405.

Rutstein, S. O. (1983), 'Infant and child mortality: Levels, trends and demographic differentials', WFS Comparative Studies 24, ISI, Voorburg.

—— (1984), 'Infant and child mortality: Levels, trends and demographic differentials', WFS Comparative Studies 43, ISI, Voorburg.

Rwanda (1983), Enquête nationale de la fécondité, vol. 1. *Analyse des résultats*, République rwandaise, ONAPO.

Singh, S., Owusu, J. Y., and Shah, H. I. (1985), 'Demographic Patterns in Ghana: Evidence from the Ghana Fertility Survey 1979–80', WFS, ISI, Voorburg.

Sombo N'Cho (1985), *Enquête ivoirienne sur la fécondité (1980–81)*, Rapport d'évaluation, WFS Scientific Reports 79, ISI, Voorburg.

—— and Tabutin, D. (1985), 'Tendances et causes de la mortalité à Maurice depuis 1940', *Population* 40/3: 435–54.

Suchindran, C. M. and Adlakha, A. L. (1985), 'Determinants of infant and child mortality in Tunisia', in IUSSP, *International Population Conference*, Florence.

Tabutin, D. (1978), 'La Surmortalité en Europe avant 1940', *Population* 33/1: 121–48.

Togo (1986), 'Enquête sur la mortalité infantile à Lomé', Tableaux statistiques, Direction de la Statistique.

United Nations (1980), *Demographic Yearbook*, New York.

Vallin, J. (1983), 'Sex patterns of mortality: A comparative study of model life tables and actual situations with special reference to the cases of Algeria and France', in A. Lopez and L. T. Ruzicka, *Sex Differentials in Mortality: Trends, Determinants and Consequences*, Department of Demography, Australian National University, Canberra, 443–76.

Vimard, P. (1984), 'Tendances et facteurs de la mortalité dans l'enfance sur le Plateau de Dayes 1930–1976', *Cahiers ORSTOM*, Sciences Humaines 20/2.

Zambia, Republic of (1980), *Population and Housing Census of Zambia*, vol. 4. *Fertility and Mortality Levels and Trends*.

11 Twins in Sub-Saharan Africa: Frequency, Social Status, and Mortality

Gilles Pison
Musée de l'Homme, Paris

1. Introduction

In all populations where it has been possible to measure the mortality of twins, it has been noted that their mortality is far higher than that of children born in single births, at least at young ages. Their low birth-weight and the complications at delivery, which are frequent in multiple births, often condemn them to an early death in countries lacking a system of pre- and postnatal care. Where such systems have been instituted, the death rate of twins has fallen in the same way as that of single births, but remains at a much higher level.

The differences in mortality between twins and singletons seem to be rooted in biological and health care differences, although they also depend on cultural factors. No culture is indifferent toward twins. Certain cultures consider their birth to be a sign of good fortune, and celebrate it; others, a sign of misfortune, and fear it. The care given to twins varies accordingly. Traditions and behaviour toward twins probably have a measurable impact on their mortality.

Africa is a good place to conduct such a study: there is a great variety of cultures on the continent, and it is possible that the treatment accorded to twins varies considerably between them. Another advantage is that the frequency of multiple births seems to be greater in Africa than elsewhere. A study of the mortality of twins in sub-Saharan Africa is, therefore, potentially rich in insights into the factors and mechanisms of mortality. It is undoubtedly easier to separate the influence of biology, socio-economic factors, and cultural factors when analysing the level of mortality and its trends for this particular sub-group than for the rest of the population.

The first part of this study considers the frequency of twin deliveries and its geographical variation in sub-Saharan Africa. The status of twins is examined in the second part. Finally, we study their mortality, comparing it with that of single births.

This chapter deals mostly with twins, and leaves aside other multiple births (triplets, quadruplets, etc.), which are much less frequent and more

Table 11.1. *Twinning rates in sub-saharan Africa*

Country, city, or area	Date	Type of source[a]	Still births inclusion	No. of deliveries		Twinning rate (per 1,000)	Reference
				Twins	Total		
Senegal							
Dakar	1972	mat.hist.	Incl.	n.a.	6,160	15	Ferry, 1977
Pikine	1986	mat.hist.	Not incl.	86	5,070	17	Antoine and Diouf[b]
Ziguinchor	1961–3	hosp.reg.	Incl.	76	3,589	20	This study
Ziguinchor	1982–4	hosp.reg.	Incl.	238	13,456	18	This study
Fakao[c]	1965	mat.hist.	Incl.	52	2,320	16	Lacombe, 1970
Niakhar	1962–8	long.stu.	Not incl.	91	8,274	11	Cantrelle and Léridon, 1971
Paos-Koto	1962–8	long.stu.	Not incl.	55	4,626	12	Cantrelle and Léridon, 1971
Bandafassi	1975–87	long.stu.	Not incl.	29	2,383	12	This study
Fissel-Thienaba	1981–2	long.stu.	Not incl.	59	5,006	12	This study
Whole country	1955–9	hlth.sta.	Incl.	1,694	108,753	16	Senegal, 1955–9
Whole country*	1978	mat.hist.	Not incl.	193	13,686	14	This study
Gambia							
Banjul	1954–8	vit.reg.	Not incl.	57	n.a.	17	Bulmer, 1960
Farafeni	1981–7	long.stu.	n.a.	n.a.	n.a.	14	Greenwood[b]
Mali							
Whole country	1969	hlth.sta.	Incl.	749	40,071	19	Mali, 1969
Liberia							
Whole country	1984	mat.hist.	Incl.	89	5,575	16	Becker[b]
Burkina Faso							
Bobo-Dioulasso	1981–2	hosp.sur.	Incl.	166	8,586	19	van de Walle[b]
Ivory Coast							
Abidjan	1975	vit.reg.	Not incl.	60	4,204	15	Dittgen, 1979
Abidjan	1978–9	long.stu.	Not incl.	1,948	125,436	16	Antoine and Herry, 1982
Whole country*	1980–1	mat.hist.	Not incl.	296	18,693	16	This study
Ghana							
Accra	1954–6	hosp.reg.	Incl.	291	5,547	52	Hollingsworth and Duncan, 1966
Whole country*	1979–80	mat.hist.	Not incl.	286	17,634	16	This study

Region	Year	Source		No.	Births	Rate	Reference
Togo							
Lomé	1978	hosp.reg.	Incl.	382	n.a.	26	Freitas-Akolo, 1979
South-east	1976	mat.hist.	Incl.	206	7,903	26	Locoh, 1984
Benin							
Cotonou	1981	hosp.sur.	Incl.	389	16,294	24	IFORD, 1982
Whole country*	1981–2	mat.hist.	Not incl.	260	13,118	19	This study
Nigeria							
—North-east							
Whole region*	1981–2	mat.hist.	Not incl.	81	6,491	12	This study
—North-west							
Kano	n.a.	hosp.reg.	Incl.	44	n.a.	15	Jeffreys, 1953[d]
Whole region*	1981–2	mat.hist.	Not incl.	105	6,502	16	This study
—South-east							
n.a.	n.a.	hosp.reg.	Incl.	109	n.a.	33	Cox, 1963[d]
n.a.	n.a.	hosp.reg.	Incl.	90	n.a.	27	Jeffreys, 1953[d]
Whole region*	1981–2	mat.hist.	Not incl.	135	9,269	15	This study
—South-west							
Ibadan	1953–6	hosp.reg.[e]	Incl.	603	n.a.	45	Bulmer, 1960
Ibadan	1967–8	hosp.reg.	Incl.	722	n.a.	60	Nylander and Corney, 1969
Ilesha	n.a.	hosp.reg.	Incl.	158	n.a.	54	Knox and Morley, 1960[d]
Igbo-Ora	1964–8	long.stu.	n.a.	216	4,791	45	Nylander, 1969
Whole region*	1981–2	mat.hist.	Not incl.	207	7,172	29	This study
Cameroon							
n.a.	n.a.	hosp.reg.	Incl.	72	n.a.	16	Jeffreys, 1953[d]
Yaoundé	1978	hosp.sur.	Incl.	194	9,682	20	IFORD, 1979
Whole country*	1978	mat.hist.	Not incl.	361	24,471	15	This study
Congo							
Brazzaville	1980–1	hosp.sur.	Not incl.	355	18,425	19	Bitemo et al., 1984
Zaïre							
Kinshasa	n.a.	hosp.reg.	Incl.	500	n.a.	22	Bulmer, 1960
Kinshasa	1981–2	hosp.sur.	Incl.	658	26,329	25	Nzita Kikhela, 1986
Lubumbashi	n.a.	hosp.reg.	Incl.	270	n.a.	17	Bulmer, 1960
Kenya							
Machakos	1975–8	long.stu.	Incl.	52	4,716	11	van Ginneken and Muller, 1984
Whole country*	1977–8	mat.hist.	Not incl.	337	30,023	11	This study

Table 11.1. *(cont.)*

Country, city, or area	Date	Type of source[a]	Still births inclusion	No. of deliveries Twins	No. of deliveries Total	Twinning rate (per 1,000)	Reference
Tanzania							
n.a.	n.a.	hosp.reg.	Incl.	39	n.a.	24	Roberts, 1964[d]
Zimbabwe							
Harare	n.a.	hosp.reg.	Incl.	100	n.a.	29	Ross, 1952[d]
Lesotho							
Whole country*	1977	mat.hist.	Not incl.	211	11,088	19	This study
Botswana							
n.a.	n.a.	hosp.reg.	Incl.	40	n.a.	18	Jeffreys, 1953[d]
South African Republic							
Transvaal	n.a.	hosp. reg.	Incl.	28	n.a.	28	Jeffreys, 1953[d]
Transvaal	n.a.	hosp. reg.	Incl.	41	n.a.	41	Jeffreys, 1953[d]
Transvaal	n.a.	hosp. reg.	Incl.	29	n.a.	27	Jeffreys, 1953[d]
Johannesburg	n.a.	hosp. reg.	Incl.	710	n.a.	20	Jeffreys, 1953[d]
Johannesburg	n.a.	hosp. reg.[e]	Incl.	290	n.a.	27	Bulmer, 1960
Pretoria	n.a.	hosp. reg.	Incl.	197	n.a.	20	Stevenson et al., 1966[d]
Natal	n.a.	hosp. reg.	Incl.	116	n.a.	21	Stevenson et al., 1966[d]
Nqutu (Natal)	n.a.	hosp. reg.[e]	Incl.	92	n.a.	21	Bulmer, 1960
Durban	n.a.	hosp. reg.	Incl.	66	n.a.	21	Jeffreys, 1953[d]
The Cape	n.a.	hosp. reg.	Incl.	40	n.a.	13	Stevenson et al., 1966[d]

* World Survey.

[a] hosp.reg.: maternity hospital register; hlth.sta.: health statistics; hosp. sur.: survey in maternity hospital; long.stu.: longitudinal survey or surveillance system; mat.hist.: maternity history in retrospective survey; vit.reg.: vital registration.

[b] Personal communication.

[c] Adjusted using standard age at maternity (from Bobo-Dioulasso survey).

[d] From Bulmer, 1970.

[e] Deliveries booked in advance only.

difficult to study. The results concerning twins also apply, in general, to other multiple births, and their excess mortality is even greater.

2. The Twinning Rate in Sub-Saharan Africa

How common an occurrence is the birth of twins in sub-Saharan Africa? For the calculation of the twinning rate (i.e. the proportion of twin deliveries among all deliveries) in the countries of this region, one does not have access to national vital statistics as in developed countries. Fortunately, other sources of information do exist. Table 11.1 presents a series of estimates of the twinning rate for several regions or cities in sub-Saharan Africa from various sources.

(*a*) **Imperfect measures**

These sources are flawed, as are most of the sources of data for African populations. For certain countries or regions, there are several measures of the twinning rate that can be compared. Important differences can be observed between them; sometimes they differ by as much as a factor of two, as in Senegal, or south-eastern or south-western Nigeria. The variation appears largely because the different rates are not obtained in the same way. The third column of Table 11.1 indicates the source for each estimate. The records from maternity hospitals (referred to as 'hosp. reg.' in Table 11.1) generally yield higher estimates than other sources. Difficult deliveries have a tendency to be over-represented, and this leads to an overestimation of the twinning rate. With demographic surveys, underestimation is common. In Appendix 11.1 we review the different data sources and their attendant biases.

One of the principal difficulties arises from the fact that the two sources do not record the same thing: observations contained in the records of maternity hospitals deal with women who gave birth, while those gathered by demographic surveys generally deal with the babies that were born. In a delivery which results in two children, the physician or the midwife records one observation, whereas the demographer records two. This difference in point of view is a source of confusion. The word 'birth' is sometimes used mistakenly to mean 'confinement', and certain statistics leave some doubt concerning the nature of the event recorded. The twinning rate can evidently vary by a factor of two according to the definition used. The definition most commonly used is the proportion of all deliveries that are deliveries of twins, and we adopt it here.

Additional difficulty is caused by the occurrence of still births, which raise special problems in cases of multiple deliveries; reporting varies from one study to the next. Still births are always counted in hospital studies; births of twins in which one or both are stillborn are thus classified as deliveries of twins. In demographic surveys, however, still births, which are difficult to observe, are not always recorded, and when they are, are often considered separately. In cases of twin births where one is born alive and the other is stillborn, the second is often not recorded, and the first is recorded as a single birth. If both twins are stillborn, they both risk being missed. In either case, a twin delivery has been overlooked.

Under-registration of twins in surveys is not limited to still births, but can also occur when twins are born alive but die soon afterwards. This risk, shared with all children who die early, results similarly in the misclassification of the surviving twin as a single birth, or in the omission of both if both die.

With the help of a simple model, we have estimated to what degree the twinning rate would be reduced by the non-registration of still births and the omission of some of the children who die early (Pison, 1987). Under the current conditions of mortality in West Africa, if one supposes that the real twinning rate (still births included) is 20 per thousand, it appears that the observed rate will fall to 16.2 if still births are excluded; furthermore, if 10 per cent of live births who die in the first month of life are not registered, the observed twinning rate will be 15.7 per thousand.

The under-registration of twins can also be measured indirectly through the proportion of monozygotic twins, or the frequency of identical twins' deliveries. (A succinct account of the biology of twinning appears in Appendix 11.2.) The proportion of monozygotic twins is more or less constant in humans, at about 3.5 to 4 per thousand (Bulmer, 1970). This proportion can be estimated by the Weinberg method, provided the sex composition of pairs of twin births is known.

Table 11.2 gives the distribution of twin births by sex in several countries of sub-Saharan Africa according to the World Fertility Survey. In total, 129, 391 births were recorded, of which 2,135 were births of twins. 60 per cent of them were pairs of the same sex. If we apply the Weinberg method, we obtain a proportion of monozygotic twins of 3.2 per thousand. This estimate is lower than the norm of 3.5 to 4 per thousand in other human populations, indicating a probable overall under-registration of 10–20 per cent which corresponds closely to the under-registration predicted by our model.

Let us conclude from this review of sources of data on twin births in Africa that the demographic surveys which do not report still births probably underestimate the proportion of twins in Africa by 20 per cent. Those surveys which attempt to report still births undoubtedly omit some, and so also underestimate the proportion of twins, although to a lesser degree. The omission of live births who die at an early age results in additional underestimation: about 5 per cent if the proportion omitted is 10 per cent, and higher if the proportion omitted is greater. These figures are only averages, and the under-registration undoubtedly varies according to

Table 11.2. *Distribution of twin deliveries by sex of twins, World Fertility Surveys*

Country	Sex and reporting order of twins				Twins of same sex	Twins of different sex	Total	% with different sex
	2 boys	2 girls	1 boy 1 girl	1 girl 1 boy				
Senegal	60	57	46	30	117	76	193	39
Ivory Coast	93	83	71	49	176	120	296	41
Ghana	96	84	66	40	180	106	286	37
Benin	80	72	67	41	152	108	260	42
Nigeria	164	142	125	97	306	222	528	42
Cameroon	113	95	106	47	208	153	361	42
Lesotho	65	70	47	29	135	76	211	36
Total	671	603	528	333	1,274	861	2,135	40

the type of survey and the region. Under-registration is less in longitudinal studies, which are in general the most reliable, and also in regions where twins are welcomed.

(b) Level and variations in the twinning rate in sub-Saharan Africa

Level. Taking into consideration the various biases mentioned previously, the twinning rate, still births included, seems to be approximately 20 per thousand for all of sub-Saharan Africa. Thus, with more numerous and more representative data, we confirm the former estimate of Bulmer (1970), which was based only on unreliable hospital records. This proportion is four to five times higher than for Asia, and twice as great as for Europe and North America. In addition, it is $1\frac{1}{2}$ times higher than for the black population of the USA.[1]

Geographical variations. The indices listed in Table 11.1 offer only imperfect coverage of Africa south of the Sahara. For East Africa, we have access to national figures for only one country, Kenya. The proportion here is much lower than the African average, but it is impossible to say if this is a characteristic unique to Kenya, or if it applies to a larger region. Our information is hardly better for Central and southern Africa.. The few available measures, especially that for Lesotho, which is relatively reliable, indicate a rate close to the African average.

For West Africa, we are far better informed, thanks in particular to the World Fertility Survey which covered most of the coastal countries from Mauritania to Cameroon. The zone for which we are presenting national or regional figures covers nearly 80 per cent of the population of West Africa.

Map 11.1 shows the twinning rate by region for each country, as estimated from the World Fertility Survey. It must be kept in mind that the WFS did not take still births into account. The rates were not corrected for under-registration, and are therefore 'crude'. For the whole zone, the twinning rate is a little above 17 per thousand. By adding 20 per cent to correct for non-registration of still births, the true rate, still births included, can be estimated at 20 to 21 per thousand.

The following points may be made about the variations from one region to another in the uncorrected rates. First, the rate is always lower in the

---

[1] In the US the proportions of twins among Whites and Blacks are respectively 10.0 and 13.5 per 1,000. These proportions were calculated from proportions by age for 1938 (McArthur, 1953), and standardized on the distribution of the ages of African mothers at the birth of their children, in order to compare them to African figures. Here we have used the distribution of ages at birth in the 1981–2 baseline survey of Bobo-Dioulasso as our standard. The proportion of twins among Black Americans is between that of White Americans and that of Africans, probably as a result of high rates of racial admixture.

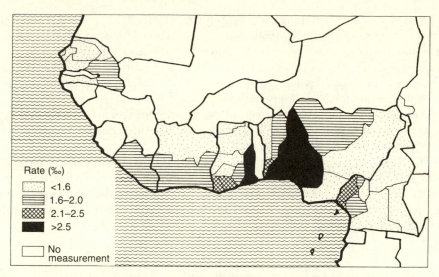

Rate (‰)
  <1.6
  1.6–2.0
  2.1–2.5
  >2.5

No measurement

MAP 11.1. The twinning rate in national fertility surveys of West Africa

interior than in coastal regions.[2] These variations could be the result of the more frequent omission of twins in the interior, where the health and education infrastructure is frequently less developed, and where mortality is higher. Large cities and capitals are often found in coastal regions, where the level of education is higher and mortality is lower.

The differences between coastal and inland regions are, however, too large to be only a reflection of better registration. Regions with low twinning rates correspond more or less to the savannah, while regions with high twinning are forest regions. A low proportion of twins, when compared with the African average, could therefore be a characteristic of the savannah populations of West Africa.

For certain countries (Ghana, Benin, and Nigeria), the northern and the southern regions differ by a factor of two. The southern regions of these countries form a contiguous coastal band with an average width of two hundred kilometres, stretching from the border between the Ivory Coast and Ghana to the mouth of the Niger river. The uncorrected twinning rates there are nearly always greater than 20 per thousand and sometimes they even exceed 25 per thousand. In south-east Ghana and south-west Nigeria, the rates reach a very high level, 29 per thousand, and they are also high in the middle region, for south Togo and south Benin. Several reliable local studies of the Yoruba, the principal ethnic group of south-west Nigeria, had

[2] The only exception, eastern Senegal, has a relatively uncertain figure, because it is based on fewer than one thousand deliveries; it is, furthermore, contradicted by another study of the same region in the area of Bandafassi, which furnishes an estimate that is clearly lower.

reported very high twinning rates (still births included) on the order of 40 to 45 per thousand (Bulmer, 1960; Nylander, 1969). The data of the Nigeria Fertility Survey, which are representative of the entire population of that region and not only of the Yoruba, confirm this result. Map 11.1 shows that the zone of high frequency of twins, which could have its centre in Yorubaland, extends well beyond to Ghana in the west.

To the east, the coastal strip of high twinning seems to stop in the south-eastern region of Nigeria. The uncorrected rate observed there is low (15 per thousand). However, high proportions of twins are again found further east, in western Cameroon. The proportion in south-eastern Nigeria, low in comparison with those of the neighbouring regions to the west and east, is somewhat surprising. The traditional unpopularity of twins in this region may have something to do with this. The study of the status of twins in sub-Saharan Africa will allow us to examine this hypothesis.

3. Social Status of Twins in Sub-Saharan Africa

In Africa, what explanation is given to twin births? How are they treated? What is their social status? The answers to these questions from various ethnographic accounts (in particular Forde, 1950 and following years; CNRS, 1973; Sindzingre, 1984; Granzberg, 1973) indicate that in nearly all societies, twins are considered as special beings. Their birth is accompanied by particular rites, which are often repeated in the course of their lives, and which are intended to restrain the powers that twins are supposed to harbour. Twins are frequently thought to have special talents as fortune-tellers or faith-healers.

Their social status varies a great deal according to culture. Here we give two extreme examples:

For the Dogon, the Bambara and the Malinke (Western Africa), twins are a reminder and an incarnation of the mythical ideal. It is as though they are representatives of a state of ontological perfection, a state which the non-twins have completely lost. The first living creatures were couples of twins of opposite sexes. The loss of twinhood . . . is the price that man had to pay for a sin committed by one of the ancestors. But the birth of twins is a reminder of that happy condition, and that is why it is celebrated everywhere with joy (Cartry, 1973).

By contrast, among certain peoples of Central Africa, the Ndembu and the Lele for example, twins belong to the animal world and are looked upon with revulsion. The Luba of Zaïre call them 'children of misfortune' and the Tonga traditionally did away with one of the two (De Heusch, 1973).

We have made a tripartite classification of the ethnic groups for which information is available (Pison, 1987). The first set comprises ethnic groups in which twin births are thought to bring luck and where they are the pride of mothers and families. Their birth is celebrated, and the twins as well as their parents are respected; they often receive presents, and eventually attain high positions close to the chief or king. In western Africa, this category includes in addition to the Dogon, Bambara, and Malinke already mentioned, the various Akan groups as well as the Ga, the Ewe, the Watchi, and the Mina who live in south Ghana and south Togo; and farther east in Nigeria, the Yoruba, the Igala, and the Katab, and in Cameroon, the Bamileke, the Bamum, and the Tikar.

The second category groups together those peoples who, according to the literature, practised infanticide or exposure of one or both of the twins. The mother was sometimes killed with them, or expelled from the village; at best, she would be considered impure for a certain period and have to follow rites of purification. In West Africa this category includes the Igbo, Ibibio, and Isoko, who are the main groups in south-eastern Nigeria, and also farther west the Edo and the Ife, and farther north the Gbari and the Kamuku. The Benafiab, one of the Konkomba subgroups in north Ghana, also fall into this category.

The third category lies between the two extremes. Here we have grouped all those peoples for whom the available information about twins either does not indicate that they were killed or left to die, or indicates that they were not killed. The evidence on these suggests that twins were at once feared and revered, feared because they could be the source of misfortune, but revered because of their powers. We have also placed in this category populations for which it is indicated that twins receive specific names. In many populations of sub-Saharan Africa, twins bear special names which identifies them immediately. Where they are considered not to be human beings but evil spirits to be suppressed, no name is given to them at all. Thus, the fact that particular names are given to twins probably indicates the absence of infanticide.

Our classification is not perfect, and for the majority of ethnic groups, we have no information. Moreover, the descriptions given by anthropologists often rest solely upon the statements of a few informants. It sometimes happens that the observers do not agree with each other. In addition, the statements may not correspond to practice, but to more or less mythical traditions which had no actual applications within human memory. Moreover, our intermediate category is heterogeneous and includes all the ethnic groups for which neither infanticide nor reverence is mentioned in the literature.

Map 11.2 indicates the location of ethnic groups in each category. Except for southern Africa, groups of the first category, that looks favourably on twins, exist in all regions. Groups in the second category, that traditionally practised infanticide of twins, are well represented in southern Africa, but are encountered here and there in several regions of western and eastern Africa as well, for example in south-east Nigeria and the southern Sudan.

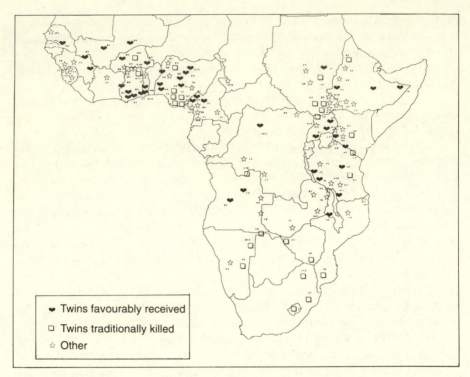

Map 11.2. Attitudes towards twins in the anthropological literature of sub-Saharan Africa

Authors such as De Heusch (1973) contrast the cultures of western Africa, for whom twinhood is often an ideal of perfection and who look favourably on twins because they evoke mythical times of joy, with the Bantu cultures of South and Central Africa, for whom twins represent disorder and unhappiness. But the three categories are represented in each of the regions, although unequally.

A comparison of Map 11.2 with Map 11.1 shows that in West Africa, the zones with high proportions of twins are also those inhabited by ethnic groups who venerate them. In south-eastern Nigeria, a zone of abnormally low twinning compared with neighbouring zones, the ethnic groups are hostile to twins.

It is difficult to know whether the old traditions mentioned by the anthropologists of doing away with twins in certain populations (e.g. among the Igbo and their neighbours) were practised on a large scale, and whether they are still practised nowadays. The low proportion of twins reported in the World Fertility Survey could, in any case, arise from a tendency to avoid declaring twins in surveys or to report them as single births out of fear of misfortune or shame. One could imagine at the other extreme, that when twins are desirable as among the Yoruba, more are declared than are born.

Hospital figures allow a check on whether twin births were over- or under-reported in the World Fertility Survey for south Nigeria. We have already mentioned reliable hospital studies which show a very high twinning rate among the Yoruba, and the hypothesis of over-reporting in south-west Nigeria is to be rejected. Concerning under-reporting in the south-east, we have the study of Nylander (1971) which compared the proportions of twins for women of different ethnic or geographical origins in Nigeria. The women of south-eastern Nigeria, the Igbo in particular, seem to have a very high proportion of twins, approaching that of Yoruba women, although perhaps slightly lower. Other hospital studies, such as those mentioned in Table 11.1, also indicate rather high proportions among the Igbo, although lower than the proportions observed in south-west Nigeria. It is thus possible that the low uncorrected twinning rates reported by the World Fertility Survey in south-east Nigeria are the result of selective under-reporting of twins, in keeping with the tradition of considering them as a sign of misfortune and, formerly, of killing them. At the other extreme, in those regions which have traditionally been well disposed towards them, all twins, even those who die early, are declared in surveys. This could explain in part why the uncorrected twinning rates are so markedly different between south-east Nigeria and the neighbouring coastal regions to the east and west. However, the variations in the proportions of twins observed by the World Fertility Survey in this region may very well be real. We lack the reliable hospital data necessary to draw definite conclusions.

4. The Mortality of Twins

In this section, we shall systematically compare the mortality of twins with that of singletons.

(a) Still births

There is no reliable source of data on still births. We can, therefore, only estimate orders of magnitude. Health statistics of Senegal (1955–9) and of Mali (1969) show about 40–50 still births per thousand births, with the mortality of twins triple or quadruple that of singletons. The survey of 1981–2 in Bobo-Dioulasso, with a somewhat lower overall proportion of still births, 30 per thousand births, shows a ratio of the same order of magnitude, 1 to 3.7 (van de Walle, personal communication). In England and Wales, by contrast, the proportion of still births for the period 1939–57 was 26 per thousand among singletons, and 58 per thousand among twins (Heady and Heasman, 1959, cited by Bulmer, 1970), a ratio of 1 to 2.2.

Excess still birth mortality among twins seems therefore to be particularly marked in Africa, but other measures from a greater number of countries would be necessary to verify this.

(*b*) **Mortality of infants and children**

Table 11.3 presents estimates of infant and child mortality for twins in several countries or regions. These figures are the probabilities of dying, expressed as percentages. We have chosen to express the measure per hundred rather than per thousand, because the levels of mortality encountered are high and the measures are inexact: twins are in fact rare, and often these figures are based only on the observation of a few hundred or, at most, of a thousand. Two significant digits, therefore, seem sufficient.

The mortality of twins is rather high: overall, 30–40 per cent of them die before 1 year of age, or 3–4 times more than singletons. Similar rates were calculated for historical France between 1700 and 1829 (Gutierrez and Houdaille, 1983): the infant mortality of twins exceeded 50 per cent, as compared with approximately 24 per cent for singletons, or more than double. In Africa, the mortality of twins is close to 50 per cent under the age of 5, as opposed to 15–20 per cent for singletons in most countries. The gap between the two seems, therefore, even wider than in historical France. Even so, these measures probably underestimate the actual mortality of twins: for those deliveries in which one twin is born dead, the surviving twin, who is weaker than average, is classified as a singleton in most surveys.

The excess mortality of twins is especially high during the first month of life, about four to five times that of singletons. It remains quite high between 1 month and 1 year of age, but the gap narrows after that, or even disappears. In this respect, Africa follows the general pattern: twins have the greatest handicap at birth and immediately afterwards.

Geographical variations in the mortality of twins. We now compare the mortality of twins in various countries. The mortality of twins follows a pattern similar to that of singletons: It is higher where mortality is generally high, for example in Senegal, and lower where mortality is lower, for example in Ghana.

The countries covered by the World Fertility Survey show two patterns in the excess mortality of twins aged 0–1 years: on one side, there are Mauritania, Senegal, Ivory Coast, Ghana, Benin, Nigeria, and Cameroon, where the mortality of twins is less than three times that of singletons, and on the other side are Rwanda, Kenya, and Lesotho, where it is more than triple. Thus, on one side we find western African, and on the other eastern and southern African countries. The same pattern is not found for mortality after one year of age. The excess mortality of twins as a whole for the first five years together is highest in Kenya and Lesotho.

Table 11.3. *Comparative mortality of twins and singletons (probability of dying in %)*

Country	City, region, or area	Date	0–1 month			1–12 months			0–1 year			x in yrs	1–x years			0–x years		
			T	S	R	T	S	R	T	S	R		T	S	R	T	S	R
Mauritania	Whole country*	1981							25	8	2.96	5	18	11	1.64	39	19	2.08
Senegal	Bandafassi	1975–87	42	8	5.01	39	11	3.71	65	18	3.58	3	37	16	2.27	78	32	2.47
	Fakao	1965	25	8	2.98	32	13	2.51	49	20	2.44	3	23	17	1.31	61	34	1.78
	Niakhar	1962–68	23	5	5.11	32	16	1.98	48	20	2.39	3	30	31	0.97	63	44	1.42
	Fissel-Thienaba	1981–84	26	4	6.74	16	6	2.46	37	10	3.77	2	7	7	1.10	42	16	2.63
	Pikine-Dakar	1986							29	4	6.72	5	6	6	1.07	33	10	3.46
	WFS	1978	20	5	4.00	16	6	2.50	33	11	2.96	5	30	18	1.70	53	27	1.98
Bourkina Faso	Bobo-Dioulasso	1981–84	18	3	6.29	14	5	2.94	29	7	3.91	2	5	4	1.41	33	11	3.02
Liberia	National Survey	1984											5			54	25	2.16
Ivory Coast	Whole country*	1980	26	7	3.91	20	8	2.51	41	14	2.90	5	11	10	1.18	48	22	2.12
Ghana	Whole country*	1979	13	4	3.80	9	4	2.23	21	7	2.87	5	7	7	1.07	27	13	1.97
Benin	Whole country*	1981	19	4	4.39	16	7	2.24	32	11	2.86	5	18	12	1.50	45	22	2.02
Nigeria	Whole country*	1981	13	5	2.79	9	5	2.00	22	9	2.32	5	15	9	1.72	33	17	1.94
Cameroon	Whole country*	1978	19	5	3.65	17	7	2.49	32	11	2.81	5	14	11	1.18	42	21	1.98
Rwanda	National Survey	1983	29	6	5.25	11	5	1.98	37	11	3.47	5	13	12	1.07	45	22	2.09
Kenya	Whole country*	1977	20	4	5.13	16	6	2.83	33	9	3.50	5	11	7	1.61	41	16	2.58
Lesotho	Whole country*	1977	25	5	4.70	19	6	3.11	39	11	3.53	5	8	6	1.37	44	16	2.70

Notes:
T = twin.
S = singleton.
R = ratio.

Sources: See Table 11.1; also Rwanda, 1984, and Rutstein (1984).

It is tempting to compare these variations in mortality with those in the status of twins. As we mentioned above, certain anthropologists do in fact contrast West Africa, where twins are valued, with Central and South Africa, where they are generally not welcome. Map 11.2 shows some of this contrast. The only countries of East and southern Africa covered by the World Fertility Survey are Kenya and Lesotho. Twins were not well looked upon among the Kikuyu of Kenya or among the Sotho of Lesotho, and this could explain their greater excess mortality in these countries.[3]

A comparison of geographical variations in the excess mortality of twins and in the twinning rate also shows a certain correspondence between the two for the zones studied. The mortality of twins is higher in regions where the proportion of twins is low, and more moderate where the proportion is high. The comparisons must be made at the country level, however, because we do not have rates of mortality by region available to us, as we do for proportions of twins.

Variations in the mortality of twins by birth order and sex. Table 11.4 presents rates of mortality of twins according to their birth order, their sex, and the sex of the other twin. The order in which twins are reported undoubtedly corresponds more to the order of death, when one or both twins has died, than to the order of birth; the first twin to be declared tends to be the surviving one, or the one who survived the longest, and not the one who was born first. This explains why in surveys the first twin almost always has lower mortality than the second.

There is no clear difference in mortality observed between twins of the same sex and twins of mixed sex, unless we group the data from different countries together, in which case the mortality of mixed sex twins is a little higher. This goes counter to the usual observation that mortality of twins of the same sex is higher. The latter include monozygotic twins who are generally weaker than dizygotic twins (Bulmer, 1970).

The only consistent difference seems to be between boys and girls. Twin boys seem to have a slightly higher mortality, but the difference is not significant.

(c) Mortality of twins and evolution

World-wide variations in the proportions of twins remain unexplained. The results of our study of twins and of their mortality in sub-Saharan Africa

---

[3] The measures of twins' mortality in Nigeria are difficult to interpret because of a lack of detail by region. In this big country, one finds in the south simultaneously groups which honour twins like the Yoruba, and groups which traditionally spurn them, like the Igbo. There is no information for the populations of the north. At the level of the whole country, one would expect a moderate excess mortality of twins, while in fact, it is rather low. This result could be explained if we could verify our hypothesis of a significant under-count of twins in south-east Nigeria. Since the uncounted twins are those who died, the uncorrected mortality rate for twins should be too low.

Table 11.4. *Mortality of twins by order, sex, and sex of the other twin (probability of dying before age 5 in %)*

Country	Order		Twins of same sex			Twins of different sex			All twins		Singletons	
	1st twin	2nd twin	Boys	Girls	Total	Boys	Girls	Total	Boys	Girls	Boys	Girls
Senegal	48	58	55	53	54	54	49	51	55	51	28	26
Ivory Coast	51	44	45	43	44	51	54	53	47	48	24	21
Ghana	23	30	28	27	27	24	26	25	27	26	14	12
Benin	40	50	46	43	44	50	40	45	48	42	23	21
Nigeria	28	38	39	34	36	29	28	29	35	31	18	16
Cameroon	31	52	38	39	39	48	45	46	42	42	22	20
Kenya	36	45	40	38	39	42	43	43	41	40	17	15
Lesotho	39	49	47	41	44	50	41	45	48	41	17	16

allow us to propose a hypothesis for the variations observed in that region. We have identified a correlation between the twinning rate, the status of twins, and their mortality. This correlation suggests the following mechanism of evolution.

The predisposition to have twins is in part hereditary for dizygotic twins, the ones observed most frequently in Africa. Giving birth to twins should a priori lead to numerous offspring, but as twins die more often than singletons and maternal mortality is higher for such births, the total benefit in terms of net reproduction is generally weak. Twinning can even have a negative effect under high mortality conditions. Bulmer (1970) estimates its effect as zero for Europe in the eighteenth century. Under the very high mortality conditions which prevailed in Africa several decades ago and which still exist in certain regions, the effect of twinning was certainly negative. One can imagine that under such conditions, the genes predisposing to twinning are negatively selected. That they do not disappear entirely is due to their genetic link with certain characteristics favoured by natural selection.

The frequency of genes predisposing to twinning is surely the result of numerous forces, one of which is the excess mortality of twins and of their mothers. Where the excess mortality of twins is the highest, the frequency of twinning genes is undoubtedly the lowest. Conversely, a lessening of excess mortality can increase their frequency.

This model does not specify the source of the relative excess mortality of twins and their mothers. It may be the result of genetic or nutritional factors which affect physical size, making the birth of twins more dangerous and twins relatively feeble at birth, or of social factors such as the treatment accorded to twins and their mothers.

The change in the twinning rate under the influence of selective mortality can only be slow, like all evolutionary mechanisms. With such a scheme the excess mortality of twins must have been maintained for long enough in the past for the current differences in twinning to result.

(d) Twins and maternal and child health programmes

In all countries of the world, regardless of the level of maternal and child health care, the mortality of twins remains higher than that of singletons. Because of the higher frequency of twins in Africa, the reduction of early mortality might be more difficult than elsewhere. With a twinning rate of 20 per thousand and a mortality of twins aged under one year three to four times that of singletons, deaths of twins represent 11 to 14 per cent of all infant deaths.

The problem is especially difficult in regions such as south-west Nigeria where nearly one birth in 20 is a twin birth, and thus one child in 10 is a twin. With the same excess mortality, deaths of twins make up 25–30 per cent of all deaths at this age. In order to achieve the same drop in infant mortality as elsewhere, efforts to provide maternal and child health care must be greater.

In the regions traditionally unfavourable to twins, the situation is, on one hand, better because twinning is often less common, but on the other hand, the handicap due to their status may well take a long time to disappear. The large contribution that twins make to the mortality of children, especially in the first year of life, certainly justifies the organization of special programmes of surveillance, nutrition, and vaccination.

5. Conclusion

Studies of the populations of sub-Saharan Africa have rarely focused on twins. In this they resemble studies from other regions of the world. Our work shows that this is undoubtedly a mistake, especially in the case of Africa. Twins hold an important place in the populations of sub-Saharan Africa. More are born there than elsewhere: twice as many as in the populations of Caucasian origin, and four to five times more than in populations of Asian origin. Their social status is also unusual in Africa. Often suspected of holding supernatural powers, they may be cherished or rejected, with very differing chances of survival.

Numerous obstacles stand in the way of the demographic study of twins, however. For example, demographic surveys do not record them well: very high early mortality, a wish to hide them from interviewers in places where they are poorly looked upon, and the shortcomings of questionnaires all conspire to omit many of them, or to misclassify them as single births.

For this study of the mortality of twins in sub-Saharan Africa, we had to be content with relatively unreliable information from the World Fertility Survey and other local surveys and hospital studies which cover this region only imperfectly.

The principal results are:

1. The high proportion of twins in sub-Saharan Africa is confirmed, with nearly 20 twin deliveries per thousand total deliveries.

2. The very high proportion of twins observed in south-west Nigeria is also confirmed. Yorubaland may be the centre of a region of high twinning which extends from the Gulf of Guinea in the west to Ghana, and perhaps even as far east as Cameroon. The surprisingly low proportion of twins in south-east Nigeria could result from an under-reporting of twins in that region, due to their poor status, but it is possible that the proportion is genuinely low. The variations in the twinning rate in other regions of Africa remain poorly documented.

3. The overall mortality of twins is very high. 40–50 per cent of them die before 5 years of age, a rate more than twice that of singletons. Their

excess mortality seems higher in eastern or southern Africa than in
western Africa, and this is probably related to a better general
acceptance of twins and their mothers in the latter area. This lower
mortality of twins in West Africa could explain their higher frequency
in that region, the result of a selection of genes which predispose
women towards twinning.

These results suggest several recommendations for future studies of the
determinants of mortality in Africa:

1. It is necessary to improve the data collection by reducing the risk of
   omitting twins from surveys. One way of doing this would be to ask
   systematically for each birth, 'Was this child born with a twin?' This
   was done in a survey conducted in the south-eastern region of Togo.
   The proportion of twins thus obtained, 26 per thousand, is identical to
   that provided by a hospital study in the neighbouring capital, Lomé,
   and not lower, as one generally observes in surveys (Locoh, 1984). The
   future Demographic and Health Survey in Togo will ask this question
   again.
2. The analysis could be improved further by systematically taking into
   account the effect of the type of birth, single or multiple, on the risk of
   death of infants. Especially in multivariate analyses, this factor should
   be one of the first to be considered because its effect is usually more
   important than other factors that are commonly studied: age of
   mother, birth order, and level of educational attainment.
3. The public health problem posed by twins must be taken into account
   when making predictions of the trend in infant mortality in Africa. This
   issue seems minor at first glance: these births represent only
   approximately 4 per cent of total births in Africa. But the excess
   mortality of twins is such that their part of total infant mortality is, on
   average, 11–14 per cent and goes as high as 30 per cent in the
   south-west region of Nigeria. The burden on programmes of maternal
   and infant care imposed by this high frequency of twinning may well
   become increasingly heavy as mortality drops in Africa.

Appendix 11.1   Sources of Data for Twins

I   Hospital sources

A   Hospital studies

The hospital studies (referred to as 'hosp.reg.' in Table 11.1) mentioned here use the
maternity registers of large hospitals. The proportions of twins they document are,
therefore, biased, because difficult births, including multiple births, are over-
represented. Therefore the proportions of twins tend to be overestimated.

One can try to correct for this bias by eliminating the statistics for those births that had not been booked in the admissions register of the hospital. This eliminates births which started at home but, because of complications ended up at the hospital, or those who came *in extremis* from other hospitals or maternity clinics that are less well equipped for difficult births.

Unfortunately, this correction, occasionally used in Table 11.1, does not totally expunge the risk of bias, because the problems that justify delivery at the hospital can manifest themselves during the pregnancy, leaving the woman time to reserve a place at the maternity clinic; moreover, women who had problems with previous deliveries would be more likely to sign up for a hospital birth than those who had not, as the risk of complications would be higher for them.

B Health statistics

Health statistics (hlth.sta.), compiled from the registers of health units, often have information on multiple births. Even when they cover the whole country, they record only the births which took place in health units, and therefore have the same drawbacks as the measures obtained in a single hospital or maternity unit; their wider coverage, however, reduces the overestimation of the proportions of twins.

C Studies in maternity clinics

With the growing tendency to have a child in a maternity clinic, registers and investigations in maternity clinics cover a larger and larger proportion of all births, and the measures are more and more reliable. A series of surveys (hosp.sur.) on infant and child mortality have been carried out over the last 10 years in the hospitals and maternity clinics of several large cities of Africa. These surveys, sometimes called 'IFORD surveys', all followed the same method, which consists of registering infants at the moment of their birth in a maternity clinic, and thereafter following them up to their second birthday (van de Walle, 1990). As they systematically use information about births in a certain number of hospitals or clinics, the investigations of this type give rise to information that should be biased in the same way as hospital registers. The selection of difficult births is, however, less likely because these investigations are carried out in all the clinics of a city, or in a majority of them. (The hospital studies mentioned above are, by contrast, often only concerned with one site, the principal hospital of the city.) IFORD-type surveys are, moreover, recent, and the majority of births were taking place in clinics in the cities where they were carried out. Thus, the investigation covered 88 per cent of the births in Yaoundé (Disaine and Garssen, n.d.), and over 85 per cent in Kinshasa (Nzita Kikhela, 1986).

The over-representation of difficult births and the overestimation of proportions of twins will therefore be less pronounced in these surveys. It is even possible, in fact, that the proportions of twins are underestimated due to a bias in the opposite direction: the under-registration of difficult births. In this type of investigation, the interviewers come every morning to the clinic to ask about new deliveries, and to register the new-born. The women for whom childbirth was not easy are not in a state to answer questions, or are disinclined to do so; some of them will even have been transferred to other wards—to the surgical section, for example, for those having to undergo a Caesarian section—and they are not accessible to the interviewers (Ouaidou and van de Walle, 1987). To sum up, the proportion of twins could be underestimated or overestimated depending on the relative importance of the biases.

D   Vital registration

Table 11.1 cites two studies that used vital registration data (vit.reg.). When complete, vital registration has the advantage of covering the whole population and not just that part which used hospitals and clinics. In some cities of Africa where registration is nearly complete, partial information on the frequency of twins has sometimes been tabulated. The resulting proportions seem to be underestimates, because of the frequent early death of twins. The Abidjan study suffered an additional risk of underestimation because the classification of births as single or multiple does not appear on the vital registration certificate; it is determined indirectly by comparing each infant with the next one on the register. If they have the same characteristics—father, mother, date of birth, etc.—one deduces that these are twins from the same pair (Dittgen, 1979). This method is unfortunately the only one possible here; it is tedious and uncertain, and allows some twins to go uncounted.

II   Demographic surveys

A   Follow-up studies

Follow-up studies (long.stu.) record the events which occur in a population while it is followed for a certain period of time. The information culled on births is more complete than that from vital registration because one does not wait for spontaneous reporting of events but regularly visits the families to collect the data. Nevertheless, under-registration of twin births is not excluded, in particular if the visits are very far apart.

B   Maternity histories

Another type of bias is at work in retrospective surveys where the women are asked about their maternity histories (mat.hist.), i.e. biographies including their pregnancies and their outcomes. Dead women are excluded from the survey, and one has information only for those who survived. Giving birth to twins is more difficult, and so maternal mortality is higher for these women, three times higher, for example, in historical France between 1700 and 1829 (Guttierez and Houdaille, 1983), and 4.5 times higher between 1757 and 1784 in Dublin (Clarke, 1786, cited by Bulmer, 1970). Thus, the number of births of twins reported by surviving women will be lower than in the total population. Births of twins have a tendency to repeat for the same women, which raises still higher their risk of death before the survey, and thus the under-representation of twin births among the survivors. A model shows, however, that the bias is not very important, reducing the proportion of twins by only 0.2 or 0.3 per thousand when the real proportion is 20 per thousand (Pison, 1987).

In closing, we will mention another difficulty in the comparison of the different measures of twinning: the variation by age of the mother. This effect should be eliminated either by comparing proportions at each age one by one, or by comparing overall proportions standardized by age of women at the birth of their children. These calculations are impossible for hospital studies because the publications do not give details by age. For demographic surveys that do give results by age, distributions of age of women at the birth of their children are similar no matter what type of survey was done. The distribution has an average age at maternity of 26 to 27 years of age, with 45 to 55 per cent of the births happening to women under 25 years old, and 7 to 15 per cent happening to those over 35 years of age. The corrections that need to be applied when calculating the proportions for the same age distribution usually are no greater than 5 per cent, which gives a difference of 1 per 100 if the proportion of twins is about 20 per 1,000. Adjustments of this order are more or less illusory given the errors in age reporting that are still frequent in Africa.

Appendix 11.2   The Biology of Twinning

The existence of two sorts of twins—identical twins and false twins—has been known for some time. Biologists call them monozygotic and dizygotic twins, in reference to their origins, which are not the same.

Monozygotic twins (identical twins) originate in a single egg, the product of the fertilization of an ovum by one spermatozoon; the single egg then divides in the course of its development, before the end of the second week after fertilization. The two embryos that result from this division are genetically identical, which explains the great resemblance of monozygotic twins, and the difficulty in distinguishing between them. In particular, they have the same sex.

Dizygotic twins (false twins) are the products of the ovulation and fertilization of two ova in the same cycle. Each ovum is fertilized by a different spermatozoon, and the twins who come from these two eggs or zygotes, therefore, resemble each other genetically no more than brothers and sisters. In particular, they can be of the same or of different sex, and the two combinations occur roughly with the same frequency.

Monozygotic and dizygotic twinhood, therefore, corresponds to two quite different biological phenomena: monozygotic twins result from a developmental anomaly which is related to asexual reproduction, or cloning, whereas dizygotic twins are the result of the ovaries producing more than one ovum in a cycle. Even if they end in the same result, the two phenomena are unrelated, and have their own 'laws'. An examination of variations in the frequencies of the two types of twin will show this.

The birth of twins of all types is a rare event for humans. In France, for example, there were 10.1 twin births per thousand births in 1984. The other multiple births, triplets and quadruplets, are even more rare: 0.20 and 0.017 per thousand respectively in France in the same year.

The frequency of twin births, or the proportion of twins, is not the same everywhere. It varies according to various factors, some of which are well known from observations made in developed countries, and particularly in Italy, where the statistics on twins are very detailed (McArthur, 1953).

The proportion of monozygotic twins, or the frequency of births of monozygotic twins, always lies between 3.5 and 4 per thousand, and does not vary by age of mother, birth order, or world region (Bulmer, 1970). More or less the same proportion is found among all mammals, with the exception of some armadillos which systematically give birth to monozygotic quadruplets or octuplets. All women seem to be equally exposed to the risk of monozygotic twinning, whether or not they have previously had twins.

Dizygotic twinhood, on the contrary, can vary a lot. The principal factors by which it varies are (Bulmer, 1970):

Age of the mother. In present-day populations of European origin, the proportion rises regularly from about 0 at menarche to the maximum of 10 per thousand at age 37, and then falls rapidly to zero again at menopause. This change is a reflection of the abundance of gonadotropic hormones which control the activities of the ovaries, particularly ovulation. The level of these hormones in the blood rises steadily with age. The fast drop in the frequency of dizygotic twinhood after the age of 37 is linked to the decline of the ovarian functions, which progresses as menopause approaches.

Birth order. At a given age, the proportion of dizygotic twins rises with birth order. These variations are, however, less important than those which depend on age. As these factors are highly correlated, especially in natural fertility populations, one can often control only for the most important factor, the mother's age.

World region. All the populations for which we have reliable data show the same variations by mother's age and birth order, but the overall level varies from one region to another. At the global level, for example, for the same age and birth order, the proportion of dizygotic twins is about twice as high in sub-Saharan Africa as in Europe, and four or five times higher than in China or Japan. The cause of these differences is not well understood.

Individuals and families. Deliveries of dizygotic twins have a tendency to be repeated for some women. If a woman has given birth to dizygotic twins, the risk of a dizygotic twin birth is raised by a factor of four for her subsequent pregnancies. This predisposition to twinning can also be found among her sisters and her daughters. The risk of dizygotic twinning thus varies within a population, and these variations seem controlled, at least in part, by genetic factors.

These laws of twinning have been established on the basis of data from countries with reliable statistics, and it is likely that they apply to the countries of sub-Saharan Africa.

References

Antoine, P. and Herry, C. (1982), *Enquête démographique à passages répétés: Agglomération d'Abidjan*, Direction de la Statistique de la Côte d'Ivoire, Centre ORSTOM de Petit-Bassam.

Bitemo, M., Kimpouni, D., and Mvila, G. (1984), 'Bilan de la collecte de l'EMIJ de Brazzaville', Fourth technical meeting on infant and child mortality surveys, IFORD, Yaoundé.

Bulmer, M. G. (1960), 'The twinning rate in Europe and Africa', *Annals of Human Genetics*, 24: 121–5.

—— (1970), *The Biology of Twinning in Man*, Clarendon Press, Oxford.

Cantrelle, P. and Léridon, H. (1971), 'Breast-feeding, child mortality and fertility in a rural zone of Senegal', *Population Studies* 25/3: 505–33.

Cartry, M. (1973), 'Introduction', in CNRS (1973), 15–32.

Clarke, J. (1786), 'Observations on some causes of the excess of the mortality of males above that of females', *Philosophical Transactions of the Royal Society*, 76: 349–64.

CNRS (1973), *La Notion de personne en Afrique Noire*, Paris.

De Heusch, L. (1973), 'Le Sorcier, le Père Tempels et les jumeaux mal venus', in CNRS (1973), 231–42.

Disaine, B. and Garssen, M. J. (n.d.), 'Niveau et structure de la mortalité avant 2 ans à Yaoundé', mimeo, IFORD, Yaoundé.

Dittgen, A. (1979), 'Étude de la natalité et de la fécondité à Abidjan en 1975 à partir de l'état civil', *Actes du Colloque de démographie d'Abidjan*, 22–6. Jan., 1: 135–52, IFORD and CIRES.

Ferry, B. (1977), *Étude de la fécondité à Dakar (Sénégal): Objectifs, méthodologie et résultats*, ORSTOM, Dakar.

Forde, D. (ed.) (1950), *Ethnographic Survey of Africa*, International African Institute, Oxford University Press.

Freitas-Akolo, A. (1979), 'Contribution à l'étude d'accouchements gémellaires au service de gynéco-obstétrique du C.H.U. de Lomé: A propos de 764 jumeaux', Mimeographed thesis, Lomé.

Granzberg, G. (1973), 'Twin infanticide: A cross-cultural test of a materialistic explanation', *Ethos* 1/4: 405–12.

Gutierrez, H. and Houdaille, J. (1983), 'Les Accouchements multiples dans la France ancienne', *Population* 38/3: 479–90.

Heady, J. A. and Heasman, M. A. (1959), *Social and Biological Factors in Infant Mortality*, General Registrar's Office, Studies on medical and population subjects, HMSO, London.

Hollingsworth, M. J. and Duncan, C. (1966), 'The birth weight and survival of Ghanaian twins', *Annals of Human Genetics* 30: 13–24.

IFORD (1979), 'Enquête sur la mortalité infantile et juvénile à Yaoundé', Document for the meeting of 22–6 Oct., Yaoundé.

—— (1982), 'Enquête démographique sur la petite enfance à Cotonou (EDPEC)', Mimeo, Yaoundé.

Lacombe, B. (1970), *Fakao (Sénégal): Dépouillement de registres paroissiaux et enquête démographique rétrospective. Méthodologie et résultats*, Travaux et Documents de l'ORSTOM 7, Paris.

Locoh, T. (1984), *Fécondité et famille en Afrique de l'Ouest: Le Togo méridional contemporain*, Travaux et documents 107, INED–PUF, Paris.

McArthur, N. (1953), 'Statistics of twin births in Italy, 1949 and 1950', *Annals of Eugenics* 17: 249.

Mali (1969), Statistiques sanitaires du Mali.

Nylander, P. P. S. (1969), 'The frequency of twinning in a rural community in Western Nigeria', *Annals of Human Genetics* 33: 41–4.

—— (1971), 'Ethnic differences in twinning rates in Nigeria', *Journal of Biosocial Science* 3: 151–7.

—— and Corney, G. (1969), 'Placentation and zygosity of Twins in Ibadan, Nigeria', *Annals of Human Genetics* 33: 31–40.

Nzita Kikhela, D. (1986), 'Techniques de collecte et d'analyse de la mortalité périnatale en Afrique noire: L'Expérience d'une enquête à Kinshasa', IDRC, Department of Demography, University of Louvain.

Ouaidou, N. and van de Walle, E. (1987), 'Réflexions méthodologiques sur une enquête à passages répétés: L'EMIS de Bobo-Dioulasso', *Population* 42/2: 249–66.

Pison, G. (1987), 'Les Jumeaux en Afrique au sud du Sahara: Fréquence, statut social et mortalité', *Dossiers et recherches* 11, INED, Paris.

Rutstein, S. O. (1984), 'Infant and Child Mortality: Levels, Trends and Demographic Differentials', Comparative Studies 43, World Fertility Survey, International Statistical Institute.

Rwanda (1984), *Enquête nationale sur la fécondité*, vol. 1. *Analyse des Résultats*, Office national de la population.

Senegal (1955–9), Statistiques sanitaires du Sénégal.

Sindzingre, N. (1984), *Les Jumeaux*, Encyclopedia Universalis.

van de Walle, E. (1990), 'The IFORD surveys', in J. Vallin, Stan D'Souza, and A. Palloni (eds.), *Measurement and Analysis of Mortality: New Approaches*, Clarendon Press, Oxford, 35–47.

van Ginneken, J. K. and Muller, A. S. (eds.) (1984), *Maternal and Child Health in Rural Kenya: An Epidemiological Study*, Croom Helm, London.

12 Child Fosterage and Child Mortality in Sub-Saharan Africa: Some Preliminary Questions and Answers

Caroline H. Bledsoe and Anastasia Brandon
Northwestern University, Evanston, and University of Pennsylvania, Philadelphia

1. Introduction

Child fostering, a common phenomenon in parts of West Africa, removes a child from its biological parents and places it in a home with other people. Unlike Euro-American adoption, West African parents usually retain parental rights and visit the child and may make financial or material contributions to his or her upkeep. Fosterage is attracting increasing demographic attention because of its likely influence on fertility and mortality. Although most approaches to fertility deal with prenatal or perinatal means of controlling completed family size, in reality people find many ways, including fosterage, to adjust family size and composition *post*-natally. African families are particularly flexible in this regard. In Sierra Leone, a woman with several small children can ask a relative or friend, or even one of her grown children, to raise and educate a child. For parents, these outlets sustain a high demand for children and decrease their interests in birth control.

Concerning guardians, a woman who has married recently, set up a new home, or borne several small children can bring in an older girl to help with household chores. Fosterage is also useful to people with no surviving children or with grown children who have left home. Often parents give children to elderly people as companions and for help with physically demanding tasks such as fetching water, splitting firewood, cleaning house, and marketing. But regardless of their own fertility status, many adults seek to invest in other people's children, either through fosterage or contributions to their schooling, to widen their network of potential supporters. Hence, fosterage questions the common assumption that parents are the only ones interested in, or willing to support, their children (see also Caldwell, 1977). (For discussions of West African fosterage, adoption, or relocation, see Oppong, 1973; Schildkrout, 1973; Fapohunda, 1978; Goody,

1982; Isaac and Conrad, 1982; Locoh, 1982; Étienne, 1983; Frank, 1984; Brydon, 1985; Antoine and Guillaume, 1986; Page, 1986; Bledsoe, 1987a; Bledsoe and Isiugo-Abanihe, 1985; and Silk, 1987.)

While West African parents send children out to be raised or to experience the hardship and discipline thought to determine their chances for success (Bledsoe, MS), they want the children to live to take care of them in their old age. However, a foster-child necessarily faces a new diet, care provider, and disease environment. Besides undergoing a psychological trauma, the child may be fed less nutritional food and receive poorer medical care than children with mothers present. These conditions may contribute to high rates of morbidity and mortality among young fosters.

Harmful effects of fosterage and child neglect are not restricted to Africa. (See Lees, 1964, and Rawson and Berggren, 1973, for the Caribbean; Oomen, 1953, for Jakarta; Said, 1955, for Malaya; Scrimshaw et al., 1957, for Central America; and Neave, 1968, for Samoa.) Nor are they confined to the contemporary Third World. Flandrin (1976) argues that the practice of putting out children doubled the mortality of the infants who were subjected to it among urban families in nineteenth-century France. And a recent study of fostering in London (Cross and Ibru, 1978) noted that physicians and social workers often see neglect and emotional disturbance among West African children fostered into English homes. Finally, in the United States Wilson et al. (1980) found the highest rates of child abuse and neglect in father-only homes, while Lightcap et al. (1982) found high rates of abuse in homes with one stepparent and one natural parent.

As these findings suggest, the fact of fosterage or parental absence undermines Western stereotypes about who cares for children and necessitates a fresh look at resource distribution within households. After examining some background African literature on social factors underlying child malnutrition, we turn to data from Sierra Leone to examine different kinds of fosterage and their possible morbidity and mortality consequences. Because fosterage is a relatively unexplored topic for demographers and nutritionists, we highlight a number of methodological problems in data collection and interpretation, in our own study as well as in others, as an aid to future research.

This study bears relevance on several levels. First, although fosterage appears to deviate from the 'normal' situation of maternal care, many studies throughout the world that look closely at household patterns are now finding that fosterage is not as rare as a Western model of the intact nuclear family would assume, even in Western societies themselves. Hence, we take as our central problem a topic that is usually treated as deviant from otherwise stable parent–child bonds. Fosterage is much more easily relegated to the 'qualifications' section at the end of a tightly woven study.

Second, and more broadly, we are concerned with the flexibility and adaptability of families to respond quickly to economic and social exigencies that arise. Such points are articulated clearly in topics such as social responses to drought (e.g. Seaman and Caldwell, in this volume). By combining the potentials of a culturally sensitive microstudy with larger scale quantitative data, our work applies an adaptation perspective to very commonplace household strategies. The combined strength of these two approaches allows us to build a fuller explanation of basic social processes from which specific demographic outcomes emerge. In this task, however, we confront a basic problem in social science analysis: how to determine cause from effect—fosterage and child mortality, in this case. We do not claim to solve this problem in our study. Rather, we suggest that both are outcomes of social and demographic adaptational strategies.

2. Defining Fosterage

By 'fosterage', we shall refer to arrangements in which children live in different households from their mothers. We use this application advisedly for two reasons. First, our definition of fosters includes children whom many Africans would hesitate to classify as such. For example, the Mende of Sierra Leone, like many other African groups, have a patrilineal ideal. This would suggest that a child with its natural father and, perhaps, a stepmother is inappropriately called a foster-child. However, since most studies in Africa indicate that fathers participate only indirectly in child care and since the mother's income is frequently the basis of a child's support, we use maternal absence as a working definition of fosterage. Moreover, small children who go to grandmothers, aunts, or older married sisters are simply considered as being 'with' those particular relatives, who have rights in the children much like those of parents. Similarly, many children who are sent away to undertake trade apprenticeships, Muslim religious instruction, or formal schooling are simply 'away' for those purposes. And finally, many children whom our definition would not include as fosters live in the same households with their mothers but are cared for by other people: elderly women, older sisters, or other wives.

To circumvent definitional problems, some scholars prefer the term 'child relocation', emphasizing the physical removal of a child from the mother's household. But this excludes cases in which a pregnant woman goes to her mother's or sister's home to deliver and receive help with the new-born, then leaves the weanling with her relatives when she returns to her husband. 'Relocation' also excludes cases in which a child is given to be raised by its mother's subfertile co-wife or another resident in the same house. Finally, it fails to capture the important social ties that families attempt to consolidate by exchanging a child.

A few scholars have argued that 'adoption' is the most appropriate label for such child transactions, since in many cases the children are sent permanently and are treated like 'born children', a Krio phrase in Sierra

Leone. However, West African children are seldom 'adopted' in the sense of a formal transfer of parental rights. Rather, they are sent with the understanding that they can be retrieved, if the parents desire. And even parents who never retrieve their children usually maintain strong interests in them.

3. Literature Review

Studies from different areas of Africa suggest that family structure affects the risks of child morbidity and mortality, especially for young children. In many African societies, weaning represents a decision by the mother and the father to terminate breast-feeding since breast milk is said to be contaminated by semen during sexual relations. Fostering out a weanling is thought to minimize the distress of a child when the mother, fearing the effects of contaminated breast milk on the child, refuses to let it nurse, particularly if the caretaker pacifies it with her own breast. However, weaning often results in diarrhoea or protein–calorie malnutrition when a child is sustained on a diet of bulky carbohydrates (Jelliffe, 1968; Winikoff, 1980). The nutritional problems common to weanlings place those sent to guardians at double risk. Namboze (1967) and Goodall (1979) found that in Uganda kwashiorkor was especially high for newly weaned children living away from parents (for Tanzania see Schmutzhard *et al.*, 1986).

Besides exacerbating vulnerabilities at weaning, fosterage can be linked to health problems for small children. Williams suggested early that kwashiorkor in East Africa was linked to broken homes (Williams, 1933; see also Sachs, 1953). More recently, Goodall (1979) concluded that Ugandan children with kwashiorkor were likely to be attended by someone other than their mother, to have changed attendants when ill, to have a pregnant mother, or to have separated parents. (See also Moodie, 1961, and Kahn, 1962, for South Africa, and G. C. Thomas, 1981, for Ciskei; Gupta and Mwamba, 1976, for Tanzania; and Dixon *et al.*, 1982, for Kenya.) The mother's employment outside the home is another alleged contributor to child malnutrition (e.g. Moodie, 1961; Jelliffe, 1962).

Although most USAID-sponsored national nutrition studies in Africa deal only peripherally with fosterage (favouring more traditional variables such as mother's education, household head's occupation, and so on), those we reviewed (Swaziland, Cameroon, Liberia, and Sierra Leone) reported poorer nutritional status among children without mothers. For instance, the Cameroonian nutrition survey (1978) showed that nationally, although only about 13.7 per cent of the children under 5 years were not with their mothers, 24.8 per cent of these had chronic malnutrition (measured by height for age), compared with 20.6 per cent for children with mothers—a significant difference. In the North, the differences were greater: 29.5 and 20.1 per cent, respectively.

Sierra Leone's National Nutrition Survey (1978) is quite sketchy on fosterage and its possible link with malnutrition. It states that among children from 3 months to 5 years of age, 'The prevalence of undernutrition [*defined by height for age*] in the Sierra Leone Sample was found to be significantly greater when . . . someone other than the mother was primarily responsible for the child's care and feeding' (p. xiii). However, no supporting figures are given.

The 1976 Liberia National Nutrition Survey has more precise data on these questions. However, it includes few foster-children. The 1974 census shows that about 36 per cent of all surviving children of women from 15 to 19 (children mostly two and under) are away from their mothers (Isiugo-Abanihe, 1983*b*), but only 3.7 per cent of the rural children from 0 to 5 years whose mothers were dead or away found their way into the national nutrition survey sample. Still, almost twice the number of these children (32.0 per cent) had chronic protein–calorie malnutrition as children with mothers (18.1 per cent).

We must utter a word of caution about interpreting the effects of the mother's absence. First, maternal absence itself is difficult to assess. As Thompson and Rahman's (1967) study of Mandinka villagers in Senegal showed, even household membership does not provide a completely satisfactory definition. During periods when mothers worked from dawn to dusk in the fields, they were present only at night, leaving their young children in the care of older children and the aged. Converse problems may have arisen in some of the national nutrition surveys. Since they focused on mother/child pairs, some mothers may have been summoned from other households where they lived, apart from their children, to answer the questions on mothers.

Even if the mother's absence can be measured reliably, how does it cause malnutrition? Many researchers argue that psychological factors are paramount: that young children react adversely to the sudden deprivation of the mother's nurturance and to the new environment. In Uganda, Geber and Dean (1955) reported that many young children separated from their mothers reacted with an appetite loss and a weight loss leading to kwashiorkor (see also Ainsworth, 1967). In our own data from Sierra Leone, local observers themselves associate increased health risks with psychological trauma among small children, as a nurse at an under-fives' clinic emphasized:

The child is used to the mother, then suddenly it is sent to the granny [*a real or fictive grandmother*], whom it may not know well. Therefore, children get sick often when they are first sent to grannies. Also, the change in diet brings upsets to the child, no matter what it was eating before.

Yet we should note also that children removed from mothers do not necessarily suffer psychologically. Many African children are cared for by other people from infancy; thus, an older sibling, an older foster-child, or a grandmother may be more familiar than a biological mother. Although they were not interested in morbidity or mortality, Weisner and Gallimore (1977) concluded that the phenomenon of older sibling caretakers often had positive outcomes for both children in later personality development and educational performance.

For young children, a more basic explanation for what is most harmful about the mother's absence is simply a lack of breast milk. Thompson and Rahman (1967) showed that young children were most apt to suffer nutritionally at peak farm labour periods when women's physical exertions decreased their milk. An explanation pertaining more to older children, one of a more social nature, comes from Ainsworth (1967), who found that young Ugandan foster-children often became malnourished when they were placed in large households where no one was deeply committed to their welfare. Similarly, a Peace Corps Volunteer working in nutrition in rural Sierra Leone reported to us that during a recent measles epidemic, most children who died had absent mothers, leaving no one to nurse them and make sure they ate and drank. These observations provide clues to ways in which children with absent mothers are excluded, often unintentionally, from scarce household resources.

On the other hand, maternal absence can actually benefit children, under certain conditions. In northern Ghana, Tripp (1981) implied that poor women's employment absences benefited their children by producing more income, as long as they had adequate time for child care. The Swaziland National Nutrition Status Survey (1983: 4.14–4.15) provides an interesting case. As we would expect, it suggested that rural children with mothers who were members of the homestead but were absent most of the time, presumably for employment, suffered less nutrition-related growth stunting (25.4 per cent) than children whose mothers were not members of the homestead (34.2 per cent). But it also found that these children suffered less stunting than children whose mothers were present most of the time (29.9 per cent); presumably because the latter spent more time in child care but had little external income. (The confidence intervals, however, were not significant. This could be explained by the fact that in comparison to many other areas, the Swaziland population is well off. Furthermore, the survey was conducted primarily during the season of food abundance.)

Focusing on maternal absence as a background factor in child malnutrition is natural for Africa, where women generally nurse their children for extended periods and where polygyny induces wives who compete for household resources to take primary responsibility for their children. Yet many studies of malnutrition also point to lack of paternal economic support, through desertion, divorce, or illegitimacy (see Williams, 1933, Sachs, 1953, Pretorius *et al.*, 1956, Scragg and Rubidge, 1960, and Moodie, 1961, for South Africa; G. C. Thomas, 1981, for Ciskei; Burgess *et al.*, 1972, for

Malawi; and Levine and Levine, 1981, for Kenya). Our own qualitative evidence from Sierra Leone, however, suggests that causation in these cases is quite complex since resource allocations may symbolically reflect social relationships. People who resent an illegitimate child may withhold from it resources they can afford. However, analogous circumstances sometimes apply even to children with their own mothers. We encountered cases wherein a woman would attempt to prove her current marital loyalty by slighting children by her previous husband at mealtimes in favour of those by her present one. Such children might well be better off with other caretakers.

A number of factors, then, bear on the nutritional and morbidity effects of fosterage: the attention devoted to a child, access to medical resources, the child's familiarity with the new caretaker and surroundings, the abruptness of the transition, and the adequacy of the new diet. We shall return later to this tension between the possible benefits of fosterage versus the drawbacks, since it has important implications for child mortality rates within households as well as in the population as a whole.

4. Data Problems

Although we have gleaned some data on the relationship of fosterage to child morbidity and mortality from a number of sources, this has not been the subject of concerted, focused attention, and many studies simply note in passing that foster-children seem to exhibit high rates of malnutrition. A number of methodological problems make the phenomenon of fosterage undeniably difficult to investigate. First, it is difficult simply to identify enough foster-children to analyse. In hospital studies, from which most of the above data come, small numbers are problematic. Second, the representativeness of these numbers is seldom clear. Hospital patients are unlikely to represent the population at large, and little attempt is made to compare these patterns with those in the wider society. Sampling problems also arise in studies that select malnourished children in the hospital or the wider population, then examine their characteristics.

Several of the national nutrition studies, which do collect large numbers, attempt to select children with mothers, probably because mothers would best be able to answer the surveys' background social, economic, and health questions. But even those that systematically include fosters contain data problems. Especially in large households with many attached dependants, the senior occupant of the household—usually a man uninterested in the details of domestic life—may be asked about the children with absent mothers: their birth circumstances, consumption patterns, etc. A female guardian who is asked about her foster-child could better explain the child's consumption patterns, but her information on the circumstances of the child's birth, mother's education, and so on, would be unreliable. (Of course, similar problems arise even with children with their mothers, because their actual caretakers are older siblings or fostered girls.)

As this implies, although most attention to the social factors involved in child malnutrition has focused on the mother's absence or lack of paternal support, there have been few attempts in African studies to identify the caretakers of foster-children (see, however, Waterston's (1982) findings in Ghana on malnourished children with grandmothers). The studies that attempt to examine the socio-economic features of guardians are even fewer, although Kahn (1962) found many cases of protein malnutrition among children with relatives who were poorer and less educated than the mother herself.

We note also that little attention has been devoted specifically to the possible relationship between fosterage and mortality. An exception is Oppong (1983), who suggested that Ghanaian parents who foster out their children experience more infant deaths than those who do not. And Cantrelle *et al.* (1986: 110) found in their Senegalese study area that more children from age 0 to 4 died who were not with their mothers than did those with mothers.

Even large-scale retrospective data collected from mothers have short-comings. Data on maternal characteristics such as education, ethnic group, and religion must be used cautiously; for maternal characteristics may be largely irrelevant to the welfare of children who are away when they become ill or die. Variables that are customarily related to child mortality such as mother's type of toilet facility, source of water supply, and roof dwelling type are even less relevant. Moreover, such data would consist of easily forgotten items that were collected retrospectively from the mother, who may have had little idea of the guardian's living conditions at that time.

To move beyond some of the difficulties of using women as the unit of analysis, it is possible to examine the chances of survival of individual children. Here, instead of simply asking whether a particular child has ever been away, the duration of the child's fosterage should ideally be taken into account, for this is likely to affect the child's condition. However, another basic methodological problem emerges: the longer a child lives, the greater its likelihood of being fostered. In a 1985 survey we conducted in Bo (a large city), 92 per cent of the dead children had died by the age of 3, and 50 per cent of the children who had ever been fostered were first sent away by the age of 5. Therefore, most of the deceased children died before they had a chance to be fostered; and the children who were ever fostered were already a selected group of survivors. Also, it is misleading to rely on data on children's residence (or their relationship to caretakers) at their time of death. Children who become seriously ill with caretakers are usually sent home, biasing the responses in favour of residence with parents at time of death. A more useful question is the following, 'With whom was the child staying when he or she got sick?'

Finally, because fosterage is such a casual feature of domestic life, mothers and caretakers quickly forget dates and other events associated with fosterage. More useful would be data that traced children to other households and noted at regular time intervals the economic and social characteristics of the foster-parents and their access to public health improvements and medical resources. These data could be compared with the biological parents' situation. Yet problems of interpretation still arise because neither the household characteristics of the guardians *nor* of the parents may be reasonable indicators of a foster-child's mortality risks: social barriers deny the child full benefits from the guardian's wealth and geographical separation denies the benefits of the mother's characteristics.

Although attempts to analyse fosterage are fraught with analytical problems that standard surveys do not confront, fosterage poses important questions about distribution of resources *within* households that need to be considered. (For related discussions, see Sachs, 1953, Williams, 1953, and Ali Taha, 1978.) Although age and sex are commonly examined intrahousehold variables, we argue that the position of children by fosterage status is also important. We turn, then, to our own quantitative and qualitative data on social, economic, and cultural factors that affect foster children's morbidity and mortality in southern and eastern Sierra Leone.

5. Fostering and Child Mortality in Sierra Leone

Sierra Leone has one of the highest infant mortality rates in the world. A. C. Thomas (1983) estimated the 1974 rate, the date of the last census for which information is available, at 227 per thousand. There is considerable regional variation, however; some chiefdoms in the south had rates of over 300 per thousand. Ewbank (personal communication) estimated that for Pujehun District, in the south, 44.5 per cent of the children were dead by the age of 5. Although most deaths occur to infants, the age range most relevant to fosterage is 1 to 4 years. Within this group, Kandeh (1985) reports that nutritionally related diseases (measles, see Aaby in this volume, diarrhoea, malnutrition, and anaemia) account for 39.8 per cent of all deaths. (See Kandeh, 1985, for a more comprehensive analysis of mortality among Sierra Leonean children.) We note also that infant feeding practices, including feeding bottled milk, appear to figure strongly in the deaths of small children. Often this has nothing to do with fosterage. However, many young mothers who send their young children away do so assuming that the caretaker will feed them imported 'tinned' milk from a bottle or 'pap' (see Bledsoe, 1987*b*). Hence, fosterage may lead indirectly to morbidity or mortality simply because children ingest contaminated or nutritionally inadequate breast milk substitutes.

Concerning fosterage itself, we underscore the point that even very young

Table 12.1. *Proportions of children deceased and living away from mother by age of mother, Sierra Leone and Bumpe Chiefdom, 1974 Census*

Age of mother	Sierra Leone			Bumpe Chiefdom		
	Total children	% dead	% away	Total children	% dead	% away
15–19	96,393	31.5	29.1	1,016	35.7	36.3
20–24	233,982	33.5	35.9	2,217	41.2	46.6
25–29	411,621	36.0	40.1	4,435	41.2	54.6
30–34	422,434	39.4	45.6	4,940	42.3	62.1
35–39	410,219	41.1	48.9	5,982	43.0	63.6
40–44	315,195	44.4	55.9	3,979	46.2	69.3
45–49	256,835	46.0	59.8	3,534	47.3	72.2
Total	2,146,679	39.6	46.1	26,103	43.2	60.9

Note: The percentage living away is the proportion of all living children not currently living with their mother.

children can be fostered. Using figures from the 1974 census, Isiugo-Abanihe (1983*a*) found that 29 per cent of all surviving children in Sierra Leone who were born to women aged 15–19—mostly children under 2—were away from their mothers (see Table 12.1). These percentages increase with age. In some chiefdoms, particularly in the south, half of the children under two were away from their mothers. The census figures suggest that fosterage is linked to child mortality, although causality is difficult to determine. Isiugo-Abanihe (1983*b*) found that those chiefdoms in which a large percentage of children were away from their mothers also had the highest rates of child mortality. Results from our own survey in a large town in Sierra Leone are similar: women who have ever fostered out children have a significantly higher child mortality experience than those who had not (p = 0.0005). However, as we (and Isiugo-Abanihe) have stressed, the positive relationship between fosterage and child mortality does not prove that children die because they are fostered out. Rather, an individual woman's child mortality experience may prompt her to foster out her surviving children to protect them against the alleged causes, whether economic or supernatural, of a prior child's death.

We turn now to a qualitative description of fosterage practices in Sierra Leone, and then to a set of quantitative data that bears on the issues of fosterage and child mortality. The methods used in the study consisted, accordingly, of qualitative ones (open-ended interviews, participant observation, daily records of household observations, and so on) as well as use of surveys and census data.

(*a*) **Fostering of young children**

Many factors precipitate a decision to foster out small children. Children sent out very young are likely to have mothers who are divorced (Page, 1986), dead, or unmarried schoolgirls wishing to return to school; or to have fathers who do not accept or support them. (It is unclear, however, to what extent this is particularly a problem in patrilineal societies, wherein children belong to their father's lineage; in which case their legitimacy may be more important to the family.) Some reasons for fosterage stem from parents' fears of witchcraft from jealous neighbours or relatives. Besides these 'crisis' reasons (see also Sinclair, 1972), the mother may be pregnant again (or wants to be), or she may have another small baby or several closely spaced children. Alternatively, she may find that a baby taxes her energy and interferes with her work on the farm or in the market.

How do the reasons for fostering and the characteristics of those who take in fosters affect young children's access to food and medical services? This depends in part on who fosters the children and why they do so. A woman who is barren or subfecund frequently takes in a small child of a close relative, either for an arrangement more like a permanent adoption than most fosterage, or hoping that the foster-child's presence will ritually attract the spirit of a child to her. Qualitative observations indicate that such fosterage arrangements, especially when they involve only one or two children, and those of close relatives, seldom result in discrimination.

Discrimination is more likely when a young child is placed with a woman already caring for several foster-children or a woman with her own young children to worry about, especially if the child was taken because of pressure from a lower status family, which does not contribute toward its expenses. Discrimination is also likely when a man brings in a relative's child against the wishes of his wife, who sees the child as a competitor for scarce resources against her own children. Similarly, although young children usually remain with their mothers in the case of a divorce until they can manage better on their own, an occasional man insists on keeping his young child. In the father's household, however, this child is likely to be viewed by the other wives as a competitor against their own children and, worse, as a reminder of a marriage they themselves may have helped to end (Bledsoe, 1987*a*).

In such circumstances, small fosters eat from bowls with much larger children who can eat more quickly and can grab more meat and sauce. Little attention is devoted to their appearance or their health. It is therefore not surprising that in the local idiom, unkempt children are taunted that they look like 'minded' (foster) children.

In many cases, of course, a small child's treatment with guardians who have young children of their own stems from lack of resources. A child who goes to a household of lower status than that of the mother is unlikely to be well fed, especially if the parents make no financial or material contribution to the upkeep. If poor foster-parents have children of their own, the child becomes an added burden. Medical care is also a problem. Many guardians lack the money to take a sick child to the hospital. Writing to the child's parents merely delays treatment since the postal and telephone systems are unreliable. Consequently, a guardian waits until the child's health has deteriorated seriously to bring him or her to the hospital or clinic.

These points are also relevant to the most salient caretakers of young children: 'grannies'. A 'granny' guardian can be any older woman, regardless of her exact relationship, although it is often the mother's mother. Because people maintain that a child cannot learn much before the 'age of sense', around six, they are willing to send younger children out to rural grannies. When ready for training, children come back to their parents or even go on to more urban caretakers.

In contrast with younger caretakers with children of their own to worry about, 'grannies' rarely discriminate against small foster-children, although we heard occasional reports of older women giving indifferent care to their young relatives' illegitimate children for whom there was no paternal support. In most cases, people argue that because of their experience and compassion, 'grannies' are the best caretakers of young children. They are said to love and pamper their small charges, and to know the proper foods for them and the traditional medicines for curing childhood diseases.

But the reality of small children's welfare with older grannies frequently differs from the popular image of a spoiled life of well-fed ease. In part because they are less well educated than the younger generation, older rural caretakers commonly use traditional medicine and take a child to the hospital as a last resort when it is ill. They are more likely than young urbanites to adhere to cultural food taboos, such as beliefs that small children should not have meat, fish, or eggs, which allegedly increase their desires for expensive animal protein and prompt them to steal. Also, grannies are more likely to believe that worms thrive on animal protein foods in the child's body and drain it of blood, making the child get pale: a symptom of kwashiorkor. In the cultural logic, therefore, feeding a small child animal protein does not cure kwashiorkor; instead, it exacerbates or even causes the disease.

Beyond the cultural beliefs they hold, many grannies face economic and geographical disadvantages that affect how they care for children. Grannies tend to be more rural and poorer than caretakers of older children or than the children's own parents. Many grandmothers live in villages away from hospitals or clinics, and they lack access to safe drinking water and adequate toilet facilities: conditions which increase the child's risk of contracting water-borne diseases. Moreover, while young people migrate to areas with off-farm employment, many rural grannies subsist by marginally supported subsistence cultivation or small-scale cash cropping. They have little to offer children besides cassava, yams, and rice, especially during rainy months such as August, which is translated locally as 'death time'. This poses a severe problem for very small children whose mothers assumed the grannies would bottle-feed them commercial tinned milk (Bledsoe, 1987*b*).

These geographical and social patterns are important to small children's welfare. Rural locations, greater poverty of local resources, poorer sanitation, and traditional caretakers, coupled with very young ages of fosterage, have far-reaching implications for morbidity and mortality risks among small children. (For more discussion of 'grannies', see Bledsoe and Isiugo-Abanihe, 1985.)

(*b*) Fostering of older children

The morbidity and mortality consequences of fosterage for older children are quite different. Older children, of course, are less sensitive to nutritional inadequacies than younger ones; but their fosterage conditions also differ. Most older fosters are sent to higher status families and to more urban areas than those from which they came. Through their training and contacts in these areas, they may achieve greater educational and occupational status than their siblings who are not fostered. Boys go for trade apprenticeships, Arabic learning, or schooling, whereas girls go for 'home training' (in housework) or schooling.

Fosterage can considerably improve an older child's life. A subfecund middle-aged urban woman reported that although her 7-year-old foster-child had been with her only three months, he was anxious to stay because he was better fed than with his own mother, a young woman with several small children. When the guardian—who was biologically unrelated to him—asked who his 'mother' was, he asserted that she was, a statement that attests not to his forgetfulness, but to his readiness to assign a socially appropriate label to the woman who now played a crucial role for him.

But although some older children in higher status homes are treated well, many are sent to people only distantly related to them, or even non-relatives. Moreover, they are often treated according to an ideology of hardship and deprivation. They may be poorly dressed, have heavy work assignments, and receive severe punishments. When they get sick, their initial complaints are often dismissed as faking in order to avoid work, whereas those of children with their mother present are taken more seriously. Like young fosters, older ones often receive less to eat, especially foods rich in protein, from the household pot than children with mothers. Frequently all the foster-children eat from one basin that contains smaller portions of meat sauce than that of the household's own children. Moreover, snacks, comprising a significant proportion of children's diets, go more to those with mothers present.

Food deprivation for alleged laziness or bad behaviour is a common punishment for children: especially foster-children. It also seems to be applied more to foster-girls than boys because they are assigned more of the household chores, and their mistakes and shortcomings are more immediately visible to guardians. As a result, a nutrition clinic supervisor reported that despite girls' closer proximity to the cooking pot than boys (with a resultant greater potential for snatching food), most of the mal-nutrition cases she saw, particularly kwashiorkor, were fostered girls. In contrast, the few older boys who were malnourished tended to be those sent for religious instruction with a Muslim Arabic teacher. The severity of their conditions is legendary. Explained one man:

These Arabic teachers do not take much care over these children. In fact, they [the children] feed themselves through alms. They go and beg. They do not have real food prepared for them.

In many cases, discrimination and punishment by food deprivation stem from social pressure on the guardians to enforce discipline, for society holds a foster-parent, more than the natural parent, responsible for the child's success or failure in life. Hence, a local saying notes that, 'The onus . . . is not on those who gave birth to the children but on those who reared the child.'

In general, however, the potential nutritional discrimination against older foster-children is offset by two factors: (1) they are better able than younger ones to fend for themselves by foraging in the forest, asking friends and neighbours for food, marketing, and stealing (Bledsoe, 1983); and (2) older children are more often sent to towns and cities, where foraging possibilities are generally better than in rural areas, and where hospitals and clinics are closer at hand for emergencies. Given all these factors, we believe that older foster-children fare comparably to their age peers with mothers.

6. The Serabu Hospital Study

Quantitative data bearing on these observations come primarily from a hospital study, in which we examined the relative risks by age and sex, of hospitalization, malnutrition, and death among fostered and non-fostered patients (a fuller discussion of this study is found in Bledsoe *et al.*, MS). The data consist of admissions records from Serabu Hospital, a rural Catholic mission hospital in Bumpe Chiefdom, in southern Sierra Leone. Charts were examined of patients from 0 to 12 years who were admitted to the children's ward between 1979 and 1985. Most of the analysis was restricted to children aged from 1 to 12, since this is the normal fosterage range. The nutritional diseases were restricted to kwashiorkor, marasmus, and protein–calorie malnutrition. A simplified kind of caretaking data was also obtained from the charts: children with mothers versus 'others'. Table 12.2 displays the child patients by age group and caretaking status.

Table 12.2. *Serabu child admissions by age group and caretaker*

Age	Number of admissions	% of all child admissions	% reported with mother	% reported with other
0–11 m.	1,241	41.2	96.9	3.1
1–5 yrs.	1,317	43.8	86.6	13.4
6–12 yrs.	451	15.0	73.2	16.8
Total	3,009	100.0	88.8	11.2

Concerning differences between the treatment of foster-children versus those with mothers, separate calculations suggested that the proportion of fosters in the hospital population is much less than in the population at large, as derived from census estimates. Young foster-children aged 1 to 5 years were only 16 to 23 per cent as likely as those with mothers to receive hospital treatment, and older children were 24 to 36 per cent as likely as those with mothers to be admitted.

As for the distribution of maladies, the proportions of most maladies among hospitalized fosters were similar to those of children with mothers. The major exception was malnutrition. Table 12.3 examines differences in children by age and caretaking status, according to whether they had mal-

Table 12.3. *Children diagnosed as malnourished by age group, sex, and caretaker (% distribution)*

		Caretaker					Total	t value
		Mother			Other			
1–5 yrs.		6.1			19.2		7.9	4.5
		(1,140)			(177)		(1,317)	
	Male	*Female*	*t value*	*Male*	*Female*	*t value*		
	4.6	7.9	2.4	16.7	22.7	1.1		
	(593)	(547)		(102)	(75)			
6–12 yrs.		3.0			3.3		3.1	0.0
		(330)			(121)		(451)	
	Male	*Female*	*t value*	*Male*	*Female*	*t value*		
	2.5	3.8	0.6	1.4	6.0	1.3		
	(755)	(133)		(71)	(50)			
Total		5.7			13.5		6.8	
(1–12 yrs.)		(1,399)			(281)		(1,680)	

Note: Numbers in parentheses are the number of children in the category.

nutrition among any of their multiple maladies reported. It shows sharp differences particularly among young children. Fostered children aged 1 to 5 were admitted with malnutrition over three times as frequently as non-fostered ones. Among fosters from 1 to 5, 19.2 per cent had malnutrition, compared with only 6.1 per cent of children with mothers. Much of the malnutrition among young fosters was kwashiorkor, lending some empirical validity to a local appellation of kwashiorkor as the 'granny disease'. In contrast, children aged 6 to 12 showed no differences in malnutrition by fosterage status, a finding reflecting older children's lower susceptibility to malnutrition as well as their fosterage conditions and their ability to forage.

Sex differences (shown in the same table) among child patients were striking. Fostered girls from 1 to 5 were only 49 per cent as likely to be hospitalized as fostered boys, and those who received hospital treatment were more often malnourished. Like the younger fosters, older female fosters were more malnourished than male fosters. But girls in general had higher rates of malnutrition in hospital deaths than boys (except non-fosters aged 6 to 12), perhaps reflecting their fewer opportunities to forage outside the household. This apparent sex discrimination in hospitalization, particularly against fostered girls, represents a significant finding for a continent where few sex differences in medical welfare have been observed, compared with other areas of the world. Breaking down the sexes by fostering status (and, we suspect, by whether paternity is acknowledged) reveals patterns not heretofore observed in African data. Whether differentiation by sex indicates a change from older patterns is an important question we cannot answer.

Concerning deaths in the hospital, an indicator of condition on arrival, Table 12.4 shows that foster-children were more apt than children with mothers to die, especially those aged 1 to 5, who had hospital death rates almost twice as high as children with mothers. In Table 12.5, malnutrition seems to be associated with foster-children's deaths in the hospital: of those children who died, only 20.4 per cent of those with mothers had malnutrition, compared to 42.9 per cent of fostered children. And if we were to take malnourished children as a group (including those below 1 year of age), we would see that 33 per cent of foster-children died in the hospital, compared to 26.5 per cent of children with mothers.

In addition, while malnourished foster-children rarely spent more than a day in the hospital, children with mothers stayed an average of 2.6 days. This suggests that mothers bringing in their own children are more likely than guardians to commit time and money to their treatment in the hospital. And while it underscores the difficulties in measuring comparable groups, it highlights the differences that *do* appear between the conditions of fostered and non-fostered children when they are brought to the hospital.

Some of the potentially most significant patterns in fosterage and hospitalization appear to involve change. The economic situation in Sierra Leone

Table 12.4. *Condition of children after treatment, by age group and caretaker (% distribution)*

Ages	Mother				Other				t for difference in % dead
	Cured	On treatment	Incapacitated	Dead	Cured	On treatment	Incapacitated	Dead	
1–5 yrs.	76.1 (862)	10.9 (124)	3.3 (38)	9.7 (110)	58.8 (104)	13.0 (23)	9.6 (17)	18.6 (33)	2.9
6–12 yrs.	72.1 (239)	14.2 (48)	7.6 (25)	6.1 (20)	62.8 (76)	21.5 (26)	5.8 (7)	9.9 (12)	1.3
Total	75.1 (1,101)	11.7 (172)	4.3 (63)	8.9 (130)	60.4 (180)	16.4 (49)	8.1 (24)	15.1 (45)	

Note: Numbers in parentheses represent the numbers of children in the category.

Table 12.5. *Maladies of Serabu children ages 1 to 5 who died in the hospital (% distribution)*

	Caretaker		Total
	Mother	Other	
Malnutrition	20.4	42.9	25.2
	(21)	(12)	(33)
Other maladies	79.6	57.1	74.8
	(82)	(16)	(98)
Total	100.0	100.0	100.0
	(103)	(28)	(131)

Note: Numbers in parentheses are the numbers of children in the category.

has declined precipitously during the last few years with rising prices, inflation, and shortages. These changes affect the household as a whole, making small children with grannies worse off now because of the increasing poverty and isolation of their caretakers. These changes may also affect intra-household resource allocations. Foster-children may face ·more discrimination at mealtimes if there is less to go around, and particularly those with poor rural caretakers undoubtedly encounter more delays in going to the hospital because petrol prices have driven up transportation costs to prohibitive levels.

Indeed, it is those hospitalized fosters who may be with rural grannies, children from 1 to 5 years, whose rates of malnutrition have risen most sharply. Table 12.6 shows that whereas malnutrition among 1 to 5-year-old patients with mothers actually declined by 8.3 per cent to a total of 1.3 per cent of admissions, it rose by 9.2 per cent among fosters to a total of 26.2 per cent. Sex differences have also intensified, as Table 12.7 demonstrates. Among fostered girls from 1 to 5, malnutrition rose 10.4 points (from 22.9 to 33.3 per cent), while it rose by only 6.9 points (from 16.9 to 23.8 per cent) among fostered boys. (Differences over time among 6 to 12-year-olds were less pronounced, though similar.) Such evidence suggests that young fostered children, particularly girls, bear heavy nutritional costs of economic hardship.

In interpreting the Serabu results, we add this caveat that, like most hospital data, they may not reflect high rates of morbidity and mortality in the wider population, but the results of a selective triage process, wherein foster-children come to the hospital only if they are very sick. However, because fosters in this study have disproportionately higher rates of malnutrition than children with mothers, and because more than twice the

Table 12.6. *Serabu children with malnutrition, by age groups, caretakers, and year of admission (% distribution)*

Year	Children with mother at ages		Fostered children at ages	
	1–5	6–12	1–5	6–12
1979–81	9.6	5.4	17.0	3.4
	(667)	(149)	(135)	(88)
1982–85	1.3	1.1	26.2	3.0
	(473)	(181)	(42)	(33)

Note: Numbers in parentheses are the numbers of children in the category.

Table 12.7. *Serabu children with malnutrition, by age groups, sex, caretaker, and year of admission (% distribution)*

	Mother		Other	
	Male	Fem.	Male	Fem.
1–5 yrs.				
1979–81	7.7	13.2	16.9	22.9
	(24/310)	(40/303)	(12/71)	(11/48)
1982–85	1.3	1.6	23.8	33.3
	(3/226)	(3/184)	(5/21)	(6/18)
6–12 yrs.				
1979–81	6.3	6.6	2.2	6.7
	(4/64)	(4/61)	(1/45)	(2/30)
1982–85	1.0	1.9	0.0	8.3
	(1/99)	(1/52)	(0/18)	(1/12)
Total (1–12 yrs.)				
1979–81	7.5	12.1	11.2	16.7
	(28/374)	(44/364)	(13/116)	(13/78)
1982–85	1.2	1.7	12.8	23.3
	(4/325)	(4/236)	(5/39)	(7/30)

Note: Numbers in parentheses are the numbers of children in the category.

proportion of young fosters than children with mothers who died in the hospital were malnourished (42.9 as opposed to 20.4 per cent), the evidence suggests that foster-children in the wider population are indeed sicker and at higher risk of mortality than those with mothers. The case is yet more persuasive when combined with findings from other studies and with our own ethnographic data.

7. Discussion

Studies of the relationship of fosterage to child mortality must address two basic questions. First, are foster-children more at risk than other children in the household where they are staying? The evidence we have reviewed is fairly clear that, on the whole, they are. Whether this stems from systematic daily discrimination or from periodic economic shortages in which fosters are first to feel the pinch in less clear. (Indirect support for the latter comes from Kolasa's (1978) study, which argues that food taboos for children in Sierra Leone are adhered to primarily when food is scarce.)

The second question is more difficult to answer: are foster-children at greater risk with guardians than with their own mothers? We have shown that the answer depends on the circumstances of a child's fosterage. Many young children with guardians actually appear to be at less risk than with their mothers. This may reflect mothers' poverty or lengthy absences, or competition from half-siblings by their mothers' new husbands. In such circumstances, young fosters with 'grannies', for example, are pampered with a level of love and attention they might not otherwise receive. And for older children, even if those raised by a higher status family are denied its richest resources, they may be exposed to a better environment than if they had remained at home (see Isiugo-Abanihe 1983a).

We do not mean to avoid the ultimate question of cause or effect in the relationship between fosterage and child mortality. We believe, as local people argue, that the advantages of fosterage outweigh its risks. Asking about options helps also to answer the difficult question of why parents tolerate knowing that their children are malnourished or even maltreated. They may have no better options. (Other demographic problems that are seen in conventional wisdom as simple cause–effect terms might be better approached by asking about alternatives. Mortality rates might rise instead of decline, for example, if all women in an area boiled their drinking water, because of increased costs to the household of fuel in cash or labour.)

Thus, foster-children may not suffer higher mortality rates because they are fostered. Rather (as Hill, 1987, cogently argues for analogous situations of migration during Sahelian drought) they bring their already high mortality risks with them when they come to a different home. Even so, the evidence suggests that once in these homes, they are likely to have higher morbidity and mortality risks than other children for reasons that stem from social structure.

For more immediate applied concerns, if the young children most at risk in a given household are probably those without mothers, then programmes and surveys aimed at 'women and their children' are overlooking a group that is subject to substantially elevated risks. Instead of being allowed to slip through the cracks of the formal health care system, foster-children might be a special target of creative programmes that seek to accommodate families' quite rational efforts to socially adjust their size and composition to meet their needs. Such efforts become even more important in situations of economic decline as households confront increasingly difficult resource allocation decisions.

Acknowledgements

We are grateful to the following people for help in various aspects of this research: Katherine Condon, Doug Ewbank, Uche Isiugo-Abanihe, William Murphy, Sam Preston, Daniel Sala-Diakanda, Ben Sheku, Étienne van de Walle, Jacques Vallin, and Susan Zimicki. We also thank the Population Council, the Rockefeller Foundation, the Ford Foundation, and the National Science Foundation, as well as the University of Pennsylvania and Northwestern University for generous support of the fosterage study.

References

Ainsworth, M. D. S. (1967), *Infancy in Uganda*, Johns Hopkins University, Baltimore.

Ali Taha, S. A. (1978), 'Household food consumption in five villages in the Sudan', *Ecology of Food and Nutrition* 7/3: 137–42.

Antoine, P. and Guillaume, A. (1986), 'Une expression de la solidarité familiale à Abidjan: Enfants du couple et enfants confiés', in AIDELF, *Les familles d'aujourd'hui: Colloque de Genève*, INED, Paris.

Bledsoe, C. H. (1983), 'Stealing food as a problem in demography and nutrition', Paper presented at the 1983 meetings of the American Anthropological Association, Chicago, Ill.

—— (1987a), 'The politics of polygyny in Mende education and child fosterage transactions', Paper presented to a Wenner–Gren Foundation symposium on gender hierarchies, Mijas, Spain.

—— (1987b), 'Tinned milk and child fosterage: Side-stepping the post-partum sex taboo', Prepared for a Rockefeller Foundation conference on Cultural Roots of African Fertility Regimes, Ife.

—— (MS), '"No success without struggle": Social mobility and hardship for Sierra Leonean children'.

—— and Isiugo-Abanihe, U. (1985), 'Strategies of child fosterage among Mende "grannies" in Sierra Leone', Paper presented at the meetings of the Population Association of America in Boston, Mass.

—— Ewbank, D. C. Isiugo-Abanihe, U. (MS), 'The relationship of child fosterage to child mortality and child morbidity in rural Sierra Leone'.

Brydon, L. (1985), 'The Avatime family and circulation, 1900–1977', in R. Mansell Prothero and M. Chapman (eds.), *Circulation in Third World Countries*, Routledge & Kegan Paul, London, 206–25.

Burgess, H. J. L., Cole-King, S., and Burgess, A. (1972), 'Nutritional status of children at Namitambo, Malawi', *Journal of Tropical Medicine and Hygiene* 73/8: 143–8.

Caldwell, J. (1977), 'The economic rationality of high fertility: An investigation illustrated with Nigerian survey Data', *Population Studies* 31/1: 5–27.

Cameroon (1978), *National Nutrition Survey*, Government of Cameroon, in cooperation with USAID.

Cantrelle, P. *et al.* (1986), 'The profile of mortality and its determinants in Senegal, 1960–80', in *Determinants of Mortality Change and Differentials in Developing Countries: The Five-Country Case Study Project*, United Nations: Department of International Economic and Social Affairs, Population Studies 94: 86–116.

Cross, C. P. and Ibru, C. (1978), 'A portrait of foster care: Private fostering among two generations of Nigerians', *West African Journal of Sociology and Political Science* 1: 285–305.

Dixon, S. D., LeVine, R. A., Brazelton, T. B. (1982), 'Malnutrition: A closer look at the problem in an East African village', *Developmental Medicine and Child Neurology* 24/5: 670–85.

Étienne, M. (1983), 'Gender relations and conjugality among the Baulé', in Christine Oppong (ed.), *Female and Male in West Africa*, Allen & Unwin, London, 303–19.

Fapohunda, E. (1978), 'Characteristics of Women Workers in Lagos', *Labour and Society* 3/20: 158–71.

Flandrin, J. (1976), *Families in Former Times: Kinship, Household and Sexuality in Early Modern France*, Cambridge University Press, Cambridge.

Frank, O. (1984), 'Child-fostering in sub-Saharan Africa', Paper presented at the meetings of the Population Association of America, Minneapolis, Minn.

Geber, M. and Dean, F. R. A. (1955), 'Psychological factors in the etiology of kwashiorkor', *Bulletin, World Health Organization*, 12/3: 471–5.

Goodall, J. (1979), 'A social score for kwashiorkor: Explaining the look in the child's eyes', *Developmental Medicine and Child Neurology* 21/3: 374–84.

Goody, E. N. (1982), *Parenthood and Social Reproduction: Fostering and Occupational Roles in West Africa*, Cambridge University Press, Cambridge.

Gupta, B. M. and Mwamba, A. (1976), 'Study of malnourished children in Tanga, Tanzania, 1. Socioeconomic and cultural aspects', *Journal of Tropical Pediatrics and Environmental Child Health* 22/6: 268–73.

Hill, A. G. (1987), 'Demographic responses to food shortages in the Sahel', Paper for the FAO Expert Consultation on Population and Agricultural and Rural Development: Institutions and Policy, Rome.

Isaac, B. R. and Conrad, S. R. (1982), 'Child fosterage among the Mende of Upper Bambara Chiefdom, Sierra Leone: Rural–urban and occupational comparisons', *Ethnology* 21: 243–57.

Isiugo-Abanihe, U. (1983a), 'Child fosterage in West Africa', *Population and Development Review* 11/1: 53–73.

—— (1983b), 'Child Fostering in West Africa: Prevalence, Determinants and Demographic Consequences', Ph.D. diss., University of Pennsylvania.

Jelliffe, D. B. (1962) 'Urbanization and child nutrition in Africa', *International Child Welfare Review* 16/2: 67–73.

—— (1968), *Infant Nutrition in the Subtropics and Tropics*, WHO, Geneva.

Kahn, E. (1962), 'Protein Malnutrition (Kwashiorkor) in Children of Working Mothers', *South African Medical Journal* 36/10: 177–8.

Kandeh, B. S. (1985), 'Causes of infant and early childhood deaths in Sierra Leone', Paper presented to the Joint Symposium in Medical Geography, Nottingham, England.

Kolasa, K. M. (1978), 'The nutritional situation in Sierra Leone', Report No. 1, Project on Consumption Effects of Economic Policy, Michigan State University.

Lees, R. E. M. (1964), 'Malnutrition: The pattern and prevention in St. Lucia', *West Indian Medical Journal* 13/2: 97–102.

Levine, S. and Levine, R. (1981), 'Child abuse and neglect in Sub-Saharan Africa', in J. E. Korbin (ed.), *Child Abuse and Neglect: Cross-Cultural Perspectives*, University of California, Berkeley, 35–55.

Liberia (1976), *Liberia National Nutrition Survey*, Ministry of Health and Social Welfare, Republic of Liberia, in co-operation with USAID.

Lightcap, J. L., Kurland, J. A., and Burgess, R. L. (1982), 'Child abuse: A test of some predictions from evolutionary theory', *Ethology and Sociobiology* 3: 61–7.

Locoh, T. (1982), 'Demographic aspects of the family cycle in sub-Saharan Africa', in *Health and the Family Life Cycle*, Federal Institute for Population Research, Wiesbaden, and WHO, Geneva.

Moodie, A. (1961), 'Kwashiorkor in Cape Town: The background of patients and their progress after discharge', *Journal of Pediatrics* 58/3: 392–403.

Namboze, J. W. (1967), 'Weaning practices in Buganda', *Tropical and Geographical Medicine* 19/2: 154–60.

Neave, M. (1968), 'Protein and calorie malnutrition of early childhood in western Samoa', *Tropical and Geographical Medicine* 20/3: 191–201.

Oomen, H. A. P. C. (1953), 'Preliminary survey on malignant malnutrition in Djakarta toddlers', *Documenta de Medicina Geographica et Tropica* 5/3: 193–214.

Oppong, C. (1973), *Growing Up in Dagbon*, Accra.

—— (1983) 'Paternal costs, role strain and fertility regulation: Some Ghanaian evidence', Population and Labour Policies Programme, Working Paper 134, ILO, Geneva.

Page, H. (1986), 'Child-bearing versus child-rearing: Co-residence of mothers and children in sub-Saharan Africa', IDP Working Paper 1986-2, Interuniversity Programme in Demography, Brussels.

Pretorius, P. J., Davel, J. A. G., and Coetzee, H. N. (1956), 'Some observations on the development of kwashiorkor: A study of 205 cases', *South African Medical Journal* 30/17: 396–9.

Rawson, I. G. and Berggren, G. (1973), 'Family structure, child location and nutritional disease in rural Haiti', *Environmental Child Health* 19/3: 288–98.

Sachs, S. B. (1953), 'The social aetiology of malignant malnutrition', *South African Medical Journal* 27/20: 430–2.

Said, M. (1955), 'Kwashiorkor in Negri Sembilan', *Medical Journal of Malaya* 10/1: 20–47.

Schildkrout, E. (1973), 'The fostering of children in urban Ghana: Problems of ethnographic analysis in a multi-cultural context', *Urban Anthropology* 2: 48–73.

Schmutzhard, E., Poewe, W., and Gerstenbrand, F. (1986), 'Separation from the mother at time of weaning', *Tropical Doctor* 16: 176–7.

Scragg, J. and Rubidge, C. (1960), 'Kwashiorkor in African children in Durban', *British Medical Journal*, 17 Dec., 1759–66.

Scrimshaw, N. S., Behar, M., Viteri, F., Arroyave, G., and Tejada, C. (1957), 'Epidemiology and prevention of severe protein malnutrition (kwashiorkor) in Central America', *American Journal of Public Health* 47/1: 53–62.

Sierra Leone (1978), *National Nutrition Survey*, Government of Sierra Leone, in co-operation with USAID.

Silk, J. (1987), 'Adoption and fosterage in human societies: Adaptations or enigmas?' *Cultural Anthropology* 2/1: 39–49.

Sinclair, J. (1972), 'Educational assistance, kinship, and the social structure in Sierra Leone', *Africana Research Bulletin* 2: 30–62.

Swaziland (1983), *Swaziland National Nutrition Status Survey: Full Report*, Government of Swaziland, in co-operation with USAID.

Thomas, A. C. (1983), *The Population of Sierra Leone: An Analysis of Population Census Data*, Demographic Research and Training Unit, Fourah Bay College, Freetown.

Thomas, G. C. (1981), 'The social background of childhood nutrition in the Ciskei', *Social Science and Medicine* 15A/5: 551–5.

Thompson, B. and Rahman, A. K. (1967), 'Infant feeding and child care in a West African village', *Journal of Tropical Pediatrics* 13/3: 124–38.

Tripp, R. B. (1981), 'Farmers and traders: Some economic determinants of nutritional status in Northern Ghana', *Journal of Tropical Pediatrics* 27/1: 15–22.

Waterston, T. (1982), 'What causes kwashiorkor in the older child?' *Journal of Tropical Pediatrics* 28/3: 132–4.

Weisner, T. S. and Gallimore, R. (1977), 'My brother's keeper: Child and sibling caretaking', *Current Anthropology* 18/2: 169–90.

Williams, C. (1933), 'A nutritional disease of childhood associated with a maize diet', *Archives of the Diseases of Childhood* 8: 423–33.

—— (1953), 'Kwashiorkor', *Journal of the American Medical Association* 153/14: 1280–5.

Wilson, M., Daly, M., and Weghorst, S. (1980), 'Household composition and the risk of child abuse and neglect', *Journal of Biosocial Science* 12: 333–40.

Winikoff, B. (1980), 'Weaning: Nutrition, Morbidity, and Mortality Consequences', IUSSP Seminar on Biological and Social Aspects of Mortality and the Length of Life, Fiuggi Terma, Italy.

13 Type of Feeding and Infant Mortality in Yaoundé

Hendrik van der Pol
IFORD, Yaoundé

1. Introduction

Infant feeding practices, those governing the giving of milk in particular, influence two demographic phenomena, fertility and infant mortality. With respect to fertility, breast-feeding affects the hormonal balance of the mother and delays the return of ovulation after delivery. This reduces the risk of conception and has an effect upon the inter-pregnancy interval.

With regard to infant mortality, the mother's milk gives a certain amount of immunological protection to the child and satisfies its nutritional needs better than substitute foods. These advantages, along with the fact that in most developing countries it is difficult to prepare replacement foods properly, mean that children fed from the breast run fewer risks of infection or malnutrition, and so have a lower probability of dying than those who are not breast-fed.

This chapter deals with the relationship between types of feeding and infant mortality in Yaoundé, both for the whole population and for certain sub-populations.

2. The Data

The data used here come from an infant and child mortality survey in Yaoundé (EMIJ) carried out by the *Institut de Formation et de Recherche Démographiques* (IFORD). This was a multi-round survey of a sample of infants who were born in 1978 in the maternity clinics of Yaoundé and whose mothers lived in Yaoundé. These infants were followed over a two-year period and were visited seven times, at ages 1, 4, 8, 12, 16, 20, and 24 months. The panel began with 9,774 new-borns, but 3,346—more than a third—were lost to observation before the two years were completed, and we do not know their fate. This is the most serious problem with this survey.

This chapter was translated by Mark Hereward.

To obtain information on the type of child-feeding in Yaoundé, the following questions were asked during each round of the survey:

1. What kind of milk is (was) the child given?
   breast milk?   [ ]
   bottle milk?   [ ]   since when? ____
   mixed feeding   [ ]   since when? ____
2. In addition to milk, do (did) you give the child other food?
      yes [ ]   no [ ]
         Which ones?
         ____   since when? ____
         ____   since when? ____ .

The frequency of non-response for the questions on duration was very high, and it was therefore decided not to use this information. Nevertheless, it is possible to estimate average durations from the information on current type of feeding given at each round of the survey.

(a) Difficulties encountered

The loss of children to observation poses a problem because it is probably linked to mortality. Mothers who lost their children may have moved because they feared that the house was bewitched, or they may have hidden from the interviewers to avoid embarrassing questions. We have shown that the omissions were most common in the following sub-populations: among the Béti, among the children of mothers who had low levels of education (none or primary level only), and among boys (van der Pol, 1986). We noted that the children lost to observation were more likely to have been given only breast milk before their disappearance; exclusive bottle-feeding was also common for them, and the combination of breast and bottle-feeding was less frequent. If loss to observation is positively linked with mortality, the results presented here should be affected correspondingly, but we believe that omissions are more likely to bias the estimated levels of mortality, than the relation between mortality and type of feeding which is the subject of this chapter.

The small numbers of observations in some categories limited our analysis. For example, knowledge of the employment status of the mother is important for studying the type of feeding, but only 15 per cent of the women in the sample reported an occupation.

(b) Types of child-feeding in Yaoundé

On the basis of the survey's responses, we may distinguish between different types of feeding by source of milk (maternal or artificial), and according to whether or not supplementary foods were used (such as purée, pap, or fruit):

(a) *Exclusive breast-feeding without supplement*: the child receives only the mother's milk, with no other food.

(b) *Exclusive breast-feeding with supplementary feeding*: the only milk the child receives is from the mother, but it also receives other non-dairy foods.

(c) *Mixed feeding, or combination of breast and other milk*: the child receives milk from the mother's breast as well as milk from a bottle. The child may also receive supplementary feeding.

(d) *Bottle-feeding only*: the child only receives milk given from a bottle. The child may or may not receive supplementary foods as well.

(e) In addition to these four groups are children who receive *no milk at all*. This group reaches an appreciable size only after the fourth round of the survey.

At the time of the first round, which occurred when the child was one month old, exclusive breast-feeding without supplement prevailed for fewer than half of the children, and its frequency fell very swiftly thereafter (Table 13.1). This pattern is linked with traditional customs. Among the Béti, the ethnic group native to the Yaoundé region, infants are given grated ripe banana from one week on, and around the age of a month they will eat chewed, cooked cassava (Tsama Amougou cited by Dackam-Ngatchou, 1985).

From one round to another, the child may pass from exclusive breast-feeding to mixed feeding, and vice versa. Some children start with combined feeding, and afterwards change to breast milk only. This pattern explains why the proportions of children fed exclusively on breast milk in the third and fourth rounds are higher than in the preceding rounds. These children are probably those who were primarily fed on mother's milk, in combination with cautious use of the bottle in the first rounds.

Exclusive breast-feeding (with or without supplements) is very important in Yaoundé: two out of three children receive only breast milk until the age of 1 year (the fourth round). If the infants who receive both kinds of milk are included, 80 per cent receive some breast milk. After 12 months, this proportion falls rapidly: 42 per cent at 16 months, 11 per cent at 20 months, and only 1.7 per cent at 2 years. Few children are fed only on the bottle; they make up only 14 per cent of the total at the fourth round.

3. Type of Feeding and Infant Mortality

The relationship between type of feeding and infant mortality is not clear in theory. On the one hand, breast-fed children are less likely to die than

Table 13.1. *Type of feeding per round, in per cent, EMIJ, Yaoundé*

Round	Age (months)	Breast milk only		Combined breast and bottle	Bottle only	No milk	Not reported	Number of children
		without supplement	with supplement					
1	1	45.4	13.6	38.0	2.1	0.9	0.1	7,878
2	4	10.3	46.5	37.2	5.4	0.5	0.1	7,008
3	8	2.2	63.1	23.5	10.0	1.2	0.0	6,467
4	12	0.9	64.7	14.5	13.9	5.7	0.2	6,083
5	16	0.1	38.0	4.1	9.2	48.0	0.6	5,789
6	20	0.1	8.7	2.1	2.2	86.4	0.6	5,516
7	24	—	1.3	0.3	0.2	97.8	0.3	5,889[a]

[a] The number of children is larger at the 7th round than at the 6th because of the return of children temporarily lost to follow-up.

bottle-fed children, because maternal milk confers some immunological and nutritional protection, whereas bottle-feeding carries the risks of lack of hygiene and of poor quality of milk (Population Reports, 1982). On the other hand, maternal feeding is much less common and the duration of breast-feeding is much shorter in developed countries than in countries of the Third World, and yet infant mortality is much lower there. What then is the impact of the type of feeding on the level of mortality in Yaoundé?

(*a*) **Infant mortality**

The survey was meant to collect information on age at death. Interviewers, however, were unable to determine that age in 44 cases, or for 7.6 per cent of all deaths. For this reason, we have calculated age at death from information on survival at the different rounds of the survey. The deaths recorded in the fourth round, for example, are those that took place between the third and fourth rounds, and the age at death is between 8 and 11 months. It is important to have the method of calculation in mind in order to interpret the variations in mortality by type of feeding correctly for the first month of life. Nearly all children started out by being breast-fed exclusively, but a fraction of them received a complement of milk from a bottle, or some other food, in the following weeks. The information on type of feeding represents the conditions at the time of the survey round, or, in the case of a dead child, at the time of death. As mortality is very concentrated immediately after birth, this results in a level of mortality in the first month which is relatively high for children who received only breast milk without supplement, and relatively low for those who lived long enough to receive breast milk and supplementary foods or combined breast and bottle feeding.

The different probabilities of dying, $_nq_x$, were calculated for four-month periods, using the following formula:

$$_nq_x = \frac{_nD_x}{P_x - {_nS_x}}, \text{ where}$$

$_nD_x$ = number of children dying between ages x and $x + n$, in months;
P_x = number of children who survived to age x; and
$_nS_x$ = number of children lost to observation between ages x and $x + n$.
The probability of dying in the first four months, $_4q_0$, was calculated in the following manner:

$$_4q_0 = 1 - (1 - {_1q_0}) (1 - {_3q_1}).$$

Note that children who died at the maternity clinic have been removed both from the denominator and the numerator for this computation.

(*b*) **Mortality by type of feeding**

As already stated, maternal milk has several advantages over bottle milk:

1. Maternal milk gives immunological protection against illnesses common in infancy, such as diarrhoea and respiratory diseases; it also helps in the maintenance of a protective environment in the child's intestine (Population Reports, 1982). Moreover, maternal milk contains the complete range of nutrients indispensable to the young infant, and is easier to digest than the artificial counterparts.
2. Bottle-feeding can be dangerous for infants when the substitute foods are not appropriate or when they are not given properly. The high price of good quality foods could lead parents to dilute the commercial preparations or those which are made up in the home. The water that is used is often polluted, the bottle not sterilized, and the food is not kept refrigerated. All of this adds to the health risks.

We can use these advantages of breast-feeding over bottle-feeding to classify the different forms of feeding according to the concomitant risk. The types of feeding in Yaoundé, in order of increasing risk, are therefore:

- exclusive breast-feeding with no supplements;
- exclusive breast-feeding with supplements;
- combined breast and bottle-feeding;
- exclusive bottle-feeding.

We have ranked exclusive breast-feeding with supplements before combined feeding, even though both complement maternal milk (one with supplementary food and the other with artificial milk given in a bottle). The reason is that maternal milk plays a more important role in the former case than in the latter. Giving milk in a bottle seems to carry a higher risk than giving other supplementary foods, which are often served with spoons or cups. These are much easier to clean than bottle and teats, and are safer for the child (Population Reports, 1982). Moreover, artificial milk is often

Table 13.2. *Probability of dying by age in months and type of feeding, per 1,000, EMIJ, Yaoundé*

Type of feeding	$_4q_0{}^a$	$_4q_4$	$_4q_8$	$_{12}q_0{}^a$	Number of deaths
Breast exclusively					
unsupplemented	22	7	15	39	166
supplemented	3				
Combined breast and bottle	16	19	18	53	89
Bottle exclusively	91	18	19	125	43
Total	24	11	16	50	389

[a] Does not include deaths in maternity clinics.

diluted in non-boiled water, and it may be kept in the bottle for an excessive amount of time. Supplementary foods, by contrast, are prepared at home and are often cooked, like pap, or fresh, like fruit.

Table 13.2 presents the probabilities of dying according to type of feeding. A separate calculation for the group receiving only breast milk is only possible up to 4 months. After that age, there are almost no children whose sole source of milk is the breast without supplementation; the group has, therefore, been collapsed with the next after that age.

Table 13.2 shows that $_4q_0$ is lowest for children whose only source of milk is the breast, but who receive supplements. The reason for this is probably that all the children who die soon after birth are included in the group which received exclusive breast-feeding without supplements. This phenomenon, already mentioned above, is probably also at work in the case of mixed feeding. A comparison of $_1q_0$ and $_3q_1$ in Table 13.3 shows this effect even more clearly.

The percentage of children who died of causes connected with pregnancy or confinement is relatively small for the group receiving combined feeding, and almost zero for the group receiving breast milk and supplements. These causes are, however, very important in the first few days after delivery. This explains the higher mortality in the first month of life for the children fed exclusively on their mother's milk, compared to the mortality of those who receive the same milk with supplements; but the excess mortality of the former group in the next three months of life is harder to understand. Curiously, supplementary food does not seem to be disastrous in the first four months of life, perhaps because the quantities are small, and administered in a relatively sterile way, as for example from the mouth of the mother to that of the infant.

The mortality of children receiving combined breast and bottle-feeding between one and four months lies between that of children who are exclusively breast-fed and of those who are exclusively bottle-fed. The deleterious effects of the bottle seem to outweigh the benefits of maternal milk after four months. Before that age, the benefits of mother's milk seem, by contrast, to be rather important.

Table 13.3. *Probability of dying in first month of life and between 1 and 4 months, by type of feeding, EMIJ, Yaoundé*

	$_1q_0$	$_3q_1$
Exclusive breast-feeding with no supplements	14	8
Exclusive breast-feeding with supplements	—	3
Mixed feeding	5	11
Exclusive bottle-feeding	67	26

The mortality of children fed exclusively from the bottle is very high in the first months of life. The bottle is not necessarily always the culprit: some children are too weak to suckle, and have to be bottle-fed. Their eventual death may be more the result of their frailty than of the mode of feeding.

Let us conclude that in the first year of life, children who are exclusively breast-fed have a higher probability of survival than those fed exclusively from the bottle or those who had mixed feeding; after the age of 4 months, there is little difference between the mortality of children fed exclusively · from the bottle, and that of children with combined feeding.

(c) Causes of death according to type of feeding

To shed light on the hazards of bottle-feeding, we now look at the causes of death reported for children aged under one year in Yaoundé (Table 13.4). For the first two rounds, that is the first four months of life, two results stand out. First, there are few deaths resulting from conditions associated with pregnancy or delivery among the children receiving combined breast and bottle-feeding. The majority of such deaths occur very early, before the introduction of mixed feeding (the mode of feeding recorded refers to the time of death).

Second, a very low percentage of children fed exclusively from the breast die from diarrhoea and dehydration. This result confirms the conclusions of other studies. Diarrhoea is much more common among infants fed from the bottle or from a combination of breast and bottle, and in the early months of life, diarrhoea is also more frequent among those fed only from the bottle than among those who receive mixed feeding (Cresencio and Hebert, 1987).

For rounds three and four of the survey, which cover ages 5 to 12 months, it must also be noted that a high proportion of deaths are due to diarrhoea among children who received combined breast and bottle-feeding. However, this time there are no infants who die of diarrhoea among the group who are fed exclusively from the bottle.

The proportion of deaths from measles (a disease which is uncommon among very young infants) is relatively low for children who receive combined feeding. However, the 'other causes' category is relatively well represented among these children. This category reflects symptoms—e.g. fever, vomiting, wasting—rather than genuine causes of death, and it is possible that a non-negligible proportion of children who died with these symptoms were in fact developing measles. Finally, deaths from other infectious diseases were quite frequent for the group fed exclusively from the bottle.

We have calculated mortality rates by type of feeding for the most common diseases in Yaoundé, measles and diarrhoea (Table 13.5). For measles, the level of mortality in the first year is more or less the same, no matter how milk is given. This result was also found in the Philippines

Table 13.4. *Cause of death by type of feeding per round, in per cent, EMIJ, Yaoundé*

Cause of death	Rounds 1 and 2			Rounds 3 and 4		
	Breast milk exclusively	Combined breast and bottle	Bottle only	Breast milk exclusively	Combined breast and bottle	Bottle only
Diarrhoea, dehydration	3	23	15	11	22	—
Measles	1	2	—	51	29	39
Other infectious disease	13	11	15	7	7	26
Nutritional disease	1	2	—	6	—	6
Disease linked to pregnancy and confinement	22	2	25	—	—	—
Disease of nerves and sense organs	—	—	5	3	—	9
Disease of respiratory system	13	16	—	4	2	—
Disease of digestive system	8	—	10	—	2	—
Congenital anomaly	1	—	—	1	—	—
Others	23	7	20	12	27	17
Not reported	15	25	10	3	11	4
Total	100	100	100	100	100	100
Number of deaths	78	44	20	88	45	23

Table 13.5. *Probability of dying of measles and diarrhoea by age in months and type of feeding, per 1,000, EMIJ, Yaoundé*

Cause of death and type of feeding	$_4q_0{}^a$	$_4q_4$	$_4q_8$	$_{12}q_0{}^a$	Number of deaths
Measles					
Breast exclusively	0.3	1.9	9.4	11.5	46
Combined breast and bottle	0.4	7.4	2.3	10.1	14
Bottle exclusively	—	9.2	5.9	15.1	9
Diarrhoea					
Breast exclusively	0.5	1.2	1.3	3.0	12
Combined breast and bottle	3.6	4.7	3.5	11.7	20
Bottle exclusively	12.5	—	—	12.5	3

[a] Does not include deaths in maternity clinics.

(Cresencio and Hebert, 1987). However, the children fed exclusively from the breast die from measles at an older age than those who receive combined feeding or who are fed only from a bottle. This could be due to the protection given by maternal milk. Finally, the mortality from diarrhoea is markedly lower for the group fed exclusively from the breast than for the other groups.

4. Type of Feeding and Infant Mortality, by Sub-Population

(a) The variables used

Many factors can affect infant mortality and type of feeding at the same time. In our analysis we shall take into account the effects of some of these: the mother's level of education or occupation, type of housing, the mother's age at the birth of the child, and ethnic group.

Mother's level of education. The level of education of the mother has been shown to be a crucial factor in infant mortality. A rise in the level of schooling by ten years has been said to reduce infant mortality by 34 per cent (United Nations, 1985). In the EMIJ survey, curiously, the relation is in the opposite direction: the higher the level of education of the mother, the higher infant mortality. There could be two reasons for this (van der Pol, 1986). It may be that the effect of ethnicity reverses the relationship between education and infant mortality, since when one controls for this variable, the expected relationship begins to appear. A second explanation is that the non-reporting of deaths in Yaoundé was undoubtedly most frequent among those with the least education.

Most studies show that breast-feeding is less frequent as maternal education increases (Bracher and Santow, 1982; Cameroon, 1983). This is also found in the EMIJ survey. It must be noted that, because of small numbers, we have kept only two educational categories: primary school or less, and secondary school or more.

Type of housing. For this analysis, we have distinguished between modern and traditional housing. To be considered modern, the dwelling unit must have a roof of cement, tile, or corrugated iron, floors of tile or cement, running water, and electric light. Dwellings which did not include at least one of these characteristics were classified as traditional. The types of housing thus defined reflect two kinds of variables which may be linked to infant mortality: construction materials which are an indication of the wealth of the inhabitants; and the sanitary conditions of the household, most notably the presence of running water and, to a lesser extent, electricity. In general, breast-feeding and socio-economic level have been found to be negatively associated (Behm, 1983). This relationship is also found in the EMIJ survey.

Mother's age. Infant mortality is influenced by the mother's age at the time of birth: children whose mothers are very young or relatively old (for example under 20 and over 35 years of age) have above average mortality (Behm, 1983). This is also the case in the EMIJ survey (Garssen, 1984). To analyse the relationship between types of feeding and infant mortality, taking into account the age of the mother at birth, we have distinguished between two groups of children: those whose mothers were under 25 years of age at the time of birth, and those whose mothers were aged 25 or more.

Ethnic group. Only the two largest ethnic groups in the sample have been used here:

1. the Béti, a group native to the region of Yaoundé; they include the Ewondo, Eton, and Boulou, and made up 39 per cent of the sample at the first round;
2. the ethnic groups of the western high plateaus, of which 90 per cent are Bamiléké. This group makes up 33 per cent of the sample.

The EMIJ survey shows that the western ethnic groups breast-feed more than the Béti, who are more likely to bottle-feed their babies.

Mother's occupation. Because of the constraints imposed by a job, women who are economically active are much more likely to bottle-feed their children. Table 13.6 shows that the children fed exclusively from a bottle or who receive combined feeding have working mothers more often than the children who are exclusively breast-fed. When mothers work outside the

Table 13.6. *Percentage of children whose mother has an occupation, by type of feeding and round, EMIJ, Yaoundé*

Round	Type of feeding		
	Exclusive breast-feeding	Combined breast and bottle	Exclusive bottle-feeding
1	9	26	32
2	8	27	38
3	9	31	40
4	9	33	42

home, the children are generally cared for by a third person (servant or grandparent), and this could influence their mortality. Eighty-five per cent of the women in the sample did not report an occupation, and we have distinguished only between economically active and inactive mothers.

Table 13.7. *Probability of dying from 4 to 14 months, by type of feeding and selected characteristics, per 1,000, EMIJ, Yaoundé*

Characteristic	Type of feeding			
	Exclusive breast-feeding	Combined breast and bottle	Exclusive bottle-feeding	Total
Mother's education				
Primary or less	24 (72)	27 (14)	64 (10)	28
Secondary or more	14 (15)	46 (31)	22 (10)	26
Type of housing				
Modern	20 (30)	32 (21)	19 (8)	23
Traditional	21 (49)	35 (16)	48 (8)	28
Mother's age				
Less than 25	25 (54)	58 (32)	44 (14)	33
More than 25	17 (33)	20 (13)	19 (6)	20
Ethnic Group				
Béti	24 (34)	35 (21)	37 (11)	32
Western	23 (38)	28 (7)	7 (1)	22
Mother's occupation				
Active	13 (5)	32 (12)	20 (5)	22
No occupation	23 (83)	39 (33)	40 (15)	27
Total	22 (88)	37 (45)	37 (23)	27

Note: Observed number of deaths is between parentheses.

(*b*) Results

Table 13.7 shows the levels of mortality according to the type of feeding and the characteristics discussed above. Variations in $_4q_0$ for the group with combined feeding are difficult to interpret, so we present only the $_8q_4$ values which relate to ages between 4 and 12 months. Mortality at those ages is significantly higher for Béti children and for the children of young mothers. It is also very high for children who receive combined breast and bottle-feeding and have educated mothers. This result is surprising, and it is not found for other types of feeding. It may be linked to the high level of diarrhoea mortality among those who have combined feeding, as shown in Table 13.8.

High mortality of the combined feeding group is concentrated among children who have young mothers (Table 13.9), and, more specifically, educated mothers aged between 20 and 24. Why is this so? Young mothers are perhaps less experienced than older mothers; among these women, the less educated are most easily influenced and more likely to accept advice

Table 13.8. *Probability of dying by age in months, mother's education, cause of death, and type of feeding, per 1,000, EMIJ, Yaoundé*

Cause of death, type of feeding and education	$_4q_0$[a]	$_8q_4$	$_{12}q_0$[a]	Number of deaths for cause	Percentage of all causes
Diarrhoea					
Breast exclusively					
Education:					
Primary or less	—	3	3	8	6
Secondary or more	2	2	4	4	10
Combined breast and bottle					
Education:					
Primary or less	4	1	5	5	16
Secondary or more	4	11	15	15	26
Measles					
Breast exclusively					
Education:					
Primary or less	—	12	12	35	28
Secondary or more	1	9	10	11	28
Combined breast and bottle					
Education:					
Primary or less	—	13	13	6	19
Secondary or more	1	13	13	8	14

[a] Does not include deaths in maternity clinics.

Table 13.9. *Probability of dying between 4 and 12 months by type of feeding, age of mother, and maternal level of education, EMIJ, Yaoundé*

Age of mother	Type of feeding		
	Exclusive breast-feeding	Combined breast and bottle	Exclusive bottle-feeding
Less than 25 years			
Education:			
Primary or less	29 (41)	38 (7)	112 (7)
Secondary or more	16 (12)	67 (25)	27 (7)
25 years or more			
Education:			
Primary or less	20 (30)	21 (7)	30 (3)
Secondary or more	9 (3)	19 (6)	15 (3)

Note: Observed number of deaths is between parentheses.

from older women (grandmothers, aunts, etc.) than those of the same age who have more education.

Another mechanism could be playing a role in increasing mortality for these women. The milk prepared for the bottle, in the context of mixed feeding, has to be kept much longer than the same quantity prepared for exclusive bottle-feeding. The problems of milk preservation are well known. Thus, the method of feeding that a young mother chooses is very important for the child's survival.

Mortality differences between the Béti and the western ethnic groups are not significant when one controls for the type of feeding. We can therefore conclude that the difference in mortality between these two groups is due mainly to the different pattern of child-feeding.

The mortality of children of active mothers is lower than that of children whose mothers do not work, even for the group who are exclusively bottle-fed, and that is also surprising. The socio-economic level of working mothers is perhaps higher than that of inactive women (Garssen, 1984).

For almost all of the variables under investigation, we see significant differences in mortality between the two categories of children who are exclusively bottle-fed. Mortality is very high among bottle-fed children whose mother has a lower level of education, lives in a traditional house, is younger than 25, without gainful occupation, and a Béti. This confirms the potentially high risks of bottle-feeding, probably because of its misuse or the lack of money to buy adequate substitutes for maternal milk. On the other hand, the differences also imply that these drawbacks can be surmounted.

5. Conclusion

Our aim in this chapter was to measure the effect of three types of feeding—exclusive breast-feeding, exclusive bottle-feeding, and a combination of the two—on infant mortality in Yaoundé. We were most interested in the ages from 4 to 12 months. Despite the loss of some children to observation, which may have affected the measurement of mortality levels, an interesting pattern of differential mortality by type of feeding has been revealed.

From 4 months onwards, the mortality of children who were exclusively breast-fed was not as high as for those who received combined feeding or who were exclusively bottle-fed. This confirms the deleterious effects of bottles and the benefits of maternal milk, which are particularly clear under the age of four months. The use of the bottle increases the frequency of diarrhoea, especially in the first months of life.

Measles, which is the most important cause of death in Yaoundé, seems to kill regardless of the type of feeding. Nevertheless, it does strike later among the children who are exclusively breast-fed. The children of young, educated women who give combined feeding, run a very high risk of death, mostly from diarrhoea. The inexperience of the mothers is a possible explanation for this. There is little difference in mortality between the children of working and non-working mothers, even though the bottle is much more heavily used in the former group.

Differences in mortality by socio-economic status of the mother are most visible when children are exclusively bottle-fed. Although the risks associated with the use of bottles are high, they are surmountable. It is important to educate the population concerning the hazards of bottle-feeding, in order to reduce the infant mortality that is connected with it.

References

Behm, H. (1983), *Final Report of the Research Project on Infant and Childhood Mortality in the Third World*, CICRED, WHO, Paris.

Bracher, M. and Santow, G. (1982), 'Breastfeeding in Central Java', *Population Studies* 36/3: 413–29.

Cameroon, Ministère de l'Économie et du Plan (1983), *Enquête nationale sur la fécondité au Cameroun 1978: Rapport principal*, vol. 1. *Direction de la statistique et de la comptabilité nationale*, Yaoundé.

Cresencio, E. and Hebert, M. S. (1987), 'Morbidity and nutritional status of breast-fed and bottlefed Filipino infants', in *Fertility Determinants Research Notes* 15, The Population Council, New York.

Dackam-Ngatchou, R. (1985), 'Aspects de la mortalité post-infantile en Afrique tropicale', *Annales de l'IFORD*, 9: 17–131.

Garssen, J. (1984), 'Analyse descriptive des rapports entre quelques variables biologiques, démographiques et socio-économiques, et la mortalité infantile à

Yaoundé', IFORD, 4th Technical Meeting on Infant and Child Mortality Surveys, Yaoundé.

Population Reports (1982), *Breast-Feeding, Fertility and Family Planning*, ser. J, no. 24, Baltimore.

United Nations (1985), *Socio-Economic Differentials in Child Mortality in Developing Countries*, New York.

van der Pol, H. (1986), 'Niveau et structure de la mortalité infantile à Yaoundé', Working paper, IFORD, Yaoundé.

14 Overcrowding and Intensive Exposure: Major Determinants of Variations in Measles Mortality in Africa

Peter Aaby
Institute of Ethnology and Anthropology, Copenhagen

1. Introduction

Social science research on variations in child mortality has mainly been concerned with socio-economic and cultural determinants such as urbanization, education, income, social status, food practices, attitudes, and sex-roles. However, the actual mechanisms by which these determinants affect mortality have rarely been examined. This may be because the mechanisms are considered the domain of the medical profession. However, the main reason probably lies in the view that mortality is caused by a few well-defined mechanisms, especially nutritional deficiency during pregnancy or childhood, lack of care, and lack of hygiene. Differences in nutrition are probably considered the major factor in explaining variation in mortality (McKeown and Brown, 1955). For example, the fact that infections which are relatively harmless in the industrialized countries often lead to high mortality in the less developed countries is explained with reference to the high degree of malnutrition in the latter (Walsh, 1983). In the words of Mosley (1984: 4):

Most biomedical and social scientists identify . . . infectious diseases and malnutrition as the main 'causes' of high infant and child mortality in poor populations. Biologically that is correct, but the observation is not much more useful than to say that pregnancies are a 'cause' of birth rates. It is important to note that both pregnancies and diseases are consequences of biosocial interactions.

The present chapter suggests that this 'causal' relation may be less certain than commonly assumed; at least for measles there is no indication that malnutrition determines variations in severity. Hence, other explanations are needed. Apart from malnutrition, factors such as *age at infection* and *genetic susceptibility* have been emphasized in epidemiological studies as determinants of variation in the severity of infection. These mechanisms are *host factors*; the cause of the severity of infection is assumed to be some 'inadequacy' in the response of the infected individual. Such weaknesses

Table 14.1. *Mechanisms of severe infection*

Host factors	Transmission factors
Malnutrition	Virulence
Age at infection	Dose
Sex	Synergism between infections
Genetic susceptibility	Sex
(Care)	

may be acquired through deficient nutritional intake, either temporary due to immaturity (or old age), or permanent due to genetic constitution.

For some infections, this emphasis on host factors is inadequate, and differences in care will not always be able to account for the variation in mortality. On the basis of experience in West Africa, particularly with measles infection, it is suggested that an emphasis on *transmission factors* often accounts better for the variation in mortality than a host factor approach. In particular, intensive or excessive exposure may be of critical importance for the outcome of infection. In other words, it is suggested that the problem may be more in the transmission of the infection itself than in the host (Table 14.1).

The different mechanisms will here be discussed with reference to the variation in severity of measles infection. Measles has often been employed to illustrate different mechanisms of severe infection, be it malnutrition (Morley, 1973), age at infection (Reves, 1985), or genetic susceptibility (Black *et al.*, 1977). Furthermore, measles is estimated to kill two million children each year in the developing countries, China excluded (EPI, 1986). This makes measles the single most lethal infection among diseases preventable by vaccine. There are, therefore, good reasons to focus on measles. Changing the focus from host to transmission factors has several implications for social science research on mortality.

The issues discussed in this paper emerged in a study of child health and malnutrition in Guinea-Bissau, started in 1978 at the initiative of the Ministry of Health. The objective of the study was to identify the causes of malnutrition, which was assumed to be the major cause of the estimated 50 per cent mortality before five years of age (Aschberg *et al.*, 1975). During the liberation war (1963–74), the strategy of PAIGC, Guinea-Bissau's leading party, was popular mobilization. Since liberation, popular mobilization has been attempted in other domains. It was hoped that the study of child nutrition and mortality could point to effective and feasible local activities as part of the preventive mobilization programme.

Since the beginning of the project, the populations of one urban district, Bandim, in the capital, and five ethnically and ecologically different rural areas have been followed. The study has combined censuses and the registration of vital events (pregnancies, births, and deaths) with regular preventive health care among pregnant women and small children. A population of about 4,000 children below five years of age has been regularly examined.

Of particular importance for the following analysis has been the occurrence of severe measles epidemics in Bandim and in one of the rural areas, Quinhamel. Collecting data from these epidemics involved both clinical examination of some of the children with measles and retrospective interviews in all households where measles occurred (Aaby *et al.*, 1983*a*; 1984*a*; 1984*b*).

2. Variations in Measles Mortality

(*a*) The problem

Measles is one of the major causes of infant and child mortality in Africa. A study from Senegal attributed 52 per cent of all deaths in the 1 to 4-year age group to measles (Senecal *et al.*, 1962). Other studies have indicated that measles accounted for 16 per cent of deaths in children aged less than 5 years in a village in Nigeria (Morley *et al.*, 1963); 32 per cent of deaths among children aged 1–4 years in Burkina Faso; and 9 per cent in Benin (Cantrelle, 1965). In rural Senegal, a child had an 11 per cent risk of dying of measles during its lifetime (Pison and Bonneuil, 1988). The measles case fatality ratio (CFR) was very high in the industrialized countries at the turn of the century (Aaby *et al.*, 1986*a*), but is now less than one in a thousand. Measles is clearly more severe in Africa than in Asia (Aaby, 1988*b*). A satisfactory explanation of severe measles should be able to account for the major variations in the severity of measles in Africa indicated in Table 14.2.

Table 14.3 lists all of the available community studies on measles infection in Africa. The CFR is higher in West than East Africa, a tendency also confirmed by hospital studies. The average CFR among hospitalized patients with measles was 12.3 per cent in West Africa (Morley *et al.*, 1967*a*) but only 5.7 per cent in East African countries (Morley *et al.*, 1967*b*). Table 14.3

Table 14.2. *Contrasts in the variations of measles mortality*

High mortality	Low mortality
Industrialized world 1900	Industrialized world 1980
Africa	Asia/India
West Africa	East Africa
Rural	Urban
Infants	Older children

Table 14.3. *Case fatality ratios (CFR) in measles infection in African community studies*

Country and source	Vaccination	Median age	CFRs (no. of cases)			
			0–4 years		All ages	
			%	No.	%	No.
Rural Surveys						
Burkina Faso (Anon., 1964)	NV				50	NI
Mali (Imperato, 1975)	NV				50	256
Mali (Morley, 1973)	NV				38	213
Nigeria (Ogbeide, 1967)	NV				25	NI
Guinea-Bissau (Aaby, 1984b)	NV	3.5	34	101	24	162
Senegal (Langaney and Pison, 1979)	NV		29	80[a]		
Ethiopia (Lindtjoern, 1986)	NV		27	63		
Senegal (Pison, 1982)	NV		27	160[b]		
Senegal (Debroise, 1967)						
Serer	NV	5	26	119	9	266
Wolof	NV	4	9	79	5	160
Gambia (McGregor, 1964)	NV	5	22	259[b]		
Senegal (Pison, 1987)	NV	3.5	20	44	13	68
Senegal (Stephens, 1990)	NV		18	537		
Gambia (Heyworth, 1973)	NV				10	72
Gambia (Hull, 1983)	V	3.5	9	77	5	132
Kenya (Muller, 1977)						
1st epidemic	V (20%)	2.5	8	331	6	424
2nd epidemic	V	2.5	2	532	2	665

		Median age					
Kenya (Leeuwenburg, 1984)							
3rd epidemic	V (56%)					1	734
Nigeria (Morley, 1973)	NV	3.5	7	222			
Somalia (Anon., 1980)			2	600[c]			
Gambia (Lamb, 1988)	V (>90%)		0	26		0	54
Urban surveys							
Guinea-Bissau (Aaby *et al.* 1984*a*)	NV	2.5	21	356		17	459
Guinea-Bissau (Aaby *et al.* 1988)	V	2	15	124		14	161
Zaïre (Kasongo Project Team, 1981)	V		6	1069			
Nigeria (Rea, 1968)			4	68			
Zambia (Rolfe, 1982)	V	1.5	2	316[d]			
Nigeria (Hondius, 1979)	V		0	78			

Notes: The median age at infection is in most cases estimated from tables of the age distribution of cases. There may therefore be minor inaccuracies.
NI = Not specified.
NV = No vaccination.
V = Vaccinations carried out.

[a] The mortality rate for the total population was 7.2 per cent (28/390). The CFR for the 0–4 years age group has been estimated on the assumption that 20 per cent of the population and 81 per cent of the deaths from measles were below 5 years of age as found in other studies from the same area (Pison, 1982).

[b] Only deaths have been registered. The CFRs are based on the assumption that all children in the age group caught measles.

[c] The CFR is based on the assumption that all nine children who died were under 5 years of age.

[d] It has been assumed that all children were under 5 years of age.

also suggests that the CFR is usually higher in rural than urban areas. In Africa, as elsewhere, the CFR is usually highest for children under 3 years of age, and for infants in particular (Aaby *et al.*, 1986*b*).

(*b*) Malnutrition and severe measles

The high CFR in African children is usually thought to be due to malnutrition (Walsh, 1983; Axton, 1979). And it has been suggested that the CFR in measles infection is an indirect index of the nutritional status of the community (Jelliffe, 1966: 105), and that the risk of death from measles is many hundreds of times higher among poorer children (Walsh, 1983). This view has mainly been based on hospital studies showing an association between weight-for-age (w/a) at admission and the risk of dying during hospitalization. However, this association could well be biased in several ways. The most severe cases may have lost more weight than other children prior to admission, since children begin to lose weight even during the incubation period (Meunier, 1898). Furthermore, growth faltering could be associated with other factors contributing to high mortality in measles without it being the cause of the high measles CFR. To assess the impact of the pre-morbid state of nutrition on measles mortality risk, it is necessary to have community studies where the anthropometric measurements are obtained prior to an outbreak of measles.

In Guinea-Bissau, where measles mortality is extremely high (see Table 14.3), nutritional status seemed fairly good, at least in the urban area that we studied. An analysis of the state of nutrition (weight-for-age, height-for-age, and weight-for-height) measured a few months before epidemics in both an urban and a rural area indicated no relation between nutritional status and the risk of dying of measles (Aaby *et al.*, 1983*a*; 1984*b*). For example, Table 14.4 shows that malnourished children with a weight-for-age below 80 per cent of the standard did not have a higher CFR in measles. Furthermore, we found no difference in the age-specific CFR between breast-fed and non-breast-fed children (Aaby *et al.*, 1981*b*). These results are consistent with our observations in later epidemics in Bandim, where we obtained information on w/a prior to the attack of measles. In one small study of five fatal cases, we found that the weight increase was unrelated to the risk of dying of measles (Aaby *et al.*, 1988*a*).

In contrast to these studies from Guinea-Bissau, two community studies from Africa have claimed to find support for the importance of the state of nutrition as a determinant of measles mortality. In Senegal, a study of measles outbreaks in three Sereer and three Wolof villages found that the CFR was higher in villages where the state of nutrition had been low prior to the epidemic (Debroise *et al.*, 1967). The Sereer had both more malnutrition and a higher measles CFR than did the Wolof. It is therefore possible that the same factors may have caused both a high degree of malnutrition

Table 14.4. *Case fatality ratio in measles infection according to number of cases in the household, age, and nutritional status, Bandim, Guinea-Bissau, 1979*

Age (months)	Case/fatality ratio (%)			Total
	Weight/age <80%	Weight/age 80–90%	Weight/age 100% +	
Single cases				
0–11		3/12 (25)	0/13 (0)	3/25 (12)
12–35	1/4 (25)	5/27 (19)	0/8 (0)	6/39 (15)
36–71	0/5 (0)	0/8 (0)	1/3 (33)	1/16 (6)
0–71	1/9 (11)	8/47 (17)	1/24 (4)	10/80 (13)
Multiple cases				
0–11	2/5 (40)	5/20 (25)	8/14 (57)	15/39 (39)
12–35	6/17 (35)	12/39 (31)	3/11 (27)	21/67 (31)
36–71	0/10 (0)	7/52 (14)	0/13 (0)	7/75 (9)
0–71	8/32 (25)	24/111 (22)	11/38 (29)	4/181 (24)
Total				
0–11	2/5 (40)	8/32 (25)	8/27 (30)	18/64 (28)
12–35	7/21 (33)	17/66 (26)	3/19 (16)	27/106 (26)
36–71	0/15 (0)	7/60 (12)	1/16 (6)	8/91 (9)
0–71	9/41 (22)	32/158 (20)	12/62 (19)	53/261 (20)
SMR	99	104	92	100

Note: SMR indicates standardized mortality ratio.

and high CFR. One factor which stands out, however, is the difference in clustering in these two ethnic groups. Among the Sereer, the mean number of cases per compound was 8.9 (266/30) versus only 3.3 (160/49) for the Wolof compounds. The study did not demonstrate that within each ethnic group or within each village outbreak it was the most malnourished who died of measles.

Another study of two epidemics in Kenya found support for the malnutrition hypothesis in the fact that children who died had significantly smaller arm circumferences than did children who survived (Muller *et al.*, 1977). However, the difference of 4 per cent (6 mm.) in arm circumference was not strong. Moreover, the result may have been influenced by the combination of cases from two epidemic periods with significant differences in the state of nutrition. To further support the importance of nutritional status, it was pointed out that the state of nutrition was significantly better in the last epidemic where the CFR was lower than in the first epidemic (see Table 14.3). However, the malnutrition hypothesis finds little support in this example because non-measles mortality during the second period was higher than during the first, suggesting a positive relation, and not the expected inverse one between state of nutrition and mortality from other infections. The criticism of this study has in fact been confirmed, since a subsequent reanalysis of the data from Kenya concluded that when controls were selected from the same period as the deaths, there was no difference in the arm circumference of those who died and those who survived (Leeuwenburg *et al.*, 1984). Finally, it has been claimed that a study from Zaïre documents an increased CFR for the most malnourished children (Neiburg and Dibley, 1986). Various biases affecting the survey make it hard to accept this conclusion.

A number of community studies besides our own have suggested that severity did not depend on the state of nutrition. In West Africa, where measles is particularly severe (Table 14.3), the disease frequently occurs shortly after the harvest when the state of nutrition is best (McGregor, 1964). Studying a rural epidemic in Gambia, Heyworth found only two of seven children who died to be malnourished. Since normally more than two out of seven children are malnourished in rural Gambia, state of nutrition cannot be said to have been a determinant of mortality in this epidemic (Heyworth, 1973). A more recent study from the Gambia likewise concluded that state of nutrition did not affect the clinical severity of measles (Lamb, 1988). Another study from an urban area in Nigeria found no relation between w/a and risk of severe disease (Hondius and Sutorius, 1979). A study of the Pokot in Uganda suggested that measles was a highly severe disease among relatively well-nourished children (Cox, 1973).

This apparent lack of evidence for an association between state of nutrition and measles mortality is by no means particular to Africa. A further problem with the malnutrition hypothesis is the relatively low measles CFR on the Indian subcontinent despite its state of nutrition being lower than in West Africa, where the CFR is very high. Severe forms of malnutrition may be correlated with more severe measles, but this has not been substantiated by any community study. Even if it is found to increase the risk of a fatal outcome, severe malnutrition will only explain a small part of the measles problem, since very few children are severely malnourished in most developing countries. In Bandim, none of the 75 fatal cases whose nutritional status before death was known were marasmic, and we found no case of kwashiorkor in Bandim prior to the large epidemic, where the CFR was 25 per cent for children under 3 years of age (Aaby *et al.*, 1983*a*; 1987*a*).

It has also been suggested that specific nutritional deficiencies, e.g. of vitamin A and zinc, which may not be strongly correlated with anthropometric indicators of the state of nutrition, might affect the outcome of infection (Neiburg and Dibley, 1986). However, no community study has provided any data on the problem. West African countries such as Gambia and Guinea-Bissau have the highest measles mortality in the world, yet these countries show little indication of severe vitamin A deficiency (Le François *et al.*, 1980; Smedman *et al.*, 1983; Bates, 1983). One would expect some association between nutritional status and risk of dying of measles, because background factors such as crowding, poor hygiene, insufficient care, and previous infections are likely to be associated with both malnutrition and high risk of mortality from measles. Since virtually no association has been found in any community study, it is suggested that malnutrition, as measured by the common anthropometric indices, is not a major determinant of measles mortality. Instead, there are good reasons to look at other mechanisms explaining severe measles infection.

(c) Age at infection

The CFR in measles is highest among the youngest children, and the greatest number of measles deaths occur before 2 or 3 years of age. The age pattern of measles infection has been suggested as one of the major determinants of variation in measles mortality; high measles mortality in developing countries has been related to young age at infection (Walsh, 1983). Following the same line of reasoning, it has been suggested that the major drop in measles mortality which occurred in the first decades of this century in England and other industrialized countries was essentially related to a change in the age at infection (Reves, 1985). Reduced family size due to lower fertility is supposed to have raised the age at infection, thereby leading to a fall in the case fatality ratio.

The mechanism of age at infection has also been used to predict that the CFR should be lower in rural outbreaks than in urban areas because age at infection is lower in the urban areas (Foster, 1984; Davis, 1982). However, as documented elsewhere (Aaby, 1988*b*), all community studies suggest the opposite tendency; the CFR has been higher in rural areas (Table 14.3).

There seems to be little prospect that variations in age at infection will allow us to explain major variations in measles mortality. None of the other host factors such as sex or genetic susceptibility seem to have the potential to explain major differentials in measles mortality. Although genetic susceptibility has been shown to have some impact on the severity of measles infection (Coovadia *et al.*, 1981; Black *et al.*, 1977), genetic changes are unlikely to have accounted for the rapid fall in mortality in the industrialized nations. Furthermore, as will be explained below, there are several features of the epidemiology of severe measles which cannot be explained by genetics. Hence, there are good reasons to look for non-host factors which may explain variation in measles mortality.

(d) Crowding and intensive exposure

Older epidemiological studies often stressed that measles was particularly severe among poor people living under bad housing conditions, in small overcrowded apartments and in crowded institutions (Debré and Joannon,

1926; Picken, 1921; Brincker, 1938; Halliday, 1928). For example, the CFR has been higher on immigrant ships, in refugee camps, in child institutions, and military camps. However, there have been few attempts to determine why overcrowding is associated with high mortality. One underlying principle in these associations may have been that measles is more severe when several children are sick simultaneously. This possibility was first suggested during our analysis of clinical measles cases seen during the epidemic in Bandim (Aaby *et al.*, 1983*a*). The CFR for Bandim children aged less than 3 years was 14.1 per cent (9/64) for single cases and 34.0 per cent (36/106) in houses with multiple cases (Table 14.4).

More recent studies in Bandim have confirmed the same tendency (Aaby *et al.*, 1987*a*). In the rural area of Quinhamel, we found that mortality at all ages was significantly higher (p < 0.001) in the huts with multiple cases than in the huts with only a single case (Aaby *et al.*, 1984*b*). In logical agreement with these results, we have found that twins have a higher CFR from measles than singletons. It was not the most malnourished twins who died (Aaby *et al.*, 1983*d*).

In line with this tendency, recent studies from Senegal (Pison and Bonneuil, 1988), Gambia (Hull, 1988), and Guinea-Bissau (Aaby *et al.*, 1984*b*) have also found that the CFR increased with the number of cases in the compound. Thus, there is systematic evidence that mortality is high in families with several cases of measles. Several older studies have shown that the CFR for measles is inversely related to the number of rooms per family. Morley (1973) has suggested that children living in a one-room family are likely to have had poor nutrition. However, inasmuch as recent community studies have been unable to show that the pre-morbid state of nutrition determines the outcome of infection, there are reasons to look for other causes of the association between case clustering and severity of infection. In Bandim, the CFR was not associated with indicators of the socio-economic position of the family, i.e. quality of housing and schooling of parents, when clustering was taken into account (Aaby *et al.*, 1983*a*; 1984*a*).

However, there is another factor in severity of infection which seems to be important. In homes with multiple cases, mortality is especially high among the so-called *secondary cases*, i.e. those who have been infected within the house, usually from a sibling. In houses with multiple cases, the first children infected, the so-called *index cases*, have mortality equivalent to that of single cases. Index cases and single cases, who usually contract the infection in a brief contact outside the home, have relatively mild cases of the disease. It therefore seems unlikely that the difference in mortality between single and multiple cases is mainly due to socio-economic, cultural, or genetic differences between families with many and few children. A major determinant of severe disease among secondary cases may therefore be intensity of exposure (Table 14.5).

Similar tendencies were also observed in the years following in Guinea-

Table 14.5. *Case fatality ratio (CFR) in measles infection according to age and type of exposure, Bandim, Guinea-Bissau, 1979*

Age (months)	Case fatality ratio (deaths/no. ill)					
	Isolated cases		Houses with multiple cases			
			Index cases		Secondary cases	
	%	Ratio	%	Ratio	%	Ratio
0–5	0	0/1			24	14/17
6–11	14	1/7	0	0/15	42	11/26
12–23	11	2/19	21	3/14	33	14/43
24–35	0	0/10	14	2/14	8	14/37
36–59	0	0/10	5	2/38	13	5/39
60+	33	1/3	6	2/36	0	0/50
Total	8	4/50	8	9/117	23	48/212

Bissau (Aaby *et al.*, 1988). Furthermore, studies from Gambia, Senegal, Bangladesh, England, and Denmark (Aaby 1988*b*; Bhuiya *et al.*, 1987) have now confirmed this tendency, and no study has contradicted it. We have not been able to find any confounding factor, such as size of family or difference in treatment, which could explain the higher mortality of secondary cases. These observations in crowding and intensive exposure suggest that infection somehow increases in severity during the transmission process. What is emphasized with 'crowding' is not so much the number of persons per room as the number of susceptible individuals living in a dwelling. The more there are susceptible individuals living together, the greater the risk that someone will be exposed intensively.

(*e*) Variations in measles mortality

If intensive exposure is a major determinant of measles mortality, it should also be able to account for the most important variations in disease severity as outlined in Table 14.2. In other words, the incidence of intensive exposure should be high where the CFR is high and vice versa. Table 14.6 summarizes the available community studies which have some information on both the CFR and the proportion of all cases which are secondary cases. There are some differences in the age groups covered, and the definition of secondary cases is not always clearly stated. However, the table does suggest a general association between a high proportion of secondary cases and high mortality and vice versa. Particularly interesting is the fact that West Africa, which has the world's highest CFRs, has also the highest percentages of

Peter Aaby

Table 14.6. *Frequency of secondary cases and case fatality ratio*

Country, authors	Age in months	Ratio of secondary to all cases		CFR (dths/cases)	
		As %	As Ratio	%	Ratio
Guinea-Bissau (Aaby, 1984a)	6–35	58	91/157	27	42/157
Senegal[a]	0–35	56	96/171	20	34/171
England (Aaby, 1986a)	4–35	46	41/90	14	14/100
Guinea-Bissau (Aaby, 1988a)	5–35	45	35/77	14	11/77
Guatemala (Gordon, 1965; Scrimshaw, 1966)	0–59	38	99/260	5	15/292[b]
Kenya (Muller, 1977; Leeuwenburg, 1984)	0–35	22	216/999[a]	6	34/592
Bangladesh (Bhuiya, 1987)	0–59	20	630/3181	2	61/3458
USA (McCormick, 1977)	0–59	14	10/71[d]	10	3/30
Bangladesh (Koster, 1987)	0–35	14	22/156	3	5/156
Gambia (Lamb, 1987)	6–35	8	1/13	0	0/13

Notes: In Guinea-Bissau secondary cases have been counted within the house. In all other studies, secondary cases have been infected in the household.
[a] Michel Garenne and Peter Aaby. Differentials in measles mortality among rural Senegalese children, preliminary data.
[b] For the age group 0–2 years, this ratio is probably 7 per cent.
[c] There is no indication of age group, the ratio presumably applies to all ages.
[d] This ratio refers to all ages.

secondary cases. The only study from East Africa suggests a considerably lower level of intensive exposure in accordance with its lower mortality. It is also noteworthy that two studies from Bangladesh (both in the Matlab area) have indicated many fewer secondary cases than in West Africa.

The other contrasts indicated in Table 14.2 may also be related to differences in exposure. The high mortality of the youngest children has usually been explained in terms of immunological immaturity (Omonulo, 1965) or the high proportion of malnourished children in this age group (Lancet, 1983). However, another reason for the excessive mortality of the youngest children could be that they are particularly likely to be exposed intensively to infections. Infections are commonly spread at the ages where there is frequent interaction among susceptibles. For example, in Bandim it was particularly children 3 and 4 years old who spread measles between the houses. The smallest children, on the other hand, usually caught the infection after exposure to an older sibling (Aaby *et al.*, 1986*b*). Similar tendencies have been observed elsewhere and apply to other infections as well (Aaby *et al.*, 1983*c*). In line with this emphasis on exposure, a recent study from South Africa reported no difference between infants and older children in their immunological response to measles. This would suggest that among infants, immunological immaturity is not the major cause of high mortality from measles (Coovadia *et al.*, 1984).

In rural African areas several years often pass between epidemics of measles. The age at infection will therefore be higher in rural than in urban areas, where the disease is often endemic. Since mortality is usually lowest for older children, it has been predicted that the measles CFR will be lower in rural areas, where age at infection is higher (Davis 1982; Foster, 1984). However, as evidenced by the studies in Table 14.3, the CFR is usually highest in rural outbreaks. This tendency has also been found in countries where there have been both urban and rural studies of measles infection (Aaby, 1988*b*). This apparent contradiction between patterns observed and expected from hypotheses about age at infection may be related to differences in exposure in urban and rural areas. The interval between epidemics affects the number of susceptibles in a family. In endemic situations it is likely that other siblings are already immune when measles is introduced into the household. With an increasing interepidemic interval, more individuals in a household are likely to be susceptible simultaneously; this would tend to increase the risk of multiple cases and intensive exposure. This kind of pattern is found in remote areas. For example, there are several indications that measles is more severe on islands, where many persons get sick at the same time (Staermose and Kofoed, 1938; MacGregor *et al.*, 1981). Nearly all community studies indicate long intervals between epidemics in rural areas, as attested to by the high median age at infection, and an association between long intervals and high measles mortality. Many other factors, including reduced access to medical care, may contribute to higher mortality in rural areas. Nevertheless, multiple cases have higher mortality than single cases in both rural and urban areas (Aaby *et al.*, 1984*a*; 1984*b*). It seems likely, therefore, that the higher mortality reported in virtually all rural epidemics compared to urban outbreaks is related to the greater degree of clustering of cases observed in rural areas.

One of the interesting implications of the clustering pattern is that vaccinations should reduce the CFR even among unvaccinated children. If some of the children in the population are vaccinated, it should reduce the number of multiple cases and intensive exposures and also reduce the CFR for unvaccinated children. This tendency is clear in all of the community studies where measles has been studied both before and after the introduction of vaccination (Aaby, 1988*b*). In Bandim, for example, the proportion of isolated cases under 5 years of age increased from 16 per cent before the introduction of measles vaccination to 28 per cent in the three years following the introduction of measles vaccination (p < 0.005). At the same time the CFR for measles fell from 20 to 15 per cent.

(*f*) Theories of severe disease and the policy of immunization

The theories of severe infection discussed here have quite different implications for a policy of prevention. Since measles mortality is usually associated with both poor living conditions and malnutrition, it has often been suggested that measles kills mostly the weak children, who would be likely to die of other infections if not from measles (Hendrickse 1975; Kasongo Project Team, 1981). Consequently, it is claimed that measles immunization may increase child survival only to a limited extent (if at all) because deaths prevented through immunization may be 'replaced' by deaths from other causes. Hence, according to Mosley (1983, 44):

even when a child is succesfully immunized, the protection is only against one specific agent. The child remains at risk to all other causes of death and, *all things being equal*, a certain proportion will go on to die of these 'competing' causes . . . But, all things are not equal. Specifically, the children whose deaths might be prevented by measles vaccine are at risk of dying not because of the severity of measles per se, but because they are on the 'road to death', and their nutritional status is so poor that they are more likely to die of any infectious disease. Thus preventing a death among these children may not necessarily save a life, but only change the cause of death.

However, if the emphasis on crowding and exposure is correct, it is not the particularly weak children who die. From the exposure perspective, measles immunization should lead to a reduction in mortality corresponding to the proportion of deaths attributed to measles.

There are a few studies from Africa which have compared the general mortality of measles-immunized and unimmunized children. Unfortunately, the selection of controls is a major problem in most of these studies.

Nigeria. The only controlled study was a small experiment carried out by Hartfield and Morley (1963) in the early 1960s in Nigeria. They observed that during an 18-month follow-up, no one died in the small group of 23 children receiving measles vaccine, whereas 3 died (2 of measles) among the 25 controls who received pertussis/tetanus vaccine (p = 0.27; Fisher's exact test).

Zaïre. The major comparative study was the one carried out in Kasongo, Zaïre, where 83 per cent of the children in one district received immunization. Their survival was compared with that of children born in the same period in an adjacent district and that of children born in the same two districts in the preceding year. While this study claimed to have shown that the initial 'gain in survival probability [in the vaccinated group] tended to diminish afterwards, to approach that of the unvaccinated group', the data did not support this conclusion. The mortality risk was 2.6–3.5 times higher in the three control groups than in the immunized group during the first year of life after starting the study, corresponding to a 62–71 per cent reduction in overall mortality. The subsequent diminution of this difference was interpreted as indicating that the weak children who had not died from measles died of other infections. However, the number of cases was clearly insufficient to permit such a conclusion (Aaby *et al.*, 1981*a*). The fact remains that mortality was 1.8–2.5 times lower in the immunized group than in the three control groups during the critical period of child mortality (from 7 to 35 months), corresponding to a 45 to 60 per cent reduction in mortality. After 3 years of age very few children die. Furthermore, most of the children were immunized before 9 months of age, which means that 20 to 30 per cent may not have seroconverted. The reported vaccine efficacy was only 69 per cent (Kasongo Project Team, 1981). Assuming that the children with vaccine failure had the same mortality as the control group, the reduction in mortality between the effectively vaccinated children and the three control groups would have been of the order of from 63 to 73 per cent and not from 45 to 60 per cent. There may have been some selection bias in who agreed to have their children immunized. However, since the unimmunized children in the area where vaccination was introduced continued to experience the same level of mortality as the control groups, it is unlikely that the unimmunized represent those who had a high risk of dying anyway. The study did not report the proportion of deaths due to measles in the immunized and control groups. However, a reduction of 45 to 60 per cent seems to be more than the share of deaths attributed to measles between 7 and 35 months of age.

Guinea-Bissau. Studies from Guinea-Bissau have compared mortality after immunization, where the controls were children who had not had measles and did not participate in the immunization campaign (Aaby *et al.*, 1984*c*). While this selection may entail obvious biases, those not attending were mainly children temporarily out of the community on the days of

immunization. In the year prior to the introduction of measles immunization, there was no difference in mortality between those attending a general
examination and those absent. Since measles immunization was the only
intervention introduced, there should be no confounding due to the simultaneous initiation of other preventive measures. The results (Table 14.7)
show clearly a reduction in mortality associated with immunization against
measles.

Another study from a rural area of Guinea-Bissau suggested a twofold
reduction in mortality in the immunized group compared with all other
children in the community (Aaby *et al.*, 1984*b*).

Senegal. Garenne and Cantrelle (1986) have recently reanalysed their data
from the Khombole area in Senegal, one of the first zones where the
measles vaccine was used in Africa. Measles vaccine was given in two
campaigns, one in 1965 and the other in 1967, in some of the villages in the
zone. Children from villages without immunization were used as controls.
Among the immunized they observed a mortality risk of 0.232 between 6
months and 3 years of age. This was 31 per cent lower than the risk of 0.336
for the control group (p = 0.028). If measles deaths had been suppressed in
the control group, only a 12 per cent reduction in mortality should have
been expected. This tendency seems due not merely to higher mortality in
the control villages, as the mortality of unimmunized children in the villages
with immunization was at least as high as that of children in the control
group.

Given these data from Africa and a few other studies from Bangladesh
and Haiti (Aaby *et al.*, 1987*a*), it seems reasonable to conclude that measles
immunization reduces mortality by at least as much as (and very likely more
than) the proportion of deaths attributed to measles infection. Those who
die of measles are therefore not the particularly weak children likely to die
anyway.

Table 14.7. *Mortality risk during one year of follow-up (1980) according to measles
immunization status, Bandim*

| Age at vaccination (months) | Mortality risk (deaths of children) | | | | Odds ratio (95% confidence interval) |
| | Vaccinated | | Not vaccinated[a] | | |
	%	Ratio	%	Ratio	
6–11	3.4	4/119	21.3	5/23	8.0 (2.7–27.3)
12–35	1.2	3/242	10.5	5/47.5[b]	9.4 (2.7–32.2)

[a] Children who did not attend the vaccination session in their district. Children with a history
of measles have been omitted from the table.
[b] Children who moved during the period of observation have been counted as followed for
six months.

(*g*) **Delayed impact of measles infection**

The fact that the measles vaccine seems to reduce mortality by more than the share of deaths ascribed directly to acute measles suggests that measles entails long-term excess mortality which may also be prevented by measles vaccination. There have been very few studies of long-term morbidity and mortality among measles patients compared to controls. Hull *et al.* (1983) reported a village outbreak in the Gambia where they went back three and nine months later to assess the impact of measles. Children aged 3 months to 6 years who had had measles had a mortality of 12.3 per cent (13/106) during the following eight months, whereas mortality for other children in the community was only 1.4 (9/654) (OR = 10.0; 95 per cent CI = 4.8–20.9). Their results could be confounded by background factors distinguishing the measles cases from the other children in the community. For example, it seems clear that deaths occurred mainly in domestic compounds where many children lived close together (Hull, 1988), and the risk of measles infection as well as general mortality may have been greater in larger compounds. Parental attitudes could play a role, since many of the controls had been immunized. However, the odds ratio was particularly high for children under 1 year of age; in that age group very few of the controls had been immunized prior to the outbreak (Aaby *et al.*, 1987*a*).

In a study from Nigeria, Osagie (1986) reidentified 106 cases of measles and the 106 controls who had visited a hospital clinic the previous year. Among the 106 measles cases, 11 had died (10.4 per cent) versus only two from the control group (OR = 6.0; 95 per cent CI = 1.5–23.4). Acute mortality was only 1 per cent (1/106), whereas ten died between the second and the sixth months, usually on the second or third month after contracting measles.

In a demographic follow-up study from Burkina Faso, children were visited every fourth month (van de Walle, 1986). Children declared to have had measles during a four-month period had a mortality risk of 3.6 per cent (22/615) in the following four-month interval. This was significantly higher than the non-measles mortality risk of 1.4 per cent (79/5555) experienced by children who had not had measles during the previous four months (OR = 2.6; 95 per cent CI = 1.6–4.2).

Whereas these studies observed differences in mortality during the first year after measles infection, a study from Guinea-Bissau (Aaby *et al.*, 1984*c*) reported excess mortality in the following year as well (OR = 4.9; 95 per cent CI = 1.4–16.9) (Aaby *et al.*, 1987*a*).

The available data strongly suggest that previous measles cases have significant excess mortality compared with community controls. Since these studies are obviously not randomized trials, it would be desirable to have further analyses in order to control for background factors which might increase both the risk of measles infection and mortality due to other causes.

The differences in mortality reported in existing data are so great, however, that it seems improbable that background factors could account for the mortality difference.

Severe measles has usually been understood to work through natural selection, taking the weaker children (Aaby *et al.*, 1984*c*). However, the data now available, particularly the studies of the impact of measles immunization and long-term consequences of measles, suggest a quite different interpretation. Not only does measles kill many normally healthy children in the acute phase of infection, it may also weaken many children so that they become susceptible to delayed morbidity and mortality.

(*h*) Mechanisms of severe infection

Studies of measles have systematically shown intensive exposure to be responsible for increased severity. Since this approach is also capable of accounting for a large part of the variation in severity of measles infection (Table 14.2), it seems warranted to examine the possible mechanisms of this association between exposure and severity.

None of the possible confounding factors seems to explain the higher CFR of secondary cases. It is therefore likely that intensive exposure somehow aggravates the infection itself. This could be due perhaps to the increased virulence of the measles virus with exposure over time. However, this would mean that the CFR increases throughout the course of an epidemic. This we did not observe. It therefore seems more likely that the effect of intensive exposure is due to a higher dose of measles virus and/or a higher rate of

Table 14.8. *Factors affecting the risk of intensive exposure*

High risk of exposure	Low risk of exposure
Polygyny	Monogamy
Extended family	Nuclear family
Large compound	Small compound
High birth rate (large sib)	Low birth rate (small sib)
Twins	Singletons
Short child spacing	Long child spacing
Multi-family houses	Single family dwelling
Small apartment	Large apartment
Joint beds, bedroom	Separate beds, bedrooms
Epidemic	Endemic
Rural	Urban
	Extra-family contact
	Public child care
	Immunoglobulin prophylaxis

intercurrent infections. Index cases may transmit a number of other infections besides measles, thereby worsening the condition of the secondary cases. Another possibility is that the intensive exposure of the secondary case causes the child to receive a stronger dose of the measles virus (Aaby *et al.*, 1985). Animal studies show a clear link between high dose of infection, short period of incubation, and high mortality. While the role of dose of viral infections in humans has not been systematically studied, there are many indications that dose influences the period of incubation and that a short period of incubation is associated with a severe course of the infection (Aaby *et al.*, 1986*a*).

Regardless of the pathogenic mechanisms involved, the observations presented here suggest the importance of overcrowding and intensive exposure in severe disease. Secondary cases of chicken-pox have been shown to be more severe than index cases (Ross, 1962). Otherwise there are few studies of the importance of exposure for the severity of infection.

3. The Crowding Pattern

The data clearly suggest that intensive exposure is an important risk factor for severe measles and may be important in other infections as well. It is therefore important to understand what socio-economic and cultural processes lead to the clustering of many susceptible individuals. Table 14.8 lists some factors which may increase the risk of intensive exposure.

Several of these factors are illustrated by studies of measles. In Bandim, monogamous families were found to have the lowest risk of measles mortality. However, polygynous families had a higher frequency of multiple cases. When the CFRs were standardized for clustering, no differences existed in mortality for monogamous and polygynous families (Aaby *et al.*, 1984*a*). Several studies also show that the CFR is higher in large compounds (Aaby, 1988*b*).

Studies from Copenhagen and Guinea-Bissau have suggested that residence in multi-family dwellings is associated with an increase in the measles CFR (Aaby *et al.*, 1988; Aaby, 1988*a*). There is also consistent evidence that mortality was higher in small apartments (Picken, 1921; Wilson, 1905; Debré and Joannon, 1926). When several children sleep together the risk of intensive exposure is presumably increased. Thus, one of the highest fatality ratios ever recorded was among the Mandingas, where all women and children sleep together (McGregor, 1964).

It should also be valuable to study general child mortality in terms of units like large compounds, extended families, polygynous households, and also with an eye to child spacing. There are relatively few studies concerning the health implications of large extended families and polygyny. However, several retrospective studies have measured child mortality by means of the

proportion of dead children among all births of the mothers interviewed. In
Zambia, the proportion of dead children rose according to the number of
wives the husband had. In monogamous families, the death rate was 22 per
cent compared with 29 per cent in polygamous families; this tendency
applied to six of seven major ethnic groups examined (Wenlock, 1979). Two
studies in Nigeria have reported that mothers from polygynous families have
a higher proportion of dead children (Caldwell, 1979; Gans, 1963). Brass
found in Kenya and Tanzania that in five of six groups there was no
difference in mortality between monogamous and polygynous families. In
the last group, the Kisii, child mortality under 5 years of age was 31 per cent
in the monogamous families and 40 per cent in the polygynous ones (Brass,
1959).

These studies indicate that higher mortality is often connected with
polygamy, though the relation is not invariable. In a rural environment,
polygynous households will often be older and more established. It is therefore unlikely that increased mortality is due to a negative association between productive capacity and polygyny. The number of children may be
the more critical variable, and our data from Bissau show large monogamous families to have the same nutritional status and child mortality as
polygynous families (Aaby *et al.*, 1981*c*). House size and construction traditions may also be important. Where each wife in a polygynous household has
her own separate house, the crowding effect may be minimal. Larger houses
seem to be associated with lower child mortality (Brass 1959; Chen *et al.*,
1980).

If bringing many children together is a critical factor, a high birth rate
may contribute to increased child mortality (McKeown and Brown, 1955).
The higher birth rate is often merely a reflection of higher child mortality
(Billewicz *et al.*, 1981), and not of a different child-spacing pattern. However, Brass's survey (1959) from Tanzania–Kenya suggests a real difference
in child spacing and a corresponding difference in child mortality; i.e. the
Kisii, the only group with high fertility, had the highest child mortality.

These examples suggest that ethnic, regional, and historical differences in
mortality may be related to variation in the crowding pattern.

(*a*) East and West Africa

There seem to be major differences in mortality between West and East
Africa; for example, measles and whooping cough are much more severe in
West Africa. Much of this variation may be due to differences in social
structure and customs of housing construction; polygyny, for example,
appears to be less common in East Africa. One study reported that married
men had on the average 1.2 wives in East Africa, versus 1.5–1.6 in West
and Central Africa (Goody, 1973). We found an average of 1.7 to 1.8 wives
per married man in Guinea-Bissau (Aaby *et al.*, 1983*b*). Similar data have

been reported from rural Senegal (Pison and Bonneuil, 1988). In addition, settlement patterns tend to be more dispersed in East Africa, whereas West Africa often has large, dense villages. In East Africa, polygynously married women normally have separate huts, and this is not always the case in West Africa. The implication of these tendencies is that children in West Africa have a higher risk of being intensively exposed, and the proportion of secondary cases in measles was found to be much higher in the two studies from West Africa than in the study from Kenya (Table 14.6).

(*b*) The Balanta case

The different elements of the crowding paradigm may be illustrated with a comparison of some of the groups followed in Guinea-Bissau; namely, the Balanta in the Tombali region and the Mandinga and Fula in the Oio region. In our study of child health in Guinea-Bissau, we were initially puzzled by the story of the Balanta, the major ethnic group, comprising about a quarter of the total population. During this century, the Balanta have expanded territorially at the expense of other ethnic groups. This has happened in spite of the fact that the Balanta have a lower birth rate than other ethnic groups (Brito, 1953). None the less, the national censuses indicate that the Balanta have maintained their share of the national population relative to the Mandinga, the other ethnic group we studied (see Table 14.9). The paradox of lower birth rate and equal population growth suggests that the Balanta have lower mortality and/or that other groups have emigrated at a higher rate. We initially thought that lower mortality among the Balanta could be due to their better nutrition. Being wet rice cultivators, the Balanta have a more regular food supply than the Mandinga, who depend mainly on swidden agriculture. However, these ethnic groups are different in many other respects.

While rural Mandinga and Fula breast-feed for 30 months on average, the rural Balanta breast-feed for as long as 38 months (Table 14.9). In all groups there is a taboo on sexual intercourse during the period of lactation, since semen is believed to contaminate the milk and kill the breast-fed child. We do not know to what extent this taboo is obeyed. If women merely breast-fed until they got pregnant, amenorrhea being the major spacing mechanism, length of breast-feeding would presumably be quite equal in the different ethnic groups. Therefore, the fact that Mandinga in Guinea-Bissau breast-feed longer than in the Gambia (Billewicz *et al.*, 1981) and that the Balanta have an even longer period of breast-feeding suggests that abstinence plays some role in spacing. The observed differences in breast-feeding length correspond to variations in cultural prescriptions on the period of lactation. The result is that the Balanta have fewer children than the Mandinga (Table 14.9).

A high degree of polygyny increases crowding in all groups. However,

Table 14.9. *Duration of breast-feeding, crowding, and child mortality for three ethnic groups, Balanta, Mandinga, and Fula in a rural setting, Guinea-Bissau, 1979–1982*

Indicators	Balanta	Mandinga	Fula
Mean duration of breast-feeding[a]	38 months	30 months	30 months
No. of children 0–4 yrs. of age by women aged 15–44 yrs.[b]	0.55	0.78	—
Population of 0–14 yrs.	35.3%	47.8%	—
Mean no. of women/married man[b]	1.7	1.6	—
Mean no. of persons/household[b]	6.1	10.6	—
No. of children 0–4 yrs. by household[b]	0.93	1.91	—
No. of persons sleeping in bed with mother and child[c]	0.17	0.69	
Weight-for-age as % of WHO standard for children aged:[a]			
0–12 months	106% (32)	105% (15)[d]	
3–5 months	104% (30)	92% (25)	
6–17 months	90% (88)	82% (108)	
18–35 months—breast-fed	86% (71)	77% (49)	
18–35 months—weaned	89% (16)	81% (43)	
Mortality during 1 yr. for children aged 0–5 months at examination from Dec. 1980 to Feb. 1981[e]	8% (7/97)	16% (13/80)	24% (5/20)
% of national population, 1979	24.9	12.6	

Note: Number of cases in parentheses.

[a] Data from general child examination, 1979.
[b] Census 1979. No census made in the Fula village.
[c] Data from general child examination, 1982.
[d] Mandinga constituted 68% and Fula 29% of the children in the nutritional survey.
[e] Included are all children aged less than five months at the time of the general child examination in the villages. Children who moved within the following 12 months have been counted for six months.

whereas adult men among the Balanta have separate households, Mandinga brothers often live together in the same household; hence, their households and living compounds tend to be larger (Table 14.10). On average, there were twice as many children below 5 years of age in Mandinga households as among the Balanta. Among the Balanta, each wife ideally has her own

Table 14.10. *Weight-for-age as per cent of standard of children aged 0–5 months according to size of household and ethnic group, Guinea-Bissau, January–March 1980*

Region (ethnic group)	Small households		Large households	
	%	No. of cases	%	No. of cases
Oio (Mandinga, Fula)	104.6	26	96.5	22
Tombali (Balanta)	105.5	29	90.0	13

Note: Household size has been assessed from the number of persons in the household who fetch water; 'small' means one or two, and 'large' means three or more water-carriers.

room, while wives in Mandinga households live together, often with five to ten women staying in the same circular hut. The difference in crowding is reinforced with the birth of new siblings. When their mother gives birth to a new child, Balanta children are said to leave their mother's bed and move to the bed of their father or grandmother. Mandinga and Fula mothers may have several children in the bed at the same time. These cultural patterns yield significant differences in the mean number of persons sleeping in the same bed.

While Balanta and Mandinga–Fula children aged 0–2 months had similar nutritional status, the fall in weight-for-age began earlier among the Mandinga and Fula and was more far-reaching. In 1980 and 1981, when no major epidemic occurred in the population surveyed, Balanta children below 6 months of age had a better chance of survival during the following years than did Mandinga and Fula children.

The difference in mortality comes about while all children are still being breast-fed. The Balanta probably have a more reliable food production system than the Mandinga, and the divergence in nutritional status which occurs before supplementary feeding becomes important could be due to Balanta mothers having more and better breast milk. While differences in quality of milk may have some impact, social factors are also essential, for the state of nutrition in the critical first six months of life was much lower in larger families in both ethnic groups. A higher risk of intensive exposure and early infection in large families could be the cause of these differences. In Bandim, where other ethnic groups had larger families, we observed that the Balanta had a lower risk of dying of measles. The Mandinga of the Gambia, on the other hand, have had one of the highest measles mortality rates ever reported (Table 14.3); and in Guinea-Bissau their CFR in whooping cough was likewise extremely high.

Therefore, it seems that differences in mortality can partly explain the Balanta paradox of low birth rate and high relative growth rate. If mortality is high, it may be self-defeating to try to increase the population by increasing the birth rate and reducing the birth interval (McKeown and Brown, 1955).

4. The Social Production of Health and Disease

The present study has suggested that for measles infection, a disease-transmission perspective accounts for the major variations in mortality better than a host-factor approach. Since there are so few studies of other infections from this perspective, it is premature to judge the relative importance of these two approaches for other infections. If disease-transmission factors are important, this will give more emphasis to the dimensions of social life that have been summarized under the heading 'overcrowding'. This perspective implies that socio-cultural processes may have a profound impact on health and disease.

African subsistence economies usually attempt to build viable units of production and mutual assistance. To maintain household production it is indispensable to control labour, and in the case of major crises such as famine or war, reliable support is necessary. These requirements invariably involve control of kinship relations and the old men enlarge their households by extending kinship connections and by bringing in more women. Women hold important roles in this system as labourers and mothers of future labourers. For men and women in African cultural systems, social success and prestige are guaranteed by the strength of the family and the number of offspring. Trying to achieve these goals often leads to increased overcrowding, which can generate higher morbidity and mortality.

However, there appear to be countervailing cultural forces which limit overcrowding. Long periods of breast-feeding are important for their impact on nutrition. In none of the groups followed in Guinea-Bissau did older breast-fed children have better nutritional status than weaned children; on the contrary, the weaned were better nourished (see Table 14.9). This may be due to the fact that weak children were breast-fed for longer periods than healthy children. None the less, it is clear from the figures that children aged 18–36 months can manage in the local environment without being breast-fed. In view of the fact that most adults claim to want as many children as possible, prolonged breast-feeding of 2–4 years may seem counter-productive. However, as reported in one study from Zambia, some Africans have experienced that too many children born close together 'burn' each other and kill each other by passing diseases easily, and that in such families many children die (Lovel *et al.*, 1983). While origins are difficult to discover, cultural rules prescribing prolonged breast-feeding and sexual abstinence during lactation apparently serve to limit overcrowding of households with small children.

The frequency of co-residing polygynous unions is lower in the cities than in the rural areas, partly because many men have their wives living in separate houses (Aaby *et al.*, 1983*a*). Furthermore, where diseases are endemic, as they are in urban areas, siblings tend to become ill at different times. This may reduce the risk of child mortality in the cities. Nevertheless, there are also adverse developments. In Guinea-Bissau, breast-feeding lasts between two and four years in the rural areas. Most groups can cite customs which indicate that the lactation period used to be longer. Comparison among the same ethnic groups shows breast-feeding to be 6–12 months shorter in the urban areas. Parents will often indicate their desire to have more children as the motivation for reducing breast-feeding. The reduction of house size in urban areas and the reduced spacing of children may well increase health problems.

In Africa, ideology and social control are intimately linked to concepts of health and disease. High morbidity and mortality undoubtedly lead to suspicions and even accusations of witchcraft and sorcery, and to the break-up of families. Social control as exercised by old men is often a question of communicating with ancestral spirits who can cause disease. As discussed above, extended family arrangements may contribute to increased morbidity and mortality. In so doing, overcrowding may provide part of the foundation for the ideology and the system of social control.

Our suggestion that severe disease is due to excessive antigen stimulation rather than immune incapacity caused by nutritional deficiencies or other host factors is no doubt controversial (Neiburg and Dibley, 1986; Lepage *et al.*, 1983; Lancet 1983). Only future studies can determine the extent of its applicability. The emphasis on overcrowding and intensive exposure has several practical consequences, some of which have been discussed elsewhere (Aaby *et al.*, 1984*c*; 1986*b*; 1987*b*). In general terms, the implication is that reduced exposure to infection due to improved housing, sanitation, better hygiene, longer birth spacing, specific prophylaxis, and a better immunization coverage may have a very significant impact on child mortality. Social scientists and historians studying the variations and changes in family and compound size and composition, village patterns and housing traditions, child spacing practices and birth rates will better understand the social production of health and disease.

References

Aaby, P. (1988*a*), 'Severe measles in Copenhagen, 1915–1925', *Reviews of Infectious Diseases* 10: 452–56.
—— (1988*b*), 'Malnutrition and overcrowding-exposure in severe measles infection: A review of community studies', *Reviews of Infectious Diseases* 10: 478–91.
—— Bukh, J., Lisse, I. M., and Smits, A. J. (1981*a*), 'Measles vaccination and child

mortality', *Lancet* 2: 93.

—— —— —— —— Smedman, L., Jepsson, O., and Lindeberg, A. (1981*b*), 'Breastfeeding and measles mortality in Guinea-Bissau', *Lancet* 2: 1231.

—— —— —— —— (1981*c*), 'Child mortality in Guinea-Bissau: Malnutrition or overcrowding', Institute of Ethnology and Anthropology, Copenhagen (mimeo).

—— —— —— —— (1983*a*), 'Measles mortality, state of nutrition and family structure: A community study from Guinea-Bissau', *Journal of Infectious Diseases* 147: 693–701.

—— —— —— —— (1983*b*), 'Spacing, crowding and child mortality in Guinea-Bissau', *Lancet* 2: 161.

—— —— —— —— (1983*c*), 'Les hommes sont-ils plus faibles ou leurs sœurs parlent-elles trop? Essai sur la transmission des maladies infectieuses', *Anthropologie et Société* 7: 47–59.

—— —— —— —— Gomes, J., Fernandes, M. A., Indi, F., and Soares, M. (1983*d*), 'High case fatality rate in twins with measles', *Lancet* 2: 90.

—— —— —— —— (1984*a*), 'Overcrowding and intensive exposure as determinants of measles mortality', *American Journal of Epidemiology* 120: 49–63.

—— —— —— —— Gomes, J., Fernandes, M. A., Indi, F., and Soares, M. (1984*b*), 'Determinants of measles mortality in a rural area of Guinea-Bissau: Crowding, age, and malnutrition', *Journal of Tropical Pediatrics* 30: 164–8.

—— —— —— —— (1984*c*), 'Measles vaccination and reduction in child mortality: A community study from Guinea-Bissau', *Journal of Infection* 8: 13–21.

—— Coovadia, H., Bukh, J., Lisse, I. M., Smits, A. J., Wesley, A., and Kiepiela P. (1985), 'Severe measles: A reappraisal of the role of nutrition, overcrowding and virus dose', *Medical Hypotheses* 18: 93–112.

—— Bukh, J., Lisse, I. M., and Smits, A. J. (1986*a*), 'Severe measles in Sunderland, 1885: A European–African comparison of causes of severe infection', *International Journal of Epidemiology* 15: 101–7.

—— —— Hoff, G., Leerhoey, J., Lisse, I. M., Mordhorst, C. H., and Pedersen, I. R. (1986*b*), 'High measles mortality in infancy related to intensity of exposure', *Journal of Pediatrics* 109: 40–4.

—— Clements, J., and Cohen, N. (1987*a*), 'Key issues in measles immunization research: A review of the literature', Expanded Programme on Immunization, Geneva.

—— Bukh, J., Hoff, G., Lisse, I. M., and Smits, A. J. (1987*b*), 'Humoral immunity in measles infection: A critical factor?' *Medical Hypotheses* 23: 287–303.

—— —— Lisse, I. M., and da Silva, M. C. (1988), 'Measles mortality: Further community studies on the role of overcrowding and intensive exposure', *Reviews of Infectious Diseases* 10: 474–7.

Anonymous (1964), 'Protection against measles in West Africa', *Public Health Reports*, 79: 862.

—— (1980), 'Epidemiology of measles in a rural community', *Weekly Epidemiological Records*, 55: 85–7.

Aschberg, S., Bygren, L. O., and Lindeberg, A. (1975), *Haelse i Oio*, Sida, Stockholm.

Axton, J. H. M. (1979), 'Measles and the state of nutrition', *South African Medical Journal*, 55: 125–6.

Bates, C. J. (1983), 'Vitamin A in pregnancy and lactation', *Proceedings of the*

Nutritional Society 42: 65–79.

Bhuiya, A., Wojtyniak, B., D'Souza, S., Nahar, L., and Shaikh, K. (1987), 'Measles case fatality among under-fives: A multivariate analysis of risk factors in a rural area of Bangladesh', *Social Science and Medicine* 24: 439–43.

Billewicz, W. Z. and McGregor, I. A. (1981), 'The demography of two West African (Gambian) villages, 1951–75', *Journal of Biosocial Science* 13: 219–40.

Black, F. L., Pinheiro, F. de, Hierholzer, W. J., and Lee, R. V. (1977), 'Epidemiology of infectious diseases: The example of Measles', in *Health and Disease in Tribal Societies*, Elsevier, Amsterdam, 115–35.

Brass, W. (1959), 'Differentials in child mortality by marriage experience of the mothers in six African communities', *International Population Conference*, Selbstverlag, Vienna, 384–95.

Brincker, J. A. H. (1938), 'A historical, epidemiological and aetiological study of measles (Morbilli; Rubeola)', *Proceedings of the Royal Society of Medicine* 31: 807–28.

Brito, E. (1953), 'Aspectos demographicos dos Balantas e Brames do territorio de Bula', *Boletin Cultural da Guine Portugesa* 8: 417–69.

Caldwell, J. C. (1979), 'Education as a factor in mortality decline: An examination of Nigerian data', *Population Studies*, 33/3: 395–413.

Cantrelle, P. (1965), 'Mortalité et morbidité par rougeole dans les pays francophones de l'Ouest Africain', *Archives fur Gesamter Virusforschung* 16: 35–45.

Chen, L. C., Rahman, M., and Sarder, A. M. (1980), 'Epidemiology and causes of deaths among children in a rural area of Bangladesh', *International Journal of Epidemiology*, 9: 25–33.

Coovadia, H. M., Kiepiela, P., and Wesley, A. G. (1984), 'Immunity and infant mortality from measles', *South African Journal of Medicine* 65: 918–21.

—— Wesley, A., Hammond, M. G., and Kiepiela, P. (1981), 'Measles, histocompatibility, leukocyte antigen, polymorphism and natural selection in humans', *Journal of Infectious Diseases* 144: 142–7.

Cox, P. S. V. (1973), 'Geographical variation in disease within a single district', *East African Medical Journal* 50: 712–19.

Davis, R. (1982), 'Measles in the tropics and public health practice', *Transactions of the Royal Society of Tropical Medicine and Hygiene* 76: 268–75.

Debré, R. and Joannon, P. (1926), *La Rougeole: Epidémiologie, Immunologie, Prophylaxie*, Masson, Paris.

Debroise, A., Sy, I., and Satge, P. (1967), 'La Rougeole en zone rurale', *L'Enfant en Milieu Tropical* 38: 20–36.

EPI (1986), *Measles: Spots that kill*, Expanded Programme of Immunization, WHO, Geneva.

Foster, S. O. (1984), 'Immunizable and respiratory diseases and child mortality', Supplement to vol. 10 of *Population and Development Review*, 119–40.

Gans, B. (1963), 'Some socio-economic and cultural factors in West African paediatrics', *Archives of Diseases of Childhood* 38: 1–12.

Garenne, M. and Cantrelle, P. (1986), 'Rougeole et mortalité au Sénégal: Étude de l'impact de la vaccination effectuée à Khombole 1965–1968, sur la survie des enfants', *Estimation de la mortalité du jeune enfant (0–5 ans) pour guider les actions de santé dans les pays en développement*, Séminaire INSERM 145, Paris, 515–32.

Goody, J. (1973), *The Character of Kinship*, Cambridge University Press, Cambridge.

Halliday, I. L. (1928), 'An Inquiry into the Relationship between Housing Conditions and the Incidence and Fatality of Measles', Medical Research Council, Report Series 120, London.

Hartfield, J. and Morley, D. (1963), 'Efficacy of measles vaccine', *Journal of Hygiene* 61: 143–7.

Hendrickse, R. G. (1975), 'Problems of future measles vaccination in developing countries', *Transaction of the Royal Society of Tropical Medicine and Hygiene* 69: 31–4.

Heyworth, B. (1973), 'Pathogenesis of measles', *British Medical Journal* 3: 693.

Hondius, A. J. K. and Sutorius, D. M. (1979), *Severe Measles in Nigeria*, Stichting WSO, Utrecht.

Hull, H. F. (1988), 'The effect of crowding on measles mortality in the Gambia, 1981', *Review of Infectious Diseases* 10: 463–7.

—— Williams, P. J., and Oldfield, F. (1983), 'Measles mortality and vaccine efficacy in rural West Africa', *Lancet* 1: 972–5.

Imperato, P. J. (1975), *A Wind in Africa*, Warren H. Green, St Louis.

Jelliffe, D. B. (1966), *The Assessment of the Nutritional Status of the Community*, WHO, Geneva.

Kasongo Project Team (1981), 'Influence of measles vaccination on survival pattern of 7–35-months-old children in Kasongo', *Lancet* 1: 764–7.

Lamb, W. H. (1988), 'Epidemic measles in a highly immunized rural West African (Gambian) village', *Review of Infectious Diseases* 10: 457–62.

Lancet (1983), 'Measles mortality and malnutrition', *Lancet* 2: 661.

Langaney, A. and Pison, G. (1979), 'Rougeole et augmentation temporaire de la masculinité des naissances: Coincidence ou causalité?' *Compte rendu des Séances de l'Académie des Sciences* 289: 1255–8.

Leeuwenburg, J., Muller, A. S., Voorhoeve, A. M., Gemert, W., and Kok, P. W. (1984), 'The epidemiology of measles', in J. K. van Ginneken and A. S. Muller (eds.), *Maternal and Child Health in Rural Kenya*, Croom Helm, London, 77–94.

Le François, P., Chevassus, A., Benefice, E., Dyck, J. L., Maire, B., Parent, G., Seymat, G., Ndiaye, A. M. (1980), 'Vitamin A status of populations in three West African countries', *International Journal of Vitamin and Nutrition Research* 50: 352–63.

Lepage, P., Mol, P. de, and Hennart, P. (1983), 'Measles mortality and malnutrition in Rwanda', *Lancet* 2: 965.

Lindtjoern, B. (1986), 'Severe measles in the Gandulla area of South-West Ethiopia', *Journal of Tropical Pediatrics* 32: 234–9.

Lovel, H., Mkandla, M., and Morley, D. (1983), 'Birth spacing in Zimbabwe a generation ago', *Lancet* 2: 161–2.

McGregor, I. A. (1964), 'Measles and child mortality in the Gambia', *West African Medical Journal* 14: 251–7.

MacGregor, J. D., MacDonald, J., Ingram, E. A., McDonnell, M., and Marshall, B. (1981), 'Epidemic measles in Shetland during 1977 and 1978', *British Medical Journal* 282: 434–6.

McKeown, T. and Brown, R. G. (1955), 'Medical evidence related to English population changes in the Eighteenth Century', *Population Studies* 9/2: 119–41.

Meunier, H. (1898), 'Sur un symptôme nouveau de la période précontagieuse de la rougeole et sur sa valeur prophylactique', *Gazette Hebdomadaire de Médicine Chirurgicale*, 1057–61.

Morley, D. C. (1973), *Paediatric Priorities in the Developing World*, Butterworths, London.

—— Martin, W. J., and Allen, I. (1967a), 'Measles in West Africa', *West African Medical Journal* 16: 24–31.

—— —— —— (1967b), 'Measles in East and Central Africa', *East African Medical Journal* 44: 497–508.

—— Woodland, M., and Martin, W. J. (1963), 'Measles in Nigerian children', *Journal of Hygiene* 61: 115–34.

Mosley, W. H. (1983), 'Will primary health care reduce infant and child mortality? A critique of some current strategies. With special reference to Africa and Asia', Paper prepared for the IUSSP Seminar on Social Policy, Health Policy and Mortality Prospects, Paris, 28 Feb.–4 Mar. 1983.

—— (1984), 'Child survival: Research and policy', Supplement to vol. 10 of *Population and Development Review*, 3–23.

Muller, A. S., Voorhoeve, A. M., 't Mannetje, W., and Schulpen, T. W. J. (1977), 'The impact of measles in a rural area of Kenya', *East African Medical Journal* 54: 364–72.

Neiburg, P. and Dibley, M. J. (1986), 'Risk factors for fatal measles infections', *International Journal of Epidemiology* 15: 309–11.

Ogbeide, M. I. (1967), 'Measles in Nigerian children', *Journal of Pediatrics* 71: 737–41.

Omonulo, A. (1965), 'Child health in Western Nigeria', *West African Medical Journal*, 255–68.

Osagie, H. F. (1986), 'Delayed mortality and morbidity 12 months after measles in young children in Nigeria', M.Sc. thesis, Institute of Child Health, University of London.

Picken, R. M. F. (1921), 'The epidemiology of measles in a rural and residential area', *Lancet* 1: 1349–53.

Pison, G. (1982), *Dynamique d'une population traditionelle: Les Peul Bandé (Sénégal oriental)*, INED Cahier 99, PUF, Paris.

—— and N. Bonneuil (1988), 'Increased risk of measles mortality for children with siblings among the Fula Bandé, Senegal', *Review of Infectious Diseases* 10: 468–70.

Rea, J. H. (1968), 'Measles in Africa', *Lancet* 1: 356.

Reves, R. (1985), 'Declining fertility in England and Wales as a major cause of the twentieth century decline in mortality: The role of changing family size and age structure in infectious disease mortality in infancy', *American Journal of Epidemiology* 122: 112–26.

Rolfe, M. (1982), 'Measles immunization in the Zambian Copperbelt: Cause for concern', *Transaction of the Royal Society of Tropical Medicine and Hygiene* 76: 529–30.

Ross, A. H. (1962), 'Modification of chicken pox in family contacts by administration of gamma globulin', *New England Journal of Medicine* 267: 369–76.

Senecal, J., Aubry, L., and Falade, S. (1962), 'Infectious diseases in the child of pre-school age in Senegal', *West African Journal of Medicine*, 93–105.

Smedman, L., Lindeberg, A., Jeppsson, O., and Zetterstroem, R. (1983), 'Nutritional status and measles: A community study in Guinea-Bissau', *Annals of Tropical Pediatrics* 3: 169–76.

Staermose, V. and Kofoed, S. E. (1938), 'Morbili in adults', *Acta Medica Scandinavica* 97: 608–16.

Stephens, P. W. (1990), 'Reliability of lay reporting of morbidity and case-of-death data: An evaluation of reported cases and deaths from measles in rural Senegal', in J. Vallin, S. D'Souza, and A. Palloni (eds.), *Measurement and Analysis of Mortality: New Approaches*, Clarendon Press, Oxford, 143–54.

van de Walle, E. (1986), 'Anatomie d'une épidémie de rougeole vue par la lorgnette d'une enquête à passages répétés', *Estimation de la mortalité du jeune enfant (0–5 ans) pour guider les actions de santé dans les pays en développement*, Séminaire INSERM, Paris, 419–28.

Walsh, J. A. (1983), 'Selective primary health care: Strategies for control of disease in the developing world, IV. Measles', *Review of Infectious Diseases* 5: 330–40.

Wenlock, R. W. (1979), 'Social factors, nutrition and child mortality in a rural subsistence economy', *Ecology of Food and Nutrition* 8: 227–40.

Wilson, J. G. (1905), 'Measles: Its prevalence and mortality in Aberdeen', *Public Health* 18: 65–82.

15 Famine Mortality in Ethiopia and Sudan

John Seaman
The Save the Children Fund (UK)

1. Introduction

The popular image of famine is of mass starvation resulting directly from failures of subsistence cultivation. Paradoxically, it is now well documented that even profound and prolonged failures of food production do not always lead to human starvation. For example, mortality following a succession of harvest failures from drought in the West African Sahel between 1968 and 1973 was of the order of 100,000 (Caldwell, 1977), much less than the millions which had been predicted by the media.

As is now well known, the reason for this is to be found in the ability of many populations to secure their food supplies even in the face of severe and recurrent shortage. The strategies followed vary, but in general include the storage of food in good years against the bad; the accumulation of cash and saleable assets such as livestock; the increased use of wild foods; the sale of assets to buy food; the redistribution of food within populations by charity, gifts, and credit; the selective or wholesale migration of populations to seek work and food in less affected areas; the remittance of cash by migrants, and often the receipt of food aid from government and international sources. From this perspective, excess mortality may be seen not as an inevitable corollary of production failure in a simple subsistence economy but as only one possible outcome of a complex response to shortage. That mass starvation has not been seen more often in Africa in the face of severe and recurrent drought is a measure of the extraordinary economic resilience of many rural populations. This chapter describes the economic effects and the population reaction to food shortages in Sudan and Ethiopia from 1980 to 1985 and the impact of this on mortality. The account is limited to the main famine areas of northern Sudan and Ethiopia. Other areas of southern Ethiopia were also affected by drought and famine during the same period.

2. Sources of Information

Relief agencies increasingly accept the need for information to allocate relief efficiently. An unusually large amount of information was collected during the famine in East Africa. However, most of this information was collected for operational rather than research purposes, and its quality and geographical coverage is uneven.

A few relief agencies devoted considerable resources to information collection, most little or none. Where there was no perceived crisis no information is usually available and because of the generally late start to relief operations little information was collected during the early stages of the crisis. In wide areas of northern rural Ethiopia information could not be systematically collected because of restricted access due to war. The result is an unusual depth of understanding of the impact of drought in some areas, such as Darfur in western Sudan, and only a sketchy understanding elsewhere.

Much of the information collected in Sudan and Ethiopia is still being processed or is in draft and much is available only in the form of internal agency working documents. It is to be expected that some of the information presented here will be revised and more information will become available. This paper should be seen only as a preliminary review.

3. Drought and Economic Crisis in Ethiopia and Sudan

(a) Geography, agriculture, and economy

Map 15.1 shows the long-term pattern of rainfall and the major topographical features of the region. Passing from north to south, rainfall is generally less, with some variation in this pattern around the Ethiopian highlands. In Sudan, the rainfall is received in a single annual peak, roughly between June and September. In Ethiopia the onset of the main rains is generally later and in the northern and eastern parts of the country part of the rain is received as a separate 'spring rain'.

In Sudan, the major cereal crops are millet, grown in drier northern areas, and sorghum, the 200 mm. isohyet marking the approximate northern and eastern limit of cereal cultivation. Sesame, groundnuts, vegetables, and other cash crops are grown in wetter areas. The main harvest is in September and October. Livestock production, as at similar latitudes elsewhere in Africa, tends to be the dominant activity in areas too dry for reliable cultivation but is also an important activity for farmers in wetter areas.

In northern Ethiopia, as in Sudan, production varies from north to south, livestock being more important in Eritrea and Tigray than in the wetter areas to the south. In Ethiopia, however, there is the additional complexity of variation in production with altitude. The classification of land varies with both altitude and rainfall but a broad division may be made into highland, over 2,400 metres above sea-level, where barley is the chief cereal; inter-

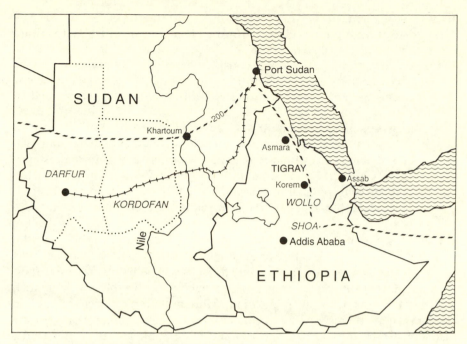

MAP 15.1. Map of Sudan and Ethiopia showing approximate limit of pre-drought 200 mm. isohyet and main areas and towns

mediate altitudes, where teff (a cereal), wheat, oil-seeds, and pulses are grown; and lowlands, where sorghum and millet are the main crops. The main harvest is gathered in November and December. In Wollo and Tigray the terrain is mountainous and all types of production may be found within a small area. To the east of the highlands, roughly along the line of the main Addis Ababa–Asmara road, the land dips through intermediate zones of semi-arid agriculture to the pastoral lowlands of the Danakil Desert.

Large commercial irrigated farms are to be found at Gezeira to the south and east of Khartoum and on the Ethiopian border. Large-scale rain-fed commercial sorghum farms are located in South Kordofan, Blue Nile, and the Eastern Region. Gedaref in the Eastern Region is also the centre of the commercial grain trade and storage in Sudan. In Ethiopia the large, formerly commercial, farms at Setit Humera on the Sudan border, on the Awash, and in the south of the country, have been nationalized.

Communications within the region are very restricted. In western Sudan road communications are poor and the area is linked unreliably by rail and road with central Sudan and with Port Sudan. Road communications within the famine area of northern Ethiopia are restricted to a single all-weather road connecting Addis Ababa and Asmara and a limited, in the northern areas very limited, feeder-road network. In northern Wollo and Tigray many roads have been closed by warfare to regular civilian traffic for some years. The rural areas of northern Wollo, Tigray, and Eritrea have been controlled to a variable but often considerable extent by anti-government forces, which restricts access to and from these areas. A poor quality motor road connects eastern Sudan with the western lowlands of Ethiopia and to the interior as far as western Tigray.

Although small-scale agriculture is the chief occupation of the region, people's access to food is determined out only by local production but also by complex relationships within a local and wider economy. In understanding the effects of food shortage additional complexity is introduced by the effects of increasing population, national political and economic changes, and the fluctuating but generally reduced rainfall in the region since the late 1960s.

Livestock provide from milk and meat a food resource, but may be reared primarily for sale and exchange for cereals. It is probable that most 'pastoral' peoples of the region normally subsist chiefly on grain and their food supplies are therefore vulnerable to fluctuations in the prices of stock and grain. Stock kept by populations who are primarily agricultural in economy may represent an accumulation of capital rather than a food resource. Cash crops such as tobacco and gum arabic are grown for trade, but sesame, groundnuts, and vegetables may also be grown for trade rather than consumption. In the Wollo Region of Ethiopia, barley is produced at higher altitudes and is exchanged for animal products and other cereals from lower zones of production.

Exchange may be local, or with a wider national or international market. In Sudan, a large proportion of cereal production is commercial and crops are marketed both locally and abroad. The geographical isolation of western Sudan and northern Ethiopia and their lack of integration with the more general food trade of the region were important features of the crisis.

For many people, wage employment, mostly in agriculture, is an important source of income. A small proportion of the population depends wholly on petty trade, manufacture, and non-agricultural sources of income. In the far west of Sudan much paid work is found locally on small commercial farms and migration to the commercial farms of the centre and east of Sudan has, because of the long distances involved, a long-term or permanent character; in Kordofan and other areas of the centre and east local work on larger commercial farms forms a more important part of the normal 'subsistence economy and migration is entirely seasonal. Because of the long distances and poor communications migrants from the far west also have problems in remitting cash to their home areas.

In northern Ethiopia, the nationalization of land and the extension of the area of military insecurity have reduced the opportunities for migrant labour within the country, although seasonal labour migration continues to the south-west and to the commercial farms of eastern Sudan. Officially organized resettlement from the northern areas to the south began in the late 1970s but was, prior to 1985, on a modest scale. Food-for-work schemes have also provided some additional local employment.

The decline in rainfall across the north of the region through the 1970s has had profound, if generally poorly documented, effects on the subsistence economy. Across wide areas of northern Sudan and Ethiopia average rainfall has fallen to the extent that subsistence from agriculture alone is now often impossible. In northern Darfur, the effects were sufficiently severe by 1977–8 for Holy (1980) to describe a 'catastrophic' situation in one area. In northern Ethiopia the population has for several decades been spilling into formerly pastoral grazing areas particularly in the eastern lowlands, areas which are drought-prone and unsuitable for sustained agriculture.

An essential, if broad, distinction may be drawn between the rural economies of the two countries. In much of Sudan, excepting possibly the Red Sea Hills, the effects of the decline in the northern economy have been moderated by the possibility of population movement towards wetter southern areas, by the opening up of new land, to an extent by the introduction of improved agricultural technology, and, notwithstanding the decline in the national economy, by sustained commercial grain production and continued opportunities for off-farm work. In contrast, in northern Ethiopia, the growing pressure on land of a population subsisting by primitive agricultural methods has been accompanied by increasing restrictions on movement and alternative employment. The effect of the reduction in rainfall is of severe and general impoverishment.

(b) Drought and production failure

The crisis in Ethiopia and Sudan did not begin at a single time. For a part of the population of northern Wollo and central Tigray, a crisis in the sense of failed production and the need to take more or less desperate measures to find food had begun at least by 1980.

The crisis first became evident to outside observers in mid-1982 with reports of drought and lowland harvest failure in parts of northern Wollo and Tigray, areas which in the past 20 years have twice suffered starvation. The progress towards the more widely publicized crisis of mid-1984 was one of continued drought in these areas and an extension of the area of drought which brought production failure both to a larger southern area of the highlands and to higher altitude production zones. Crop failure affected areas of the west and south-west highlands where it was previously unknown, and it affected not only the historically drought-prone lowlands but all altitudes of production.

The population directly affected by drought cannot be accurately defined but may reasonably be taken to be the entire population of northern Shoa, Wollo, Tigray, and Eritrea, in total not less than 7 million people.

In Sudan the onset of crisis was more clearly marked by the widespread drought, loss of livestock, and harvest failure across the country which began in northern areas in 1983 and spread to more southern latitudes in 1984. In 1983, the cereal crop in north Darfur was estimated to have met only 18 per cent of the needs of the population and to have been only 25 per cent of the production level in the 1970s. In 1984, south Darfur was estimated to have met only 60 per cent of its grain needs. Livestock loss in Darfur was estimated at over 50 per cent. Losses were certainly greater in the Red Sea Hills and some other northern areas. 1984 was a year of national crop failure in Sudan. Commercial cereal production was estimated to have fallen from a 1979–83 average annual tonnage of 1.4 million tonnes to 0.4 million tonnes.

Again, the affected population cannot be accurately estimated. The most severely affected northern areas have a total population of approximately 5 million.

(c) Responses to drought

Ethiopia. In highland Ethiopia, the options open to a farmer faced with a shortfall in production over needs are limited by poor communications and the fact that at times of general shortage the competition for access to the limited alternative sources of income are intense. The options are to sell livestock and other capital goods, to use wild foods to eke out grain supplies, for adult males to seek work elsewhere and to return with cash to buy food, and for women and children to migrate to towns to seek work or charity.

Increased commercial sale of cattle at Korem in northern Wollo was noted from mid-1982 (Cutler, 1984) although this had certainly begun in northern areas before this. Interviews by the author with famine migrants in Sudan in late 1983 found that they had been progressively selling off livestock, in some cases over several years, in order to buy food. It is noteworthy that many of these migrants were people who had owned 20 or more cattle and who might, in terms of highland Ethiopia, be regarded as normally prosperous and secure. For many poorer highland people their 'capital' would be no more than a few small stock, agricultural implements, and the materials of their house.

The market prices of livestock appear to have held up reasonably well (Cutler, 1984) although many stock were lost to drought. The price of grain rose in northern markets by 1982 and by mid-1983 was over double the pre-famine price throughout the region.

In most areas supplies of wild foods, chiefly seeds winnowed from grasses,

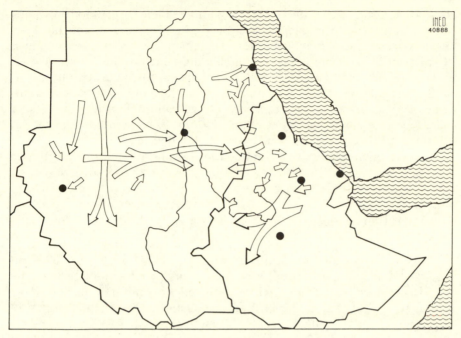

MAP 15.2. Chief routes of migration, 1984–1986

are very small. The options for alternative local employment in the highlands are few. In eastern lowland areas where some tree cover remains, firewood-selling attracted many people, but the market was rapidly glutted and prices were low. Because of the lack of alternative sources of income within the highlands, the most widely adopted strategy was migration. A large proportion of the highland population, perhaps 1.5 million people, decamped to other areas of Ethiopia and to Sudan. As might be expected, migration within and from Ethiopia developed in sequence, as economic distress extended and deepened within the area. The routes of migration are shown in Map 15.2.

Migration to towns on the main Addis Ababa–Asmara Road began from areas of central Tigray and northern Wollo in late 1982 and early 1983. The initial government relief policy of giving rations for people to take home was quickly overrun by numbers and a refusal by people to return to their homes. The first camps were established at Korem and Makalle by early 1983. The progressive extension of drought led to the establishment through 1984 and 1985 of camps in most of the main roadside towns along the length of Wollo and into northern Shoa and on the Kombolcha–Assab road. Camps also developed in Gondar.

The population of these camps is unknown. By March–April 1985 the population 'in and around' the camps was estimated to have been about

800,000 (Jansson *et al.*, 1987), although the resident population in camps was certainly less than this. It is clear that particularly in the northern and less secure areas only a selected population approached these camps. Migrants in Sudan from areas of Ethiopia adjacent to relief centres, when asked why they had not sought relief at camps on the main road nearer to their home villages, showed a combination of fear of the Ethiopian authorities and ignorance of the existence of the camps. Further, supplies of relief food reaching the northern camps prior to the main international relief effort in 1985 were variable but often grossly deficient, and many people stayed only briefly. Substantial variation in the numbers and the nutritional condition of new arrivals was seen over time. A marked seasonal variation, with new arrivals being highest in the second half of the year, was noted in Korem (Nash, 1986).

Westward migration from the highlands may be divided into four main parts.

1. A movement into western Tigray, chiefly from northern Wollo and central Tigray organized, sustained, and possibly initiated by the Relief Society of Tigray (REST), the relief organization of the Tigray People's Liberation Front. Between October 1982 and spring 1983 approximately 400,000 people passed through REST checkpoints (Jansson *et al.*, 1987). These were supported by a combination of local production, food purchase in Ethiopia, and the importation of relief food through Kassala in Sudan.
2. A spontaneous movement, chiefly of adult men seeking field work, into eastern Sudan in late 1983. The scale of this migration is unknown as there was little attempt to register or assist these people, but judging from the 20,000 or more who did not find work and who remained in camps it probably numbered between 50,000 and 100,000. It is of interest that many of these migrants were clearly inexperienced in migration. All the adult men with a few unmarried women from whole villages had chosen to move together, leaving the residual food and livestock with the remaining women and children.
3. A migration in late 1984 and early 1985 to camps in eastern Sudan. Most of this population were of entire villages from northern Wollo and central Tigray, the movement being organized by REST.
4. A substantial population movement into western and south-western Ethiopia, areas largely inaccessible to observation by outsiders. The scale of this movement is unknown as the population was dispersed but is thought to have been numbered in the hundreds of thousands. The origins of these migrants are to be found in wide areas of central highland Ethiopia.

To these must be added the arrival of approximately 100,000 Eritreans to camps at Kassala in Sudan. There is no doubt that Eritrea was severely affected by drought as were the neighbouring areas of Sudan and Ethiopia but no clear account of this is available.

Sudan. The situation in Sudan was radically different from that in Ethiopia. The factors which distinguished Sudan from Ethiopia may in general terms be listed as the large reserves of capital available in richer villages, such that food supplies through one year of production failure were often not in doubt; the possibility of successful movement of cattle and population to more distant southern pastures; the abundance of supplies of wild foods particularly during the rainy season, when food supplies were otherwise least; and the considerable opportunities for alternative work. The range of strategies employed varied widely between and within villages of different economy, wealth, and agricultural opportunity. Very detailed descriptions of the responses of several groups in Darfur are given by de Waal (1987).

This is not to say that much of the population of Sudan did not face extraordinary difficulties and hardships but it does account for the much less dramatic impact of the drought than was seen in Ethiopia.

The point may be illustrated by taking a 'worst case' village described by de Waal (1987) in northern Darfur. This village, Jebel Si, had suffered declining agricultural production since the 1950s and had been in grain deficit from drought since the 1960s. The village had survived by a combination of long-term male migration to central Sudan, and dry season work including work by women in harvesting and threshing in southern and western Darfur. Distant migrants would sometimes remit money or return when they had earned enough cash, using this to subsidize deficit grain production. These strategies made up, if unreliably, the grain deficit from the 1960s and were supplemented by the gradual sale of livestock. Between 1980 and 1984, when livestock numbers were generally rising in Darfur they were falling in Jebel Si.

In 1983 the harvest failed, the crops meeting under 10 per cent of needs. The strategy pursued was again to search for outside work. By the time of the survey in 1986, 46 per cent of 140 households were headed by women: of 74 men who had left during the preceding two years 46 were long-term migrants to central Sudan. By the dry season of 1984–5 only a handful of people remained in the village. The work found was, as before, in harvesting and on irrigated farms to the south, and in the late dry season, when no agricultural work was to be found, the sale of firewood and fodder, water-carrying, and building work in a local town provided a living. Seventy per cent of the sample was found to have had income from one of these sources. The consumption of wild foods was general, and for the small remaining population who could not find alternative occupation it was the chief means of subsistence.

In 1984–5 the number of productive animals fell by 75 per cent, of which the number which died were twice the number sold. One-third of the sample, mainly richer people, had successfully obtained credit and one-third had obtained charity including remittances from central Sudan. By the rains of 1985 nearly all households were able to return to the village in order to plant.

Population movements within Sudan were on a substantial scale. Movements were chiefly to urban areas and were of people seeking assistance from relatives, or work. The general pattern was for numbers to rise from 1983 and to peak in the first half of 1985. It is estimated that in Darfur, 50,000 to 100,000 people visited the town of Geneina alone and a similar number Nyala and El Fasher, a pattern which was repeated at towns across northern Sudan. Many people, particularly from nearer areas, went to Khartoum, where shanty towns grew up on the periphery of Khartoum North and Omdurman. The population of the camp at Omdurman was periodically transported back to Kordofan by the government. It is estimated that approximately 200,000 migrants came to the city. Increased labour migration occurred to the centre and east of Sudan, and of livestock to the wetter southern areas of Bahr El Ghazal.

The Red Sea Hills Province was severely affected by drought. The greater part of the rural population moved to camps on the main road and to Port Sudan. In the Eastern Region, signs of distress were less evident, presumably because of greater access to work and the generally more consistent supplies of grain. Employment fell because of the harvest failure in 1984. Signs of economic stress were evident from rising tensions between the established refugee populations and local Sudanese when the former were given free food.

(d) Relief food distribution

It is well known that the international relief response to the East African crisis was very late. In western Sudan, small quantities of food averaging a few kilograms per person were sold at subsidized rates from May 1984. Substantial shipments did not begin until late 1984. In Darfur, 47,351 tonnes of grain were distributed between December 1984 and July 1985. In Ethiopia significant deliveries of food aid were not made until late in 1984. Although the quantities supplied eventually reached many hundreds of thousands of tonnes the distribution of this food was very uneven, much going to drought-affected areas and resettled populations in the south of the country. Rainfall and harvests across the region were much improved in 1985.

4. Mortality

Estimates of mortality are available for (1) populations in camps and (2) the general population. These are presented separately as the pattern and determinants of death are different for each.

(*a*) Camps of refugees and displaced people

Information on mortality, changes in mortality with time, and in some cases age-specific mortality, was collected in several camps in Sudan. In camps formed by a single substantial influx of population over a short space of time the pattern of mortality was similar, being characterized by an initial peak, sometimes reaching very high rates, and then falling over a period of weeks or months to more normal levels. This pattern has been observed in other parts of the world and a recent review is available (Toole and Waldman, 1987).

Fig. 15.1 shows two examples, from Umballa in Darfur, a camp with a population of approximately 25,000 Chadian refugees and displaced Sudanese, and Wad Kowli, a camp of approximately 80,000 Tigrayan refugees on the Ethiopian/Sudan border. The data shown are reasonably accurate as they were obtained by the direct enumeration of funerals by a '24-hour watch'. The population data for Wad Kowli are less certain, as there are differences between 'official' figures and those obtained subsequently by census; there was considerable movement in and out of the camp over the period shown. The higher population total, yielding a lower death rate, has been used.

The reasons for this pattern of mortality are largely understood. The high initial mortality can be explained in terms of the condition of people on arrival, and of their concentration on sites without adequate water supplies or organized systems of sanitation and adequate supplies of food. Deaths resulted chiefly from epidemics of measles, diarrhoea, and dysentery and from respiratory infections compounded to a variable degree by malnutrition. As would be expected mortality is much higher in children. The decline in mortality results from the improvement of conditions with time and the removal of individuals who are susceptible to measles and other infections by the survival of infection or death.

Conditions at Wad Kowli were as bad as any described. Many refugees reached the camp seriously ill and malnourished. On arrival, the effects of gross overcrowding and poor water and food supplies were compounded by a lack of sanitary provision. Scurvy, which has been comparatively rare in other famine-affected populations, was common (Yates, 1986). Crude mortality rates reached approximately 8.2/10,000 per day and mortality of under-fives over 30/10,000 per day in February 1985 (Yates, 1986). It is estimated that approximately 5 per cent of the population of eight camps in eastern Sudan died during the first three-month period (Toole and Waldman, 1987). Conditions at Umballa were much better.

In camps in Ethiopia, mortality was also high, essentially for the same

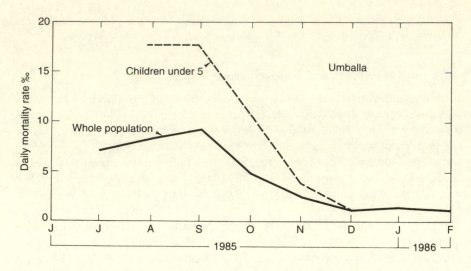

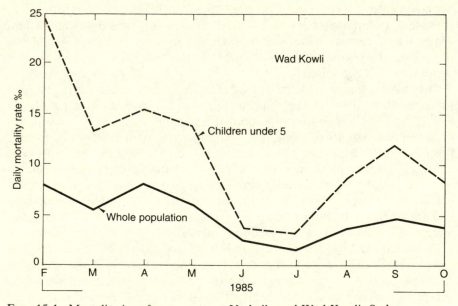

FIG. 15.1. Mortality in refugee camps at Umballa and Wad Kowli, Sudan

reasons, although because of the high rate of population flux at some sites it is difficult to establish meaningful mortality rates. Deaths at Korem camp numbered 100 or so a day at different times, representing 'spot' crude mortalities on the basis of rough estimates of population of the order of

20–30/10,000 per day, of which a large proportion was accounted for by child deaths. A very large proportion of children registered at Korem were malnourished: 70 per cent were found to be less than 80 per cent of reference weight-for-height values at one period (Nash, 1986), i.e. below approximately the third percentile of Western norms. Further, Korem is at 2,400 metres altitude, there was little shelter or fuel, and the high mortality was due, at least in part, to exposure. An extreme case was that of Harbu camp in Wollo, where 2,612 of 7,200 people were reported to have died between 29 October 1984 and the end of January 1985 (Jansson *et al.*, 1987), for an average rate of 49/10,000 per day over that period.

(b) The general population

Ethiopia. The only systematically obtained information on mortality currently available from a rural population in highland Ethiopia is from a draft report of a survey by Otten (1986). This survey was conducted in the Awraja (District) of Yifata na Timuga in the Shoa Region, on the border with Wollo. The area of the district is approximately 4,400 square kilometres, spanning a range of production zones from highland to desert, approximately 40 per cent of the population being resident within the highland zone. The total population of the area was 382,385. The survey was conducted on a total of 51,274 rural families representing a population of 256,369. Mortality and the cause of death by a restricted list of causes (diarrhoea, measles, neonatal tetanus, respiratory infections, lack of food, and 'other causes') was estimated by recall for a 7-day and 30-day period as part of a broader investigation to select families for food distribution. Different parts of the population were surveyed at different periods between February and October 1985. The results of the first survey therefore represent a 'famine affected' but 'unfed' population.

The crude rates of mortality were found to be equivalent to an annual rate of 91.6 per thousand on the 7-day recall and 106.1 per thousand on the basis of the 30-day recall. Additionally it was noted that in one surveyed group of 2,857 people, 24 had died in a 10-day period up to registration and interview immediately prior to the first food distribution. This, expressed as an annual rate, is equivalent to a crude death rate of 306.6 per thousand.

Causes of death in 87 per cent of cases were given as diarrhoea, measles, and lack of food. Outbreaks of diarrhoea with blood, thought to be shigella dysentery, were noted. Cholera was prevalent in the area but accounted for only a small proportion of deaths.

Unfortunately, no information is available on variation in mortality within the survey area, or on the age structure of the population. There was substantial variation in the nutritional status of children in different areas but it is not possible to relate this finding to variations in mortality. The relative mortality by age group was, for each thousand deaths recorded, 111 (0–12 months of age); 208 (1–4 years of age); 198 (5–14 years); 263 (15–50 years); and 219 (above 50), which suggests a higher mortality of children and the old than of younger adults. Following the introduction of food distribution and community health services, the crude death rate fell to reach a rate equivalent to approximately 10 per thousand by December 1985.

A survey conducted in an adjacent smaller area showed, on a three-month recall, a crude death rate equivalent to 68.2 per thousand. Information obtained by Cutler (1985) in December 1984 on 100 famine-affected families by interviewing migrants to the Sudan from Eritrea, Gondar, Wollo, and Tigray gave a mortality estimate of 70 per thousand in the year prior to migration.

In the 1973 famine in Wollo and Tigray, the only systematically obtained rural mortality data (Raya and Kobbo, northern Wollo) gave an estimated crude death rate for the year covering the worst period of the famine of 82 per thousand (Seaman and Holt, 1975).

No comparable 'normal' mortality rates are available for rural highland Ethiopia, but those observed are clearly much higher than any which would be expected. The relative contribution of starvation and disease to this increased mortality cannot be exactly known. It is possible that patterns of disease were altered by population movements—cholera for example appeared to affect a wider area and higher altitude than the 'normal' seasonal outbreaks—and it may be that the observed outbreaks of dysentery arose in the same way. However, there is evidence for a substantially raised risk of death in the malnourished (Chen *et al.*, 1980), and the rapid fall in mortality observed by Otten (1986) on the introduction of relief food distribution suggests that starvation was the major factor. That the population remained in their villages under such conditions presumably reflected the lack of any better alternative. In more northerly famine areas relief food was less in quantity and much later to arrive and it is impossible to gauge its effect.

Sudan. De Waal (1987) conducted a survey of 1,182 households at 8 sites in Darfur. He estimates that the crude death rate in this population averaged 28.2 per thousand over the two-year period from June 1984 to June 1986. For the calendar year 1985 he estimates the crude death rate at 40.15 per thousand. Taking a normal figure of 18 per thousand, which he argues is a high estimate of normal mortality in the pre-crisis period, he concludes that the excess mortality in Darfur between June 1984 and June 1986 amounted to 95,000 people, of which 85,500 died in 1985. The population of Darfur is estimated at approximately 3.1 million of which 1.3 million live in the northern area.

De Waal found that most of the excess mortality occurred in the dry

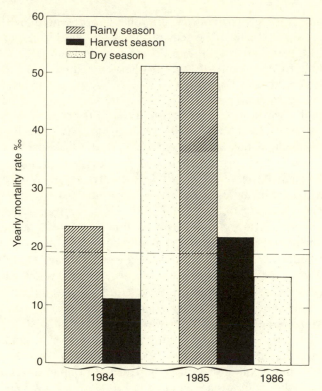

FIG. 15.2. Death rates in Darfur at different seasons from 1984 to 1986

season of 1985 and during the rains (see Fig. 15.2) and that only during these periods was mortality significantly elevated above normal. This seasonal variation in mortality is a normal pattern due to disease in the late dry season which was grossly exaggerated in 1985.

Mortality was found to be significantly different within male- and female-headed households (55.6 and 66.9 per thousand respectively), although the difference was not significant when the results for 11 women widowed within the preceding two years were removed. There was no important difference in the age structure of these households.

Excess mortality was closely related to age. Infant mortality in the 1984–5 period was estimated at 119 per thousand. The age-specific death rate averaged over two years was 115 per thousand. Even in the rains of 1985, when infant mortality was highest, it was thought not to be significantly elevated above normal. The chief reason for this observation was thought to be the practice of late weaning of infants, which is not until 12–18 months of age.

Over half the excess mortality occurred in children between the ages of

1 and 4 years. This age group was also under-represented in the study population. Set against the 1973 census, mortality in this group had increased from 15.7 to 79.5 per thousand between 1984 and 1986. This was attributed chiefly to the effects of the 1984 harvest failure in north Darfur, and specifically to the fact that children of this age group are weaned but unable to consume an adult diet.

Excess mortality was found to be less marked in the 5–9-year age group and the excess mortality noted in that age group was entirely of boys. Seventy-five per cent of these deaths occurred in the first eight months of 1985. This was attributed to the fact that in Darfur, women and therefore young girls who remain in the household have greater access to food than do boys. Adolescents, adults, and the old were only at marginally elevated risk.

Mortality was not found to be related to the destitution of a group, or to the type of survival strategy followed. Wealth was found to be a poor predictor of mortality. For example, mortality in the village of Jebel Si, already described, was no higher than in much richer groups. The one economic factor found to be related to mortality was livestock ownership. People owning one or more 'economic livestock unit', i.e. a minimum of two large or five small animals, had a significantly lower child mortality (49.8) than those owning less. This difference was attributed to access to milk.

A survey (McLean, 1985b) of 780 mothers aged between 15 and 44 years in Kordofan in September and October 1985 found that 56 of 186 live births during the preceding six-month period had died (301 per thousand). For north Kordofan, the rate was estimated at 310 per thousand live births. Mortality in the 1–4-year age group was estimated at 40 and 44 per thousand for south and north Kordofan respectively. It is not clear why the high infant mortality rate was observed.

A preliminary report of the results of a survey in north Kordofan (SCF (USA) and University of Khartoum, 1985) of 36 randomly selected households in each of 81 villages in one district in mid-1985, with a total population of approximately 400,000, gave estimates of crude mortality during the period May to October 1985 in different areas in the range 41 to 92 per thousand. Mortality under the age of 5 was estimated at 105 to 254 per thousand as measured over the period July to October 1985.

No information has been found on famine mortality in other areas of northern Sudan, but it appears likely that the pattern observed in Darfur and Kordofan was repeated across the northern areas to the Red Sea coast. The evidence suggests that although rates of malnutrition were high in some areas (McLean, 1985a) and that death from starvation certainly occurred, most deaths arose not from food shortage as such, but from the risks of migration and particularly of movement to peri-urban camps. In a sense the greater part of the excess mortality may be seen as incidental to the generally successful survival strategies of the population, a point which is confirmed by de Waal's observation that the greater part of the population of Darfur did not feel itself threatened by starvation. Their concern was destitution rather than starvation, and this conditioned their responses to drought. People did not know about the risk to children in camps and were quite explicit that 'if they had known so many children would have died in these places they would not have come'.

The observation that child deaths may have occurred from poor food quality rather than quantity, and the widespread occurrence of vitamin deficiency diseases, suggests that this may also have been a contributing factor to mortality in Ethiopia. Relief food for general distribution was in both countries usually only cereals.

5. Estimates of Total Excess Mortality

Given the limited number and mixed quality of the observations available, extrapolation from these to an estimate of total famine mortality can only be tentative. If the observed mortality in Darfur was representative of the northern affected areas of the country, this suggests an excess mortality of the order of 250,000 people. If the limits of the 'affected' population are taken as 5–10 million people, perhaps 2.5 to 5 per cent died during the famine period.

In Ethiopia, the famine mortality was clearly much greater. The conservative assumptions are of an 'excess' mortality of 50 per thousand per year in an affected population of 7 million; calculating over one year and adding 150,000 deaths in camps suggests a low estimate of mortality of approximately 500,000. If a higher mortality is taken, and a longer period of raised mortality, which is certain, this total might be doubled. If to this is added the 600,000 people officially resettled after 1985 from the north to the south of the country, it suggests that by 1986, the population of the northern highlands was reduced by 15–20 per cent of pre-famine levels.

References

Caldwell, J. C. (1977), 'Demographic aspects of the drought: An examination of the African drought of 1970–74', in D. Dalby, R. J. Harrison Church, and F. Bezzaz (eds.), *Drought in Africa*, International Africa Institute, London.

Chen, C. C, Chowdhury, A. K. N., and Huffman, S. L. (1980), 'Anthropometric assessment of energy-protein malnutrition and subsequent risk of mortality among preschool aged children', *American Journal of Clinical Nutrition* 33: 1836–45.

Cutler, P. (1984), 'Famine forecasting: Prices and peasant behaviour in northern Ethiopia', *Disasters* 8/1.

—— (1985), 'The use of economic and social information in famine prediction and response', Report to the Overseas Development Administration, London.

de Waal, A. (1987), 'Report on drought in Darfur, Sudan', Report to the Save the Children Fund (UK).

Holy, L. (1980), 'Drought and change in a tribal economy: The Berti of northern Darfur', *Disasters* 4/1.

Jansson, K., Harris, M., and Penrose, A. (1987), *The Ethiopian Famine*, Zed Books, London.

McLean, M. (1984*a*), 'A report on the nutritional status of 1,888 children in Kordofan Feb./Mar. 1985', Report of OXFAM/UNICEF and Kordofan Regional Government Nutritional Status and Drought Monitoring Project.

—— (1985*b*), 'A report on the nutritional status of 4575 children in Kordofan Region September/October 1985', Report of OXFAM/UNICEF and Kordofan Regional Government Nutritional Status and Drought Monitoring Project.

Nash, T. (1986), 'Report on activities of the child feeding centre in Korem', Report to the Save the Children Fund (UK).

Otten, M. W. (1986), 'Nutritional and mortality aspects of the 1985 famine in north central Ethiopia', Draft report to Save the Children (USA).

Seaman, J. and Holt, J. F. J. (1975), 'The Ethiopian famine of 1973–4, 1. Wollo province', *Proceedings of the Nutritional Society* 34: 114A.

SCF (USA) and University of Khartoum (1985), 'Preliminary findings of a harvest/health survey in Um Ruwaba Distict, North Kordofan', Draft report.

Toole, M. J. and Waldman, R. J. (1987), 'Mortality trends in refugee emergencies', Report to Center for Disease Control, Atlanta.

Yates, R. (1986), 'Medical review of the refugee camps, Wad Kowli, Sefwa I and II and Umballa, Jan. 85–April 86', Report to Save the Children Fund (UK).

16 Famine in Africa: A Global Perspective

John C. Caldwell and Pat Caldwell
Australian National University

1. Introduction[1]

In our report on experience in the Sahel in 1973 (Caldwell, 1975: 23–31) we discounted the common newspaper headline of that year (e.g. above a *New York Times* editorial: 'Six Million Facing Starvation') and cited an estimate made in August 1973 by a team of the Center for Disease Control (1973: 4) that an upper bound for the excess deaths arising from the famine would be 101,000 for 1973 in Mauritania, Mali, Niger, and Burkina Faso. This would have meant a rise in the death rate for the four countries from perhaps 25 to 31 per thousand, removing the equivalent of three months' natural increase. The researchers, however, were at pains to point out that this was an upper bound based on the proven experience of nomads on the Saharan fringe and that other nomads may have suffered less while the evidence suggested no excess mortality among sedentary agriculturalists.

There were higher estimates from Ethiopia but our investigation of the source of these figures convinced us that they were completely unreliable. We concluded about the excess mortality that

no one knows; the figures in the newspaper headlines were figments of the imagination and many apparently serious reports were little better. The statistical systems did not meet the challenge and demographers utilizing survey methods did not fill the breach . . . [We] became increasingly convinced that the drought publicity hid the vital truth. The real lessons were not how easily man succumbed to the drought but how tenacious he was in managing his survival (Caldwell, 1975: 26).

That tenacity had not always proved successful. In northern Ghana it was said that the 1913 drought killed men as well as cattle while in 1972–3 it was mostly cattle that died. We adduced evidence to show that the changes had been brought about by improvements in communications, the development

---

[1] This paper will update and interpret four previous reports (Caldwell, 1975, 1977, 1981, 1984). Caldwell (1984) was commissioned by the Desertification Section of the United Nations Environmental Programme for two purposes: (1) as a decennial update of new findings since the research centring on the 1978 Sahelian drought; and (2) to analyse the *Desertification Questionnaire* distributed to all United Nations member countries in 1982 by UNEP Desertification Section.

of a market economy, and the coming into being of independent national states in Africa and of an international system more conscious of disaster and more capable of delivering help. There are more markets than was the case 60 years ago, price rises are known, and there are roads and trucks so that food can flow to where the prices are highest. The national and international communities hear of rural famines; national governments inevitably give aid to the hungry who migrate to the capital and other major urban areas; international food aid eventually reaches areas which have become known for their suffering (and food trickles to the residents and helps to lower prices). This analysis concurs with that of Watkins and Menken (1985; also Watkins, 1985), who have examined the historical record to conclude that the main check on population growth has not been the great famines but the normal levels of mortality and fertility.

Nevertheless, there is new evidence from beyond Africa that should give us pause before we conclude too quickly that Africa's famines are not a major determinant of mortality. That evidence comes primarily from China and Bangladesh, but we shall also draw on Indian and Sri Lankan evidence.

2. Famine and Mortality: The New Evidence from Outside Africa

(a) China in 1959–61

The magnitude of the African and Asian famines has frequently been a matter of guesswork because of the lack of adequate vital registration systems and because of the blurring effect of age misstatement in subsequent censuses. However, we now have data of stark clarity delineating the huge Chinese famine of 1959–61 that marked the end of the Great Leap Forward. The important demographic information was released only in 1983–4, when the 1953, 1964, and 1982 census findings were made available for the first time, providing accurate single-year data (of such high quality because of the importance to the Chinese of the animal signs of the date of birth and the ability of the census office to translate these into conventional ages). When the publication of the One-in-a-thousand Fertility Survey provided good retrospective annual measures of nuptiality and fertility (Caldwell and Srinivasan, 1984; Caldwell, Bracher, Santow, and Caldwell, 1986; Ashton et al., 1984; Coale, 1984; Kane, 1987, 1988), this information made possible the adjustment of the vital registration data.

The Chinese information made it clear that contemporary famine can still cause major demographic disaster and that the extent of that disaster can be greatly underestimated by eyewitness reports at the time without the evidence provided by demographic data collection systems (cf. Ashton et al., 1984; 630–2). Admittedly, China was a much more closed society than is drought-prone Africa. The Chinese censuses revealed a gap of around 60 million persons in the age structure (Ashton *et al.*, 1984; Coale, 1984; Calot, 1984; Banister, 1984), or the equivalent of around four years' natural increase at the levels prevailing immediately before the famine. By 1960 the death rate had doubled from 20 per thousand only two years earlier to nearly 40 per thousand, and annual natural increase was minus 1.4 per cent (Coale, 1984: 47 and 69). Several aspects of the Chinese famine demographic experience are probably general and should be sought in Africa too.

1. Only half the check to population growth can be attributed to excess mortality, for fully half was caused by a collapse in the birth rate from around 38 per thousand in 1958 to 22 per thousand in 1961.
2. The reduction in the birth rate resulted both from a decline in marital fertility in a population with little access to modern family planning at the time and a fall of 20 per cent in marriage rates with a consequent impact on first birth rates (Caldwell and Srinivasan, 1984: 73).
3. Ultimately, the check on population growth was equivalent to less than four years of natural increase, and probably less than three years, for two reasons. The first, and most important reason was that, in conditions where there had been an unusual number of married women neither pregnant nor lactating (because of a reduced pregnancy rate and an unusually high infant mortality rate) and where there had been an unusual number of young women of marriageable age still single, there occurred marriage and baby booms. The 1962 marriage rate was 60 per cent higher than three years earlier, and the 1963 birth rate at 47 per thousand was almost double that of 1961 and 13 per cent above the 1950–7 average. The second reason is that immediately after the famine the death rate fell to a level not only two-thirds below the peak famine level but at least one-third below the pre-famine level presumably mostly because of excess famine deaths among the old or the sick and weak.
4. Proportionately the greatest rise in the death rate was among the very young and the very old. In the first year of the crisis the infant mortality rate rose 60 per cent, while, during the whole period of famine, deaths to persons under 10 years of age almost doubled compared with a rise of less than two-thirds among persons over that age (Ashton *et al.*, 1984: 619).

(b) Matlab District in Bangladesh, 1974–5

No other Third World Asian or African country has national data that can allow a comparable analysis. Nevertheless, in Bangladesh, where widespread flooding caused a famine in 1974–7, the Cholera Research Laboratory (now the International Diarrhoeal Diseases Research Centre,

Bangladesh) maintained a unique demographic surveillance system covering 228 villages in the Matlab District with just over a quarter of a million inhabitants. The demographic impact of the famine has been reported by Ruzicka and Chowdhury (1978: 16–25) and Chen and Chowdhury (1977). The Matlab data show a doubling of the death rate between the first quarter of 1974 and the first quarter of 1975 and excess deaths equal to about one year's normal mortality. In 1975 natural increase fell almost to zero, and for the whole year there was population loss arising from the added impact of migration (a factor which was controlled in China). The population lost almost one year's natural increase of which excess deaths accounted for just over one-half and deficient births for just under half. As a result of the famine, marriage rates fell and divorce rates rose, both processes reversing as normal conditions returned. Comparing age-specific death rates from mid-1974 to mid-1976 with mid-1968 to mid-1971 rates (i.e. those before either war or famine mortality crises), we find rises during the famine of around 45 per cent for the population under 10 years and over 45 years, with very low rises for the ages in between. The general picture is similar in outline if not in magnitude to China. There are three additional points which are of importance to Africa.

1. Even rural populations who produce a great deal of their food are greatly affected by market prices, especially during famine. Because of a steep rise in prices (caused both by the flood and inept government policy), death rates are reported to have risen almost as much outside as within the flood area (i.e. at Companyganj, the other CRL centre).
2. In an open society one defence against famine is out-migration, so that in the first quarter of 1975 2 per cent of the population left the area (predominantly adult males), with the result that net migration was over five times the level of natural increase.
3. In Bangladesh, where the lack of an adequate vital registration system and the occurrence of massive age misstatement rival the situation in sub-Saharan Africa, the 1974–5 famine was not apparent in the 1981 census age structure, although the WFS survey of 1975 evidenced current low fertility (as did that of Ghana which was also carried out in a crisis period).

(c) Bengal in 1943–6

The recent period has also seen for the first time the publication and analysis by Greenough (1982; see also Caldwell, 1983, from which some of these calculations are taken) of the mortality data from the remarkable survey of 13 thousand households undertaken by P. C. Mahalanobis and the Indian Statistical Institute in the latter part of the 1943–4 Bengal famine in the 30 worst affected subdivisions (mostly now in Bangladesh). In the 1943–6 period excess deaths probably amounted to 3.5 million in a Bengal population of 60 million, taking the crude death rate from a pre-famine level of 26 or 27 to 53 in 1943 (and to 150 in some areas). By 1944 the birth rate had fallen by about 30 per cent. Excess mortality among the population under 10 and over 50 years was several times that of those of intermediate age. Greenough attributed most excess deaths in 1943 to starvation, in 1944 to ensuing epidemic disease, and in 1945 to the resulting dislocation and impoverishment. Once again the mortality crisis was not simply the result of crop failure but also of wrong-headed government decisions and of the rise in prices.

(d) Recent observations in south India and Sri Lanka

In a study of a south Indian rural area affected by the 1980–3 drought (Caldwell, Reddy, and Caldwell, 1986), we examined a population which suffered little excess mortality, partly because the drought was not extreme and partly because of self-help and governmental assistance in a large diversified country where all areas are rarely affected at the same time. Nevertheless, marriage rates declined markedly in 1983 and birth rates in 1984. Families who had resisted the famine by cancelling nearly all ceremonies, including religious ones, explained that they just could not meet the expected dowry payment or pay for wedding celebrations in such hard times. The study also showed a rise in weakness and sickness with hunger, a greater reliance on the market for food in spite of rising prices, the severest impact on the poor and landless, and the importance of having migrant members of the family elsewhere—especially in the towns—so as to send remittances for the purchase of food.

A recent micro approach study of Indian Tamil estate workers in Sri Lanka (Gajanayake *et al.*, 1991) focused part of the work on the 1974–5 famine, when infant mortality rates among the population doubled and fertility halved. The families explained that the hard times made it impossible to meet dowry and wedding costs, but also that marriage in such sad times was most inappropriate. They also took it for granted that marital fertility levels would have fallen explaining that there was little sex in these hard times when everyone was sad, tired, and weak.

3. Famine in Africa in a Comparative Perspective

The above summary is striking in terms of the common elements between countries and clearly should relate to Africa as well. The following is a summary of what we might anticipate both in terms of similar patterns and in terms of modifications.

1. Famine, induced by drought, and compounded by civil strife or poor administration, almost certainly causes very considerable rises in African mortality levels. Compared with Asia, the upswings may be less dramatic because of the extraordinary flexibility of African migration, where mass movements begin when disaster threatens rather than waiting until it is too late. Nomadism, shifting cultivation, and a long tradition of men engaging in other, and often distant, pursuits during the dry season give Africa greater protection than does the identification of families with a fixed small plot to be protected at all costs as tends to be the situation in peasant Asia. Nor, on the other hand, are there such large almost defenceless groups as Asia's landless labourers, who constitute almost half the rural population of Bangladesh. However, this does mean that the picture reported for Burkina Faso during the 1973 drought that the sedentary population was not exposed like the nomads and had probably experienced no rise in mortality (Caldwell, 1975: 24, reporting USA Department of State, 1973) was almost certainly wrong.

2. In African famines the check on population growth probably parallels that of Asia in that half of all the pause in growth originates in lower fertility levels. There are just as many problems in raising bridewealth as dowry, and greater difficulties still in those parts of the savannah where bridewealth or marriage settlements are constituted by cattle, the very resource that is most catastrophically affected by drought. We have also been told by African women that of course there is little sex during such disasters either because the spouses are separated or because conditions render it undesirable or inappropriate. If one employs the data reported by the Faulkinghams for the Niger village they studied (Faulkingham, 1977*a*: 153) to calculate 'normal' birth and death rates by averaging the 1969–71 rates, and then uses these rates to provide 'expected' figures for 1972–5, then the actual rates show a four-year increment of population only one-third of what would have been expected (i.e. an average annual rate of natural increase around one per cent instead of 3 per cent with negative levels in 1974 and 1975) with approximately half the efficiency explained by a birth deficit and the other half by excess deaths. Faulkingham discounts the role of marriage in the fertility reduction (Faulkingham, 1977*b*: 169) and shows a decline in the proportion of fecund women currently married only in the 15–19 age group (Faulkingham, 1977*b*: 170), but in an early marrying population that is the only age group that can be affected in the short run, and between 1973 and 1975 the proportion fell by one-quarter. He also reported that 'the regulation of fertility is not perceived to be governed by choice during marriage . . . [and hence to explain the fertility decline in this way is a] hypothesis which must be rejected' (p. 169). This, however, does not necessarily cover a

reduction in sexual relations because of separation, weakness, and general lack of good cheer. Faulkingham (1977*a*) supported an explanation based on subfecundity arising from malnutrition.

3. There is a succession of causes of higher deaths from starvation to disease and perhaps ultimately to more general impoverishment. Here, again, in their work in the Niger village of Tudu the Faulkinghams were sanguine at first about the mortality impact of the drought, for death rates continued to fall during the driest years, only to rise dramatically after the rains came and even when the first good harvest had been gathered (Faulkingham, 1977*a*: 151–3).

4. Those most vulnerable to excess famine deaths are the young and the old. In Africa this is almost certainly true in the case of the nomads when faced by a disaster situation because these are the least mobile groups. Elsewhere, especially in sedentary populations, it may be the young who are most exposed, partly because of the lengths to which Africans will go to protect the old (Caldwell, 1982; Caldwell and Caldwell, 1987*a*) and partly because children beyond infancy, especially the 1–4-year-olds, are peculiarly exposed even in normal times with mortality levels much higher relative to other groups than is common in other parts of the world (Cantrelle, 1975). Recent work in rural Mali has identified adult mortality as much lower relative to child mortality than any standard tables of the age structure have exhibited (Hill, 1985). Certainly, when famine-related high mortality came at last to Tudu, 68 per cent of all deaths were children under 10, 20 per cent were in the 10–49 age range and only 12 per cent in the population over 50 years (Faulkingham, 1977*a*: 154)—although, given the age structure, the sudden high mortality levels, and the normal African mortality pattern, this is not an unexpected distribution.[2]

5. Mortality levels, even in remote largely subsistence areas, will react not merely to the success of harvests but also to the price of food. Indeed the market becomes more important in crisis both for the purchase of critically needed food and for the sale of animals and other possessions in order to be able to buy food (Caldwell, 1975; Hill, 1987; Turton, 1985). In the short run it is high market prices which ration food, albeit unevenly, but in the longer run it is those higher prices which attract food from afar and begin to provide a solution to the crisis. The market's ability to assist during famine has progressively increased as information systems improved so that the knowledge of higher prices filtered further afield and as the transport system, especially roads and trucks to travel on them, grew so as to be able to meet the demand. In the Sahelian drought of the early 1970s entrepreneurs from the coast were bringing food to inland markets long before

---

[2] Calculations based on Coale and Demeny (1966), North family of life tables.

national or international assistance schemes were organized. The most serious limitation placed on the market is government action which limits such trade either internally or across borders.

6. Even very considerable mortality crises are likely to remain invisible in demographic data collection systems because of age misstatement and other data defects. Indeed only good registration system or censuses with excellent age statement will suffice (it might be noted that, while China had the latter, its somewhat defective vital registration system completely collapsed during the crisis of 1959–61, which was one reason that it took so long to gauge the seriousness of the situation). In the censuses carried out in 1976 in Mali, Mauritania, and Senegal and in 1977 in Niger there is no evidence of the Sahelian drought either in the age structure nor, where included, in retrospective mortality statements. More surprisingly, the detailed survey information collected in Mali in 1981 and 1982 by the team from the London School of Hygiene and Tropical Medicine in conjunction with the International Livestock Centre for Africa (Hill, 1985) revealed in the retrospective mortality information no sign of the Sahelian drought. This does not necessarily mean that the impact of the drought was slight because the retrospective information also shows no secular trend in mortality even though comparison with demographic surveys carried out in 1956–8 and 1960–1 shows that there have been very significant mortality declines. The lesson is probably that the analysis of retrospective mortality information in order to establish mortality trends is unsuited to sub-Saharan African demographic data and that mortality change is best shown by successive surveys. It might be added that work of an anthropological type shows that populations caught in a famine are aware of the danger but have little idea of excess mortality. In good times one couple in five might lose a baby, and in bad times one in three, but there is always such capriciousness about where death strikes as to make such contrasts far from clear to the people most involved.

7. African famines are even less Malthusian than are those of Asia in the sense that levels of population growth are higher and continue to be largely unchecked. The major component of mortality remains the 'normal' mortality as exhibited in the average non-famine year. The elimination of excess famine-mortality will improve living standards, and is one approaching a necessarily multi-faceted assault on mortality. But even the elimination of famine mortality peaks will probably not dramatically lower African mortality. In the period 1950–70, the Chinese famine probably accounted for less than one-tenth of all deaths and for an addition of no more than 2 points to the crude death rate; indeed, if the subsequent low death rates can be ascribed to the preceding high famine mortality, then these figures overstate the

position. Even in the Sahelian countries all excess famine deaths since 1970 are unlikely to account for as much as 10 per cent of all deaths, and perhaps not as much as 5 per cent. We have little way of knowing, although the kinds of comparison made in the next section are of interest.

One important point should first be made. The most influential village study carried out during the Sahelian drought was the study by the Faulkinghams of Tudu, in Niger, a village which they had studied before the drought. That experience produced an important paper (Faulkingham and Thorbahn, 1975), which showed that, although rainfall in the area was in 1971–3 only 58 per cent of the 1969–70 average (and only 33 per cent in 1973) and the 1971–3 per capita crop yield only 39 per cent of the 1969–70 average (5 per cent in 1973), the crude death rate in 1971–3 was actually 12 per cent lower than in 1969–70 (and in 1973 alone it was 23 per cent lower). They explained the continuing drop in mortality as being due to 'the increasing availability of good emergency and maternity care' at a nearby dispensary and maternity clinic or at a hospital at a somewhat greater distance. Yet, two years later Faulkingham (1977*a*) was able to report that though the monsoon in 1974 was adequate, and indeed that the crop yield per capita was not only more than three times the average for 1971–3 (and 33 times that for 1973) but 25 per cent up on the 1969–70 figure, the crude death rate for both 1974 and the first half of 1975 had soared, averaging three times the 1971–3 figure and 2.6 times the 1969–70 one. The explanation was an epidemic of cerebro-spinal meningitis which is far more likely to attack weakened populations than healthy ones and which killed one-quarter of all 1–4-year-olds. Certainly this excess mortality, not from the starvation stage of the drought but from the subsequent epidemic stage, has to be attributed to the famine, although it is far from clear just how typical the Tudu experience was or whether it suffered an unusual disaster. If we now calculate excess mortality for the period from the beginning of 1971 to mid-1975 by comparing the death rate with 1969–70 average mortality, we find a rise of one-third in death rates, while if we compare the period with 1973 the rise is almost threefold. If the whole of the most exposed populations of the Sahelian countries (probably around 15 million people) experienced the same rise in mortality during these four and a half years, then excess mortality would have been close to half a million or about 3 per cent of the population (compared with $4\frac{1}{2}$ per cent in China in 1959–61). If the same four and a half years in Tudu are compared with 1969–70 in terms of natural increase, noting a marked fall in the birth rate in 1974 and 1975 (ascribed by Faulkingham to physiological reasons but possibly affected by marriage rates), then the rate fell from 3.5 to 2.0 per cent. If this is applied to the whole exposed Sahelian population, it would check population growth by almost two and a half years' increments (although if the total national populations of the Sahelian countries are taken into account, this would amount to about one and a half years' increments). This may well prove to be an overstatement. Because of the practice of both long breast-feeding and long postpartum female sexual abstinence in much of sub-Saharan Africa, high infant and child mortality can be followed by compensatory high births because of the unusually early resumption of sexual activity and possibly of ovulation too. Thus Thompson reported of the village of Keneba in the Gambia that high levels of infant and child deaths from measles in 1961 led to a doubling of the birth rate to 87 per thousand in 1962 (Caldwell and Thompson, 1975: 525).

4. African National Demographic Patterns

Because of the lack of small-scale studies and of vital registration schemes, there is little alternative when trying to assess the long-term impact of

Table 16.1. *A comparison of selected data for 32 sub-Saharan African countries, comparing the poorer and richer populations (unweighted averages)*

Characteristics	16 poorer countries[a]	16 richer countries[b]
1985 per capita GNP (US$)	210	533
1965–85 average annual growth of real GNP per capita	0.2%	1.8%
1965 % girls in primary school	25%	50%
1985 expectation of life at birth	47.5 years	51.3 years
1965–85 increase in expectation of life at birth	6.2 years	6.8 years
1985 total fertility rate	6.6	6.6
1965 crude birth rate (per thousand)	48	47
1965 crude death rate (per thousand)	24	22
1965 rate of natural increase (per thousand)	24	25
1985 crude birth rate (per thousand)	48	47
1985 crude death rate (per thousand)	18	16
1985 rate of natural increase (per thousand)	30	31
1965–85 change in rate of natural increase (per thousand)	+6	+6
1965–80 annual rate of population growth	2.6%	2.8%
1980–85 annual rate of population growth	2.9%	3.2%
Change	+0.3%	+0.4%

[a] Ethiopia, Burkina Faso, Mali, Chad, Mozambique, Malawi, Zaïre, Burundi, Togo, Madagascar, Niger, Benin, Central African Republic, Rwanda, Somalia, Uganda.
[b] Kenya, Tanzania, Sudan, Guinea, Sierra Leone, Senegal, Ghana, Zambia, Lesotho, Liberia, Ivory Coast, Zimbabwe, Nigeria, Cameroon, Botswana, Congo.

Source: World Bank, *World Development Report: 1987*, Oxford University Press, New York, 1987.

famine to attempting an assessment of national population trends. An attempt was made in 1982 by the United Nations Environment Programme to encourage countries to analyse separately demographic data from their arid or drought-prone (and presumably famine-prone) and non-arid areas, but analysis (Caldwell, 1984: 21–3) showed that the returns were unusable either because the questions were misunderstood or data were not normally kept in this form. The only alternative is to compare famine-prone and non-famine-prone countries as a whole.

First, however, it is necessary to make some important points about demographic parameters and their interrelations with socio-economic variables for African countries, as has been attempted in Table 16.1 employing World Bank data. The per capita income figures are, on the whole, less plausible indicators of real living standards than is the social and demographic information on the nature of society. It is hard to take seriously the proposition that the populations of Sierra Leone and Guinea are economically better off than those of Kenya and Tanzania. Nevertheless, the simple dichotomy, with the average income of the second group 2.5 times that of the first, should suffice to identify certain characteristics of sub-Saharan Africa. Not only are the countries in the second group richer but the gap is growing.

The important fact about sub-Saharan Africa, in contrast to Asia or Latin America, is that, at least at the national level, there is little economic determination of demographic behaviour. This is an important point to establish before going on to examine the situation of arid, famine-prone countries.

(a) Poor and rich countries

The richer countries are characterized by an expectation of life at birth less than four years greater than the poorer ones and the gap is growing only slowly. Relative wealth has been difficult to translate into health. Nigeria's expectation of life at birth is lower than that of Ghana or Togo even though its income is over twice Ghana's and thrice Togo's. Nigeria has not been able to convert its income into a national health system, in common with most other sub-Saharan African countries, but in contrast for instance, to take an Asian comparison, with Sri Lanka, which, with less than half the per capita income, has a universal health system and a life expectancy 20 years greater. At the individual level, in the city of Ibadan, it can be shown that, once the mother's education is controlled, family income plays no role in determining child survival (Caldwell, 1979). Indeed, this may be true at the national level as well (in the Tables the level of primary schooling 20 years ago has been taken as the best indicator of current and recent maternal education—cf. Caldwell, 1986).

Similarly, at both the national and individual levels, income has practically no impact on fertility. One reason is undoubtedly that a greater level of contraceptive practice among the better-off is often counterbalanced by shorter periods of lactation and postpartum sexual abstinence (Caldwell and Caldwell, 1987*b*).

The result of such similar levels of mortality and fertility is that the rates of natural increase are even closer to each other and have been rising at the same pace over the two decades from around 2.5 per cent to around three per cent. The rate of population growth in the poorer countries is slightly below that of the richer countries because of net emigration from the latter to the former.

(*b*) Famine-prone and other countries

Having established that poverty alone does not determine high mortality or low levels of natural increase, we can now proceed to contrast the famine-prone countries with the others. The selection of ten famine-prone countries in Table 16.2 is based on reports of famine deaths relative to the population of each country but one could certainly argue about marginal cases. Most are relatively arid, but some have experienced the additional problem of civil strife. Most do not have a strong economy in a non-arid part of the country—a factor which has been important in limiting deaths in the arid parts of Nigeria and Kenya.

Seven of the ten famine countries belong to the poorer group already identified in Table 16.1, and hence the whole group is on average relatively poor. None is found among the richest ten countries. It is not famine which has kept them poor. It is aridity, which has reduced the resource base for agriculture and which has thus led to both poverty and famine. Nor are these arid countries coping well with the challenge of development; only three—curiously the three poorest—are believed to have increased their per capita income over the last two decades. As a result they have been relatively unsuccessful in providing education.

There is a modest gap of four years between life expectancies in famine and non-famine countries, perhaps largely explained by lower parental education, but interestingly, and perhaps surprisingly, mortality improvement over the last 20 years has been of the same order in both groups of countries—at about 0.35 years gained per elapsed year (not the 0.5 years that the United Nations used to anticipate but a level that seems to characterize much of sub-Saharan Africa). Here is evidence of a sort that the famines which have racked the famine-prone countries since 1970 have done practically nothing to dint the rate of mortality decline. This suggests both that in terms of excess mortality the famines were not cataclysmic and also that mortality levels and rates of change are determined largely by normal rather than crisis mortality.

Once again, fertility levels are almost identical. Thus, there is a small, but

Table 16.2. *A comparison of selected data for sub-Saharan African countries contrasting 10 countries subject to famine with 22 countries not subject to famine (unweighted averages)*

Characteristics	10 famine countries[a]	22 non-famine countries[b]
1985 per capita GNP (US$)	$229	$448
1965–85 average annual growth of real GNP per capita	0.4%	1.2%
1965 % girls in primary school	16.0%	47.0%
1985 expectation of life at birth	47	51
1965–85 increase in expectation of life at birth	6.9 years	7.0 years
1985 total fertility rate	6.5	6.6
1965 crude birth rate (per thousand)	48	47
1965 crude death rate (per thousand)	25	22
1965 rate of natural increase (per thousand)	23	25
1985 crude birth rate (per thousand)	47	48
1985 crude death rate (per thousand)	19	16
1985 rate of natural increase (per thousand)	28	32
1965–85 change in rate of natural increase (per thousand)	+5	+7
1965–80 annual rate of population growth	2.7%	2.8%
1980–85 annual rate of population growth	2.7%	3.2%
Change	0.0%	+0.5%

[a] Ethiopia, Burkina Faso, Mali, Mozambique, Niger, Somalia, Tanzania, Sudan, Senegal, Chad.
[b] Malawi, Zaïre, Burundi, Togo, Madagascar, Benin, Central African Republic, Rwanda, Kenya, Guinea, Sierra Leone, Ghana, Zambia, Uganda, Lesotho, Liberia, Ivory Coast, Zimbabwe, Nigeria, Cameroon, Botswana, Congo.
Source: as for Table 16.1.

significant, difference in the levels of natural increase, 2.8 per cent compared with 3.2 per cent per annum, three-quarters of the difference arising from the mortality differential. Yet, a level of natural increase close to 3 per cent per annum (and likely to reach that level in 1993 if the recent change is maintained) can hardly be described as Malthusian and provides little evidence that the great famines of the 1970s and 1980s substantially checked population growth. The basic question still remains why that check did not occur. One could, of course, ascribe the entire mortality differential between famine and non-famine countries of three points per thousand to famine and calculate for the ten countries involved, with a 1985 combined population of 140 million, an annual level of excess deaths since 1970 of almost half a million, but it seems almost certain that the whole discrepancy can be ascribed to greater poverty, fewer health services, and lower levels of parental education.

A final caution is in order. The estimates of Tables 16.1 and 16.2 are far from certain and the possible margin of error may constitute a large part of some of the differentials we have been emphasizing. For the famine-prone countries the United Nations *Demographic Yearbooks* present for 1965 life expectancies averaging 1.6 years below those of the World Bank (and averaging, irrespective of sign, 4.5 years disagreement) and for 1985 an average 0.6 years lower (1.9 years difference irrespective of sign). Nor do these two authorities derive their estimates from independent sources. Nevertheless, the best guides to demographic change in the arid countries remain periodic censuses with their count of total numbers, retrospective fertility and mortality questions in some cases, and age structures (affected more by age misstatement than in the better educated, less arid countries), supplemented by occasional, and often local, surveys. A major difficulty is that some have only had one national census. The 1976 census of Mali found 10 per cent more people than had been anticipated, leading international organizations to raise their estimates of both fertility and mortality levels. United Nations and World Bank estimates still differ by over four years in their estimates of Mali's expectation of life at birth, but this is less than half the discrepancy for 1965.

5. Drought, Famine, and Subsistence Crisis in Africa

(*a*) Historical famine and the climatic situation

In terms of rainfall and freedom from famine in the West African savannah the 1950s were unusually good years, and, to a lesser extent, so were the 1960s up until 1968, when rainfall was less than at any time since the 1930s (Glantz, 1987: 38). Indeed, with one possible exception, every year from 1969 until 1985 had less rain than any year between 1950 and 1967. The dry years 1971–5 reached their nadir in 1973, while each year during the 1980s was drier than the previous one, culminating in the drought-stricken years of 1984 and 1985 which had even less rain than 1973 or 1978. The good period was the time when first, colonial governments and then, independent governments became conscious of the need for planned development, and hence has come, partly for this reason, to be regarded as the norm. The fragmentary historical record suggests that the good years were probably more atypical than the 1970s and 1980s and that future planning may have to be based on the acceptance of present conditions rather than regarding the 1970s and 1980s as a transient period of crisis.

What has changed has been man's ability to cope with famine, at least in terms of containing excess mortality if not in terms of containing stock losses and crop failures. No one in northern Ghana or Burkina Faso doubts that the 1912–14 drought killed a bigger proportion of their population than did that of the early 1970s. The former drought was responsible for a famine which may have reduced the population of Bornu Province by 28 per cent although no one knows what the division was between deaths and out-migration (Watts, 1983: 291). In West Africa the evidence to date seems to be that the drought of the mid-1980s, although severer than that of the early 1970s, has killed fewer people still.

(*b*) Agriculture and nutrition

As FAO has continued to produce figures on rising African food imports and declining food production, these figures have become inextricably linked in the public mind with intensifying famine and climbing mortality. Lofchie and Commins (1982: 1) have written:

Sub-Saharan Africa is the only region in the world where food production per capita has declined during the past two decades. As a result, the average calorie intake per capita has now fallen below minimal nutritional standards in a majority of African countries. By current estimates, approximately 150 million out of Africa's 450 million people suffer from some form of malnutrition originating in an inadequate supply of foodstuff.

The situation has been assessed by Goliber (1985: 15–17) as one where falling food production has set conditions for drought famine. He put the blame both on government intervention policies and tradition-bound agricultural practices, pointing out that by 1984 the region was importing 20 per cent of its cereal requirements.

Yet, the situation is far from simple. Wheat and rice dominate cereal imports (Eicher, 1982: 156), and this is largely a question of changes in food tastes brought on by urbanization and even by aid programmes. Other components of the import stream are canned goods, reflecting the low level of African manufacturing, and sugar. To a considerable extent these imports reflect a rising standard of living or a diversification of the way of life. In places they serve as a bulwark against famine deaths.

There probably has been some decline in regional food production but a major review article by Berry (1984) shows that subsistence food production estimates are often little more than wild guesses and there is no certainty about trends in food production. The major constraint on food production is probably limited general development and the lack of growth of a market which can afford to pay the prices needed to make non-labour inputs worth while (Eicher, 1982: 156–7).

While the evidence is merely weak that food production per capita has declined, it is non-existent that food consumption per capita has fallen. It is pointless to argue that consumption would have fallen but for food imports and food aid because these are both realities of the African scene. What is even less proven is that nutritional levels have declined. Trends are uncertain even for specific areas during drought (Caldwell, 1975: 10–11) and far from being assessable across the region. Even where two skilled investigators carried out studies some years apart in a specific district there can be problems. Brabin (1985) was able to show that two such investigations of the Akamba in Kenya arrived at incompatible conclusions about the levels and determinants of malnutrition and certainly could not establish the trend.

(c) Ancient and new methods of protection

Traditional methods of protection against famine are largely based on easy mobility and owe much to the nature of the family and the relationship to the land. Lineage-type families have always been structured so that young men could go off to warfare or to seek work. In times of famine, larger numbers travel in order to be able 'to eat out the hungry period elsewhere' (Prothero's translation of the Hausa expression). Conjugal ties are not of the type that hinders such movement. Nor is there the kind of attachment to a single land holding which encourages the Asian peasant to cling desperately to it regardless of increasing danger. Shifting cultivation and nomadism have seen to that, although there is a great attachment to the ancestral locality. There are a range of other defences: belt tightening and even organized fasting, searching for plants and animals eaten since before the neolithic revolution, and the sale of valuables and of animals. Much depends on security networks, and these are established with relatives, friends, and patrons during the good times by giving social relations priority over economic ones. This is why one's foodstocks must be shared even during famine and why there are limitations to the gains possible in being far-sighted in storing food.

The newer methods have largely been a product of the expansion of communications and the monetization of the economy. Markets now respond to food shortage with rapid rises in prices. Modern governments and international agencies ultimately also react to dire need.

(d) Disequilibrium and migration

A persistent theme, especially in the geographical literature, has been that of disequilibrium. For instance, Garcia (1981: 185) writes: 'overproduction introduces a disequilibrium with the environment which may not be noticed until drought strikes. Droughts do not generate the disequilibrium, they merely reveal a pre-existing one.' Yet many of the changes suggested for greater food production are clearly disequilibrating (e.g. Eicher, 1982: 156 ff.).

In one sense, Africa's greatest defence against drought is a form of disequilibrium. Migration, both in its volume and its composition by marital status and sex, is savannah Africa's traditional and effective answer to famine. A study for the World Bank of West African migration (Zachariah and Condé, 1981) showed that Burkina Faso has coped with its aridity and poverty by the migration of one-sixth of its population and that Mali has similarly exported one-sixteenth of its numbers. The number of migrants rose steeply during the drought of the early 1970s.

6. Some Case Studies

(a) Ethiopia

Estimates from an expert medical group in Harerghe Province (Ethiopian Government, 1974) suggested a death rate in 1973–4 of close to 75 per thousand. Although the survey work was generally good, the mortality estimate was based on a single question about mortality over the previous twelve months. Because of the usual problem with regard to such reference periods, it is doubtful whether much reliance can be placed on the estimate.

Perhaps the most important anthropological work has been that carried out by Turton on the Mursi of south-west Ethiopia and reported in a series of articles (Turton, 1977, 1979, 1980, 1985; Turton and Turton, 1984). The earlier study identified the problems of pastoralists in remote areas with hostile neighbours both in terms of moving cattle during crisis and of cattle raiding. Of all deaths to men over 30 years of age during the dry years of 1970–4, over one-quarter could be attributed to violence, much of which was specifically related to the crisis conditions (Turton, 1977: 180). Clearly, if the calculation had been restricted to excess deaths, the proportion would have been still higher.

In a later paper, after further field work, Turton (1985: 334) wrote:

[In 1969–70] they themselves insisted that, although they were often hungry, no one among them ever died of starvation. They told me a very different story when I returned three years later in November, 1973 . . . As I went through the census of 367 married men and their families which I had collected in 1970, I was given vivid and macabre accounts of people dying of starvation, committing suicide, abandoning their relatives and gorging themselves to death on meat and fish after weeks of hunger. Almost 20 per cent of the married men alone in the census had died since 1970—not all of them, of course, from starvation. The death rate among young children . . . must have been enormous.

It might be noted that, given the length of time between the two counts and the previous mortality level, excess deaths may have been no more than 50 per cent above what would have been anticipated in normal times.

Turton's later study is important because it shows the subsequent, largely successful adjustments made by the Mursi as drought became a normal condition. Even for these isolated people the distant market had been important from early in the famine because they bought food by selling rifles, agricultural implements, tobacco, hides, honey, even walking-sticks (1985: 355). By 1979 they had begun a mass migration to a place 50–60 kilometres away, closer to the market and in an area where higher rainfall promoted agriculture, but, because this meant the presence of tsetse flies, prohibited pastoralism. They changed their way of life, and, in due course, reached a settlement with their new neighbours. Turton (1985: 340–1) concluded that they had successfully solved their problem because they did not receive continuing food aid.

(*b*) Karamoja in Uganda

Biellik and Henderson (1981) reported on the area of Karamoja in north-east Uganda where an acute famine occurred arising from drought and civil strife and compounded by remoteness. They reported that they had randomly chosen a sample of 150 households and had identified deaths taking place during the previous year by relating them to a local events calendar. It might be noted that the use of such calendars in sub-Saharan Africa has not proved in the past to be a certain way of restricting events to a single year. If they did succeed, then they have reported on famine conditions of an intensity hardly any longer known in the world. They calculated a crude death rate of 212 per thousand, or more than 60 per cent above the highest figure reported by any district in the Bengal famine of 1943–4. They also found an infant mortality rate of 607 per thousand. It is not clear how representative these figures were of a broader area but they may well reflect the possible impact of famine prior to the development of a market economy, aid programmes, or safe long-distance migration. In this case 78 per cent of deaths were attributed by the survivors directly to starvation, 20 per cent to disease, and only 2 per cent to violence.

(*c*) The Sahel Region

The most important demographic finding to come from the Sahelian drought was that the lack of both earlier baseline demographic data and current vital statistics rendered it impossible even to make an informed guess about the magnitude of the mortality crisis which had occurred. In the circumstances, caution was appropriate. Our own studies on the region (Caldwell, 1975, 1977) led us to conclude that the drought had not measurably increased mortality.

This sanguine estimate was supported by other evidence. The Faulkinghams (Faulkingham and Thorbahn, 1975) had gone back in 1973–4 to the Niger village that they had studied in 1968–9 and were able to report crude death rates during the drought years of 1972 and 1973 around 30 per cent lower than they had been during the 1969–71 period, which had enjoyed double the annual rainfall (i.e. 12 per thousand compared with 17 per thousand). A relocation in 1973 of adult Saburu males in northern Kenya after a lapse of 15 years from an earlier study showed survival rates no lower than would have been anticipated from pre-drought mortality levels (Spencer, 1973). Mortimore (1973) reported of a village in Kano State:

Although all village heads in Danbatta reported that no deaths or epidemics could be attributed to the famine, they all agreed unequivocally that people were leaner and weaker than normal, and hardship and suffering were very considerable.

The USA Department of State's (1973) information about Burkina Faso was that 'deaths from starvation have apparently been limited to a few thousand, mostly in remote areas which became inaccessible'. The one point that seems certain is that the Sahel drought of the 1970s killed fewer people than might have been anticipated in circumstances where rainfall and food production were a small fraction of normal.

Successive droughts, with attendant famine, have not prevented rapid population growth during the present century in the West African savannah. French West Africa (which included all Sahelian countries except Chad but in addition contained Guinea, Ivory Coast, Togo, and Benin) had, according to official censuses and head counts, a population of around 13 million in 1921, 17 million in 1947, 39 million in 1974, and 57 million in 1987. Such growth had occurred in spite of the world's most persistent continuing mortality. Even in 1970, at the end of the good period, the crude death rate in the Sahel was probably still over 39 per thousand, the expectation of life at birth under 40 years, and the infant mortality rate above 20 per thousand.

Much of our difficulty in demographic interpretation arises from the extent of our uncertainty about these baseline levels. Subsequently there has been no improvement. There were neither death registrations nor anything resembling a body count during the droughts. Outside observers soon learnt that the local people had a keen appreciation of the bad times and of misery but no real appreciation of mortality trends. These are necessarily a statistical matter and not one of personal experience. Even if infant mortality rates had jumped from 200 to 300 per thousand, this would mean only that one extra baby from every ten births died. In high mortality countries this is well within the limit of chance bad luck even in good seasons.

The most important new investigation on demographic processes in savannah Africa is that which was carried out in 1981–2 by the London School of Hygiene and Tropical Medicine in and near the Inland Delta of the Niger river in Mali and reported by Hill and colleagues in a subsequent book (Hill (ed.), 1985). They were able to compare their results with a 1956–8 survey in the same area and a 1960–1 demographic survey of Mali (analysed by Brass *et al.*, 1968).

The project collected data on 37 thousand persons belonging to five groups. There was a sample of Bambara farmers north of Segou, a largely sedentary Fulani group on the Delta west of Mopti, a group of Tamasheq or Tuareg who spent the dry season on the Delta but were nomadic during the wet season, and two more nomadic groups away from the river and near the Burkina Faso border, the Seno-Mango Fulani and the Gourma Tamasheq. The project's publications have not made it easy to produce overall indices of mortality, but it is clear that mortality levels in rural Mali are still very high and this evidence supports the United Nations Demographic Year-book's estimate of a national expectation of life at birth for 1980–5 around 41.5 years rather than the World Bank's estimate for 1985 of 46.5 years.

With regard to famine the retrospective mortality data did not disclose higher mortality during the famine years of the early 1970s, although this is probably evidence of poor retrospective data rather than of little excess famine mortality. On average, infant mortality rates were around 250 per thousand with 350 births resulting in death by 5 years of age. It was not aridity that produced higher mortality but continuous residence on the Delta, for the Delta Fulani evidenced an infant mortality rate close to 350 with almost half of all births resulting in deaths by 5 years of age. Much lower infant and child mortality was experienced by the Delta Tamasheq, who spent the wet season away from the Delta. This was not the result of poorer nutrition on the delta, for, on the contrary, nutritional levels seemed better there (Wagenaar-Brouwer, 1985; Hildebrand, 1985). It would appear that closely settled residence during the wet season in a riverine situation can be particularly dangerous. Perhaps both malaria and diarrhoeal diseases played roles. This does suggest that medical and sanitary intervention may have more impact than nutritional intervention. The project took advantage of different levels of child care among different social strata to attempt to examine the interrelation between child mortality and levels and types of child care (Hildebrand *et al.*, 1985). They threw some interesting light on the matter but a great deal more research yet needs to be done.

The retrospective data showed no sign of decline over time in infant and child mortality but did evidence adult decline. The comparison with earlier surveys suggests that all age groups have experienced mortality decline. When two villages were compared, it appeared that this was particularly the case for the village which had become more linked with the outside through migration and the development of the market. The evidence seems to be that it is social and economic change which will reduce mortality in drought-prone Africa.

7. Conclusion: Mortality Decline in Famine-Prone Africa

There is no evidence of a close association between the frequency of famine and mortality levels in sub-Saharan Africa. Famine-prone areas tend to be poorer because of their lower levels of resources, particularly rainfall. It is this lower level of income, particularly in the relatively low levels of education that have been affordable, which entirely accounts for the fact that mortality is moderately higher in the famine countries. The only long-term answer is general economic development. In the last two decades incomes have not been growing in the famine-prone countries. Nevertheless, it does appear, rather unexpectedly, that mortality has improved in these countries as rapidly as in less arid lands. There is, however, a possibility that this partly reflects over-optimistic assumptions by international agencies about current mortality levels in famine Africa.

Demographers are a long way from being able to estimate excess famine mortality arising from African droughts and civil disaster. It still seems plausible that excess mortality during the Sahelian drought of the early 1970s might not have exceeded 100,000 even in the worst year in spite of the publicity given to six million facing death. Possibly such exaggerated statements helped to contain the excess mortality. Certainly Africa's long experience of droughts played a major role. The reduction of the great peaks of famine mortality in sub-Saharan Africa presents the challenge. Success will do something to reduce long-term mortality but one should not exaggerate the famine component in total mortality. Even in the Sahelian countries over the last two decades it is unlikely to have constituted as much as 10 per cent of all causes of death, and part of that fraction is made up of old people whose lives were not much shortened.

The timing of Africa's reaction to famine and its success in lowering both famine and general mortality levels depend upon being able to measure mortality. In the short run this probably means standardizing surveys, but ultimately only national mortality registration systems will suffice. There would seem to be an obvious need for some kind of early warning system so that measures can be taken to meet a coming crisis. One demographic method would be to detect changes in migration streams by age, marital status, and sex. Non-demographic detectors include market prices and rainfall figures. Yet, the evidence seems to be that all these detection systems lag behind local knowledge and the advice that good district administrators can give to a central government.

References

Ashton, B., Hill, K., Piazza, A., and Zeitz, R. (1984), 'Famine in China, 1958–61', *Population and Development Review* 10/4: 613–45.

Banister, J. (1984), 'An analysis of recent data on the population of China', *Population and Development Review* 10/2: 241–71.

Berry, S. S. (1984), 'The food crisis and agrarian change in Africa: A review essay', *African Studies Review* 27/2: 57–112.

Biellik, R. J. and Henderson, P. L. (1981), 'Mortality, nutritional status and diet during the famine in Karamoja, Uganda, 1980', *Lancet*, 1330–3.

Brabin, L. (1985), 'Malnutrition among the Akamba of Kenya—problem or response to a problem', *Disasters* 9/2: 115–21.

Brass, W., Coale, A. J., Demeny, P., Heisel, D. F., Lorimer, F., Romaniuk, A., and van de Walle, E. (1968), *The Demography of Tropical Africa*, Princeton University Press, Princeton.

Caldwell, J. C. (1975), *The Sahelian Drought and its Demographic Implications*, Occasional Paper 8, Overseas Liaison Committee, Washington.

—— (1977), 'Demographic aspects of drought: An examination of the African drought of 1970–74', in D. Dalby *et al.* (1977), 93–100.

—— (1979), 'Education as a factor in mortality decline: An examination of Nigerian data', *Population Studies* 33/3: 395–413.

—— (1981), 'Perspectives on fertility and mortality in Africa', in UN Economic Commission for Africa, *Population Dynamics: Fertility and Mortality in Africa*, UN, Addis Ababa, 32–48.

—— (1982), *Theory of Fertility Decline*, Academic Press, London.

—— (1983), Review of Paul R. Greenough, *Prosperity and Misery in Modern Bengal: The Famine of 1943–1944*, Oxford University Press, New York and Oxford, 1982, *Population and Development Review* 9/3: 541–2.

—— (1984), *Desertification: Demographic Evidence, 1973–83*, Occasional Paper 37, Australian National University, Canberra.

—— (1986), 'Routes to low mortality in poor countries', *Population and Development Review* 12/2: 171–220.

—— and Caldwell, P. (1987a), 'Family system, their viability and vulnerability: A study of intergenerational transactions and their demographic implications', Paper presented to the IUSSP Seminar on Changing Family Structures and Life Courses in LDCs, East–West Population Institute, Honolulu, 5–7 Jan. 1987.

—— —— (1987b), 'The cultural context of high fertility in sub-Saharan Africa', *Population and Development Review* 13/3: 409–37.

—— and Srinivasan, K. (1984), 'New data on nuptiality and fertility in China', *Population and Development Review* 10/2: 71–9.

—— and Thompson, B. (1975), 'Gambia', in J. C. Caldwell *et al.* (eds.), *Population Growth and Socioeconomic Change in West Africa*, Columbia University Press, New York, 493–526.

—— Reddy, P. H., Caldwell, P. (1986), 'Periodic high risk as a cause of fertility decline in a changing rural environment: Survival strategies in the 1980–83 South Indian drought', *Economic Development and Cultural Change* 34/4: 677–701.

—— Bracher, M., Santow, M. G., and Caldwell, P. (1986), 'Population trends in China—a perspective provided by the 1982 census', in C. Li, D. Tie, H. Wu, and J. Sun (eds.), *A Census of One Billion People: Papers for International Seminar on China's 1982 Population Census*, Population Census Office under the state Council, Beijing, 352–91.

Calot, G. (1984), 'Données nouvelles sur l'évolution démographique chinoise 1: Les Recensements de 1953, 1964 et 1982', *Population* 39/4–5: 807–35.

Cantrelle, P. (1975), 'Mortality', in J. C. Caldwell *et al.* (eds.), *Population Growth and Socioeconomic Change in West Africa*, Columbia University Press, New York, 98–118.

Center for Disease Control, US Public Health Service (1973), 'Nutritional surveillance in drought affected areas of West Africa (Mali, Mauritania, Niger, Upper Volta), August–September 1973', mimeographed report, Atlanta.

Chen, L. C. and Chowdhury, A. K. M. A. (1977), 'The dynamics of contemporary famine', in International Union for Scientific Study of Population, *International Population Conference, Mexico, 1977*, IUSSP, Liège, 409–26.

Coale, A. J. (1984), *Rapid Population Change in China, 1952–1982*, National Research Council, Committee on Population and Demography, Report 27, National Academy Press, Washington.

—— and Demeny, P. (1966), *Regional Model Life Tables and Stable Populations*, Princeton University Press, Princeton.

Dalby, D., Harrison Church, R. J., and Bezzaz, F. (eds.) (1977), *Drought in Africa*, African Environment Special Report 6, International African Institute, London.

Eicher, C. K. (1982), 'Facing up to Africa's food crisis', *Foreign Affairs*, 61/1: 151–74.

Ethiopian Government Relief and Rehabilitation Commission (1974), *Harerghe under Drought: A Survey of the Effects of Drought upon Human Nutrition in Harerghe Province*, Report to the Ethiopian Government by the London Technical Group (J. Seaman, J. Holt, and J. Rivers), Addis Ababa.

Faulkingham, R. H. (1977a), 'Ecological constraints and subsistence strategies: The impact of drought in a Hausa village, a case study from Nigeria', in Dalby *et al.* (1977), 148–58.

—— (1977b), 'Fertility in Tudu: An analysis of constraints of fertility in a village in Niger', in J. C. Caldwell (ed.), *The Persistence of High Fertility*, Australian National University, Canberra, 153–88.

—— and Thorbahn, P. F. (1975), 'Population dynamics and drought: A village in Niger', *Population Studies* 29/3: 463–77.

Gajanayake, I., Caldwell, J. C., and Caldwell, P. (1991), 'Why is health relatively poor in Sri Lanka's tea estates', *Social Science and Medicine* 31, in press.

Garcia, R. V. (1981), *Drought and Man: The 1972 Case History*, vol. 1. *Nature Pleads Not Guilty*, Pergamon, Oxford.

Glantz, M. H. (1987), 'Drought in Africa', *Scientific American* 256/6: 34–40.

Goliber, T. J. (1985), 'Sub-Saharan Africa: Population pressures on development', *Population Bulletin* 40/1.

Greenough, P. R. (1982), *Prosperity and Misery in Modern Bengal: The Famine of 1943–1944*, Oxford University Press, New York and Oxford.

Hildebrand, K. (1985), 'Assessing the components of seasonal stress amongst Fulani of the Seno-Mango, central Mali', in Hill (ed.) (1985), 254–87.

—— Hill, A. G., Randall, S., and van den Eerenbeemt, M. L. (1985), 'Child mortality and care of children in rural Mali', in Hill (ed.) (1985), 184–206.

Hill, A. G. (1985), 'The recent demographic surveys in Mali and their main findings', in Hill (ed.) (1985), 41–64.

—— (ed.) (1985), *Population, Health and Nutrition in the Sahel: Issues in the Welfare of Selected West African Communities*, Routledge & Kegan Paul, London.

—— (1987), 'Demographic responses to food shortages in the Sahel', Paper presented for the FAO Expert Consultation on Population and Agricultural and Rural Development: Institutions and Policy, Rome, 29 June–1 July 1987, mimeo.

Kane, P. (1987), *The Second Billion: Population and Family Planning in China*,

Penguin, Melbourne.

—— (1988), *Famine in China 1959–61: Demographic and Social Implications*, Macmillan, London.

Lofchie, M. F. and Commins, S. K. (1982), 'Food deficits and agricultural policies in tropical Africa', *Journal of Modern African Studies* 20/1: 1–25.

Mortimore, M. B. (1973), 'Famine in Hausaland 1973', Paper presented to Symposium on Drought in Africa, Centre for African Studies, School of Oriental and African Studies, University of London, 19–20 July 1973.

Ruzicka, L. T. and Chowdhury, A. K. M. A. (1978), *Demographic Surveillance system—Matlab*, vol. 4. *Vital Events and Migration—1975*, Scientific Report 12, Cholera Research Laboratory, Dakha.

Spencer, P. (1973), 'Mortality Rates among the Samburu of Northern Kenya 1958–73', Symposium on Drought in Africa, Centre for African Studies, School of Oriental and African Studies, University of London, 19–20 July 1973.

Turton, D. (1977), 'Response to drought: The Mursi of Southwestern Ethiopia', in J. P. Garlick and R. W. J. Keay (eds.), *Human Ecology in the Tropics*, Taylor & Francis, London.

—— (1979), 'War, peace, and Mursi identity', in K. Fukui and D. Turton (eds.), *Warfare amongst East African Herders*, National Museum of Ethnology, Osaka, 179–210.

—— (1980), 'The economics of Mursi bridewealth', in J. Comaroff (ed.), *The Meaning of Marriage Payments*, Academic Press, New York.

—— (1985), 'Mursi responses to drought: Some lessons for relief and rehabilitation', *African Affairs* 84: 331–46.

—— and Turton, P. (1984), 'Spontaneous resettlement after drought: An Ethiopian example', *Disasters* 8/3: 178–89.

United States Department of State (1973), 'Drought relief aid to Upper Volta', Collection of eight unclassified cables.

Wagenaar-Brouwer, M. (1985), 'Preliminary findings on the diet and nutritional status of some Tamasheq and Fulani groups in the Niger Delta of central Mali', in Hill (ed.) (1985), 226–52.

Watkins, S. C. (1985), 'A skeptical view of the demography of famines: Results from a simulation model', in IUSSP, *International Population Conference*, Florence, vol. 4, pp. 339–51.

—— and Menken, J. (1985), 'Famines in historical perspective', *Population and Development Review* 11/4: 647–75.

Watts, M. (1983), *Silent Violence: Food, Famine and Peasantry in Northern Nigeria*, University of California Press, Berkeley.

Zachariah, K. C. and Condé, J. (1981), *Migration in West Africa: Demographic Aspects*, Oxford University Press for World Bank, Oxford.

17 The AIDS Epidemic in Sub-Saharan Africa

Michel Caraël and Peter Piot
World Health Organization

1. Introduction

The World Health Organization estimates that five to ten million people in the world are presently infected by the Human Immunodeficiency Virus (HIV). This estimate is based on the 215,000 cases of AIDS which had been reported to it by early 1989, and on the hypothesis that there is an important underestimation due to lack of diagnostic facilities, the lack of systematic surveillance, and the hesitation of certain governments to recognize the reality of the epidemic.

By February 1990, more than 40,000 cases of AIDS had been reported to the WHO by countries in the African continent (World Health Organization, 1990). Burundi, Congo, Ivory Coast, Kenya, Malawi, Rwanda, Tanzania, Uganda, Zaïre, Zambia, and Zimbabwe have each reported 1,000 or more cases. The actual number of cases of AIDS in Africa is probably much higher, possibly approaching the hundreds of thousands (Piot *et al.*, 1988). The annual incidence of AIDS in Kinshasa, one of the large cities of Africa, was estimated to lie between 55 and 100 new cases per 100,000 people in 1984–5 (Mann *et al.*, 1986*a*). In this city, the ratio of women to men in-patients afflicted with AIDS was 1.3:1, but between the ages of 15 and 30, the ratio was reversed, to 1:3–5 (Ryder and Piot, 1988). In general, in Africa, the average age of female AIDS patients is significantly lower than that of the male. In Kinshasa, the average ages are 30 and 37, respectively, and in Kigali they are 33 and 36. This phenomenon is also found in studies of seroprevalence. The illness is most common in urban areas, but important rural epidemics have been described in some countries, such as Uganda (Serwadda *et al.*, 1985), Ivory Coast (Gody *et al.*, 1988), and Tanzania (Mhalu *et al.*, 1987).

If the modes of transmission and the biology of infection of HIV are fundamentally the same the world over, there are nevertheless considerable differences in the epidemiology and clinical aspects of HIV. Central and East Africa are at present the regions of the world where the prevalence of HIV infection is highest in the general population. For the reasons mentioned above, HIV seroprevalence gives a better indicator of the seriousness of the epidemic and the future mortality than the number of

This chapter was translated by Mark Hereward

Table 17.1. *Prevalence of HIV antibodies in various populations of sub-Saharan Africa*

Type of population Country: City	Year	Numbers examined	% seropositive	Source
General population				
Cameroon	1985	1,273	1	Durand et al., 1986
Centr. Afr. Rep.: Bangui	1985	1,263	4	Merlin et al., 1986
Congo: Brazzaville	1986	368	5	Merlin et al., 1986
Uganda: Kampala	1985	716	15	Carswell et al., 1986
West Nile District	1986	71	1	Carswell, 1987
Mukono	1986	289	5	Carswell, 1987
Zaïre: Kinshasa	1987	2,011	4	Ryder and Piot, 1988
Equateur	1986	389	1	Nzila et al., 1988
Hospital staff				
Ivory Coast: Abidjan	1986	42	5	Deni et al., 1987
Rwanda: Kigali	1985	180	19	Van de Perre et al., 1987
Zaïre: Kinshasa	1984	2,381	6	Mann et al., 1986
Blood donors				
Rwanda: Kigali	1984	180	18	Van de Perre et al., 1987
Tanzania: Dar es Salaam	1986	650	5	Mhalu et al., 1987
Uganda: Kampala men	1986/7	1,370	15	Carswell, 1987
Kampala women	1986/7	214	21	Carswell, 1987
Zaïre: Kinshasa	1986	400	8	Mann et al., 1986
Zambia: Lusaka	1985	207	18	Melbye et al., 1986

Pregnant women			
Ivory Coast: Abidjan	1986	331	3	Denis et al., 1987
Kenya: Nairobi	1985	1,100	3	Piot et al., 1987
Tanzania: Dar es Salaam	1986	192	4	Mhalu et al., 1987
Bukoba	1986	100	16	Mhalu et al., 1987
Arusha	1986	144	1	Mhalu et al., 1987
Uganda: Kampala	1987	170	24	Carswell et al., 1987
Zaïre: Kinshasa	1987	6,000	6	Greenberg et al., 1988
Equateur	1986	136	2	Nzila et al., 1988
Prostitutes and barmaids			
Cameroon: Meiganga	1985	221	8	Durand et al., 1986
Ivory Coast: Abidjan	1986	101	20	Denis et al., 1987
Ghana	1986	98	1	Neequarye et al., 1986
Kenya: Nairobi	1985	286	61	Piot et al., 1987
Rwanda: Butare	1984	33	88	Van de Perre et al., 1985
Tanzania: Dar es Salaam	1986	224	29	Mhalu et al., 1987
Arusha	1986	20	0	Mhalu et al., 1987
Uganda	1986	185	68	Carswell, 1987
Zaïre: Kinshasa	1985	377	27	Van de Perre et al., 1985
Equateur	1986	283	11	Nzila et al., 1988

AIDS cases officially recorded. There is an estimated seven to eight years'
lag between the first infection with HIV and the appearance of clinical
AIDS. After a period of about two years of sub-clinical infection, between 5
and 7 per cent of people who are infected show symptoms of the illness
every year, but what proportion will reach the clinical stage of AIDS at the
end of 10 or 15 years is unknown and could range from 60 to 90 per cent.
The case fatality rate of AIDS is 100 per cent.

In this chapter, we first examine the seropositivity rates in some cities in
Africa, then the modes of transmission of HIV, and finally, the influence of
the epidemic on overall mortality rates.

2. Sero-Epidemiology of HIV

The seroprevalence rates in selected groups of people in different countries
vary enormously (Table 17.1). The results of these surveys should be interpreted cautiously, because the sample selection could influence the rates of
seroprevalence. In random clustered-sample surveys, seroprevalence rates
for HIV-1 of 0.5 to 18 per cent were observed (Table 17.1). For the groups
of people with a raised risk of HIV, like patients who have sexually
transmitted diseases (STD), or prostitutes and their clients, infection rates
reaching 90 per cent have been reported. In general, the distribution of
seroprevalence by age is bi-modal, with a peak under 2 years of age, and a
peak between 20 and 30 (Ryder and Piot, 1988). The distribution reflects
sexual transmission between adults, and vertical transmission from mother
to child.

National seroprevalence surveys are being carried out in several countries.
Rwanda took a national survey of 2,605 people in December 1986 (Bugingo
et al., 1988). The seropositivity ranged from 18 per cent in the cities to 2 per
cent in rural areas (Fig. 17.1 and 17.2). In the urban areas, there were more
women than men infected. In the rural areas, the risk factors for the
acquisition of the HIV were related to travel to urban areas.

There is little longitudinal data on HIV infection in Africa. Among the
health workers in two hospitals in Kinshasa, about one per cent a year were
infected with HIV in 1984 and 1985 (Mann *et al.*, 1986*c*; Ngaly *et al.*,
1987*b*). The seroprevalence rates for the adult population in Kinshasa and
Nairobi have been rising slowly but steadily. Thus, in Kinshasa, the
infection rates for HIV-1 in pregnant women rose from 0.25 to 8 per cent
over a 16-year period (Desmyter *et al.*, 1986). However, in a region of rural
Zaïre, the seroprevalence rates have stayed steady at a low level (0.8 per
cent) over a ten-year period (Nzila *et al.*, 1988*a*). In Kigali, from 1982 to
1985, seroprevalence in blood donors has risen from 10 to 18 per cent. In
Bangui, from 1985 to 1987, the seropositivity rates quadrupled in the adult
population, rising from 2 to 8 per cent (Merlin *et al.*, 1986). It is in the

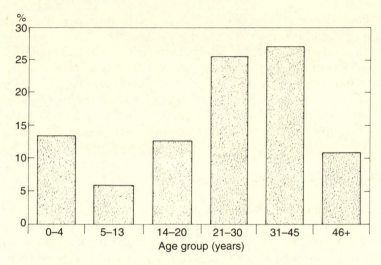

FIG. 17.1. HIV seroprevalence by age, urban areas of Rwanda

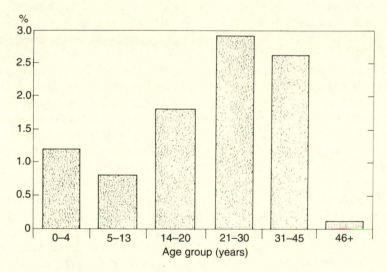

FIG. 17.2. HIV seroprevalence by age, rural areas of Rwanda

sexually very active populations that the virus has spread most spectacularly, as among prostitutes in Nairobi, who in four years have had seroprevalence levels rise from 4 to 61 per cent (Piot *et al.*, 1987).

Current data lead one to think that HIV-1 started to spread swiftly in urban areas of Central Africa from the second half of the 1970s, although serum taken in Zaïre in 1959 was shown to test positive for HIV-1 (Nahmias *et al.*, 1986; Quinn *et al.*, 1986). It will probably be impossible to establish where and when HIV-1 started this massive spread.

The discovery of HIV-2 has considerably increased the complexity of the epidemiology of HIV, particularly in West Africa. HIV-2 infection is particularly common in southern Senegal, Guinea-Bissau, and in the Cape Verde islands. The Ivory Coast has an epidemic of the two viruses which seem often associated. The results suggest that HIV-2 infects the same groups of people that HIV-1 does (Denis *et al.*, 1987).

3. Heterosexual Transmission

A ratio of males to females approaching unity in the infection rates at the ages of greatest sexual activity and among populations most at risk for STDs are, as we have already stated, a reflection of the predominance of heterosexual transmission, which is responsible for at least 80 per cent of the new cases of HIV infection (Ryder and Piot, 1988). The seroprevalence and AIDS rates vary by age and sex. Women are, in general, infected at an earlier age than men. In Kinshasa, the infection rate for women 15 to 25 years old is five times higher than that of men in the same age group. After the age of 35, however, the men have twice as high a rate of infection. In the absence of studies of risk factors and of anthropological observations of sexual behaviour, these data are difficult to interpret; they suggest that, at least in Kinshasa, young women are more sexually active than men, and that these women have sexual relations with men older than themselves. However, it is equally possible that biological factors, such as easier transmission from man to woman than in the other direction, or the unequal presence of co-factors such as STD, also play a part in this situation (Kreiss *et al.*, 1986).

Epidemiological studies have brought to light some risk factors such as a high number of sexual partners, sex with a prostitute, and a history of STDs (Clumeck *et al.*, 1985; Van de Perre *et al.*, 1987). Prostitutes probably play an important part in the propagation of HIV in many African cities (Kreiss *et al.*, 1986; Van de Perre *et al.*, 1987; Plummer *et al.*, 1987). They have, more or less, the highest rates of seroprevalence, and are a known reservoir of other STDs (D'Costa *et al.*, 1985; see also Table 12.1). Their probability of being infected is closely correlated with the number of clients they have, and the level of seroprevalence in the general adult population. In some cities of East and Central Africa, premarital virginity is a cultural norm still largely respected, and marriage itself is a relatively stable institution. For men, sexual initiation is almost necessarily with a prostitute. In Kigali, in a group of soldiers and blood donors, 70 per cent said that they had had at least one sexual encounter with a prostitute in the year before the survey, and only 2 per cent with non-prostitutes (Caraël *et al.*, 1988*a*). The

Table 17.2. *Number of sexual contacts with prostitutes by age during the last 12 months, urban Rwanda*

	Age in years						Total	
	19–24		25–29		30 +		No.	%
	No.	%	No.	%	No.	%		
No contacts	33	19	41	23	65	49	139	29
1–23 contacts	113	65	107	61	54	41	274	57
24 or more	27	16	28	16	12	9	67	14
Total	173	100	176	100	131	99	480	100

Note: χ square = 37.5, p < 0.01.

frequency of visits to prostitutes varied considerably with age and marital status (Tables 17.2 and 17.3). The average age of entry into a permanent union was 28 years in this group of men whose age at first sexual contact was 19 years.

In other cities, like Kinshasa or Dar es Salaam, where sexuality before and after marriage is not regulated by strong cultural norms, prostitutes— defined as women exchanging sexual favours for money—are less numerous and concentrated in only a few places (bars, hotels, and night-clubs, etc.). Tolerance in sexual affairs applies to both sexes in a wide variety of unions. Between being a friend and being a spouse lie various intermediate categories—mistresses, outside wives, girls with 'sugar-daddies', etc.— which reduce the need to resort to prostitutes (Parkin and Nyamwaya,

Table 17.3. *Number of sexual contacts with prostitutes by group and marital status during the last 12 months, urban Rwanda*

	Blood donors (n=182)				Military (n=301)			
	Single		Married		Single		Married	
	No.	%	No.	%	No.	%	No.	%
No contacts	29	28	50	64	21	9	42	60
1–23 contacts	57	55	21	27	170	74	26	37
24 or more	18	17	7	9	40	17	2	3
Total	104	100	78	100	231	100	70	100

Notes: Single vs. married: χ square (blood donors) 34.2; χ square (military) 85.5; p (blood donors) < 0.001; p (military) < 0.001.

1987). This different situation is reflected partly in the number of clients prostitutes have, which varies very much from city to city: on average, they have fewer clients in Kinshasa—158 clients a year—than in Butarc (Rwanda) or in Nairobi—528 and 1,440 respectively. These differences could be due to the sampling method, but we think they reflect, at least in part, socio-cultural differences (Piot and Caraël, 1988). In any case, it is clear that female prostitution plays an important role in the HIV epidemic.

Among couples, if one partner is HIV seropositive, the other partner is also positive in 20 to 90 per cent of cases (Caraël *et al.*, 1988*b*; Nzila *et al.*, 1988*b*). The transmission rate among couples appears to depend first on the stage of clinical development of the HIV infection in the infected partner, and to a lesser extent on the amount of sexual activity. In Zaïre, more than 60 per cent of couples in which one partner had contracted AIDS had serologically concordant status (the two partners were infected), but if the infected individual was asymptomatic, his or her partner was seronegative approximately 80 per cent of the time (Nzila *et al.*, 1988*b*). In Rwanda, a comparative study of seropositive and seronegative couples showed the same risk factors already mentioned: sexual activity of the husband with prostitutes and a history of STDs (Table 17.4). In this study, in 90 per cent of the couples in which the woman was seropositive, the husband was also seropositive (Caraël *et al.*, 1988*b*). The efficiency of male–female transmission compared to female–male transmission is not well established. If HIV acts in the same way as other STDs, sexual transmission from man to woman seems to be more efficient than in the other direction. In the presence of factors favourable for transmission, the risk of a man acquiring HIV from vaginal intercourse with an infected woman could reach 5 to 10 per cent, as shown in a prospective study in Nairobi (Cameron *et al.*, 1987). Cross-sectional and longitudinal studies carried out in Africa show that

Table 17.4. *Risk factors among seropositive and seronegative couples, urban Rwanda*

	Seropositive couples (n=124)		Seronegative couples (n=150)	
	No.	%	No.	%
Husbands had contacts with prostitutes during last year	101	82	41	27
Had STD episodes during last two years				
Husbands	80	65	22	15
Wives	59	48	17	11

Note: Seropositive vs. seronegative couples: p < 0.001.

genital ulcers—the most common being chancroids—do not only increase the risk of getting HIV, but also the infectivity (Cameron *et al.*, 1987; Greenblatt *et al.*, 1988; Simonsen *et al.*, forthcoming). A prospective study of prostitutes in Nairobi also suggests that Chlamydia trachomatis infections (but not gonorrhoea) make the woman more open to infection with HIV (Plummer *et al.*, 1987). Genital ulcers and chlamydia infections could help the HIV to enter the body through a break in the mucosa or perhaps through a mobilization of T-lymphocytes carrying the CD4 receptor in the genital tract, as has been suggested by a study in Rwanda (Van de Perre *et al.*, 1988). It should be underscored that heterosexual transmission also takes place in the absence of these co-factors.

4. Perinatal Transmission

In populations where HIV is mostly transmitted by heterosexual contact, a considerable proportion of fecund women are infected by this virus. Between 2 and 24 per cent of the pregnant women in the large cities of Central and East Africa are seropositive, and seroprevalence rates as high as 3 per cent have been seen in West Africa (see Table 17.1). For this reason, perinatal infection is more and more frequent in Africa, as is shown in the seropositivity levels reaching 11 per cent in children in a large hospital in Kinshasa (Mann *et al.*, 1986*b*) and 12 per cent in children 0 to 4 years old in urban areas of Rwanda (Bugìngo *et al.*, 1988). The rates and the mode of perinatal transmission are still not well known. Several prospective studies on the generational transmission of HIV are in progress in Africa. As opposed to an observation made in the US, congenital malformations are not more common among children born to seropositive women in Kenya (Embree *et al.*, 1987). Although the studies are, as yet, incomplete, it is more and more clear that the likelihood of *in utero* infection depends, at least in part, on the degree of immunodeficiency in the infected mother. Children born to seropositive mothers more often have a general lymphadenopathy at birth (Braddick and Kreiss, 1988), and their birth-weight is lower than that of control groups (Serwadda *et al.*, 1985).

5. Transmission by Blood

Transfusions constitute the second mode of transmission of AIDS in Africa, responsible for 5 to 10 per cent of the adult cases of AIDS, and up to 25 per cent of the paediatric cases (Ryder and Piot, 1988). Blood transfusions are relatively frequent in this region: in 1984, in Rwanda, a short time before blood donations were tested, the Red Cross of the country collected 28,000 units of blood for transfusions, which is almost one unit per 200 people per year. Transfusions are given chiefly for nutritional or parasitic anaemia and for obstetric complications. For example, in Kinshasa, anaemia caused by a serious bout of malaria accounts for two-thirds of all transfusions to children under 12 (Kayembe *et al.*, 1986). Another group at risk for HIV infection by blood transfusion is that of sickle-cell anaemia patients (Izzia *et al.*, 1984; Ngaly *et al.*, 1987a). Testing for HIV antibodies in blood donations, which has now been introduced in the majority of African countries (at least in the big cities), will probably prevent more cases of AIDS in Africa than it did in Europe.

6. Injections and Other Modes of Transmission

In many developing countries, parenteral treatment is preferred over oral therapy by both medical personnel and patients. Often disposable needles and syringes are not available, and if they are, they are reused. Moreover, sterilization of instruments is often badly done. Use of other instruments that break the skin for medical or ritual reasons (circumcision, tattoos, etc.) is also quite common. Presently available data do not allow us to ascertain the exact role that injections play in the spread of HIV in Africa, because of the high use of injections in the general population, and the possibility that the association between the risk of infection from HIV and the injections comes from the treatments for clinical problems that are associated with the HIV infection. Although cross-sectional studies often, though not always, find an association between injections and infection from HIV (Kayembe *et al.*, 1986; Lepage *et al.*, 1986; Mann *et al.*, 1986a; Van de Perre *et al.*, 1987), no association of this type has been found in the prospective studies of incidence of HIV infection in Kinshasa or Nairobi (Cameron *et al.*, 1987; Ngaly *et al.*, 1987b; Plummer *et al.*, 1987). In view of the difficulties in proving this causal relationship, it is not likely that contaminated injections are responsible for a large proportion of HIV infections.

In Africa, as elsewhere, no study has given evidence for transmission of HIV by social contact, insects, or in the home outside of sexual relations (Mann *et al.*, 1986a, 1986c; Piot and Schofield, 1986).

7. Effects on Mortality

The major biological modes of transmission of the virus from human to human by sexual contact or blood, highlight its socio-cultural dimension. The diffusion of HIV is thus loosely associated with the structure of sexual relations in a community: the values associated with this or that way of living, the type and number of sexual partners, the variety of behaviour between men and women, within social groups, and the permanence or fragility of unions. Loosely, because the diffusion also varies to the extent that the virus has barely entered some communities, although it has been present in others for ten years or more. Loosely also because its diffusion varies to the extent that the co-factors which help transmission—genital ulceration—are not distributed in the same way throughout sub-Saharan Africa. Add to these factors a disproportionate role played in the spread of the epidemic by very sexually active people in contact with travellers, like women prostitutes in the cities where this function is specialized.

These characteristics explain why, as opposed to most other epidemics, which usually have most effect on children and the old in rural areas, HIV infections affect young adult urban residents most of all. Cities where the HIV epidemic is more advanced are, in general, in countries where the urban sector is not above 5 to 15 per cent of the population; nevertheless, the growth of the urban population is very fast, with a rate of increase of 5 to 7 per cent per year, of which a half is due to rural migration (United Nations, 1987). The future course of the epidemic in rural areas is largely unknown, but anthropological research leads one to believe that the necessary conditions for the development of an epidemic are not yet met (Piot and Caraël, 1988).

In the absence of long-term longitudinal studies which would let us discover what proportion of the people with HIV infection then go on to develop clinical AIDS, it is extremely difficult to project mortality from the seroprevalence rates. In the cities, where the crude mortality rate for adults (aged 20–49) is on the order of five per thousand, and where the seroprevalence rates are on the order of 10 per cent, in the next five years, one can anticipate a doubling of the adult mortality rate and an increase in the mortality rate of childen under 5 from 25 to 40 per thousand. A seroprevalence of 20 per cent would bring about an adult mortality rate of 15 per thousand in 1991 (Carballo and Caraël, 1988).

Female mortality from the HIV epidemic will directly affect the birth rate, and in particular the births to mothers in the age group 30–35 years. Maternal sickness due to the infection and the dangers of perinatal transmission could also bring about an important reduction in fertility. Marriage itself could be strongly affected by the dangers of having casual sex partners weighing on people's mind. In areas where HIV is highly prevalent, disruption of marriage due to suspicion could become more frequent, and the remarriage of divorced or widowed people could become more difficult. In the absence of prospective studies to evaluate changes in behaviour due to HIV information and education programmes, it is difficult to predict sociodemographic effects of the HIV epidemic, but there is no doubt that there will be major consequences on the mortality of the urban populations of sub-Saharan Africa.

References

Braddick, M. and Kreiss, J. (1988), 'Perinatal transmission of HIV', in P. Piot and J. M. Mann, *AIDS and HIV Infection in the Tropics*, Baillière–Tyndall, London.

Bugingo, G., Ntilivamunda, A., and Nzaramba, D. (1988), 'Enquête nationale séroépidémiologique', *Congrès africain des maladies infectieuses*, Kigali, 2–5 Feb.

Cameron, D. W., Plummer, F. A., Simonsen, J. N., *et al.* (1987), 'Female to male heterosexual transmission of HIV infection in Nairobi', Abstract MP. 91, Third International Conference on Aids, Washington, DC, 1–6 June.

Caraël, M., van de Perre, P., Allen, S., *et al.* (1988*a*), 'Sexually active young adults in Central Africa', in R. Schinazi and A. J. Nahmias (eds.), *AIDS in Children, Adolescents and Heterosexual Adults*, Elsevier, New York.

—— —— Lepage, P., *et al.* (1988*b*), 'HIV transmission among heterosexual couples in Central Africa', *AIDS* 2/3: 201–5.

Carballo, M. and Caraël, M. (1988), 'The social impact of AIDS', in *The Global Impact of AIDS*, London.

Carswell, J. W. (1987), 'HIV infection in healthy persons in Uganda', *AIDS*, 1: 223–8.

—— Sewankambo, N., Lloyd, G., and Downing, R. G. (1986), 'How long has AIDS virus been in Uganda?', *Lancet*, 1: 1217.

Clumeck, N., van de Perre, P., Caraël, M., Rouvroy, D., and Nzaramba, D. (1985), 'Heterosexual promiscuity among African patients and AIDS', *New England Journal of Medicine* 313: 182.

D'Costa, L. J., Plummer, F. A., Bowmer, I., *et al.* (1985) 'Prostitutes are a major reservoir for sexually transmitted disease in Nairobi, Kenya', *Sexually Transmitted Diseases* 185/12: 64–7.

Denis, F., Barin, F., Gershy-Damet, G., *et al.* (1987), 'Prevalence of human T-lymphotropic retroviruses type III (HIV) and type IV in Ivory Coast', *Lancet* 1: 408–11.

Desmyter, J., Goubau, P., Chamaret, S., and Montagnier, L. (1986), 'Anti-LAV/HTLV III in Kinshasa mothers in 1970 and 1980', Abstract 110, Second International Conference on AIDS, Paris, 23–5 June.

Durand, J. P., Garrigue, G. P., Bonloumie, J., *et al.*, (1986), 'AIDS in Cameroon: Poster 377' *International Conference on AIDS, Paris, 23–5 June 1986.*

Embree, J., Braddick, M., Ndinya-Achola, O., *et al.* (1987), 'Does prenatal human immunodeficiency virus infection produce infant malformations?', Abstract, Third International Conference on AIDS, Washington, DC, 1–5 June.

Gody, M., Ouattara, S. A., and Thé, G. de (1988), 'Clinical experience of AIDS in relation to HIV-1 and HIV-2 infection in a rural hospital in Ivory Coast, West Africa', *AIDS* 2: 433–6.

Greenberg, A. E., Nguyen-Dinh, P., Mann, J. M., *et al.* (1988), 'The association between malaria blood transfusions and HIV seropositivity in a pediatric population in Kinshasa, Zaïre', *Journal of the American Medical Association*, 256: 545–9.

Greenblatt, R. M., Lukehar, S. A., Plummer, F. A., *et al.* (1988), 'Genital ulceration as a risk factor for human immunodeficiency virus infection', *AIDS* 2: 47–50.

Izzia, K. W., Lepira, B., Kayembe, K., and Odio, W. (1984), 'Syndrome d'immunodéficience acquise et drépanocytose homozygote', *Annales de la société belge de médecine tropicale* 64: 391–6.

Kayembe, K., Mann, J. M., and Francis, H. (1986), 'Prévalence des anticorps anti-HIV chez les patients non atteints de SIDA ou de syndrome associé au SIDA à Kinshasa, Zaïre', *Annales de la société belge de médecine tropicale* 66: 343–8.

Kreiss, J., Caraël, M., and Meheus, A. (1988), 'Role of STD in transmitting Human Immunodeficiency Virus', Editorial, *Genitourin Medicine* 64: 1–2.

—— Koech, D., and Plummer, F. A. (1986), 'AIDS virus infection in Nairobi prostitutes', *New England Journal of Medicine* 314: 414–18.

Lepage, P., van de Perre, P., Caraël, M., *et al.* (1986), 'Are medical injections a risk factor for HIV infection in children?' *Lancet* 2: 1103–4.

Mann, J. M., Francis, H., Davachi, F., *et al.*, (1986*a*), 'Risk factors for human immunodeficiency virus seropositivity among children 1–24 months old in Kinshasa, Zaire', *Lancet* 2: 654–7.

—— —— —— (1986*b*), 'Human immunodeficiency virus seroprevalence in pediatric patients 2 to 14 years of age at Mama Yemo Hospital, Kinshasa, Zaire', *Pediatrics* 78: 673–7.

—— —— Quinn, T. C., *et al.* (1986*c*), 'HIV seroprevalence among hospital workers in Kinshasa, Zaire', *Journal of the American Medical Association* 256: 3099–102.

—— —— —— (1986*d*), 'Surveillance for AIDS in a central African city, Kinshasa, Zaire', *Journal of the American Medical Association* 255: 3255–9.

—— —— —— (1986*e*), 'HIV seroincidence in a hospital worker population: Kinshasa, Zaïre', *Annales de la sociéte belge de médecine tropicale* 66: 245–50.

Melbye, M., Njelesani, E. K., Bayley, A., *et al.* (1986) 'Evidence for heterosexual transmission and clinical manifestations of human immunodeficiency virus infection and related conditions in Lusaka, Zambia, *Lancet*, 2: 1113–15.

Merlin, M., Gonzalez, J. P., Josse, R., Josserand, R., Ivanof, B., and Georges, A. J. (1986), 'Evaluation of the prevalence of anti LAV-HTLV-III antibodies in the central African populations: About 12 sample surveys', Poster 374, Interntional Conference on AIDS, Paris, 23–5 June.

Mhalu, F. S., Bredberg-Raden, U., Mbena, E., *et al.* (1987), 'Prevalence of HIV infection in healthy subjects and groups of patients in Tanzania', *AIDS* 1: 217–22.

Nahmias, A. J., Weiss, J., Yao, X., *et al.* (1986), 'Evidence for human infection with an HTLV-III/LAV-like virus in Central Africa, 1959', *Lancet* 1: 1279.

Neequarye, A. R., Neequarye, J., and Mingle, J. A. (1986), 'Preponderance of females with AIDS in Ghana', *Lancet*, 2: 978.

Ngaly, B., Kayembe, K., Mann, J. M., *et al.* (1987*a*), 'HIV infection in African children with sickle cell anemia', Abstract, third International Conference on AIDS, Washington, DC, 1–5 June.

—— Ryder, R. W., Kapita, B., *et al.* (1987*b*), 'Continuing studies on the natural history of HIV infection in Zaire', Abstract M.3.6, Third International Conference on AIDS, Washington, DC, 1–5 June.

Nzila, N., De Cock, K. M., Forthal, D., *et al.*, (1988*a*), 'The prevalence of infection with human immunodeficiency virus over a 10-year period in rural Zaïre', *New England Journal of Medicine* 318: 276–9.

—— Ryder, R., Colebunders, R., *et al.*, (1988*b*), 'Married couples in Zaïre with discordant HIV serology', Abstract, Fourth International Conference on AIDS, Stockholm, June.

Parkin D. and Nyamwaya, D. (eds.) (1987), *Transformation of African Marriage*, International African Seminars, Manchester University Press.

Piot, P. and Caraël, M. (1988), 'Epidemiological and sociological aspects of HIV-infection in developing countries', *British Medical Bulletin* 44: 68–88.

—— and Schofield, C. J. (1986), 'No evidence for arthropod transmission of AIDS', *Parasitology Today* 2: 294–5.

—— Plummer, F. A., Mhalu, F. S., *et al.* (1988), 'AIDS: An international perspective', *Science* 239: 573–9.

—— —— Rey, M. A., *et al.* (1987), 'Retrospective epidemiology of HIV infection in Nairobi populations', *Journal of Infectious Diseases* 155: 1108–12.

Plummer, F. A., Simonsen, N., Ngugi, E. N., *et al.* (1987), 'Incidence of human immunodeficiency virus infection and related diseases in a cohort of Nairobi prostitutes', Abstract, Third International Conference on AIDS, Washington, DC, 1–5 June.

Quinn, T. C., Mann, J. M., Curran, J. W., and Piot, P. (1986), 'AIDS in Africa: An epidemiologic paradigm', *Science* 235: 955–63.

Ryder, R. W. and Piot, P. (1988), 'Epidemiology of HIV-1 infection in Africa', in P. Piot et J. M. Mann, *AIDS and HIV Infection in the Tropics*, Baillière–Tyndall, London.

Serwadda, D., Mugerwa, R. D., Sewankambo, N. K., *et al.* (1985), 'Slim disease: A new disease in Uganda and its association with HTLV-III infection', *Lancet* 2: 849–52.

Simonsen, J. N., Plummer, F. A., Ngugi, E. N., *et al.* (forthcoming), 'Human immunodeficiency virus infection among lower socioeconomic strata prostitutes in Nairobi', Submitted for publication.

United Nations (1987), *The Prospects of World Urbanization*, New York.

van de Perre, P., Caraël, M., Nzaramba, D., *et al.* (1987), 'Risk factors for HIV seropositivity in selected urban-based Rwandese adults', *AIDS* 1: 207–11.

—— P., Clumeck, N., Caraël, M., *et al.* (1985), 'Female prostitutes: A risk group for infection with human T-cell lymphotropic virus type III', *Lancet* 2: 524–6.

—— De Clerq, A., Cogniaux-Leclerc, J., *et al.* (1988). 'Detection of HIV p 17 antigen in lymphocytes but not epithelial cells from cervicovaginal secretions of women seropositive for HIV: Implications for heterosexual transmission of the virus', *Genitourin Medicine* 64: 30–3.

WHO (1990), 'Acquired immunodeficiency syndrome (AIDS)', *Weekly Epidemiological Record*.

18 Theories of Mortality Decline and the African Situation

Jacques Vallin
INED, Paris

To begin, I submit that *theories* should be written in the plural. In the singular form, the word suggests that a theory of mortality decline should stop at the rather simplistic notion that an early stage of economic and social development corresponds to a high level of mortality and that the passage from this first stage to a more advanced one (accomplished by most European countries during the last 150 years and by other countries more recently) leads to a much lower mortality level. A theory of mortality decline, like the more general theory of the demographic transition of which it is a part, is of interest only in so far as it provides a useful description of the various components of social and economic development which affect mortality trends and, above all, an evaluation of the relative importance of each of these factors in accounting for these trends: the progress of medicine, improvements in nutrition, the development of education, increases in standards of living, changes in the environment, policies of sanitation and public health, and so on. There is little point in providing an exhaustive list; while everyone agrees that the list is long, there is little consensus regarding its exact limits. It is even more difficult to weigh the relative importance of the pieces of the puzzle. While certain authors have simplified a great deal to demonstrate the supposed dominance of one or another factor, others have stressed the interconnection of a large number of causal variables, without necessarily illuminating the debate. Thus there are several theories of the mortality decline on record and while I do not refuse to take a stand, I do not intend to treat one of them dogmatically as the dominant one. Even less do I presume to elaborate the theory that was lacking until now. On the contrary, the very diversity of theories seems worthy of our attention. After all, as I discuss the prospects for mortality change, and evaluate the likelihood of success of current health and social policies or suggest minor or major mid-course adjustments, it is probably better to examine various hypotheses than to follow blindly a single theory on which there is no consensus. This is all the more true since these theories are often partial, operating at various levels of interpretation, and are thus complementary (Palloni, 1987). Hence, my first concern will be to review the existing literature.

This chapter was translated by Laudan Aron

Secondly, these theories are often based on varying empirical evidence. Does the experience of Europe in past centuries resemble or differ from that of developing countries today? Are there more differences or similarities between more and less developed countries with respect to progress in public health? Should we give more weight to an argument based on a detailed study of the historical facts that influenced the mortality decline in a particular country, at the risk of being overwhelmed by context-specific factors, or to broad analyses of large international data sets that may be confounded by background noise? And where does Africa fit into the picture? Confining ourselves to a single theory would imply that all of these questions can be fully answered. Conversely, if we consider all theories rather than only one, the discussion can progress even if no definitive answer emerges.

A basic question is whether there has been or there is now a decline of mortality in Africa. If so, what are the driving forces? Are these factors the same as for Europe or for other developing countries? In the second section I shall hazard some speculations on Africa's chances of rapidly catching up with the levels of life expectancy of industrial countries and an increasing number of developing nations.

1. Theories of Mortality Decline

At the risk of oversimplification, it might be said that the debate over the causes of the mortality decline has long opposed the supporters of the primacy of public health (the individual or collective implementation of medical resources) and those who emphasize increased access to economic resources and improved nutrition. In the last ten years, certain authors have attempted to go beyond this dichotomy. Thus they have made room for at least the recognition of the complexity of existing relationships, if not a theory.

(*a*) Public health technology or standards of living?

As far back as human behaviour can be traced, man seems to have demonstrated the desire to conquer disease and to postpone death, initially by placating the gods or the forces of evil, but increasingly by accumulating knowledge, and by searching for medications which would first improve the effectiveness of prayers or incantations, and later replace them. Did this secular quest affect the level of mortality prior to the eighteenth century? In the absence of conclusive evidence, demographic historians will no doubt continue to discuss this at length.

At any rate, at the beginning of the eighteenth century, life expectancy was still close to the minimum level allowing high fertility populations to maintain themselves. In France, for example, we know from the work of Henry that life expectancy was only 25 years between 1740 and 1749 (Blayo, 1975). And Molière had no qualms about satirizing the medicine of his era, which was closer to quackery than to a science.

Evidence in favour of the primacy of health technologies. The situation is very different with respect to modern medicine. Between Molière's time and the era of Pasteur, there was a true revolution in the art of combating disease and death. From the introduction of inoculation in Europe, which Razzell (1965, 1969, 1977a) considers to be one of the first decisive factors, medical progress and its diffusion to the masses have certainly played a fundamental role in the steep mortality decline that has occurred in the old world since the end of the eighteenth century and more recently, with even greater force, in developing countries. As van de Walle (1985: 355) has emphasized:

Individual access to resources and the collective allocation of resources into public health programmes has clearly played an important role since the end of the nine-teenth century. The transfer of health technology has been partly responsible for the fast decline of world mortality since the Second World War.

From the discovery of micro-organisms to the invention of antibiotics, the victory gained in Europe over infectious disease and the extraordinary gains in life expectancy that have resulted, have powerfully influenced our thinking. The development of efficient and cheap techniques of prevention and treatment led us to believe that it was possible to push mortality back everywhere, regardless of the level of economic and social development. Inequality in the face of death seemed to be even less acceptable (since it was quite preventable) than social inequality, which was more difficult to avoid. Social security systems have emerged in most developed countries, while at an international level the World Health Organization has com-mitted itself to freeing Third World populations from the burden of the main parasitic and infectious diseases. Health intervention programmes implemented after the Second World War are particularly illustrative of the philosophy that appropriate health technologies are capable of eradicating certain major causes of mortality at low cost, benefiting even the poorest populations. Vaccination permitted a victory over smallpox, complete now that the Indian subcontinent and Africa are rid of it. Insecticides have led to the near elimination of malaria in a number of countries. The example most often cited is that of Sri Lanka, where life expectancy rose from 42 to 54 years during a three-year campaign to spray DDT (1946–8).

Thus, until the 1960s the dominant thesis was that mortality declines were primarily due to the success of health technologies. In the mid-1960s, Stolnitz (1965) was emphasizing the remarkable neutrality of economic events in influencing mortality trends, and Demeny (1965) held as negligible the potential links between the evolution of per capita income and mortality:

The large amount of statistical material on underdeveloped countries which is available for the past three decades reveals the almost complete absence of such a relationship . . . There is a high degree of uniformity between mortality trends through time and in different countries, a uniformity not existent as far as trends in per capita income is concerned.

And yet, no one today, especially not a sociologist or a demographer, would dream of explaining mortality decline in terms of medical progress alone. Experience has shown that the remarkable public health successes achieved here or there, at least at face value independently of decisive improvements in living standards, are rather exceptional and difficult to replicate in different contexts. When advanced medical technologies appear, they are only the translation into the field of medical science of a more general evolution of society (towards more rationality, but also towards greater control over its destiny). Furthermore, in order to induce a mortality decline, these technologies must be implemented for the benefit of the masses. Varying ecological, economic, social, and cultural factors can delay or accelerate this implementation. Moreover, we know today that even a primitive state of medical knowledge can result in some decline of mortality. The success of the fight against the major epidemics of the pre-industrial period depended more on the degree of state organization than on the still very imprecise knowledge of mechanisms of contagion. Similarly, eighteenth-century improvements in agriculture and therefore in diet have probably contributed more to the first important declines of mortality than the slow progress of a medical knowledge that was more theoretical than applied.[1]

Evidence for the primacy of living standards. Some researchers have reversed the argument completely, and argued that only increasing living standards have played a determining role in the rise of life expectancy. The most interesting example here is undoubtedly that of McKeown (1976a). Although his book, *The Modern Rise of Population*, was only restating a thesis developed in several articles by the author and his colleagues (McKeown and Brown, 1955; McKeown and Record, 1962; McKeown, 1965; McKeown, Brown, and Record, 1972), it triggered a heated debate ten years ago. The debate included critiques published by Razzell (1977b) in the *Economic History Review*, Schofield (1977) in *Population Studies*, and van de Walle (1977) in *Science*, and the author's rejoinder in *Population Studies* (McKeown, 1978). Criticizing Razzell for having wrongly attributed

---

[1] Prior to the Industrial Revolution, the greatest successes of Western medical science were probably in anatomy and surgery, due to the contributions of Ambroise Paré and others. These advances were to a great extent ineffectual before the discovery of asepsis and anaesthesia.

such a large role in the eighteenth-century mortality decline to inoculation, McKeown intended this book to lead to an exclusive explanation of this progress by an improvement in food supply. (The work was complemented by another book focusing specifically on a discussion of the role of medicine, McKeown, 1976*b*.) Without explicitly raising his thesis, which rested only on the case of England in the eighteenth century, to the rank of a theory, he considered the study of a particular context to be richer in general lessons than all-encompassing discussions such as those of Glass and Eversley (1965),

a field of research to be cultivated more or less indefinitely, like botany or chemistry, and from which a comprehensive interpretation of the modern rise of population can be expected only in the remote future if at all! (McKeown, 1976*a*: 11)

McKeown bases his argument on the identification of three groups of factors which could have affected mortality from infectious disease, the main cause of mortality decline during the first phase of the demographic transition:

1. medical intervention (immunization and treatment);
2. a decrease in the virulence of micro-organisms;
3. improvements in living standards leading to:
    (*a*) lower exposure to infection
    (*b*) increased capacity for resistance.

McKeown rejects successively each factor except one. First, he argues that only inoculation would be relevant in this period, and it could not have been effective; furthermore, it could not have explained lower mortality from infections other than smallpox. The second explanation is highly improbable since there is no disease for which it can be said with certainty that the relation between infective agent and host changed. McKeown also rejects the first part of the third explanation, since a reduction in the exposure to risk through improvements in hygiene and sanitation appeared, according to him, only towards the end of the nineteenth century. He therefore attributes the largest part of the mortality decline to an increase in resistance to infection resulting from improved nutrition.

While admitting that data do not exist to verify that food consumption per head increased, or that the nutritional status of the population improved during this period, he bases his theory on two *a contrario* arguments and one analogy. On the one hand, he disagrees with several historians who believe that the rise of European populations cannot be explained by a single common factor since increases occurred in such differing economic contexts. He argues from this very diversity that a common element that induced the overall demographic change should be identified; and this element must be the increase in food resources resulting from improvements in agriculture and transportation which everywhere typifies the eighteenth and nineteenth centuries. Moreover, he challenges the notion that the dominant factor could be one that did not modify the very conditions that made infection the most common cause of morbidity and mortality for more than 10,000 years. Immunization, therapy, and more importantly, a random decline in the virulence of disease are, in his opinion, too flimsy to account for a demonstrably irreversible phenomenon.

McKeown's third argument, by analogy, is probably the most perplexing:

The most useful evidence of the relation between nutrition and infectious diseases comes from the experience of physicians who have worked extensively with infants and children in developing countries. This experience leaves no doubt that . . . malnutrition is a major determinant of infection rates and of the outcome of infections.

In order to understand the current situation in Africa, must we really resort to a theory of mortality decline which argues from observations made in developing countries today to explain the European experience two centuries ago? Is this not circular reasoning?

Whether the stress laid by McKeown on nutrition was justified or not, it has strengthened the conviction that health intervention programmes should do more than promote purely medical tools such as immunization and therapy. The idea may now appear commonplace, but was less so at the time. Since then it has been incorporated into the primary health care strategy adopted by WHO at the Alma-Ata conference in 1979.

McKeown must also be credited with having advanced the discussion on one of the intermediate variables (nutrition) through which living standards influence mortality. Socio-economic differentials in mortality, which are quite pronounced in developing countries (Behm and Vallin, 1982), must operate through such intermediate variables. Writers before and after McKeown have been less successful in formulating theories in which economic factors play a crucial role in mortality decline. As early as 1961, Frederiksen had gone so far as to claim that the rise in life expectancy in Sri Lanka after the Second World War was exclusively due to a rise in living standards. Although this point was easily refuted by Newman (1965), Frederiksen (1966) generalized the thesis to Mauritius, British Guyana, and twenty-one other countries.

Certain authors who consider the link between mortality and standard of living as indisputable even treat mortality measures as indicators of the standard of living. Their only doubt centres around whether it is preferable to use infant mortality (United Nations, 1970), mortality between ages 1 and 2 (Gordon *et al.*,), or between ages 1 and 5 (Frederiksen, 1966).

The importance of economic variables was popularized by Illich (1975) a few years later in *Némésis Médicale*. He boldly wrote that 'the study of the evolution of the structure of morbidity has proved that it was as superficially affected by physicians in the last century as it was by priests in previous centuries'; and in even stronger terms: 'medical enterprise [today] has become a major threat to health'.

Unfortunately, explanations which rest solely on increased living standards can no more serve our purpose than those based exclusively on improvements in public health technologies. The common mistake of those who have attempted to isolate a single set of dominant factors has been either to focus on the experience of one population at a given time without considering other contexts, or to look at sets of statistics that were too heterogeneous to shed light on actual relationships.

(*b*) Beyond the Debate

To quote Chesnais (1986), the opposition between public health technologies and socio-economic development is a 'false dichotomy'. Rather than search for *the* key factor which is supposed to dominate all others, it is surely more useful (as is often the case in the social sciences) to acknowledge the importance of several factors. This is what most scholars now try to do.

There are certainly many ways of approaching a multi-faceted phenomenon and it would be tedious to review all of the writers who have attempted to do so in this instance. I shall focus on three approaches which, in different ways, have significantly contributed to a clarification of the debate.

Preston's contribution. Preston has devoted several publications to a complete re-examination of the causes of mortality decline on the basis of an impressive collection of international statistics. His purpose has been twofold. On the one hand, he has tried to measure the relative importance of various causes of death. Expanding on work done with Keyfitz and Schoen (Preston *et al.*, 1972), he has examined the relationship between mortality levels from all causes and mortality from seven large groups of causes, using data on 165 populations from different countries and different periods (Preston, 1976). He fitted a straight line to these data and assumed that different slopes for each group of causes indicated the percentage of the overall decline attributable to that group. On that basis, he estimated that 25 per cent was due to the complex *influenza, pneumonia, and bronchitis*, 10 per cent to *tuberculosis*, 10 per cent to *diarrhoeal diseases*, and 14 per cent to *other parasitic and infectious diseases*. In other words, the decline of parasitic and infectious diseases alone explains about 60 per cent of the decline in mortality. It should be noted that this estimate is on the low side, since the remaining 40 per cent is attributable to ill-defined causes, some of which are undoubtedly of parasitic and infectious origin. Conversely, the trend in tumours and cardio-vascular disease, which have negative coefficients, appears to have acted as a break on mortality decline.

These results are only applicable to the data set considered, and therefore to the periods and places which are represented. Preston himself (Preston and Nelson, 1974) has shown that at comparable mortality levels, the cause structure of mortality varies significantly over time and space. The problem of the ill-defined causes of death certainly distorts the picture for *cardio-*

vascular diseases. It is quite likely that an examination of more recent data based on countries with advanced sanitation and controlling for ill-defined causes, would reveal that the trend in cardio-vascular disease is a major element in the overall mortality decline (Vallin and Meslé, 1988). Nevertheless, this result is suggestive of the considerable weight of parasitic and infectious diseases in the overall mortality decline during the last two centuries and in developing countries today.

The importance of this conclusion becomes fully apparent if we consider Preston's other line of research (Preston, 1975, 1976, 1980, 1982, 1985; Preston and van de Walle, 1978). What were the mechanisms behind this victory over infectious diseases? As Demeny (1965) or Stolnitz (1965) have shown, the relationship between income per head and mortality is very loose when we consider all countries globally at different time periods; but Preston has shown that there is a non-negligible relationship when we group the data by successive time periods. Fig. 18.1, taken from Preston (1975), illustrates this clearly. It shows the relationship between expectation of life at birth and income per head for 10 countries during the period 1900–10, 38 countries during 1930–40, and 57 countries during 1960–70. The three sets, chosen on the basis of data reliability, are not strictly comparable. The first set is particularly unrepresentative of the world situation since it consists only of countries which are developed today. The relative shapes of the trend lines for the three sets of points none the less illustrate the transformation of the relationship between mortality and living standards, probably since the beginning of the century but certainly since the 1930s.

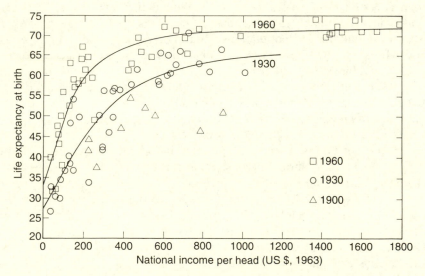

FIG. 18.1. Relation between life expectancy at birth and national income per head for nations in the 1900s, 1930s, and 1960s (after Preston, 1975)

By comparing the average world life expectancy which would have prevailed in the 1960s if the structural relationship of 1930 had been maintained,
and conversely that which would have prevailed in the 1930s with the
relationship of the 1960s, to actual observed life expectancies, Preston com-
putes the share of increases in life expectancy attributable to higher per
capita income and the share attributable to changes in the relationship
between mortality and living standards. He concludes that

factors exogenous to a country's current level of income probably account for 75–90
per cent of the growth of life expectancy for the world as a whole between the 1930s
and the 1960s. Income growth *per se* accounts for only 10–25 per cent (Preston,
1975: 237).

Similar results are found when income per head is replaced by such measures
as adult literacy or calorie consumption per person. Even though the contribution of these three factors is in fact significant, they cannot account for
the declines in mortality. Preston (1975: 240) writes:

Income, food and literacy were unquestionably placing limits on level of life
expectancy attained in the 1930s, as they do today. But they are not the only factors
operating, and we must look elsewhere to account for the majority of recent trends.

The widespread belief that increases in life expectancy are dependent on
increases in living standards, and are thus slower in developed countries, but
are mainly the result of technological transfer, and thus faster, in developing
countries, is by no means a sufficient explanation (Davis, 1956; Omran,
1971). While mortality declines were very rapid in certain developing
countries during the 1940s and 1950s, they also picked up speed in developed countries during the same period. In both cases, factors other than
economic growth played a part. Preston suggests that the concept of technological transfer may not be limited to developing countries. Pointing to
the fact that historically Europe 'imported' inoculation from China, he
stresses that generalizable public health technologies which are perfected in
a given country will tend to spread rapidly to all others. Even though the
technologies in question differ (vaccination, sulpha drugs, and antibiotics in
developed countries; insecticides, sanitation, and Maternal and Child Health
in developing countries), the role of technological transfers has been very
important in both situations. Preston (1975: 243) concludes that 'factors
exogenous to a nation's level of income per head have a major effect on
mortality trends in more developed countries as well as in less developed
countries'.

He does not deny the importance of increases in living standards. Beyond
what has been said, they intervene in less visible ways. Three of these
deserve mention. First, the study of the relationships between life expectancy
and standards of living drawn from national averages ignores internal differentials in the distribution of national income. At the same level of income

per head, some countries have a lower expectation of life because of greater social inequality. Secondly, Fig. 18.1 shows not only that there is a threshold level beyond which mortality is virtually independent of living standards, and that this threshold level has dropped considerably, but also that relatively small changes in living standards at the lower end are sufficient to trigger considerable increases in life expectancy. It therefore appears that where mortality is highest and a decline is most needed, improvements in economic circumstances remain essential. Finally, a change in the relationship between life expectancy and standard of living has been accompanied by a change in the cause structure of mortality. The share of those causes of death most closely linked with living standards and difficult to reduce through public health measures is larger in those countries which achieved a given level of life expectancy in the 1960s than it was for those which attained the same level in the 1930s. For example, in those countries which today have life expectancies of around 60 years, diarrhoeal diseases are much more prevalent than was the case in European countries when they were at comparable levels of mortality. Conversely, the share of respiratory tuberculosis is much smaller in the former than in the latter countries.

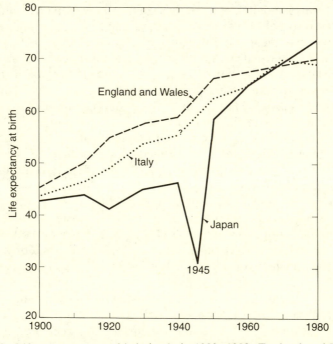

FIG. 18.2. Life expectancy at birth (males), 1900–1980, England and Wales, Italy, and Japan (after Johansson and Mosk, 1987)

The model of Johansson and Mosk. In an excellent article published recently in *Population Studies*, Johansson and Mosk (1987), building on previous work (Mosk and Johansson, 1984, 1986), have tried to understand the dual effects of economic growth and exogenous factors on mortality decline. Their work is based on case studies of three countries with very different histories of mortality decline: Japan, Italy, and England.

After 1900, a time when all three countries had strikingly similar levels of life expectancy (around 45 years) despite large discrepancies in living standards, their paths diverged sharply (Fig. 18.2). While life expectancy increased continuously in England and Italy, it was virtually stagnant in Japan until the end of the Second World War, when it increased rapidly and caught up with the other two countries. To understand the reasons for this divergence, Johansson and Mosk distinguish two categories of factors in the decline of mortality: the overall resistance of the population to disease, and the degree to which the population was protected from exposure to infection. Resistance to disease is sensitive to improvements in living standards. Exposure to infection is affected by education levels and public health measures; in addition it can be weakened or strengthened by urbanization which, in a first stage, deprives increasing portions of the population of the protection of rural life, but in a second stage affords them the benefit of better public health.

Johansson and Mosk illustrate the historical experience of the three countries in a striking graphical presentation of these two sets of factors (Fig. 18.3). For convenience, they distinguish three levels (low, medium, or high) of resistance to disease and of exposure to infection. They assume that, all other things being equal, the shift from one level to the next corresponds to an increase in life expectancy of 10 years. Thus the diagonal lines in Fig. 18.3 reflect the same level of life expectancy which can be achieved with different combinations of the two sets of factors. On the graph, Johansson and Mosk show the paths followed by the three countries from a life expectancy of about 40 to one over 60.

The top priority given to public health by the Japanese government after the Meiji restoration (Seaman, 1906; Takenata and Kitagawa, 1954) accounts for the fact that in 1900 this country had achieved a level of life expectancy almost equal to that of England and Italy, and this despite much lower levels of income per head. Up to this threshold of 45 years, life expectancy had increased in England mostly as a result of higher standards of living; however, factors leading to reduced exposure to risk (education, public sanitation) were countered by the negative effects of urbanization. Italy followed a path between those of England and Japan on both counts. Subsequently, in the first half of this century, regular increases in life expectancy were realized in England and especially in Italy as a result of progress in education and public health. In Japan, however, life expectancy stagnated: there were no improvements in standards of living as the harness-

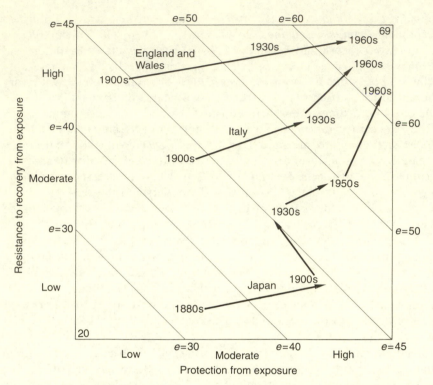

FIG. 18.3. The path history of life expectancy at birth in England and Wales, Italy, and Japan graphed as an outcome of the differential contribution of resistance factors and/or exposure factors (after Johansson and Mosk, 1987)

ing of national resources to military ends slowed down efforts to improve public health. By the 1950s and 1960s, high rates of economic growth and a renewed focus on public health policy were allowing Japan and, in a less spectacular manner, Italy, to catch up with England and Wales.

This explanatory model is perhaps most appealing in that it contrasts the situations of different countries and periods. Like all models, however, it oversimplifies mechanisms that we know to be quite complex. The opposition between factors which influence resistance and those which affect exposure is somewhat arbitrary. Is there really a fundamental difference between increased resistance to micro-organisms through better nutrition and the protection afforded by vaccination? Both serve to reinforce the body's defences. Although one is more a function of living standards and the other more of public health services, are they not both closely linked to the level of education? In practice, the various components of economic and social development all play an important role in the decline of mortality. To make further progress on the path traced by Johansson and Mosk, it would be necessary to consider additional factors and to include the experiences of other countries in the comparisons.

Mosley's framework. Along different lines, several authors have sought this broader perspective in recent years by defining a conceptual framework applicable for studies of all of the factors involved in mortality trends (Mosley, 1985*b*; Nayar, 1985; Palloni, 1985). The principal impetus in this direction has been given by Mosley (1980; 1982; 1984; 1985*a*; Mosley and Chen, 1984*a* and 1984*b*). In his view the false opposition between socio-economic and public health factors has been caused by barriers between disciplines, the social sciences on the one hand and the bio-medical sciences on the other. While social scientists have emphasized the links between mortality and aspects of social structures (income, education, economic activity, etc.), physicians concerned with measuring the effectiveness of public health measures have highlighted the biological mechanisms which cause sickness and death (Mosley and Chen, 1984*a*; see Fig. 18.4). Demographers have not always taken into account both sets of factors, which are in fact closely interlinked.

Mosley attempted to do this by proposing a general framework of the linkages between child mortality, various social and economic determinants, and different intermediate variables. Although there are several versions of this framework, and other authors have adopted variations of it, the underlying theme remains the same. Mosley's most recently published framework is reproduced in Fig. 18.5. In dealing with child mortality, the scheme is based on the malnutrition/infection dyad, which is treated as the principal medical cause of death (Scrimshaw *et al.*, 1968; Solimano and Vine, 1982). The synergism between malnutrition and infection is central to the morbidity process leading to death. Malnutrition weakens the body's capacity to resist infection while infection in turn reduces appetite and metabolic functions. This vicious circle is very likely to be fatal if it is not interrupted by appropriate therapy.

The advantage of Mosley's scheme is to illustrate in a relatively simple manner the role played by five groups of intermediate factors in this bio-medical mechanism: nutrient deficiency, environmental contamination, injury, maternal factors, and personal illness. Each of these sets of factors is a function of both individual and group behaviour: nutritional practices, hygiene, infant care, fertility patterns, attitudes toward disease. They do not, however, affect the bio-medical mechanism at the same level. Environmental pollution reduces the capacity to resist infection or may itself constitute a direct factor of contamination. Similarly, poor or insufficient nutrition decreases appetite or causes malnutrition directly; disease control measures may increase resistance to infection or cure an existing illness.

Individual and collective practices are themselves linked to different elements of the socio-economic and cultural sphere; although not introduced

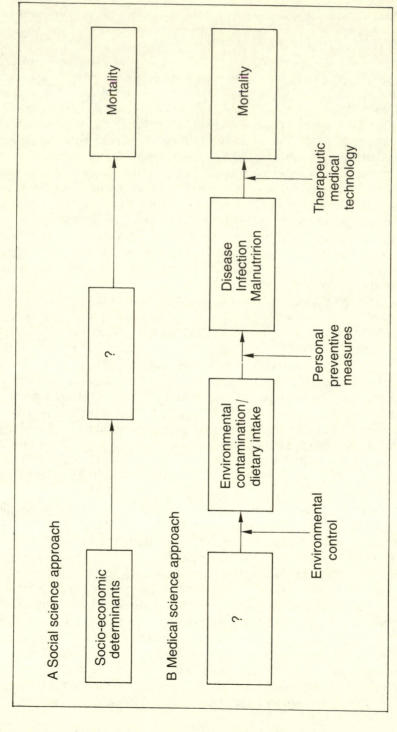

FIG. 18.4. Conceptual models of social science and medical science approaches to research on child survival (after Mosley and Chen, 1984*a*)

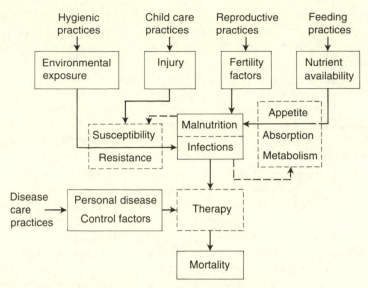

FIG. 18.5. Conceptual model of the operation of five groups of intermediate variables and their socio-economic determinants on child mortality and morbidity (after Mosley, 1985*a*)

explicitly in his framework, Mosley refers to a social synergism distinct from the biological synergism which links malnutrition and infection:

a single social determinant, poverty for example, can act independently on several intermediate variables and succeed in raising mortality risks over and above what we would expect from the simple additive effects of the intermediate variables (Mosley, 1985*a*).

By putting the emphasis on *practices* which affect the intermediate variables, Mosley's framework clearly assigns the role of major independent variables to two fundamental phenomena: the quality of the practice (hence the key role of education), and the means available to implement the practice (household income, public services). Like many other writers, Mosley underscores the importance of the mother's education for infant mortality. He writes,

this concept [social synergy] not only explains why certain direct bio-medical intervention schemes have a much more limited effect than expected, but also why a small number of fundamental social changes such as mother's education, can have significant effects on child survival.

At first glance this may appear to contradict Preston's findings, but in my view, this is a false impression. Mosley's analytical framework concerns the determinants of infant mortality in countries where it remains relatively high and is strongly linked to infectious disease. We are therefore dealing with countries which are on the left-hand side of Fig. 18.1 and in which life expectancy is very sensitive to living standards or education.

Moreover, Mosley's framework sheds light on why imported medical technologies are so effective when they are aimed at certain specific diseases with both high incidence and lethality among relatively healthy persons (programmes such as malaria campaigns in Sri Lanka, maternal immunization against neonatal tetanus in Africa). Synergistic phenomena are unimportant there, and public health programmes can be effective regardless of the socio-economic context. Conversely, with respect to measles or diarrhoea, for example, synergism is unmitigated and specific medical techniques such as vaccination and oral rehydration are likely to result in disappointment when employed alone. In the instance of measles, vaccination reduces the frequency of an otherwise relatively mild disease, which is dangerous only by virtue of the unfavourable conditions (malnutrition) of the child who contracts it. In the instance of diarrhoea, oral rehydration therapy addresses the severity of symptoms which are dangerous because of their frequent occurrence. If, as Mosley believes, this is indeed the case, it becomes clearer why certain programmes of vaccination, oral rehydration, and even nutritional supplementation have been unsuccessful when implemented in isolation (Jones *et al.*, 1985; Mata, 1985; Beghin and Vanderveken, 1985). There may also be situations of positive synergy, however, where preventive measures such as measles immunization prevent children from becoming weak and vulnerable in the first place.

Although complementary, the three theoretical perspectives that have been reviewed do not jointly constitute a general theory. Nevertheless, it appears that the works of Preston, Johansson and Mosk, and Mosley provide a basis on which to frame useful questions regarding the current situation in Africa.

2. The African Situation

In the area of mortality, the point of departure is that much less is known about Africa than about other continents. Vital registration of deaths is particularly defective. According to UN standards which are far from demanding, only Egypt, Mauritius, and five other micro-states or territories (Cape Verde, Réunion, Saint Helena, São Tomé, and the Seychelles) totalling 9 per cent of the population of sub-Saharan Africa, have 'complete' registration (i.e. officially reported omission lower than 10 per cent). Most of the available data come from retrospective surveys, which are subject to important errors of observation, or from indirect estimation. Published data should always be interpreted with caution, whether the concern is with levels, trends, or the impact of causal factors. This can be demonstrated by comparing two consecutive sets of life expectancy estimates for the period 1980–5 published by the United Nations in 1985 and in 1986 (Table 18.1). Within one year certain estimates changed by as much as 3 or 4 years, or by almost 10 per cent. This provides a warning about the uncertainty of the estimates and, of course, of any argument which might be based on them. Despite this major handicap, we shall attempt to answer several key questions about the levels and trends of African mortality: Has it declined? What accounted for this decline? What are the prospects for the future?

(a) The Lagging African Mortality Decline

We must underscore at this point that, despite what is often argued, a mortality decline is already well under way in Africa. Nevertheless, the

Table 18.1. *Countries for which United Nations estimates of life expectation at birth for 1980–5 differed between 1985 and 1986*

Country	1985 estimate	1986 estimate	Difference
Mozambique	49.4	45.3	−4.1
Rwanda	49.5	46.5	−3.0
Uganda	52.0	49.0	−3.0
Ethiopia	42.9	40.9	−2.0
Somalia	42.9	40.9	−2.0
Swaziland	48.6	48.5	−0.1
Zimbabwe	55.7	55.8	+0.1
Libya	57.9	58.3	+0.4
Morocco	57.9	58.3	+0.4
Egypt	57.3	58.1	+0.8
Benin	42.5	44.0	+1.5
Togo	48.7	50.5	+1.8
Cape Verde	57.0	59.0	+2.0
Algeria	57.8	60.1	+2.3
Burundi	44.0	46.5	+2.5
Cameroon	48.0	50.9	+2.9
Burkina Faso	42.0	45.2	+3.2
Réunion	66.4	69.7	+3.3
Ivory Coast	47.0	50.5	+3.5

Source: United Nations, 1985 and 1986.

continent is lagging behind in the level of its mortality, and the gap has recently increased.

The decline in mortality is well under way

Living standards remain mediocre and are deteriorating in almost all countries. There are many cases of endemic disease, such as the parasitic, infectious and contagious diseases which cause the death of many infants and children under five. Shortages in personnel and public health services are the main obstacles in the path of efforts aimed at reducing mortality (Economic Commission for Africa, 1986).

This is how the conference of planners, statisticians, and demographers summarized the health situation of sub-Saharan Africa in their final report of 1986. And yet, notwithstanding these oft-repeated findings, despite the Sahel drought and the recent famines in Ethiopia, African mortality seems to have improved significantly in recent decades. Despite the uncertainties about them, the UN estimates are the only ones which permit an overall picture of the African situation in terms of levels and trends in expectation of life at birth. Given the poor quality of the data, their values reflect in part the hypotheses underlying the adjustments. There is little doubt, however, concerning the reality of the mortality decline in Africa (Table 18.2).

Table 18.2. *Trends in expectation of life at birth in Africa, 1950–5 to 1980–5*

Country	Expectation of life		Improvement (in years)
	1950–5	1980–5	
North Africa	41.9	56.5	14.6
Algeria	43.1	60.1	17.0
Egypt	42.4	58.1	15.7
Libya	42.9	58.3	15.4
Morocco	42.9	58.3	15.4
Sudan	37.2	47.7	10.5
Tunisia	44.6	60.6	16.0
West Africa	35.5	47.2	11.7
Benin	32.5	44.0	11.5
Burkina Faso	32.5	45.2	13.3
Cape Verde	42.6	59.0	16.4
Gambia	30.6	35.0	4.4
Ghana	42.0	52.0	10.0
Guinea	30.7	40.2	9.5
Guinea-Bissau	33.5	43.0	9.5
Ivory Coast	36.0	50.5	14.5
Liberia	37.5	49.0	11.5

Table 18.2. *(Cont'd)*

Country	Expectation of life		Improvement (in years)
	1950–5	1980–5	
Mali	32.5	42.0	9.5
Mauritania	33.5	44.0	10.5
Niger	33.0	42.5	9.5
Nigeria	36.5	46.5	10.0
Senegal	34.7	43.3	9.6
Sierra Leone	29.0	34.0	5.0
Togo	36.0	50.5	14.5
Central Africa	36.8	47.8	11.0
Angola	30.0	42.0	12.0
Cameroon	35.9	50.9	15.0
Central African Rep.	34.0	43.0	9.0
Chad	32.5	43.0	10.5
Congo	36.0	46.5	10.5
Equatorial Guinea	33.5	44.0	10.5
Gabon	38.0	49.0	11.0
Zaïre	40.5	50.0	9.5
East Africa	36.6	47.3	10.7
Burundi	40.0	46.5	6.5
Comores	40.0	50.0	10.0
Ethiopia	32.9	47.3	10.7
Kenya	38.6	52.9	14.3
Madagascar	37.7	49.6	11.9
Malawi	36.2	45.0	8.8
Mauritius	51.0	66.7	15.7
Mozambique	37.4	49.6	11.9
Réunion	52.6	69.7	17.1
Rwanda	40.0	46.5	6.5
Somalia	32.9	40.9	8.0
Tanzania	37.0	51.0	14.0
Uganda	40.0	49.0	9.0
Zambia	37.8	51.3	13.5
Zimbabwe	41.5	55.8	14.3
South Africa	41.2	53.0	11.8
Botswana	42.5	54.5	12.0
Lesotho	37.3	49.0	11.7
Namibia	38.7	48.2	9.5
Rep. of South Africa	41.5	53.5	12.0
Swaziland	41.0	48.5	7.5
Africa	37.8	49.4	11.6

Source: United Nations, 1986.

Between 1950–5 and 1980–5, expectation of life at birth increased by about ten years in almost every country of tropical Africa, and by about 15 years in Northern Africa. Today, expectations of life at birth below 40 are exceptional, and almost all of the values for countries in tropical Africa fall between 45 and 55 years; North African countries are closer to 60 years. Compared to average life expectancies in the order of 25 or 30, which were probably the norm around the turn of the century and not uncommon even after the Second World War, these results indicate that significant progress has been made.

Concerning infant and child mortality, which still account for a very large proportion of deaths in Africa, the available data are somewhat more reliable. In the excellent critical summary by Althea Hill in Chapter 1 of this volume, indirect estimations drawn from various recent censuses and African surveys (particularly the World Fertility Survey) on child survival by mother's age strongly confirm this view of a general decline in mortality.

But recently the gap between Africa and other continents has increased.   It appears, however, that tropical Africa has fallen behind dramatically during

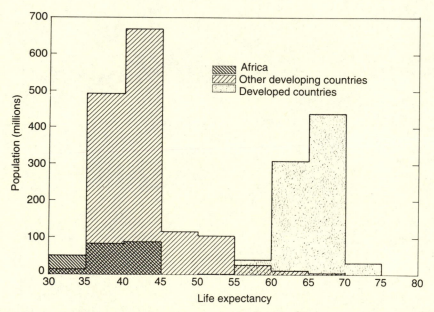

FIG. 18.6. Distribution of countries weighted by population size, by life expectancy in 1980–1985

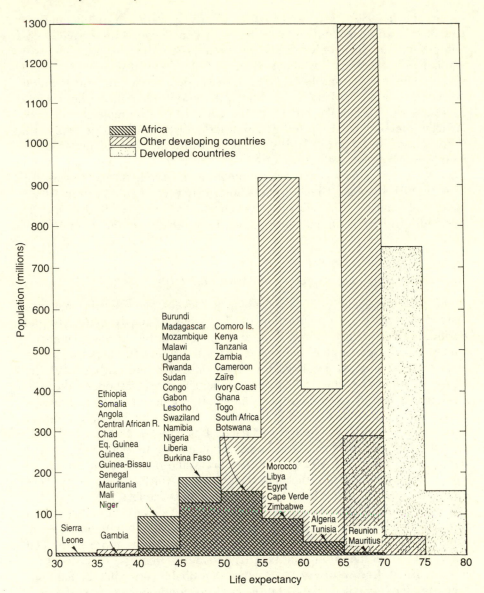

FIG. 18.7. Distribution of countries weighted by population size, by life expectancy in 1950–1955

the past 30 years. This is illustrated in Figs. 18.6 and 18.7, which present the distribution of life expectancies of different countries in the world, weighted by their populations, for the periods 1950–5 and 1980–5. Africa, other less developed countries, and the more developed countries are shown separately. In 1980–5 (Fig. 18.6) Africa clearly appeared to trail behind the rest of the world and this is even more evident if we consider only sub-Saharan Africa. (It is only because of North Africa that the continent as a whole has a life expectancy above 55 years.) Moreover, if we compare these results with those from 1950–5 (Fig. 18.7), the relative deterioration of Africa's position is striking. Even though the lowest life expectancies (below 35 years) were primarily African in the early 1950s, the majority of black African populations were found alongside other Third World countries (between 35 and 45 years). Today, in contrast, the bulk of non-African countries are either at the level of North Africa (most notably India with a life expectancy of 55.4 years) or at a much higher level (this is the case for China, at 67.8 years). Thus, on the whole, countries of sub-Saharan Africa have made considerably less progress than the rest of the Third World. Is this indicative of a unique position held by Africa on the road to low mortality?

(b) Factors explaining the decline of African mortality

If we plot the gains in life expectancy in developing countries between 1950–5 and 1980–5 as a function of the levels at the beginning of the period, we note that the most important gains occurred in those countries which had already reached life expectancies of around 50 years by 1950–5 (Fig. 18.8).[2] For countries above and below this privileged starting level, life expectancy gains become increasingly smaller. This result supports the conclusion, reached by several authors, that mortality declines follow a logistic curve, slow at the outset, rapid in the middle, and again quite slow at higher levels of life expectancy (Bourgeois-Pichat, 1966; Vallin, 1968).

From this perspective, Africa's lag appears to be both normal and temporary. Indeed, all African countries are found on the left-hand side of Fig. 18.8. They constitute the bulk of the group which, starting from very low levels in 1950–5, has been able to achieve only modest increases during the last 30 years. The prescription would then be to wait: now that Africa has reached a medium level of expectation of life, it will make more rapid progress and make up for the lag in relation to the more developed countries, while the latter will experience slower progress, now that they have reached European levels. Reality is probably less simple than this scenario, and a detailed analysis of the African situation is in order. Various aspects are detailed in different chapters of this book. Here I would like to discuss several issues raised by the general ideas discussed in the first section, as they apply to Africa.

---

[2] Like Figs. 18.6 and 18.7, Fig. 18.8 has been published elsewhere previously (Vallin 1985a). It has not been updated to conform to more recent United Nations estimates, as this would not be important for the present argument.

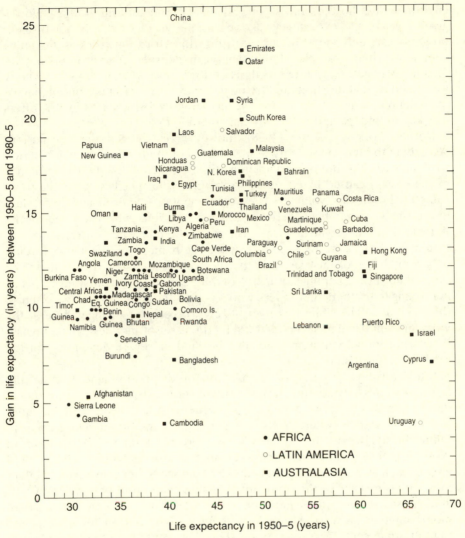

FIG. 18.8. Gain in life expectancy in last 30 years by level reached in 1950–1955

Is the malnutrition–infection dyad still the key? The vicious circle which in certain contexts links malnutrition and infection is at the core of Mosley's explanatory framework. Most authors agree that Africa over the past few decades offers one of the best examples of such a context: levels of income are low, the food supply is insufficient and irregular, hygiene is poor, education is not developed, economic development is slow, the physical environment is hostile, and so on. All of these factors imply that below a given level of life expectancy, as long as the vicious circle is not broken, progress can only be slow and difficult. In Africa, measles is the most commonly cited example of the synergism between malnutrition and infection. Measles, it is often said, is serious only when it attacks a body weakened by malnutrition, and trying to control it by vaccination campaigns, for example, will not break the vicious circle. Mosley's framework offers one key to understanding the African situation (Vallin, 1985*b*).

Recent work by Aaby (1988), however, challenges this conclusion. According to him, the severity of measles is not the result of its combination with malnutrition, but of a completely different factor: the greater virulence of the disease caused by crowding. Aaby gives the specifics of his theory in Chapter 14 of this volume. The word theory is appropriate here, and interestingly, it has been derived from observations which are specifically African. The underlying principle is simple. A child who contracts measles from a brief exposure to a carrier outside the home, will in general develop only a mild case of measles since the received dose of the virus is low. The same child, in the confines of a crowded household, will contaminate his or her younger brothers and sisters who sleep in the same room and often in the same bed. The siblings are very likely to receive a stronger dose of the virus and will develop severe and often fatal cases of measles. Thus, regardless of nutritional status, measles can be mild or severe depending on the mode of transmission.

While Mosley's framework is based on observations made in Asia and Latin America, where infant mortality is primarily linked to diarrhoeal diseases, the alternative scheme proposed by Aaby could well be more suitable for Africa, where measles is particularly important. Differences in family lifestyles explain why measles is more dangerous in Africa than in Asia. Moreover, differences between ethnic groups within Africa could also explain why the severity of measles and, by extension, overall infant mortality varies across the continent. The cohabitation of polygynous wives, and the sharing of rooms and even beds by several young children, are all more common in West Africa than in East Africa and in the countryside than in urban centres. Aaby's thesis, therefore, could help to explain two of the most striking differentials of African mortality.

Peter Aaby further argues that the crowding phenomenon is not limited to measles, but extends to other infectious diseases and even to certain parasitic diseases. It may be that this is not the case and that it is only for measles that this explanation competes with the malnutrition–infection synergism so dear to Mosley. Even so, by replacing a biological mechanism depending on socio-economic factors (nutrition) with another biological mechanism depending on socio-cultural factors (degree of contact between children), the thesis reminds us of the potential importance of the cultural context in demographic studies in Africa.

Is the importance of the mother's education a universal law? Preston, as well as Johansson and Mosk, has underscored the role of education. Mosley considers the educational status of the mother as the most important explanatory variable of infant mortality. Caldwell also places education at the top of the list of factors contributing to an improvement in the status of women, to which he attributes most of the spectacular successes achieved in health by certain poor areas such as Sri Lanka, Kerala, and Costa Rica (Caldwell, 1986). Many surveys in Africa, most notably the World Fertility Survey, confirm this nearly unanimous opinion. Mbacké and van de Walle give yet another description of the modalities of this relation by writing in Chapter 5 of this volume that 'level of education is the principal explanatory factor behind observed differences in the use of public health services'.

We know that this relationship holds after controlling for possible confounding variables. In particular, it holds for urban centres, as Caldwell (1979) showed in Nigeria, and Antoine and Diouf (1987) showed more recently in Senegal. Even within a city the relationship holds after controlling for other variables. Thus, Antoine and Diouf demonstrate that in Pikine, a lower class suburb of Dakar, within households that have piped water, child mortality is halved when the mother is literate, and conversely, when both parents are illiterate, mortality is unaffected by the source of water supply.

The influence of the mother's education on infant mortality is particularly evident in African towns where bottle-feeding tends to reduce the practice of breast-feeding. For various reasons (lack of hygiene, excessive dilution of the formula), bottle-feeding constitutes a severe hazard for children of illiterate mothers, but is much less dangerous for the children of educated mothers who know how to use it properly.

In more general terms, as Tabutin and Akoto indicate in Chapter 2, education has a direct impact on behaviour towards children. These authors add that although the impact of education on mortality is universal, the magnitude of its effect varies from one country to another, and the level of education beyond which mortality declines markedly is not everywhere the same.

Certain recent findings even appear to contradict the accepted wisdom on education and infant mortality. Dackam Ngouatchou's (1987) analysis of the survey taken by IFORD in Yaoundé is a case in point. Noting no link between the mother's education and infant mortality in this case, Ngouatchou does not attribute this unexpected result to poor data quality. Rather, he argues that formal education is sometimes a very poor indicator of knowledge of sanitation or nutrition, which have strong effects on mortality. The connection between formal education and knowledge about health depends strongly on a number of socio-cultural factors, the most important of which, according to Dackam Ngouatchou, is ethnic identity. In Cameroon, for example, Bamileke mothers, though relatively less educated, are more likely to have their children vaccinated than the better educated Beti mothers. Thus, the diversity of the African situation is so great as to throw into question even such a well-accepted finding as the link between education and child mortality. This can only prompt demographers and anthropologists to re-evaluate the universality of even the most firmly established theories.

Does ethnicity play a major role in Africa? The most recent studies underscore the importance of ethnic factors in accounting for mortality differences. Akoto and Tabutin even conclude, after reviewing World Fertility Survey data from Kenya and Cameroon, that of the eight variables considered, ethnicity of the mother turns out to be the most predictive of infant mortality. Is this not one of the factors of mortality decline which is, if not exclusively African, at least particularly marked in Africa? The great civilizations (Judaeo-Christian in Europe and America, Arab–Islamic in North Africa and the Middle East, Buddhist in the Far East, etc.) made fewer inroads in Africa than in most other parts of the world, and colonial influences appeared later than elsewhere. This may explain Africa's cultural mosaic which generates a wide array of attitudes in the area of health.

The diversity of attitudes is underscored by Adegbola (1988) in connection with extramarital births, and by Pison (Chapter 11 of this volume) in connection with the fate of twins (they were either revered or killed). Although mortality differences by sex are less drastic, Gbenyon and Locoh (in Chapter 10) suggest that some ethnic groups do not discriminate against girls, while others do so quite markedly.

Even more importantly, as we mentioned earlier, ethnic diversity and the fundamentally different lifestyles that result are behind Aaby's mechanism explaining differences in the severity of infectious disease, especially of measles, a primary cause of mortality in Africa.

For most African countries, the complex social structures which have evolved out of the mix of ethnic groups and the diversity of their customs and attitudes, can block the adoption of effective modern health technologies. To achieve its goal, a health policy must be sensitive to the socio-cultural factors which affect morbidity and mortality; otherwise even the most effective public health measures run the risk of failure. Understandably, centralized decision-making structures of the state are poorly connected with the grass-roots level, and cannot easily satisfy local needs in a multi-ethnic society. A policy appropriate for the Bamileke may have little or no success among the Fulani or the Beti. In responding to emergencies, authorities often devote too little attention to adapting their strategies to suit different contexts.

Urbanization as the crucible of modernization? Mortality has declined much more rapidly in urban areas of Africa, particularly in the large urban centres, than in rural areas. All studies of mortality differentials acknowledge this fact as commonplace (Akoto and Tabutin, Chapter 2; Ewbank *et al.*, 1986; Cantrelle *et al.*, 1986). The role played by urbanization in African mortality declines, however, is the inverse of the one it played in nineteenth-century Europe: there, city residents were exposed to higher health risks (Davis, 1973). Also found in other developing countries, this phenomenon has taken on exceptional importance in Africa. The authors of a case study on mortality in Senegal, published by the United Nations (Cantrelle *et al.*, 1986), confirm that among all demographic, socio-economic, cultural, and environmental factors, residence in an urban area is the most important one in reducing mortality. Even within cities, mortality is not the same for those who have been there for a long period and for those who have arrived recently. Thus, in Pikine, children who were born in greater Dakar experienced half the mortality of children who had come to the region after their birth.

This urban advantage can be explained only in part by the large socio-economic differences between urban and rural areas. When controlling for income, education, and occupational status, the differentials weaken but rarely disappear. It is usually pointed out that cities monopolize basic medical resources and that the urban environment is more favourable to public health programmes. This may account for the contrast with historical Europe, where the medical–sanitation context put city-dwellers at a disadvantage. We must perhaps go beyond these well-established linkages, and investigate the unique role of African cities as melting-pots of diverse ethnic groups where people are exposed to modern ideas, particularly through education. Education is more developed in the cities, and the educated find work in the urban economic activities which are less bound to tradition than agriculture. Filled with ethnic variation, African cities are an environment which is more receptive to effective medical and public health measures; in this sense they are truly the melting-pots of modernization.

(c) Can Sub-Saharan Africa catch up?

If Fig. 18.8 warrants a certain optimism, it fails to convince that health will soon make rapid strides towards improvement in Africa. On the one hand, it is possible that factors particular to Africa render the continent especially unreceptive to the public health policies developed thus far. It was in Africa that 'vertical' intervention programmes had the least success after the Second World War (Molineaux, 1985; Jones *et al.*, 1985). It is also in Africa that primary health care strategies adopted by WHO and by most national governments have been the most disappointing (Vallin and Lopez, 1985; Garenne *et al.*, 1985; Adeokun, 1985.) Is this relative failure wholly due to the need to mobilize more forces in order to take off because Africa was starting from a lower point? Can it not be argued instead that the failure is explained by specific African constraints? The success of a primary health strategy is predicated on the extent to which the basic needs of the population have been met effectively, and it is germane to ask whether one cause of failure has not been insufficient knowledge of the context in which strategies were being implemented.

On the other hand, it is important to mention one last characteristic of the African context, which has not yet been mentioned here and is likely to weigh heavily on future mortality trends: the complete absence of a fertility decline. With reference to the frame of Aaby's theory of the lethality of infectious disease, continuing high fertility levels in themselves constitute a major barrier to mortality decline. More generally, can we imagine that the high population growth rates (3.5 per cent in Tanzania, 3.7 per cent in the Ivory Coast, 4.1 per cent in Kenya) will continue to rise because of one-sided declines in mortality? The developing countries which have experienced the fastest mortality declines during the past 30 years are also those which have had the largest fertility declines. Can we really discuss the future of African mortality without also considering the conditions which would bring on a decline in fertility? Probably not, but the debate would take us beyond the scope of this work.

References

Aaby, P. (1988), 'Malnutrition and overcrowding-exposure in severe measles infection: A review of community studies', *Reviews of Infectious Diseases* 10: 478–91.

Adegbola, O. (1988), 'A comparative analysis of mortality of children of informal and formal unions', Paper presented at the Seminar on Mortality and Society in Africa South of the Sahara, Yaoundé, IUSSP, Liège.

Adeokun, L. (1985), 'Problèmes posés par les programmes d'intervention sanitaires au Nigéria', in Vallin and Lopez (1985), 177–96.

Antoine, P. and Diouf, P. D. (1987), 'Urbanisation, scolarisation et mortalité des enfants', Paper presented at the Seminar on Mortality and Society in Africa South of the Sahara, Yaoundé, IUSSP, Liège.

Beghin, I. and Vanderveken, M. (1985), 'Les Programmes nutritionnels', in Vallin and Lopez, (1985), 77–102.

Behm, H. and Vallin, J. (1982), 'Mortality differentials among human groups', in Preston (1982), 11–39.

Blayo, Y. (1975), 'La Mortalité en France de 1740 à 1829', *Population*, special issue, Nov.

Bourgeois-Pichat, J. (1966), *Évolution et croissance démographique*, Carnegie Foundation for World Peace, European Center, Geneva.

Caldwell, J. C. (1979), 'Education as a factor in mortality decline: An examination of Nigerian data', *Population Studies* 33/3: 395–413.

—— (1986), 'Routes to low mortality in poor countries', *Population and Development Review* 12/2: 171–220.

Cantrelle, P., Diop, I., Garenne, M., Guèye, M., and Sandio, A. (1986), 'The profile of mortality and its determinants in Senegal, 1960–1980', in United Nations, *Determinants of Mortality Changes and Differentials in Developing Countries*, Demographic Study 94, New York, 86–116.

Chesnais, J. C. (1986), *La Transition démographique*, Travaux et documents 113, INED–PUF, Paris.

Dackam Ngouatchou, R. (1987), 'Causes et déterminants de la mortalité des enfants de moins de cinq ans en Afrique tropicale', Doctoral thesis, IDUP, Paris.

Davis, K. (1956), 'The amazing decline of mortality in underdeveloped areas', *American Economic Review* 46: 305–18.

—— (1973), 'Cities and mortality', in IUSSP, *International Population Conference*, Ordina Editions, Liège, vol. 3, pp. 259–78.

Demeny, P. (1965), 'Investment allocation and population growth', *Demography* 2: 203–32.

Economic Commission for Africa (1986), 'Final Report of the Conference of planners, statisticians and demographers', United Nations, Addis Ababa.

Ewbank, D., Henin, R., and Kekovole, J. (1986), 'An integration of demographic and epidemiologic research on mortality in Kenya', in United Nations, *Determinants of Mortality Changes and Differentials in Developing Countries*, Population Studies 94, New York, 33–85.

Frederiksen, H. (1961), 'Determinants and consequences of mortality trends in Ceylon', *Public Health Report* 76: 659–63.

—— (1966), 'Determinants and consequences of mortality and fertility trends', *Public Health Report* 81: 715–27.

Garenne, M., Cantrelle, P., and Diop, I. (1985), 'Le Sénégal', in Vallin and Lopez (1985), 307–30.

Glass, D. and Eversley, D. E. C. (eds.) (1965), *Population in History*, Edward Arnold, London.

Gordon, J. E., Wyon, J. B., and Ascoli, W. (1967), 'The second year death rate in less developed countries', *American Journal of Medical Science* 254/3: 357–80.

Illich, I. (1975), *Némésis médicale*, Éditions du Seuil, Paris.

Johansson, S. R. and Mosk, K. (1987), 'Exposure, resistance and life expectancy: Disease and death during the economic development of Japan, 1900–1960', *Population Studies* 41/2: 207–35.

Jones S., Waldman, R. J., and Foege, W. H. (1985), 'Le Rôle des programmes de vaccination', in Vallin and Lopez (1985), 41–52.

McKeown, T. (1965), 'Medicine and world population', in M. C. Sheps and J. C. Ridley (eds.), *Public Health and Population Change*, University of Pittsburgh.

—— (1976a), *The Modern Rise of Population*, Edward Arnold, London.

—— (1976b), *The Role of Medicine: Dream, Mirage or Nemesis?*, Nuffield Provincial Hospitals Trust, London.

—— (1978), 'Fertility, mortality and causes of death: An examination of issues related to the modern rise of population', *Population Studies* 32/3: 535–42.

—— and Brown, R. G. (1955), 'Medical evidence related to English population change in the eighteenth century', *Population Studies* 9/2: 119–41.

—— and Record, R. G. (1962), 'Reasons for the decline in fertility in England and Wales during the nineteenth century', *Population Studies* 26/2: 94–122.

—— Brown, R. G., and Record, R. G. (1972), 'An interpretation of the modern rise of population', *Population Studies* 26/3: 345–82.

Mata, L. (1985), 'La Lutte contre les maladies diarrhéiques, le cas du Costa Rica', in Vallin and Lopez (1985), 53–76.

Molineaux, L. (1985), 'La Lutte contre les maladies parasitaires: Le Problème du paludisme, notamment en Afrique', in Vallin and Lopez (1985), 11–40.

Mosk, C. and Johansson, S. R. (1984), 'Death and development: Mortality decline in Japan, 1908–1960', Technical Report, National Science Foundation.

—— —— (1986), 'Income and mortality: Evidence from modern Japan, 1900–1960', *Population and Development Review* 12/3: 415–40.

Mosley W. H. (1980), 'Social determinants of infant and child mortality: Some considerations for an analytical framework', Paper presented at the Conference on Health and Mortality in Babies and Small Children, Cairo, 18–20 May.

—— (1982), 'Biological contamination of the environment by man', in Preston (1982), 39–68.

—— (1984), 'Child survival: Research and policy', supplement to vol. 10 of *Population and Development Review*, 3–23.

—— (1985*a*), 'Les Soins de santé primaire peuvent-ils réduire la mortalité infantile? Bilan critique de quelques programmes africains et asiatiques', in Vallin and Lopez (1985), 101–36.

—— (1985*b*), 'Biological and socio-economic determinants of child survival: A proximate determinants framework integrating fertility and mortality variables', in IUSSP, *International Population Conference*, Florence, Ordina Editions, Liège, 189–208.

—— Chen, L. C. (1984*a*), 'An analytical framework for the study of child survival in developing countries', supplement to vol. 10 of *Population and Development Review*, 25–45.

—— —— (1984*b*), *Child survival: Strategies for Research*, supplement to vol. 10 of *Population and Development Review*.

Nayar, P. K. B. (1985), 'Le Kerala, Inde', in Vallin and Lopez (1985), 357–69.

Newman, P. (1965), *Malaria eradication and population growth; with special reference to Ceylon and British Guyana*, School of Public Health Economics, University of Michigan.

Omran, A. R. (1971), 'The epidemiology transition', *Milbank Memorial Fund Quarterly* 49/1: 509–38.

Palloni, A. (1985), 'Santé et lutte contre la mortalité en Amérique latine', in Vallin and Lopez (1985), 447–75.

—— (1987), 'Theory, analytical framework and causal approach in the study of mortality of young ages in developing countries', *Annales sociologiques belges de médecine tropicale* 67/1, supplement, 447–75.

Preston, S. H. (1975), 'The changing relation between mortality and level of economic development', *Population Studies* 29/2: 231–48.

—— (1976), *Mortality Patterns in National Population*, Academic Press, New York, San Francisco, London.

—— (1980), 'Causes and consequences of mortality decline in less developed countries during the twentieth century', in R. A. Easterlin, *Population and Economic Change in Developing Countries*, National Bureau of Economic Research, University of Chicago Press, 289–360.

—— (ed.) (1982), *Biological and Social Aspects of Mortality and the Length of Life*, Ordina Press, Liège.

—— (1985), 'Resources, knowledge and child mortality', in *International Population Conference*, Florence, Ordina Editions, Liège, 373–84.

—— and Nelson, V. E. (1974), 'Structure and change in the causes of death: An international summary', *Population Studies* 28/1: 19–51.

—— and van de Walle, E. (1978), 'Urban French mortality in the nineteenth century', *Population Studies* 32/2: 275–97.

—— Keyfitz, N., and Schoen, R. (1972), *Causes of Death: Life Tables for National Populations*, Seminar Press, New York.

Razzell, P. E. (1965), 'Edward Jenner: The history of a medical myth', *Medical History* 10/3.

—— (1969), 'Population change in eighteenth century England', in M. Drake (ed.), *Population in Industrialization*, London, 123–56.

—— (1977*a*), *The Conquest of Smallpox: The Impact of Inoculation on Smallpox Mortality in Eighteenth Century Britain*, Caliban Books, Firle.

—— (1977*b*), Book Review of *The Modern Rise of Population*, *Economic History Review*, Feb., 192.

Schofield, R. (1977), '*The Modern Rise of Population*, by Thomas McKeown', *Population Studies* 31/1: 179–81.

Scrimshaw, N. S., Taylor, E. C., and Gordon, G. E. (1968), *Interactions of nutrition and infection*, WHO, Geneva.

Seaman, L. L. (1906), *The Real Triumph of Japan*, D. Appleton, New York.

Solimano, G. and Vine, M. (1982), 'Malnutrition, infection and infant mortality', in Preston (1982), 83–111.

Stolnitz, G. H. (1965), 'Recent mortality trends in Latin America, Asia and Africa', *Population Studies* 19/2: 117–38.

Takenata, M. and Kitagawa, D. (1954), *The Development of Social, Educational and Medical Work in Japan since Meij*.

United Nations (1970), *Economic Survey of Europe in 1969*, Part I. 'Structure, Trends and Prospects in the European Economy', New York.

—— (1985), *World Population Prospects: Estimates and Projections as Assessed in 1982*, New York.

—— (1986), *World Population Prospects: Estimates and Projections as Assessed in 1984*, New York.

Vallin, J. (1968), 'La Mortalité dans les pays du Tiers Monde, évolution et perspectives', *Population* 4: 845–68.

—— (1985*a*), 'La Mortalité dans les pays en développement', *Espace, Populations, Sociétés* 3: 515–40.

—— (1985*b*), 'Les Facteurs de la mortalité infantile dans les pays en développement', in *Études de quelques problèmes méthodologiques liés aux enquêtes EMIJ*, IFORD, Yaoundé, IFORD, 121–9.

—— and Lopez, A. (eds.) (1985), *La Lutte contre la mort: Influence des politiques sociales et des politiques de santé sur l'évolution de la mortalité*, Travaux et documents 108, INED–PUF, Paris.

—— and Meslé, F. (1988), *Les Causes de décès en France de 1925 à 1978*, Travaux et documents 115, INED–PUF, Paris.

van de Walle, E. (1977), '*The Modern Rise of Population*, by Thomas McKeown', *Science* 197, 653.
—— (1985), 'Present patterns of demographic change in the light of past experience', in *International Population Conference*, 4, IUSSP, Florence, 355–6.

Index of Names

Index of Subjects

abortions 220, 221
accidents 180, 181
adoption 279
aetiologies 147, 148, 152, 153, 156, 176
Afghanistan 28
agriculture 42, 350–3, 378, 408, 409
   insecticides 207
   and nutrition 381
   production 357
   swidden 339
   workers in 39, 40, 61
AIDS 4, 8, 9, 391–401
Algeria 231, 237, 421, 422
altitude 350–1, 352, 353, 361, 362
   and malaria transmission 206, 207
amenorrhea 339
amodiaquine 214, 215, 216
anaemia 105, 209, 287, 400
anaesthesia 408 n.
Anopheles 204, 207, 212, 214
antenatal care 74, 145, 149, 224
antibiotics 407
antigen stimulation 343
antiseptics 162
aridity 378
asepsis 408 n.

bacteria 173, 177
   Bacillus subtilis 163
   Clostridium 162, 163
   Escherichia coli 178, 189, 192
   Shigella dysenteriae 178–9, 361
   Staphylococcus aureus 192
   Welchia perfringens 163
Bamako 77, 99–121, 232, 234, 249
   excess female mortality 244, 248
   excess male mortality 237, 243
   no significant differences 241, 247
Bangladesh:
   diarrhoeal diseases 177, 178
   excess female mortality 230, 247
   famine 368, 369–70, 372
   measles 329, 330, 331, 334
   neonatal mortality 161
   poor living conditions 66
BCG (bacille Calmette–Guérin) 72, 74
behaviour 249, 250, 253, 400, 417
   anthropophilic 211
   bad 291

Bengal 370–1, 384
Bhutan 161
birth:
   control 279
   environment 171–3
   extramarital 430
   home 129
   intervals 29, 342; spacing 336, 343
   month of 108–13
   multiple 253, 257
   order 128, 130, 132, 135, 272, 276
   previous 78, 138
   still 220, 221, 254–6, 257–8, 265–6
   trauma 180, 181
   trimester of 127, 128, 132, 138
birth rates 336, 338, 342, 379
   affected by HIV 401
   doubling 376
   fallen 369, 371, 375
   lower, and equal population growth 339
birth-weights 128, 130, 132, 135, 138
   expected effects on survival 142
   impossible to collect 84
   low 71, 108
   routinely recorded 80, 92
blood donors 392, 396, 397 n., 399–400
bottle-feeding 305, 313, 314, 316, 317, 429
   risks 307, 308
Brass:
   African standard table 232
   child survival method 1, 11, 12
breast-feeding 178, 199–200, 313, 376
   decision to terminate 282
   duration, in different ethnic groups 339,
     340, 343
   exclusive 305, 308, 309, 314, 317
   impact of 191–5, 342
   prolonged 185
   transition from, to solid foods 183
bridewealth 248, 372
bronchitis 411
bronchopneumonia 146

Cape Verde Islands 396, 420, 421, 422
carbohydrates 282
cardiac failure 107
care:
   child 49, 145–57, 271
   emergency 375

Index compiled by Frank Pert